**To Renew Books**
PHONE (925) 258-2233

# R. Murray Thomas

# Folk Psychologies Across Cultures

 **Sage Publications**
*International Educational and Professional Publisher*
Thousand Oaks ■ London ■ New Delhi

For information:

Sage Publications, Inc.
2455 Teller Road
Thousand Oaks, California 91320
E-mail: order@sagepub.com

Sage Publications Ltd.
6 Bonhill Street
London EC2A 4PU
United Kingdom

Sage Publications India Pvt. Ltd.
M-32 Market
Greater Kailash I
New Delhi 110 048 India

Printed in the United States of America

*Library of Congress Cataloging-in-Publication Data*

Thomas, R. Murray (Robert Murray), 1921-
  Folk psychologies across cultures / by R. Murray Thomas.
      p. cm.
  Includes bibliographical references (p.   ) and index.
  ISBN 0-7619-2459-0 — ISBN 0-7619-2460-4
  1. Ethnopsychology. I. Title.
  GN502 .T56 2001
  155.8—dc21

                          2001002981

This book is printed on acid-free paper.

01  02  03  04  05  06  7  6  5  4  3  2  1


| Acquiring Editor: | Jim Brace-Thompson |
| Editorial Assistant: | Karen Ehrmann |
| Production Editor: | Sanford Robinson |
| Cover Designer: | Jane Quaney |

# Contents

# Preface

The contents of this book are based on the following five assumptions:

- Everyone carries in mind a psychology in the form of an explanation of how and why events occur as they do. In effect, a psycology is the answer to the two-part question: By what thought processes do people account for the objects and events of the world, and what beliefs do people acquire by means of those processes?
- A large portion of any person's psychology is held in common with other folks with whom that person is identified either directly or else vicariously through such mass communication media as newspapers, books, radio, and television. That commonly held portion of a person's beliefs can be referred to as a group's *folk psychology*.
- That folk psychology can be regarded as part of the group's culture, when *culture* is defined as "the collective programming of the mind which distinguishes the members of one human group from another" (Hofstede, 1980, p. 25).
- Frequently the misunderstanding, confusion, and conflict in people's social interactions result from differences in people's psychologies, that is, from differences in their beliefs about life and in the way they interpret events.
- If people hope to interact with others in a constructive manner, they can profit from understanding other folks' beliefs and ways of interpreting events. That understanding is fostered by a person recognizing the likenesses and differences among the psychologies of diverse cultural groups, with the resulting knowledge promoting well-informed relationships with members of those groups.

In keeping with the five assumptions, this book (a) provides a framework for analyzing folk psychologies and (b) describes multiple forms that folk psychologies assume in different cultures—descriptions intended to help readers understand the varied ways that the people they encounter will likely view life.

# 1

# Diverse Cultures, Diverse Psychologies

The best known early study of folk psychology appeared in a massive work, *Völkerpsychologie*, by the pioneer German psychologist Wilhelm Wundt (1832-1920) in the opening years of the 20th century. Originally a 5-volume, 3,000-page publication, *Völkerpsychologie* expanded to 10 volumes by the time of its fourth edition in 1927. In this tome, Wundt pictured the psychological life of the individual as constantly determined by, and interwoven with, the social setting. For Wundt, folk psychology concerned "those mental products created by a community of human life and are therefore inexplicable in terms merely of individual consciousness, since they presuppose the reciprocal action of many" (Wundt, 1912/1916, p. 3). Although it was Wundt who was primarily responsible for popularizing the expression *folk psychology*, he credited two German editors—a philosopher, Lazarus, and a philologist, Steinthal—with creating the term in 1860 when they launched their *Folk Psychology and Philology Journal (Zeitschrift Völkerpsychologie und Sprachwissenschaft)* (Wundt, 1912/1916, p. 2).

In keeping with Wundt's definition, the term *folk psychology* is used throughout the following chapters to mean a collection of beliefs, shared by members of a cultural group, regarding how people think when they interpret life's events. Or, cast another way, a folk psychology is the answer to a pair of questions: (a) By what thought processes do the members of a cultural group account for the events of the world—including their own and other people's behavior—and (b) what beliefs (Wundt's "mental products") do people acquire by means of those processes?

Because not everyone who writes about folk psychology defines the term in the same way, we may profit at the outset from recognizing how other conceptions of folk psychology compare with the one used throughout the following pages.

## CONSTRASTING CONCEPTIONS OF FOLK PSYCHOLOGY

Three useful ways to view definitions of folk psychology are from the vantage points of (a) the kinds of people intended, (b) the components of the mind intended, and (c) the relationship between folk psychology and scientific psychology.

### Kinds of People Intended

The word *folk* is used to mean *human* whenever the modes of thinking identified as folk psychology are assumed to be universal throughout humankind. Such an intent is suggested by Place's (1996, p. 264) writing that

> Folk psychology, I maintain, is a linguistic universal. In every natural language currently spoken, in every ancient language and culture of which we have decipherable records, the same basic concepts, the same explanatory scheme, are deployed in the accounts that are given of the actions both of the speaker/writer and of other human beings.

Among speakers of English, those basic concepts are identified by such words as *believing, feeling, desiring, hoping, remembering,* and other terms that are considered to designate mental functions common to all normal people no matter where or when they've lived. Conceiving of folk psychology in this all-encompassing fashion is particularly useful for the conduct of comparative psychology, whenever the term *comparative psychology* refers to how humans "think" compared with how cats, dolphins, frogs, squid, and garden slugs "think."

However, in daily parlance—in commonsense usage—the term *folk* is typically intended in a more restricted sense. Such is the case when the word *folk* appears in the expressions *folk art, folk beliefs, folklore, folk songs,* and *folkways.* Here *folk* does not refer to all humans but, rather, to limited clusters of people, clusters frequently called *cultural groups.* In this more limited meaning, *folk psychology* concerns the ways of thinking typical of members of a particular group of people. This conception fits Jerome Bruner's (1990, p. 13) description of folk psychology as "a culture's account of what makes human beings tick." Such a meaning is the one assigned to *folk psychology* throughout this book. As the examples in Chapters 2 through 13 illustrate, one group's folk psychology can differ from another's. And because the issue of what constitutes a cultural group is a bit complex, that issue is inspected in some detail later in this chapter.

### The Intended Components of Mind

People who speak and write about folk psychology may also disagree about what aspects of mind and behavior are properly identified as *psy-*

*chology.* Should the term *psychology*—meaning the study of the mind—be limited to descriptions and explanations of thinking *functions,* such as functions identified by the English-language terms *believing, understanding, desiring, wishing, judging, remembering, forgetting, feeling (happy, afraid, guilty, at peace), planning, imagining,* and more? Or does *psychology* properly also include specific products of those functions—specific beliefs, understandings, desires, wishes, judgments, feelings, and the like that are widespread among members of a culture?

Present-day writers about the philosophy of psychology and about developmental psychology usually appear to restrict their use of *folk psychology* to the first of these possibilities—the description and explanation of mental functions. Thus, Baker (1999, p. 319) has suggested that in recent times the term *folk psychology* has most often been intended by scholars to mean "the [commonsense] conceptual framework of explanations of human behavior." Churchland (1994, p. 308) casts his version of that pursuit in these words:

> 'Folk psychology' denotes the prescientific, commonsense conceptual framework that all normal socialized humans deploy in order to comprehend, predict, explain, and manipulate the behaviour of humans and the higher animals. This framework includes concepts such as *belief, desire, pain, pleasure, love, hate, joy, fear, suspicion, memory, recognition, anger, sympathy, intention,* and so forth. It embodies our baseline understanding of the cognitive, affective, and purposive nature of persons. Considered as a whole, it constitutes our conception of what a person is.

Folk psychology, then, becomes the study of the kinds of mental processes typically found among members of a cultural group. Such study focuses on how members believe their own minds and others' minds work. Sometimes this has been called people's intuitive *theory of mind* (Wellman, 1990). It seems apparent that some individuals can talk knowingly about their assumed thinking processes. Consider, for example, the comment: "I believe in the idea of conscience, so it was my conscience that made me go back and help them fix the flat tire." Other people cannot—or at least do not—analyze their thought processes, but only reflect their intuitive conception of human thinking in what they say and how they act. "I really don't know why I went back. It just seemed like the thing to do. I would have felt bad if I hadn't."

Throughout this book, however, my conception of *folk psychology* not only involves peoples' notions about how humans think but also includes the products of mind that result from such thinking. In other words, the field of folk psychology, as intended in these pages, concerns both a cultural group's shared thinking processes and the substantive beliefs that derive from those processes—substantive beliefs about reality, about knowing, about causes, about competence, about values, about humor, about self, and more. I am convinced that our understanding of a folk psychology is diminished if we focus solely on a people's theory of how the mind operates and neglect the sorts of beliefs that result from those conceptions of mind.

The reason I adopt such a position is twofold. First, that position fits what Wundt had in mind when he wrote about "those mental products created by a community of human life." Indeed, his *Völkerpsychologie* (Wundt, 1927) is filled with a great host of specific beliefs held by particular cultural groups. Second, a group's specific beliefs serve as valuable lenses through which to view the members' shared thought processes. In effect, interpretations of how people think—people's mental functions—are typically inferences drawn from those individuals' expressed beliefs and displayed behaviors. For example, the inhabitants of a village blame their current drought on the anger of a god who controls rainfall, with that anger having been elicited by the villagers' failure to perform a ritual honoring the god. As a second example, the Judaic-Christian-Islamic version of how human life arrived on earth contends that God, by one sudden act, created a single man (Adam) in the complete form seen in the modern-day human male, then used one of Adam's ribs to create the first woman (Eve). According to that account, those two persons—Adam and Eve—were the progenitors of all humans who have since that time populated the world.

Writers who limit the expression *folk psychology* to discussions of mental functions, and do not include the products of those functions, will accept the above accounts of drought and human life as cultural beliefs, but will probably claim that neither of those examples is an instance of folk psychology. Instead, the drought explanation will likely be called *folk meteorology* and the Adam-and-Eve anecdote *folk biology*. However, it seems clear that both of those beliefs are products of the human psyche—interpretations produced by a cultural group's ways of thinking. Therefore, I would argue that both examples qualify as *folk psychology*. In particular, both can serve as lenses through which to inspect the nature of a cultural group's thinking processes. For instance, the villagers' explanation of the drought is a belief that attempts to account for a particular observed phenomenon. The mental operation to be inferred from such an explanation must include the cultural group's conviction that there are supernatural beings who possess the traits of jealousy and vindictiveness and have the power to control the weather. Furthermore, the explanation reflects a mode of reasoning that traces a three-stage, cause-and-effect path from (a) people's neglecting to honor an invisible personified god or spirit, to (b) that god's resenting being neglected, and finally to (c) the god's punishing the people by withholding rain. The Adam-and-Eve proposal about human beginnings is likewise useful as a window on people's thought patterns. That account reflects a source of knowledge on which doctrinaire Jews, Christians, and Muslims are willing to base their beliefs about reality. Their trusted source of knowledge is not empirical observation (seeing is believing) or the outcome of an experiment but, rather, is hearsay in the form of a narrative of ancient origin that has been passed down through the centuries as supernaturally revealed truth. That information about the kind of knowledge people trust is useful in deciding how to interact with them.

In summary, throughout this book I have included a great many descriptions of people's beliefs about life's events—events that are physical, biological, economic, social, personal, and more. I propose that those descriptions are properly considered aspects of folk psychology, especially because they permit inferences about how different cultural groups think about life.

## Folk Psychology and Scientific Psychology

Much of contemporary writing about folk psychology centers on questions about the relationship between folk psychology and scientific psychology. One prominent question is this: Does folk psychology qualify as a *theory*? In response, authors have often disagreed about the qualities that a proposal must display if it is to earn the title *theory*. Among notable participants in this debate, Fodor (1987) and Stich (1983) have answered *yes*, people's commonsense beliefs about the mind do form a theory. Fodor not only asserts that folk psychology is a theory, but it's a theory that science will refine. Chater and Oaksford (1996) accept the notion that folk psychology is a theory—or set of theories—but it's "bad science" for a variety of reasons and thus is not a theory in the strict sense often intended by scientists. (That sense requires that a proposal about relationships among phenomena be in the form of laws or generalizations, with hypotheses logically derived from the generalizations and with a means of empirically testing the validity of the hypotheses.) Place (1996) denies that folk psychology is a true theory. And so it goes. The dispute over folk psychology's status as a theory has not yet been settled, and the dispute can be expected to continue (Valentine, 1996).

A second question scholars debate is whether scientific psychology, as it develops into the future, will replace commonsense explanations of behavior. This has become known as the *eliminativism* issue. Such participants in the debate as Rorty (1965) have likened folk psychology to the beliefs in witchcraft that were common in Europe and the Americas in the 17th century. Thus, from Rorty's perspective, folk psychology, like witchcraft beliefs, will be "discredited and abandoned in the light of contemporary discoveries in the neurosciences" (Place, 1996, p. 264).

However, others who engage in the eliminativism dispute will disagree. Chater and Oaksford write that, no matter what scientists learn about the operation of the human brain, folk psychologies will continue to be useful because

> scientists seek out and explore just those areas where theories can be built, tested, and applied; they shy away from areas that presently appear intractable to scientific methods. The ability to choose to focus on tractable matters and ignore the intractable marks an important difference between science and common sense. Folk theories must allow us to make the best sense of our everyday world and guide our actions as successfully as possible; to do this they must face up to the full complexity of the everyday world, which, we suggest, science rightly prefers to avoid. (Chater & Oaksford, 1996, pp. 252-253)

Richards (1996, p. 275) agrees that folk psychology explanations of behavior will not be discarded. "A rich heterogeneous language drawn from all areas of human experience over many millennia will necessarily continue its Protean career for as long as we wish to talk to one another about ourselves."

Finally, it is instructive to consider an awkward fact about the language that analysts are obliged to use in their discussions of folk psychologies. This is the fact that, having grown up in a particular culture, the analysts themselves have been steeped in folk-psychology parlance. From infancy onward, they have learned to use such terms as *believe, want, intend, hope,* and *remember* as if these were real things and not merely fairy-tale fictions passed down through the ages. Consequently, those philosophers and "scientific" psychologists who now reject such terms as accurate indicators of how the human mind works find it difficult, if not impossible, to explain themselves in scientific nomenclature untainted by folk-psychology concepts. Today's most prominent proponents of eliminativism place their faith in neuroscience—in studies of the operation of the brain—as the most trustworthy source of proper descriptions of how human minds function. They expect that neuroscience terminology will replace folk-psychology terminology as the language of psychology. How this might work out has been illustrated in Richards' (1996) example of how a pair of sentences in folk-psychology language might be recast in neuroscience language that describes events in the form of brain functions (Richards, 1996, p. 271).

> Folk-language version: "I have a vivid memory of my fifth birthday party."
> Neuro-language version: "A strong resonance in my 8th peristratial cortex levels is reactivating an earlier biostate with a cognitive temporal verbal coding of 'fifth birthday party.'"
>
> Folk-language version: "You have some strange ideas."

Neuro-language version: "You've got some abnormal levels of glucose consumption in your forebrain."

How useful such a change in describing mental activity might be is a matter that readers can decide for themselves.

## Summary

In view of the foregoing sketch of controversies about folk psychology, what can be expected of the treatment of folk psychologies throughout the rest of this book?

First, as already explained, the meaning here of *folk psychology* is not confined to conceptions of how people think, for it also includes products of such thinking in the form of specific beliefs, emotions, and values. Second, I am assuming that the word *folk* does not refer to humankind as a whole but, instead, it refers to the particular cultural groups whose psychologies are being discussed. Third, no attempt is made to write in language free of traditional folk-psychology parlance. Throughout the book such terms as *reality, knowledge, beliefs, feelings, attitudes, humor,* and the like are employed on the expectation that such terms can, indeed, be interpreted by readers in meaningful ways—in ways that approximate the writer's intentions.

## CULTURAL DIVERSITY

As noted earlier, a key tenet on which the contents of this volume are built is that the folk psychology of one culture can differ from the folk psychology of another. As a result, the way the typical member of one culture interprets what people say and do can differ from the way a typical member of another culture interprets those events. In recent years, the shared beliefs held within a cultural group have sometimes been referred to as *indigenous knowledge,* defined variously as people's "cognitive and wise legacy as a result of their interaction with nature in a common territory" (Maurial, 1999, p. 62) or as "the knowledge that has evolved in a particular societal context and which is used by lay people in that context in the conduct of their lives" (George, 1999, p. 80).

As an introduction to this proposed diversity of viewpoints among cultural groups, consider the following sampling of convictions:

*Reality.* Within traditional Zulu society in South Africa, reality consists of tangible people and objects as well as spiritual beings. . . . When people are still alive, their spirit may temporarily wander from their body and engage in activities at some distance, with this departure from the body often providing valuable learning experiences. Dreams during sleep are cited as evidence of this wandering. (Thomas, 1997, p. 265)

*Living things.* In Iroquois culture, brightly painted wooden masks are thought to have magical qualities, attributes of life, so that they require periodic sustenance and are thus "fed" such matter as tobacco and sunflower oil. The Iroquois are likely to be distressed by such objects being exhibited in museums, for they fear that such things as masks will feel alienated and unhappy at being so imprisoned. (Wilson, 1959, p. 54)

*Knowing.* [Among the one million members of Chagga society living on the slopes of Mount Kilimanjaro in Tanzania], when parents teach their children how to get a good crop of bananas, they also, at the same time, teach them several other things: (a) that working hard is a blessing and a fundamental human value; (b) that certain methods must be applied to protect the farm from soil erosion; (c) that this particular farm belonged previously to family ancestors who should always be remembered, respected, and appreciated; and (d) that a good crop will feed the families and others in need. Thus, what is known and passed on has personal, social, moral, and economic implications. Indigenous knowledge is education that underscores the importance of bondedness, cooperation, altruism, generosity, and environmental protection. (Mosha, 1999, p. 213)

*Cause.* [In the Hindu culture of Nepal, the highest-status social caste is that of the priestly Brahmans.] One is born into the Brahman caste. However, one can lose one's Brahman status, or be effectively excommunicated from the caste. This would happen if a man or woman publicly violated an important rule of caste behavior. For example, if a Brahman publicly consumed rice cooked by a lower-caste person, he or she would no longer be Brahman and would assume the caste rank of the person whose boiled rice was eaten. Another way caste status can be lost is through sexual behavior. . . . A Brahman man loses his Brahman status only if he has sexual relations with a woman of an untouchable caste. In this case he, too, would become untouchable. But he may have premarital or extramarital relations with any nonuntouchable woman [Kshatriya, Vaisya, or Sudra castes] without losing his Brahman rank or his ability to reproduce Brahman children through a Brahman wife. (Stone, 1997, p. 97)

*Competence.* Japanese mothers [of young children] appeared to place higher confidence in efficacy of effort than did American mothers. Perhaps the Japanese mothers were thus expressing a belief that problems are susceptible to persistence and hard work and that responsibility for achievement lies with the individual. Mothers and children in the United States seemed less oriented toward internal sources of achievement. They emphasized the role of parents in children's success in school [and] were more likely to place blame on the school for the children's failure. (Hess et al., 1986, pp. 148, 163)

*Innate characteristics.* In Confucian tradition, each person is born with a propensity for virtue, but circumstances of life will determine whether this virtue will be nurtured or lost. Furthermore, Confucian theory proposes that most people are born with equal potential ability to succeed. But during a time of unfavorable influences, a person may abandon himself to wrongdoing. Personal intent and willpower are required for overcoming [such] difficulties. (Lin, 1988, p. 121)

*Attributes of "self."* The Gisu people of Uganda are widely known for their competitiveness and their assertive natures; their society rewards individual achievement. This is reflected in their concepts of personality [that include] *litima* [meaning violent emotion] and *bunyali*, roughly translated as 'ability' or strength of character and the implication of surmounting obstacles. (La Fontaine, 1986, p. 144)

*Esteemed traits.* [Among the Nyansongo in the Gusii region of Kenya, East Africa,] obedience rather than enterprise or initiative is considered to be the key to success. . . . Smartness or brightness by itself is not a highly valued characteristic, and the Nyansongo concept of intelligence includes respect for elders and filial piety as vital ingredients. An obedient child, according to Nyansongo thought, is also responsible, that is, he performs the tasks and chores regularly assigned to him by his parents with a minimum of supervision. (LeVine & LeVine, 1963, p. 181)

*Consequences of behavior.* The Hindu doctrine of karma [in which the quality of a person's deeds during one life span determines the quality of that person's life in subsequent existences on earth] emphasizes the principle that as a man sows, so shall he reap and that he is the maker of his own destiny. (Iyer, 1969)

*Values.* In a study of Anglo families in New Haven, Connecticut, and of Puerto Rican families in Puerto Rico's metropolitan areas, Anglo mothers more often valued young children's exploring the setting on their own, thereby reflecting the prototypical U.S. cultural values of individualism, initiative, self-control (rather than control by others), and self-maximization. Puerto Rican mothers more often valued toddlers' displaying proper social demeanor by not risking socially offensive behavior in strange situations, thereby reflecting a *sociocentric* value-commitment—a concern for maintaining harmony within the group. The proper child in the Puerto Rican setting would be "calm, obedient, and respectfully attentive to the teachings of his or her elders, in order to become skilled in the interpersonal and rhetorical competencies that will someday be expected of the well-socialized adult." (Harwood, Miller, & Irizarry, 1995, p. 98)

*Prohibitions.* [Polynesian societies display] extreme variation in the severity and also the objects of menstrual taboos. . . . The taboos range from keeping the woman out of sight [during her menstrual period], through details of strict hygienic avoidance, to her complete reintegration into daily life. Among the Marquesas a woman had to be kept out of sight for three days. Among most Maori tribes the woman moves about freely, works in the house, etc. Only the bodily secretions are tabooed. Among the Tuhoe tribe the taboo applied only to *kopa*, the cleansing material used by the women. Here the degree of precision and specialization is remarkable; only one species of moss is to be used. . . . The humiliation experienced by a woman when a man sees her *kopa* is so great that it is regarded as sufficient cause for suicide. (Steiner, 1999, pp. 129-130)

With the foregoing miscellany of beliefs as an initial taste of folk psychologies' products, we turn now to a more complete description of what this book is about and then consider in detail what folk psychologies are and what they are not.

## THE BOOK'S TWOFOLD PURPOSE

This book is designed to achieve two aims:

- Suggest a framework on which the elements of folk psychologies can be displayed so that the dominant psychology of one culture can readily be compared with that of another. In other words, the framework—represented by chapter titles and topics within chapters—is intended to reveal the structure of peoples' belief systems.
- Furnish a number of examples of belief and practice from different cultures to demonstrate the diverse forms that each component of the framework can assume across cultural groups. In most chapters, the examples are 'products of thought,' such as particular beliefs, emotions, intentions, desires, hopes, and the like that are widely held within specified cultures. The intent is not to provide an extensive catalog of illustrations for each component of the framework. Rather, the purpose is to illustrate several forms that each component assumes in representative cultures, then leave to readers' initiative the identification of additional examples from cultures with which they are acquainted.

It seems evident that when individuals communicate with each other, what each one says and does is founded on each person's underlying beliefs about the world. During a typical conversation, participants don't bother to explain their underlying beliefs, since they assume that they all hold the same unstated convictions. Either (a) they recognize that all of the conversers are members of the same culture or (b) they are unaware that some people subscribe to worldviews different from their own.

A great deal of intercultural conflict results from individuals failing to understand each other's psychological perceptions. Or, if they do understand others' psychologies, they may be unwilling to accept such beliefs. Thus, the practical application of this book's contents can be that of assisting readers in understanding the folk psychologies on which persons from different cultural groups base their thought and behavior. Such understanding could result in greater skill in social relations and perhaps greater tolerance for others' viewpoints.

This initial chapter describes the major components of the framework. Subsequent chapters dissect each component and illustrate how the elements of a component can assume different forms in various peoples' psychologies. However, before inspecting the framework, we should consider in greater detail what is meant by *folk psychology, sources of evidence,* and *the evolution of folk psychologies.*

## DELINEATING THE DOMAIN OF FOLK PSYCHOLOGIES

As noted earlier, the term *psychology* or *psychological theory,* as used in these pages, refers to a description of (a) the thought processes that determine how and why individuals explain events and (b) the beliefs about life that result from such thought processes. A folk psychology is such a description shared by a group of people. If we accept Hofstede's (1980, p. 25) definition of *culture* as "the collective programming of the mind which distinguishes the members of one human group from another," then the label *folk psychology* includes a cultural group's interpretation of how people develop their beliefs and their modes of thought and action. That interpretation is what Barth (1987, p. 1) calls an "aggregate tradition of knowledge." In addition to the term *folk psychology,* such a tradition can be identified by alternative labels—*naive psychology, commonsense psychology, ethnopsychology, everyday psychology, the psychology of the populace.*

However, defining folk psychology in only this general way can lead to confusion when we later inspect examples of people's notions of thought and action. Thus, we can profit from identifying this book's more precise meaning of folk psychology as it relates to three concepts—*group, stability,* and *science-versus-religion.*

### Group

A key consideration in recognizing a folk psychology is the question of who are the members of a group. If a group's belief system is to qualify as *folk* psychology, the group cannot consist solely of experts or authorities, that is, of those who specialize in knowledge of the system, such as professional psychologists, psychiatrists, anthropologists, philosophers, priests, shamans, medicine men, chiefs, or the like. Although the cultural group can include such specialists as these, most of its members must be "common folk," ones drawn from the lay public.

A characteristic that binds the group's members together is typically reflected in an adjective or two in the group's designator—Apache, Basque, Javanese, Muslim, Mormon, Social Democrat, Marxist, Libertarian, Nazi, pacifist, skinhead, nerd, redneck, Ivy Leaguer, or the like. Compound labels may identify subgroups that subscribe to more specific folk psychologies than do the larger congeries of which the subgroups are a part—Mongolian peasant, Irish Catholic, Southern Baptist, left-wing Democrat, right-wing Republican, university-educated feminist.

When we try to identify a person's set of beliefs as representing a particular folk psychology, we face two puzzles about groups. First, an individual may embrace only a portion of a given group's overall set of beliefs. Can we then legitimately say the person subscribes to that collective's folk psychology? One way out of this difficulty is to define folk psychology as a set of convictions held *at least in large part* by members of a group, especially when the large part includes core tenets of that psychology. Thus, individuals can still be identified as members of the group if they accept the belief system's central elements without accepting every detail. For instance, a dedicated Muslim may agree that the world is under the control of an omniscient, ubiquitous, all-powerful Allah, yet may reject the traditional Muslim belief that the contents of Islam's most revered holy book, the Qur'an, were delivered in segments to the prophet Mohammed by the angel Gabriel near the city of Mecca.

While this "core tenets" solution to the question of membership is of some use, it's still imperfect, since it allows a shadow area within which there can be doubt about whether a person embraces enough of the group's beliefs to qualify as an adherent of its psychology.

A second problem is that of multiple group membership. People usually are members of more than a single group, and the cluster of beliefs that typify one collectivity's psychology may not be identical with another's. In some instances these different views, while not identical, may still be compatible, because the aspects treated in one of the systems differ from those treated in the other. Consider the case of a middle-aged man, originally from the Foi ethnic group of Papua New Guinea's southern highlands, who has been living in Australia for the past 20 years. Like most Australians, he questions the truthfulness of advertisements seen on television, for he believes that the creators of television commercials, in order to make money, are willing to exaggerate the worth of their products. But unlike most Australians, he also subscribes to a traditional Foi belief in the meaning of dreams. According to Foi tradition, a dream of sexual intercourse is interpreted as foretelling future success in hunting. Dreaming of a house falling down in disrepair means imminent death, and a dream of red bird feathers means success in acquiring valuable pearl shells (Weiner, 1991, pp. 27-28). Whereas there is no conflict between questioning the veracity of television commercials and ascribing meanings to dreams, in other cases two cultural groups' psychologies are clearly incompatible. For instance, a member of a fundamentalist Christian denomination is, in her professional life, a research biologist. Consequently, she faces a problem in deciding which version of human origins she will embrace—the creationist interpretation of human beginnings found in the Bible (Adam and Eve were created by God in their mature human forms) or the Darwinian interpretation on which most of modern biology is founded (humans evolved over eons of time from more elemental species).

In summary, an individual's psychology can be monolithic, composed entirely of beliefs from a single established folk psychology, as would be true of a Thai who subscribes faithfully to all of the beliefs of a Theravada version of Buddhism. Or else a person's psychology can be a composite of elements of different folk psychologies, with the elements drawn from among the beliefs of disparate groups of which that person is a member, as in the case of a woman who identifies herself as a Zambian-American, global-feminist, Roman-Catholic, lesbian-rights Republican. A personal psychology may also include elements of belief based on the particular person's unique conclusions based on events specific to his or her own life.

## Stability

Because cultures are never static but are always in a state of transition, so also are folk psychologies that are embedded in cultures. Furthermore, the pace of change can differ from one culture to another and between one component of a folk psychology and another component. For instance, in a typical Christian worldview, the concepts of *soul* as an element of human personality and of *life after death* as a segment of the human life span have continued unaltered over the centuries. However, in Christian psychology the characteristics attributed to females in comparison to males—including the competencies and proper life roles of the two genders—have been changing, particularly during recent decades in advanced industrial societies. An increasing number of Christian denominations now offer women roles in the clergy that previously were available only to men because popular conceptions of female attributes have recently been revised.

Within any folk psychology there is usually some measure of tension between stability and change. The stability appears to derive, at least in part, from people's yearning for ageless, immutable truths on which to ground their lives. Hence, a folk psychology that claims to provide eternally valid wisdom can be highly attractive, since it offers a trustworthy foundation on which to base one's efforts to survive and prosper in an ominous, unpredictable world. But as conditions of the world change, beliefs proposed as immutable truths may no longer equip people to survive as they did before. Hence, folk psychologies may change under the pressures of a new reality's demand for updated answers about why life's events occur as they do.

## Science and Religion

Of both theoretical and practical interest is the place of science and of religion in folk psychologies.

### The nature of science

The term *science* or *scientific method* has commonly been used to identify a way of collecting and interpreting information about life—a way based on such precepts as the following:

- All statements about the nature of the universe, including about people's lives, should be founded on empirical evidence, that is, founded on observations and measurements of the real world rather than on speculation about what "might be."
- No conclusions about the nature of the universe are final. Each conclusion is tentative, representing "what we know at this time," and is subject to further validation and refinement based on additional empirical evidence.
- If a conclusion drawn from the study of a particular sample of phenomena (objects, people, events) is to be applied also to a broader group of phenomena than the sample is thought to represent, then care should be taken to ensure, as far as possible, that (a) the sample has accurately represented the broader group and (b) the extent of likely error in the sample's representativeness is reported.
- The belief that a statement about life is true—or at least approximately true or tentatively true—should not be based on faith in the person or document from which the statement came but, rather, should be determined by how well the statement has been derived from the application of scientific procedures.

### The nature of religion

There exists no universal agreement about the meaning of religion. Writers who conceptualize religion in a broadly inclusive way define it variously as "the collective expression of human values," as "the zealous and devout pursuit of any objective," or as "a system of values or preferences—an inferential value system." Such definitions are so broad that they encompass not only the belief systems of Christianity, Islam, and Jainism but also those of communism, democracy, logical positivism, and even anarchism.

Other writers place far greater limitations on the term *religion*, proposing that a conceptual scheme qualifying as religion must be an integrated system of specified components, including the nature of a supreme being or of gods (theology), the origin and condition of the universe (cosmology), rules governing human relations (ethics, moral values), the proper behavior of people toward superhuman powers (rites, rituals, worship), the nature of knowledge and its sources (epistemology), and the goal of life (teleology). Under this second sort of definition, Christianity, Islam, and Jainism are religions but communism, democracy, logical positivism, and anarchism are not.

The second of these conceptions of religion seems to be the one more widely adopted and is the one intended throughout this book.

Virtually all religions qualify as folk psychologies, except those few practiced solely by a coterie of specialists (monks, nuns, shamans) who make religion their life's work and whose beliefs and rituals are not embraced by a lay public.

## The place of science and religion in folk psychologies

To identify the roles of science and religion in folk psychologies, we can consider how science is similar to, and different from, religion. Science and religion share several attributes. Both (a) are founded on empirical observations, (b) require an investment of faith, and (c) account for the causes of phenomena. However, the two usually differ somewhat in their conceptions of these attributes.

*Empirical observations.* Science and religion are both concerned with interpreting what people see, hear, and feel in their daily lives. However, the typical manner in which people's observations are collected may differ between scientific and religious approaches. Scientific methods are likely to include more precise and publicly verifiable observation and measurement procedures than do traditional religious methods. The techniques of science are also more likely to involve attempts to control some of the factors that seem to influence events so that the scientist can observe what effect the remaining factor or factors exert. Religions are more likely to make observations of events in their natural settings, free from attempts to control ostensibly causal variables. However, observations from the viewpoint of science may also be made under natural conditions.

Whereas religions are apt to include people's reported dreams and visions as acceptable observations of "the real world," scientific perspectives usually regard such reports as people's opinions rather than factual accounts of reality.

*Faith.* The word *faith*, as intended here, refers to people's willingness to base their judgments and behavior on the assumption that a particular belief is true. People may or may not be able to adduce a line of logic in support of their faith. Thus, they may defend their faith either by citing evidence or by simply saying "It's the way I feel" or "It's reasonable" or "I'm compelled to believe it."

Religion and science usually differ in regard to the objects in which adherents place their faith. In a religion, the faith is often invested in a person (Mohammed for Muslims, the Pope for Catholics, Joseph Smith for Mormons, Mary Baker Eddy for Christian Scientists), supernatural beings (God, Brahman, ancestral spirits), or a document (the Torah for Jews, the Guru Granth Sahid [The Divine Word] for Sikhs, The Great Learning and Doctrine of the Mean for Confucianists, the Tao Te Ching for Taoists).

Scientists typically place their faith in "scientific methods," that is, in the sorts of principles illustrated in our earlier section on "the nature of science." But scientists don't all agree on what those methods are. For instance, in recent decades, proponents of postmodernism have differed with the advocates of logical positivism about what constitute trustworthy ways of gathering and interpreting observations. Specifically, postmodernists have questioned the widespread belief among positivists that (a) experimental conditions can be controlled in ways that enable researchers to precisely identify different variables' contribution to causing events so as to (b) permit accurate predictions of future events (Thomas, 2001, pp. 197-207). But it's not only the advocates of religions who place faith in "authoritative" people and documents. Scientists do the same, although the people and publications they honor are usually not the same as those respected by proponents of a religious persuasion. The reason scientists are obliged to trust people and documents is that no one can directly reproduce the observations about all manner of phenomena that are reported by individual scientists or are published in journals and books. Most of what any scientist knows has been accepted on the word of someone else. So whether scientists are willing to trust authorities usually depends on how closely the authorities' descriptions of their data-gathering techniques and their interpretations adhere to the tenets of scientific methodology.

*Causality.* Perhaps the most obvious difference between religious and scientific reasoning about events is that religious accounts more often attribute causes to supernatural forces. The distinction between these two viewpoints becomes apparent when we consider how people try to influence the outcome of an event. A typical religious perspective contends that many—perhaps all—events are controlled by personified supernatural forces—gods and spirits. Thus, the way to cure illness, avert a damaging windstorm, or ensure the gender of an unborn child consists of appealing to the supernatural forces by means of rituals, pleas, promises, and offerings. It is hoped that the supernatural forces, if pleased by those supplications, will then produce the hoped-for outcome. In contrast, a typical scientific viewpoint holds that events can be influenced by people's (a) understanding the operation of the tangible world's variables that are directly responsible for particular happenings and (b) trying to manipulate those variables in a manner that produces the desired results. Thus, the religious view is one of mediated causation—people do not effect events directly but, rather, they influence events by pleasing the mediators that control the world. However, the scientific view is one of immediate causation, with people directly attempting to alter the discernible factors that are assumed to determine events.

## The composition of folk psychologies

For convenience of explanation, throughout the above discussion I've drawn sharp contrasts between scientific and religious bases of folk psychologies. However, in practice, folk psychologies are a mixture of both approaches. Some observers have suggested that the particular combination of the two viewpoints found in a given cultural group's psychology is influenced by (a) how obvious and humanly controllable the causal factors seem to be and (b) how vital an event is to people's survival and well-being. Consider, for example, the dangers fishermen face at sea. Acheson notes that despite the development of better fishing and communication technology, "the sea is still a dangerous and risky environment for a terrestrial animal such as man" (1981, p. 287). Thus, as Malinowski (1922, 1948) suggested decades ago, people may cope with irreducible risk through ritual and magic. He reported that in the Trobriand Islands there was no magic associated with lagoon fishing that involved no physical danger, but "in open-sea fishing, full of danger and uncertainty, there is extensive magical ritual to secure safety and good results" (Malinowski, 1948, p. 31). As a further illustration,

> Johnson (1979) argues that a large number of witches were thought to inhabit the environs of a Portuguese fishing community before the advent of motorized fishing craft. When motors were adopted, which made it much safer to negotiate a dangerous bar at the entrance of the harbor, the witches disappeared almost immediately and the level of religious observance declined as well. (Acheson, 1981, p. 288)

## SOURCES OF EVIDENCE

The expression *sources of evidence* refers to the sorts of information on which the description of a folk psychology can be founded. Principal sources include (a) one's own observations of people's conversation and behavior, (b) explanations offered by members of the group whose psychology is being investigated, (c) written documents, such as a religion's published history and doctrine, (d) laws and regulations, (e) rites and rituals, (f) various forms of literature and art (proverbs, anecdotes, poems, songs, dances, paintings, carvings, architectural designs), and (g) other summaries of folk beliefs written by such observers as anthropologists, social psychologists, travelers, missionaries, and novelists.

## Observations of People's Behavior

Imagine the following segment of conversation between a pharmacist and a bakery owner in a small American town. The segment is followed by a description of the implied folk psychology meanings behind the two men's remarks. Such meanings are understood by typical members of the culture even though those members might not be able to articulate the meanings. The objects of the conversation are 18-year-old Mike and 17-year-old Chelsea.

> Pharmacist: "Did you ever hire that young fellow, that Mike?"
> Baker: "I did, but he didn't work out. He wasn't too bright in the first place, and then he had a bad upbringing."
> Pharmacist: "What seemed to be his trouble?"
> Baker: "Lazy. He didn't care whether he did a good job or not. He didn't seem to feel bad about doing things poorly. He never kept his mind on the work, always dreaming about something else, so he'd do a job only half consciously, not concentrating on what he was up to. But you can't do much to change kids at that age. I had to let him go. How about you? Did you hire that Scott girl?"
> Pharmacist: "Chelsea? You bet. Great girl. Lots of natural talent and energy. Her dad's a medical doctor and her mother taught math before they were married. They've done a good job with Chelsea—set a good example and expected a lot of her. Now, there's a girl with a real conscience—she's always trying to do her best. Hard working, honest, self-assured, highly intelligent, and a lot of common sense."
> Baker: "Unfortunately, a conscience and common sense are two things Mike lacked."

We can now suggest elements of the folk psychology that apparently guided the two shopkeepers' assessments of Mike and Chelsea. Each element is stated as an assumed principle of human behavior, which is accompanied in parentheses by segments of the conversation from which the principle can be inferred.

- A person's competence derives from both one's nature or genetic endowment ("he wasn't too bright in the first place") and one's nurture or environmental influences ("he had a bad upbringing").
- The quality of people's genetic inheritance can be estimated from knowing about their parents' accomplishments ("Her dad's a medical doctor and her mother taught math").
- People can concentrate on only one novel thing at a time, that is, on only one thing that requires concentrated attention ("He'd do a job only half consciously").

- Personality characteristics by the latter teen years are so ingrained that they are highly resistant to efforts to alter them ("But you can't do much to change kids at that age").
- A lot of what people learn—and what becomes part of their personality—is acquired through modeling, that is, through imitating others ("They . . . set a good example and expected a lot of her").
- People's personalities are composed of traits that influence their performance in all aspects of life. Such traits explain people's behavior and enable one to predict how people will act in the future ("lazy" and "hard-working, honest, self-assured, highly intelligent, and a lot of common sense").
- Being academically adept ("intelligent") is not the same as making good decisions in practical situations ("common sense").
- An important feature of personality is one's *conscience*, which functions as an internal rewarding and punishing system influencing one's behavior. A person's conscience can be either strong or weak. A strong conscience motivates the individual to strive toward a goal even under difficult circumstances ("she's always trying to do her best" and "Mike lacked . . . a conscience" so he "didn't care whether he did a good job or not"). Abiding by the dictates of one's conscience is rewarded by feelings of pride and accomplishment. Violating the dictates of one's conscience is punished by feelings of guilt, shame, and remorse. ("He didn't seem to feel bad about doing things poorly").

Drawing accurate inferences from observed behavior can require a precise understanding of the culture of the people who are observed. Such an understanding is most often brought to events by (a) people who are both products of that culture and adept at analysis and (b) outsiders who become intimately acquainted with the culture by living in it and studying it with the aid of native informants and published descriptions.

## Explanations by Members of a Culture

As an illustration of an explanation offered by a member of a culture, Dr. Konai Helu Thaman describes the psychological significance of flower or fruit garlands that people wear in her South Seas island home nation of Tonga.

> In Tonga, *kakala* means fragrant flowers. For most Tongans, however, *kakala* also means fragrant fruit, leaves, and wood which have sacred and mythical or legendary origins. Not only have *kakala* been 'socialized' into Tongan culture, but also ranked just as people are ranked. Furthermore, when [flowers or fruit] are strung or woven together into garlands, the end-products are themselves ranked. The different ways of stringing a *kakala* and the patterns used have been standardized and have remained relatively unchanged over hundreds of years. There exists a full and sophisticated vo-

cabulary as well as an elaborate etiquette associated with *kakala*. . . . The methods used to make a *kakala* usually depend upon a variety of considerations, including the desired type [of garland], the occasion for which it is to be worn, as well as factors relating to the rank of the person who is going to wear or receive the *kakala*. The final process is *luva* or the giving away of the *kakala* by the person who wears it to somebody else, for *kakala* is never meant to be kept indefinitely by the wearer, but to be given to somebody else, as a token of respect and love, [because *kakala* symbolizes] the values of *faka'apa'apa* (respect) and *'ofa* (love). (Thaman, 1993, p. 256)

Frequently, people's folk beliefs are formally compiled by researchers who pose questions to be answered by typical members of a cultural group.  As shown in later chapters, much of the published information about folk beliefs has been gathered in this manner.  However, it is important to recognize that what people say they believe is not necessarily the same as the tenets on which their behavior is apparently founded. A man who quite seriously asserts that he believes all ethnic groups are equally worthy of esteem may not reflect such a conviction in the way he treats people of different ethnic origins.

## Written History and Doctrine

What is considered proper human behavior in a folk psychology—and particularly in an established religion—is typically found in doctrinal accounts that either are written or, in nonliterate cultures, are inherited as oral history.

Among Jews, many of the guides to understanding human behavior are found in the Jewish Bible, particularly in (a) two books (Leviticus and Deuteronomy) among the initial five books (Pentateuch) that form the Torah, (b) the book of Proverbs, and, to a limited extent, (c) the books of Job and Ecclesiastes.

A Christian psychology draws not only on the Jewish sources that compose the Christian Bible's Old Testament, but also on the New Testament's four gospels (credited to Matthew, Mark, Luke, and John), and on the series of letters that the apostle Paul wrote to various struggling church groups in the early Christian world.

The fundamental elements of an Islamic psychology appear in the Qur'an, which is composed of holy doctrine dictated by the prophet Mohammed to scribes in the 6th century C.E. (Shakir, 1988).  Added to the psychological elements of the Qur'an are those from the collections of Mohammed's wise sayings (*hadith*) that are found in the various versions of the Sunnah (Suhrawardy, 1941).

Detailed descriptions of a traditional Hindu psychology have been passed down through the ages in the Manu Smriti (Buhler, 1886), which is a compilation of the laws or memorized traditions of Manu. According to legend, Manu was the primordial man and the Supreme Being's representative on earth, responsible for revealing to the world the Supreme Being's (Brahman's) dictates and wisdom. A similar book, the Grihya-Sutras (Oldenberg, 1886), is an aggregation of rules governing the conduct of daily domestic life and thus serves as a further guide to an age-old Hindu psychology.

## Laws, Rules, and Regulations

Laws, rules, and regulations—and particularly the rationales offered in their support—frequently reflect psychological convictions held by the people who created them. If such convictions are compatible with the society's folk psychology, those laws, rules, and regulations are likely to remain in force. If not compatible, they will not long endure.

As illustrations of edicts founded on particular psychological assumptions, consider the interpretation of human nature and of the causes of events implied in the following three laws. The description of each is followed by an estimate of the psychological principle or rationale underlying that edict.

*The law:* In the United States prior to 1920, the law prohibited women from voting in national elections. *The rationale:* Women and men inherently differ in their personality characteristics. Males, compared to females, by nature are more aggressive and outspoken, are blessed with greater physical strength and stamina, display greater initiative, have higher intelligence, are more logical and objective in their judgments, and are more resolute in their decisions. In contrast, females by nature are more retiring and emotional, lack physical strength and stamina, are followers rather than leaders, are intellectually inferior, arrive at decisions through intuition rather than logical reasoning, and often change their minds. Consequently, whereas men are properly equipped to make the judgments required in elections, women are not suitably equipped.

*The law:* In the United States, lawbreakers under age 18 are typically tried in separate courts for juveniles where the judge has considerable latitude in negotiating consequences to be faced by malefactors. *The rationale:* The central consideration behind such an arrangement is the intellectual maturity of offenders. It is generally assumed that teenagers, and particularly children below age 10 or 12, have not reached "the age of reason" and therefore cannot estimate the likely consequences of delinquent behavior. That the important consideration is immature judgment and not age itself is shown by the fact that adolescents below age 18 can be tried in adult criminal courts if prosecutors can mount sufficient evidence to convince juries that the culprits fully "knew what they were doing."

*The law:* Under such fundamentalist Islamic governments as those of Afghanistan and Iran, women are legally required to clothe all parts of their bodies but their faces. It is even preferred that they be clad in black garments covering all parts except the eyes. *The rationale:* According to the Qur'an, women's intrinsic sexual attractiveness can readily take advantage of males' intrinsically strong sexual drive, so men can be gripped by uncontrollable sex urges if not protected from women's wiles (Shakir, 1988).

## Literature and Art

The communicative and creative products of a culture—literature, languages, proverbs, paintings, architecture—often mirror important elements of the society's folk psychology.

## Literature

The following are examples of literary sources of two folk psychologies enmeshed in religious scriptures.

In Hindu tradition, the Mahabharata and Ramayana are lengthy poems detailing struggles among opposing social factions. Through the medium of these dramatic epics, followers of Hinduism over the ages have learned their culture's values and conceptions of peoples' relationships with their environments. Today, on the island of Java, the two epics continue—as they have for centuries—to provide the contents of puppet dramas that function as transmitters of tradition for the general populace (Buck, 1976; van Buitenen, 1973).

The Shinto worldview in Japanese culture assumes several forms. For the purposes of this book, it is useful to distinguish between four types of *religious Shinto* and *basic Shinto*. The four religious types are: (a) a set of rituals practiced only by the Imperial Family (*koshitsu shinto*); (b) shrine Shinto (*jinja shinto*), which is a system of beliefs and rituals held at shrines around the country in honor of gods or spirits (*kami*); (c) sect Shinto (*kyoha shinto*), a collection of 13 religious groups that came into existence in the 19th century as offshoots of Shinto tradition; and (d) folk Shinto (*minkan Shinto*), "a portfolio term for the amalgam of superstitious, magico-religious rites, and practices of the common people" (Agency for Cultural Affairs, 1972, p. 32). In contrast to these four is *basic Shinto*, which can be defined as the pervading value orientation of the Japanese people. Shinto, in this sense, is a foundation stratum of beliefs undergirding not only the four religious types but also all of Japanese society, a set of convictions that virtually all Japanese can be expected to hold, beliefs that represent a broadly encompassing folk psychology. The most basic literary sources of basic Shinto are two volumes completed in the 8th century C.E.—the Kojiki (1958) or Furu-koto-bumi (Records of Ancient Matters) and the Nihonshoki (1958) or Nihongi (Chronicles of Japan).

## Language

An accurate understanding of a people's language is often necessary for grasping the nuances of  a culture's worldview.  Such an understanding is sometimes beyond the capacity of some members of the society, particularly the younger members.  This point has been illustrated by Basil Johnston of the Ojibway Indian community in the Canadian province of Ontario.

> I learned that the words in our tribal language had meanings more fundamental than the primary ones that were commonly and readily understood. To know this character of words is crucial in understanding how the tribe perceived and expressed what they saw, heard, felt, tasted, and smelled in the world and what they thought and how they felt about the world of ideas. . . . [For instance, our ancestors] could not or dared not define God or the deities, or explain or reduce to human terms certain phenomena, [so] they invented the word *manitou*, which at times, depending upon context, might mean spirit, but which in its more fundamental senses meant talent, attributes, potencies, potential, substance, essence, and mystery. (Johnston, 1982, p. 6)

## Proverbs

Elements of folk psychologies are often reflected in adages that people regard as succinct truths about life and as guides to behavior.  The following illustrate such popular sayings in European-American culture. Each saying is followed in parentheses by an implied folk-psychology meaning that is understood by members of the culture.

> Spare the rod and spoil the child. (Without physical discipline, children's development goes awry.)
> A stitch in time saves nine.  (Taking action when a problem first arises averts greater trouble in the future.)
> The apple doesn't fall far from the tree. (Children can be expected to resemble their parents in appearance and behavior.)
> Birds of a feather flock together.  (People are likely to keep company with others whose attitudes and habits are much like their own.)
> One bad apple can spoil the lot. (In a group, one member who is ill behaved is likely to influence the other members to misbehave as well.)

Frequently, understanding an aphorism requires an intimate knowledge of the particular culture, as illustrated by two Samoan sayings whose meanings depend on a knowledge of legends transmitted orally from one Samoan generation to the next.

> *The proverb:* "Heaven was spat on" (*Ua anu Lagi*). *The proverb's foundation:* This adage is used in reference to someone who behaved improperly toward those in authority.  According to legend, the Samoan people originated in a land called Pulotu.  The king of Pulotu had a daughter named

Lagi (heaven) and a son named Fali (grass) who traveled together to visit the island of Papatea. However, on their arrival they were shocked at the rude treatment they received at the hands of the Papateans, who spat on Lagi and trampled Fali underfoot. Since then, impolite treatment of people of high rank has been expressed by the phrase, "Heaven was spat on." (Adapted from Schultz, 1965, p. 34)

*The proverb:* "Tufugauli's ears go wandering about" (*Ua tafao taliga o le Tufugauli*). *The proverb's foundation:* This saying derives from the legend of King Sun, the ruler of the islands of Atafu-mea, who was famous for the way he oppressed his subjects. One day as some girls discussed their deplorable fate and cursed the king, they were overheard by a boy named Tufugauli, who was feigning sleep in a corner of the house where they chatted. Later the boy reported the event to his relative, King Sun, who then severely punished the people of the village. And because Tufugauli was the only one not punished, everyone realized that he had been the informer. It was then that the girls remarked, "Tufugauli's ears go wandering about." (Adapted from Schultz, 1965, pp. 124-125)

The Analects (Sayings) attributed to the Chinese social philosopher Confucius (551-479 B.C.E.) are an intimate part of the folk psychology on which the government of the Republic of China on Taiwan is officially founded. The Confucian worldview is also widely held in mainland China and Korea. Here are three sayings intended as guides to interpreting life (Ware, 1955, pp. 107, 110, 111).

Those born with an understanding of the universe belong to the highest type of humanity. Those who understand it as the result of study come second. Those who study it with great difficulty come third. And the people who find it too difficult to attempt study come last.

Continuous readaptation to suit the whims of others undermines excellence.

[The traits of people when they are at their best are] humility, magnanimity, sincerity, diligence, and graciousness. If you are humble, you will not be laughed at. If you are magnanimous, you will attract many to your side. If you are sincere, people will trust you. If you are diligent, you will be successful. If you are gracious, you will get along well with your subordinates.

## Graphic and performing arts

Aspects of a people's belief system may be found in a culture's graphic and performance arts.

During 70 years of Communist rule in Russia, paintings that decorated the walls of public buildings portrayed the sorts of social relations considered appropriate in societies based on Karl Marx's dialectical materialism.

In central Java, the successive levels of the massive 9th century C.E. stone edifice known as Borobudur depict the stages of life that dedicated

Buddhists must pass through on their way to the desired ultimate state of enlightenment.

On the ceiling of the Sistine Chapel of the Vatican in Rome, Michaelangelo painted scenes representing a Christian version of human creation and of spiritual beings that affect people's fate during their life on earth.

An architectural style that conveys psychological and cosmological meanings for a cultural group is the tipi (teepee), the type of conical tent that has been the classical dwelling of Indians in North America's Great Plains.

> The shelter is understood as the universe, or microcosmically as a human person. The central open fire is the presence of the Great Mysterious, which is at the center of all existence, and the smoke hole at the top of the tipi is the place and path of liberation. Similar understandings are specific to the small dome-shaped sweat lodge wherein, as with the eastern subarctic [Native Americans], purification rites are required as for sacred ceremonies. Even though today most Plains people live in permanent frame houses, the purification lodges are usually found nearby. (Brown, 1989, p. 16)

An example of culture reflected in performing arts is the collection of Navajo Indian observances known as *sings*, which consist of chants and dances that convey a Navajo conception of the universe and of people's place within it. Sings function as mystery plays, reminding adults of their heritage and instructing the young in a tribal perception of life.

> There is a great difference between such mystery plays and the European morality plays as we know them. Navajo ceremonialism is not concerned with morality. . . . But it is concerned with the fact that the deeds of individuals are not confined to their own spheres of social action; they vitally affect the earth, the waters, the mountains—the whole web of life. Nor is the influence of a [person] restricted to the term of his physical life. It continues through his ghost to be a psychical force. This interrelation of parts within the solidarity of the whole living universe, the psychic effects resulting from physical causes, the correspondence of inner and outer forms of life, and the continuance of causal action through the realms of life and death, all combined to give meaning and validity to the sings as profound mysteries. (Waters, 1950, p. 249)

## Summaries of Folk Beliefs

The self-assigned task of scholars who study the beliefs of different peoples often consists of observing the behavior of members of a culture and estimating what that behavior means. By way of illustration, consider an account by an American anthropologist, Amy Stambach, who observed the phenomenon of *kichaa* among the Chagga people who live on the slopes of Mount Kilimanjaro, Africa's highest mountain (19,340 feet above sea level), in northern Tanzania.  In an article titled "Too Much Studying Makes Me Crazy," Stambach explains that *kichaa* is a behavioral malady that many of the Chagga believe is caused by schooling of the sort introduced by the British when they established colonies in Africa.  The present-day Tanzanian school system, rather than officially incorporating native cultural practices into schooling, separates custom and schooling in the belief that one is traditional and the other progressive.

> As a result, some Chagga students are caught in a social and moral bind that leads classmates and teachers to describe them as people torn between tradition and modernity . . . [so that such students suffer the symptoms of *kichaa*, symptoms that can include] lack of physical stability and a propensity to fall down, an excess of saliva, violent behavior, and loud speech.  In certain circumstances, particularly those involving girls, symptoms include uncontrollable laughing and crying and flailing about on the floor. . . .  Many people conceptualize *kichaa* as a process of "moving far from my father's house"—a metaphor that captures the distancing consequences often associated with formal education.  Seen as a process that takes one far away, schooling potentially isolates students from the everyday activities that define people socially.  Typical 9-hour school days remove students from household routines that many believe create meaningful relationships and, [contrary to traditional culture,] locate them conceptually in a world of books and blackboards, letters and numbers.  (Stambach, 1998, pp. 503-504)

## Conclusion

The descriptions of folk psychologies in this book have been drawn chiefly from six sources: (a) literature and art of different cultures, (b) scholars' published summaries of folk beliefs, (c) the doctrinal writings of various religions, (d) historical accounts, (e) published explanations by members of cultures, and (f) my own observations of the behavior of people of different cultural backgrounds.

## THE EVOLUTION OF FOLK PSYCHOLOGIES

In trying to account for how and why folk psychologies have assumed their particular character, I imagine that, over the ages, each psychology has acquired its nature from the confluence of at least three causal factors: (a) human needs and motives, (b) threats to people's well-being, and (c) unusually inventive and persuasive individuals.

### Human Needs and Motives

If we are willing to accept the proposition that the most basic human motive is to survive and prosper, then a folk psychology can be seen as an instrument in the service of that motive. Specific needs that derive from the survival motive appear to include needs for food, shelter, safety (harm avoidance), self-confidence, self-respect, and understanding the environment.

## Threats to People's Welfare

Threats to people's survival and need-fulfillment can differ from one culture to another and can thereby influence the character of the psychologies that societies create or adopt to cope with threats. Survival risks can result from (a) the limited human life span, (b) disease, (c) climate, (d) surrounding terrain, and (e) predators.

Perhaps the most daunting threat to survival derives from the curtailed human life span—from the fact that even the longest-lived persons die after ten decades or so, and most people expire much earlier. Although everyone beyond the age of childhood recognizes the inevitability of death, very few consider death a pleasant prospect. Thus, it is hardly surprising that most folk psychologies provide for prolonging people's survival by extending an individual's essence, the human *soul*, beyond the body's demise, even extending that essence infinitely.

Among the important concepts in folk psychologies are the proposals about the causes and cures of disease and illness.

The dangers to people's well-being vary with climate and weather conditions. The term *climate* refers to the typical dominant atmospheric temperature in a region. The word *weather* refers to short-term conditions of temperature, wind, and precipitation.

Predators are beings that seek to harm people and/or their possessions.

A typical function of folk psychologies is to offer explanations of—and ways of accommodating to—such threats.

## Inventive and Persuasive Individuals

I assume that innovative ideas, including new features of folk psychologies, do not arise spontaneously from multiple members of a culture. Instead, novel notions are introduced by particularly creative individuals who propose convincing answers to questions about human belief and behavior. Examples of such individuals are found in the histories of popular religions—Moses, David, and Solomon for Judaism; Lao-tzu for Taoism; Siddhartha Gautama for Buddhism; Mencius for Confucianism; Mahavira for Jainism; Martin Luther for Lutheranism; John Calvin for Presbyterianism; and more. Communism, as a philosophical/political persuasion that assumed the status of a folk psychology in various countries during the 20<sup>th</sup> century, was a product of the creative skills of Karl Marx and Friedrich Engels.

But it's not enough simply to furnish new ideas. If the ideas are to become part of a folk psychology, compelling disseminators must convince the populace that this new psychology is superior to the old. The spread of Christianity is a case in point. Although Jesus has been credited with inventing the novel rendition of Judaism that became known as Christianity, it was the apostle Paul and other disciples who convinced a growing body of believers that Jesus's version was the world's best guide to the conduct of life on earth and to eternal survival thereafter. Likewise, a Communistic belief system would not have been widely adopted in Eastern Europe and China without the persuasive skills of such individuals as Vladimir Lenin and Mao Tze-tung.

## THE BOOK'S STRUCTURE

Each of the following chapters, 2 through 14, bears a title indicating the aspect of folk psychologies that the chapter concerns. The 13 titles thus identify the components of the framework used for displaying significant features of folk psychologies. The nature of that framework can be summarized in a list of the chapter titles and the central question that each chapter is designed to answer.

Chapter 2.  *Reality.* What objects and what relationships among objects truly exist in the universe rather than being just imaginary?

Chapter 3.  *Knowing.* How do people come to know what they know?

Chapter 4.  *Cause.* Why do things happen as they do?

Chapter 5.  *Competence.* What constitutes competence, how are competencies identified, and what should be done about incompetence?

Chapter 6.  *Values.* How and why do people distinguish between good and bad, desirable and undesirable, proper and improper, efficient and inefficient, beautiful and ugly?

Chapter 7.  *Emotions.* Are the same types of feelings found in all cultures, does the importance of different emotions vary across cultures, and what sorts of situations are expected to elicit different types of affect?

Chapter 8.  *Humor.* What conditions and events are thought to be amusing, and why?

Chapter 9.  *Self and Not-Self.* How do people distinguish between one's-self and not-one's-self?

Chapter 10.  *Rites and Rituals.* What purposes do cultural ceremonies serve?

Chapter 11. *Time and the Life Span.* What is the nature of historical time and of the human life span?

Chapter 12. *Gender and Sex.* In what ways are females and males alike and different?

Chapter 13. *Prohibitions.* What is forbidden and why?

Certainly there are more facets of folk psychologies than are directly addressed in this book's chapters. Hence, the book offers only a limited array of *Folk Psychologies Across Cultures.* For example, here is a sampling of further topics on which additional chapters might have focused: life versus death, human versus nonhuman, happiness versus sadness, normal versus abnormal, work versus play, family structure and function, social class, etiquette, justice, and ethnicity.

In the book's closing chapter, I speculate about the value of studying folk psychologies and about their future status. Thus, Chapter 14. *Folk Psychologies' Significance and Trends* addresses the questions of what use is an understanding of folk psychologies, and what can be expected of folk psychologies in the years ahead.

To summarize, the purpose of this book is not to offer a definitive analysis of every type of component found in folk psychologies. Rather, the intention is to inspect a selection of topics and of examples from different societies that illustrate typical variations of folk thinking in the world's cultures.

# 2

# Reality

*What objects and what relationships among objects truly exist in the universe rather than being just imaginary?*

A traditional concern of philosophers is ontology—the study of *being* or of the *nature of all reality*. The basic question that ontology addresses is: What constitutes existence? In other words, what is it that exists and in what forms? Because different folk psychologies answer this question in different ways, one important distinction among versions of ethnopsychology is in the reality status that each psychology assigns to objects and events.

An essential foundation for people's notions of reality is the sort of evidence on which they base their beliefs. This is the epistemological issue of how people arrive at their conceptions of reality. Chapter 3 focuses on epistemology by offering answers to the question "How do people know what they know?"

The present chapter first describes ways reality is conceived in illustrative folk psychologies in terms of three analytical dimensions, then closes with an illustration of how a cultural conception of reality can change with the passing of time.

## DIMENSIONS OF REALITY

Three interrelated dimensions along which conceptions of reality can be viewed are those of (a) actual/constructed, (b) evident/inferred, and (c) degrees of conviction.

## Actual/Constructed Dimension

This dimension concerns the question: Is a person's perception of the world a true reflection of what exists, or is that perception a social construction, or is it the individual's personal creation? Four positions along the actual/constructed scale that can be represented in different folk psychologies may be labeled *naive realism, approximated realism, constructed realism,* and *solipsism.*

| naive realism | approximated realism | constructed realism | solipsism |
|---|---|---|---|

### Naive realism

A psychology that portrays life from a naive-realism perspective assumes that what a person sees and hears is an exact copy of what exists "out there." Thus, the image or map of reality that people carry in their minds is accepted as a precise replica of the world beyond the person's body. And because that image is considered to be an authentic replica, the mental map in one person's mind is thought to be identical to that in another's mind—except, perhaps, in the minds of people identified as "mentally deranged."

Consider, for example, the reality status of words. Are words just noises and images, arbitrarily assigned as symbols to designate objects, events, or ideas that people wish to communicate to each other? If so, then a rose by any other name would smell as sweet. Or, on the contrary, does each word have a built-in meaning—an inherent reality that could not be represented in any other word? Folk psychologies can differ in the way they answer these questions.

Most literate members of modern industrialized societies apparently believe that words are symbols with no inherent meaning in themselves. So a rose could be called *bunga mawar* (which is the term for *rose* in the Indonesian language) and still look and smell the same. However, people who thus see most words as only symbolic may still avoid using certain ones in jest or anger (*God damn, go to hell*), fearing that such terms are inherently profane or may displease supernatural forces.

But in other societies, a word does not merely represent a designated thing; rather, the word and the thing are identical.

[In many, if not all, American Indian cultures,] words have a special potency or force that is integral to their specific sounds. What is named is therefore understood to be really present in the name in unitary manner, not as a "symbol" with dualistic implication, as is generally the case with modern languages. An aspect of the sacred potency latent in words in primal tradition is the presiding understanding that words in their sounds are born in the breath of the being from whom they proceed, and since breath in these traditions is universally identified with the life principle, words are thus sacred and must be used with care and responsibility. . . . Recitation of a myth, for example, is understood to be an actual, not a symbolic, recapitulation or reenactment of that primordial creative process or event, which is not bound by time. (Brown, 1989, p. 3)

A further example of belief in words' intrinsic meanings is religious zealots' contention that doctrine translated into another language cannot have the same meaning as the meaning conveyed in the doctrine's original tongue. Thus, Muslims in such countries as Afghanistan, Iran, and Malaysia are required to memorize holy scripture—the Qur'an—in the original Arabic and, when reciting passages, to chant their recitation in a distinctive euphonious style in order to convey the passages' true meaning.

According to some folk psychologies, not only is the word the same as the thing it designates, but the word was the creator of the thing. In the cosmogony of the Iatmul, who live along the Sepik River in Papua New Guinea, the original state of the world was aquatic. At some unidentified moment in the prehistoric past, the water was stirred by wind, and land arose from the seas. From a pit within the land, male ancestors of today's humans emerged to separate the sky from the earth by means of forked branches. Those ancients then began to name all of the features that would become the contents of the earth. As they issued a name, the feature was born. "History and time effectively began with the migrations of these ancestors, who, by conferring totemic names to phenomena, created the 'path' (*yembii*) of the world. . . . As a collective memory, the physical referents of totemic names, especially the landscape, enable Eastern Iatmul to know their distant past" (Silverman, 1997, p. 102).

## Approximated realism

The term *approximated realism* refers to the assumption that there is indeed a natural world "out there" which

exists as an independent, objectively knowable reality that can be observed, analyzed, and categorized. By utilizing "the scientific method," it has been thought that we can construct, test, and confirm/disconfirm hypotheses. Further, through the incorporation of increasingly accurate empirical observations, we can produce incrementally derived generalizations that are verifiable, that cumulatively reveal the immutable laws of the universe. Thus we can generate a science that will allow us to know more and more accurately "the way the world is," [physically, socially, psychologically] through the use of observations, instruments, and generalizations that have a transcendent reliability. (Beyer & Liston, 1996, p. 138)

In recent times, such a conception of reality has often been referred to as *positivism* or *modernism*. *Positivism*, and particularly the 20th century's subvariety known as *logical positivism*, has functioned over the past two centuries as the principal paradigm guiding the conduct of modern science (Toulmin, 1994). Such a viewpoint has been incorporated into certain versions of folk psychology, particularly among scientifically informed publics in Western industrialized societies. Unlike naive realists, positivists do not believe their current version of reality is an exact copy of the natural world. Instead, they think their present understanding is no more than an estimate of the truth, an estimate that requires more refined observation and analysis in order to arrive closer to a single, objective truth. Hence, the aim of collecting empirical data and logically interpreting the data is to improve one's estimate of reality. The way people phrase their interpretations can imply that they subscribe to approximated realism. For example, a person's mentioning "sampling error," "chance factors," or "measurement limitations" is an admission that the version of reality reflected in a given set of observations has failed to identify all of the aspects of the real world that contributed to those results.

Increasingly, and particularly in advanced industrial societies, approximated realism forms a large part of folk culture, with people's beliefs founded on public opinion polls, reports of scientific experiments, lessons in school, ethnologists' analyses of cultures, news distributed via mass communication media, and television documentaries.

## Constructed realism

Such expressions as "Gypsies don't see things our way" or "He marches to a different drummer" suggest that the speaker believes in some form of constructed realism, a philosophical position representing a further step away from naive realism. Constructed realism holds that the conception of what exists and what is true is simply a human creation, a product of what people believe is true. One group or one individual can construct a version of reality that differs from the version to which another group or individual assents. And the degree to which that conception might be an accurate reflection of some "objective world out there" is a matter of debate that cannot be resolved to everyone's satisfaction.

When a rendition of reality is one to which members of a group subscribe—a version negotiated among group members and propagated by the group—that conception is typically called *socially constructed reality* or *culturally constructed reality*. On the other hand, an interpretation of reality invented by an individual—or an individual's variation of a socially constructed folk psychology—warrants the label *personally constructed reality*.

> For members of a society, "reality" is the unquestioned conceptualization of what they are doing and the context in which it is done. . . . [The academic field of] sociology, unlike metaphysics, concerns itself with the "sense of reality," not some "absolutely real," and that this "sense of" reality is a working notion that lasts only so long as members' activity sustains it. (Frank, 1979, pp. 167-168)

Therefore, people who subscribe to a social-construction conception of reality will recognize that a typical German Protestant view of the universe, a typical Turkish Muslim view, and a typical Chinese Taoist view will not be identical.

A contrast in constructed realities is seen in the difference between different folk psychologies' notions of representations. In most Western cultures, a photograph or painting of a person is considered to be a visual depiction of that individual—merely a resemblance and not the person himself or herself, or even a piece of that person. However, in some cultures, a photograph or drawing or sculpture of a human or animal is regarded as identical to the original being. Among the Loango in central Africa, a wooden image of a person has traditionally been believed to contain the soul (*masoka*) of the portrayed individual.

Likewise, in a substantial number of South American tribes and in certain regions of Eastern Europe (Bulgaria, Greece, Macedonia, Romania, Serbo-Croatia), a person's reflection in a mirror or pool of water is thought to be the person's soul. The belief that breaking a mirror is bad luck apparently derives from the notion that cracking a mirror shatters the soul and augurs a person's death. A container of water placed within or next to a grave is intended to confine the soul of the deceased to that location, preventing it from wandering aimlessly about (Barber, 1988, pp. 180-181).

George Catlin (1796-1872), who spent his life painting scenes of daily life in American Indian tribes, noted that the Mandan of the Great Plains believed that the portraits he drew "made *living beings*—they said they could see their chiefs alive in two places—those that I made were *a little* alive—they could see their eyes move—could see them smile and laugh, and that if they could laugh, they could certainly speak if they should try, and [the images] therefore must have some life in them" (Catlin in Lévy-Bruhl, 1960, p. 34).

Lévy-Bruhl proposed that this assumption of identity between a model and a person

> is not on account of a childish trust in analogy, nor from mental weakness and confusion; it is not due to a naive generalization of the animist theory, either. It is because, in perceiving the similitude, as in looking at the origi-

nal, the traditional collective [constructed] representations imbue it with the same mystic elements [as those attributed to live persons themselves]. (Lévy-Bruhl, 1966, pp. 34-35)

## Solipsism

The most extreme departure from naive realism is solipsism, the belief that there is no real world outside the person; the only reality is what is in one's mind. To assume that what is "in mind" is a reflection —accurate or otherwise—of a reality beyond the self is considered by solipsists to be an unreasonable conviction based on unsupported faith, a conviction for which there can be no proof. People are simply deluding themselves when they believe they have witnessed a "real world out there." Their belief in a palpable world beyond their own minds is nothing more than an illusion. Some writers who style themselves as postmodernists appear to subscribe to a version of solipsism (Denzin, 1997; Derrida, 1976). It seems unlikely that any cultural group's conception of the universe—any folk psychology—is solipsistic. The notion that reality is nothing more than "what's in the mind" is apparently limited to a relatively few individuals who speculate about such matters.

## Summary

Such labels as *naive realism, approximated realism,* and *constructed realism* can be applied to folk psychologies either by the insiders (the people dedicated to that psychology) or by outsiders (observers who are not ad-herents of that psychology but who propose which of the three labels fits a particular cultural group's perspective). These two viewpoints—the insider's (emic perspective) and the outsider's (etic perspective)—are often in conflict. For instance, members of a cultural group may believe that their portrayal of life is an accurate revelation of "the way things really are" (naive realism), whereas an anthropologist studying the group may conclude that the group's portrayal is merely one society's interpretation (social construction). This distinction is reflected in the analysis offered by an outsider—Brown—of the conception of reality of insiders—traditional Native Americans.

> Unlike the conceptual categories of Western culture, American Indian tradi-tions generally do not fragment experience into mutually exclusive di-chotomies, but tend rather to stress modes of interrelatedness across categories of meaning, never losing sight of an ultimate wholeness. Our animate-inanimate dichotomy, or our categories of animal, vegetable, and mineral, for example, have no meaning for the Indian, who sees that all that exists is animate, each in its own special way, so that even rocks have a life of their own and are believed to be able to talk under certain conditions. Creatures we relegate to the category "animal" or "bird" and consider infe-

rior to humans, the Indian refers to as "people" who, in a sense, have a recognized superiority to humans. (Brown, 1989, p. 71)

## Evident/Inferred Dimension

An evident/inferred dimension of analysis is based on the assumption that people's ideas about reality can be at various levels of abstraction. The most concrete, basic level is that of a person directly witnessing events and maintaining records of those events in mind as separate episodes composed of particular components (people, objects, actions). Events can be observed immediately or can be experienced vicariously (through television and radio programs, people's oral descriptions, incidents reported in books, magazines, or on a computer network). These direct-observation experiences are the *evident level*. Everyone who witnesses the event can attest to who was there and what occurred—on the condition that everyone pays careful attention to what goes on.

In addition to directly recognizing an event's observed features, people may (a) identify a characteristic (or a combination of characteristics) that several objects or episodes seem to share and (b) apply a label to that characteristic (or that combination). This is the *inferred level* that results from the process of concept construction—of deducing attributes that seem to be common to multiple objects or events, then applying a label to that inference. Most of the beliefs that comprise a folk psychology's knowledge base are concepts—abstractions regarded by members of the culture as being objectively real. Because such concepts can differ from one culture to another, inferred reality can vary across cultures. This can be illustrated by the following example.

Figure 2-1 pictures one member of a particular American household. People in that household have assigned the name *Lancer* to the pictured member. People of whatever cultural background who observe Lancer directly should be able to agree on what they see. But in addition, in American culture, Lancer is also believed to share a variety of inferred characteristics with certain other members of a household. Those shared features are known as *breed* characteristics, a collection of traits to which the culture has applied the label *Great Dane*. And a more limited selection of Lancer's breed characteristics will also be displayed by a larger number of entities whose cluster of features warrants the label *dog*. Further, even fewer inferred characteristics are assumed to be held by a much larger number of entities whose traits in common qualify them for the label *animal*. But not all cultures make these particular distinctions. Some folk psychologies will recognize the features envisioned at the American *dog* level but not at the *Great Dane* breed level; so in those cultures there will be no symbols representing distinctions among breeds, with the result that *dog breed* is not part of such cultures' reality.

Figure 2-1

**Lancer Himself—at the Evident Level of Reality**

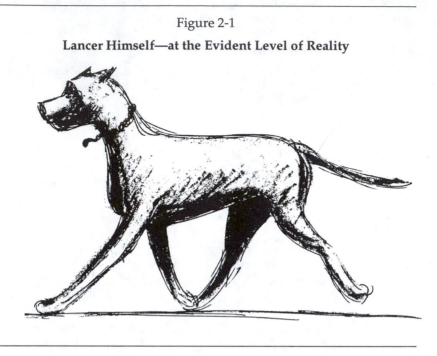

Cultures can also differ in many other characteristics that are abstracted from—or assigned to—inferred groupings of entities to which Lancer belongs. For example, the concept *edible* or *foodstuff* would be applied to Lancer in the Batak culture of Indonesia's Sumatra Island as well as in China and Korea, but it would not be an acceptable concept in typical North American or British culture. Whereas the concept *suitable household pet* would be an inferred feature applied to Lancer in American culture, it would not be an aspect of reality in traditional Muslim culture.

In summary, a great portion of people's notions of reality consists of labeled qualities (concepts) abstracted from objects and events, with those concepts shared by members of a culture and taught to each new generation as truths.

The following examples illustrate differences among representative folk psychologies in each of three types of inferred reality that concern (a) the nature of the universe, (b) supernatural beings and forces, and (c) the soul.

## The nature of the universe

Nearly all folk psychologies include a cosmogony—a set of beliefs about how the universe began, what it contains, and how it is organized.

Apparently people's need to understand their environments in order to survive and prosper in such settings motivates them to imagine principles and forces that might account for the nature of the universe they observe. The varied results of such inferences can be suggested by cosmogonies from four cultures—secular North American, Kogi, Japanese, and Navajo.

*A North American secular cosmogony.* The term *secular folk psychology* refers to a belief system that excludes (a) personified supernatural spirits (gods, jinns, angels) and (b) mystical locations (heaven, purgatory, hell) or states of existence (limbo, nirvana) in which a person's putative essence (soul) resides after death.

The North American secular cosmogony is also found in much of Europe and in other societies around the world that trace their beliefs about the universe to European and North American secular, rather than religious, sources. The following sketch identifies five features of that cosmogony as it seems to exist today. My proposal that the five are indeed part of North American folk belief is supported by the observation that (a) the five are taught in virtually all North American schools from the upper-elementary grades through the university and (b) news media (newspapers, news magazines, radio, television broadcasts) refer to the five in a manner which assumes that the consumers of news are well acquainted with the five and accept the descriptions as accurate portrayals of reality.

- *The beginning of the universe.* The universe originated millions of years ago. However, the way it started is unclear, so its origin remains a source of much speculation. One version of such speculation is called the big-bang theory.
- *The structure of the cosmos.* The earth is a large sphere, referred to as a planet, which circulates around the sun along with several other planets which appear as tiny lights in the night sky. The remaining twinkles in the sky—and millions more not visible to the naked eye—populate the cosmos. The attraction of one object for another is called gravity; gravity is the force that causes objects to fall to the earth.
- *The composition of matter.* All objects in the universe are composed of invisibly small atoms. What makes one object different from another is the pattern in which the two objects' particular atoms are organized.
- *The evolution of life.* Each plant and animal species in the universe (including humans) was not created separately and in the form seen today. Instead, all living things evolved over millions of generations by some extremely simple original cells gradually separating into complex and diversified types so as to produce the many thousands of species that exist today.

- *The nature of biological inheritance.* When a new living thing is created, the main biological characteristics which that thing will develop have been dictated by genes contributed by the thing's parents.

All of the foregoing conceptions qualify as inferred beliefs, because each includes concepts abstracted from direct observations of various kinds, with many of the observations requiring technologies beyond humans' visual, auditory, and tactile sensory equipment. In effect, none of the five statements is the description of an *evident* direct observation. Each has depended on special instruments and procedures (telescopes, microscopes, chemical analyses, carbon dating, computers, and more) and on particular ways (theories) of organizing diverse direct observations. The inventive individuals who originally proposed such beliefs have been scientists and philosophers of various sorts. They have supported their inferences about such notions as *evolution, atoms, gravity,* and *genes* with various kinds of evidence—statistical analyses, photographs, drawings, and computer simulations. If the inferences are to be accepted into a folk psychology, the general public must trust that the statistics and photographs are valid depictions of what they are purported to represent. Consequently, believing that the five statements are true requires a substantial investment of people's faith in the veracity and acumen of the individuals who have been the sources of those statements.

*A Kogi cosmogony.* The Kogi—an isolated people in the Sierra Nevada de Santa Marta mountains of Colombia—teach that a supreme Mother Goddess created the cosmos in the form of nine worlds, with the fifth and centermost the one in which we live. They believe that Good and Evil coexist and that the purpose of knowledge is to achieve a balance between Good and Evil, thereby enabling people to reach old age in a condition of wisdom and tolerance. The Kogi consider themselves the possessors of the true religion. As the "elder brothers" of humankind, they feel responsible for protecting the health of the universe (*Mysteries of the Ancient Americas,* 1986, p. 270).

*A Japanese cosmogony.* In Japanese folklore, one version of how Japan acquired its rulers distinguishes two categories of deities, the heavenly gods (*Amatsu-kami*) and the native or territorial gods (*Kunitsu-kami*). The legend describes how the Grand Goddess of the Sun, chieftainess of the heavenly gods, sent one of her offspring to rule Japan from Mount Takachiho on the southern Japanese island of Kyushu. A descendent of this earthbound deity was Jimmu, who moved northeast from Kyushu to conquer all of Japan and establish the imperial court in Yamato. Historians have speculated that the heavenly deities in the tale were actually foreign conquerors, while the native gods were the chieftains of Japan's aboriginal tribes (Egami, 1962, p. 13).

*A Navajo cosmogony.* In the folk psychologies of Navajo, Hopi, and Pueblo Indians of the southwestern United States, the universe consists of the earth and four underworlds. People originated in the lowest of the underworlds—the womb of Our Mother Earth—then ascended by stages until they inhabited the earth. A giant stone mountain protruded from the lowest underworld up through the successive underworld layers to eventually tower above the earth and serve as the core of the universe. The sides of the mountain facing the four directions of the compass glowed with distinctive hues—white on the east, blue on the south, yellow-red on the west, black on the north. When humans emerged from the underworlds, they settled at the foot of the mountain, planted seeds that made the earth spread out, and called to the Holy People to help them plant the four holy mountains that would mark the outer borders of the world. The revered peak to the east was made of sand and white shell, the one to the south of sand and blue-green turquoise, the one to the west of yellow-red sand and abalone, and the one to the north of black sand and jet. The dominating central mountain was called *The Mountain Surrounded by Mountains* or *The Encircled Mountain.* Within this defined territory, lesser mountains were placed along with plants, trees, animals, the winds, the seasons, the sun, the moon, and the stars.

Each of the four underworlds was a particular color, the same hues as those on the four sides of The Encircled Mountain. The lowest of the four was the Dark or Red World, with its sky-opening to the east. Second was the Blue World, with a sky-opening to the south. Third was the Yellow World, opening to the west. Fourth was the White World, opening to the north.

Each of the holy mountains in Navajo lore has its counterpart in today's visible world. Mount Blanca in Colorado has been identified as the holy mountain of the east, Mount Taylor of the San Mateo range as the mountain of the south, the San Francisco peaks in Arizona as the mountain of the west, and a peak in the La Plata or San Juan range as the mountain of the north. Huerfano Peak above Chaco Cañon has traditionally been considered the Encircled Mountain, even though its modest size fails to reflect its overwhelming importance in Indian folk psychology. The Grand Canyon of the Colorado River is the chasm—or "inverted mountain"—through which people originally emerged from the underworld.

This cosmogony continues to be reflected today in the sand paintings of the Hopi and in the form of the Pueblo secret underground ceremonial chamber—the kiva (Waters, 1950, pp. 163-173).

## Supernatural beings and forces

The word *supernatural*, as intended here, refers to invisible objects that are believed to influence the world's events. When the causes of events are not blatantly obvious, people are apt to conceive of causal forces that could account for such critical, unexplained happenings as illness, death, accident, crop failure, and the like. In most cultures, if not all, those causes include supernatural beings. Such supernatural entities are typically invested with certain human characteristics held in exaggerated proportions, enabling those beings to achieve spectacular feats. Supernatural entities are often credited with infinite knowledge, great speed, enormous strength, and the ability to be in many places at the same time. They may also display such human emotions as jealousy, vengeance, delight, anger, generosity, envy, and pity. Some such beings are believed capable of assuming the guise of visible animate or inanimate objects—a bear or tiger, a long-dead ancestor, a fruit or flower, a magic potion.

In some folk belief systems, certain living people are endowed not only with mundane human traits but also with supernatural qualities. Those individuals are often known by such terms as *living gods* and *witches*. For instance, Jesus Christ has been accepted by Christians as a deity in human form. In Japan, before the nation's emperor at the end of World War II was required by Allied military forces to renounce the claim that he was divine, the emperor had been officially considered godly by both the Japanese government and the general populace.

Whereas living gods are often portrayed in folk psychologies as benevolent beings, witches are generally depicted as harmful. For example, among the Nupe and Gwari tribes of northern Nigeria, witches have been seen as

> unequivocally evil, as destroying life, mainly through mysterious wasting diseases, and as implying the power of witches to "eat" the "life-soul" of their victims. Witches are active at night and cannot be seen or discovered by ordinary means. . . . [It is] only the "shadow-souls" of witches which roam about and attack victims, while their bodies remain asleep at home, thus deceiving any ordinary attempts at proving, or disproving, these mystic activities. (Nadel, 1960, p. 408)

In folk psychologies, the envisioned types of numinous beings and their functions can vary from one culture to another, as illustrated in the following cases.

*Zulu spirits.* According to the lore of the Zulu people in the Natal region of South Africa, the universe was created by a supreme being known as Nkulunkulu (the Great One) who subsequently stood apart from the conduct of the world, almost never intervening in the world's operation and rarely meddling directly in human affairs (M'Timkulu,

1977, p. 14). However, the spirits of one's dead ancestors may continually hover about to affect one's life. It is to these dead ancestors that Zulus turn for guidance and support in time of need.

Zulus believe that reality consists of both tangible objects (people, animals, plants, houses, mountains) and spirit beings which are not actually separate from the tangible universe. Instead, the two are combined to form a unified whole, with the society of living mortals seen as continuous with the society of the spirits of dead ancestors. Therefore, people's personality characteristics when they were alive are retained in their spirit state. A woman who was cantankerous while living will still be fractious when she is transformed by death into a shade. A man of authority when alive will be authoritative in his spirit state. As a result, not all ancestors are honored or solicited for aid. Only those who, while alive, achieved distinction by force of their leadership and longevity will become spirits with power over the fate of the living. The rituals practiced in Zulu culture are designed to curry the favor of these ancestral phantoms so as to promote the well-being of the group and its members.

Although the Creator, Nkulunkulu, seldom intervenes in mortals' lives, if an individual or group fails to maintain the amicable social relationships that are so highly valued in Zulu society, Nkulunkulu may suddenly punish the offenders and bring them into line. The punishment can assume any of a variety of forms—sickness, mental disorder, loss of property, drought, and more.

Belief in the influence of ancestral spirits is obviously not limited to the Zulus. Indeed, the notion that the ghosts of dead ancestors linger to affect the lives of their living relations is very widespread. Such a belief is central to the folk psychologies of such diverse peoples as Confucianists in China, Okinawans in the western Pacific, and adherents of Voodoo in Haiti.

*Jewish-Christian-Islamic spirits.* Judaic-Christian-Islamic folk belief includes a single almighty personified being (Yahweh-God-Allah) who is assisted by attendant spirits (angels, jinns, genies) and is opposed by Satan, who is the source of the world's evil. The tradition's monotheistic God not only created the cosmos but also spawned Satan, who was one of God's archangels before turning evil and falling from God's favor. Principal functions attributed to God include those of creating and supervising everything that exists, establishing moral standards of human behavior, rewarding people's obedience and punishing their disobedience (during their lifetime and in their life-after-death), and intervening in human affairs (sometimes in response to people's prayers and rituals).

*Plateau Tonga spirits.* In the southeast African nation of Zimbabwe, the Plateau Tonga are a Bantu-speaking people numbering perhaps 100,000.

Tonga tradition includes four principal types of spirits, with each assumed to perform a separate function. The most important are the *mizimu*. They are the specters of dead kinsmen who, when living, had achieved some measure of distinction and respect. Each *mizimu* is addressed by name and honored on any important occasion, such as when a family changes location or plants crops, or when a husband sets forth on a hunting trip or purchases a new plow or cooking pot. Failing to accord proper attention to *mizimu* invites misfortune—accident, illness, social dissension, or the like. The living can call for the aid of *mizimu* in time of need. Maintaining the goodwill of *mizimu* requires periodic offerings, usually of beer.

The *basangu* form a second category of spirits influential in general affairs of the community at large. *Basangu* issue their demands through people they possess. A third type are the *masabe,* considered to be the spirits of animals or foreigners that can cause illness to people they control; the illness can be cured by the affected person's learning the dances that relate to the possessing *masabe.* The fourth variety are *zelo,* ghosts of dead people but distinct from the *mizimu* of respected deceased kinfolk.

> The *mizimu* are not immortal like the ghosts (*zelo*) who are independent of the devotion of living people for their continued existence. When the living cease to remember the *mizimu* and no longer call upon them by name, they become nameless spirits wandering at large who now work only for evil. . . . Over these [wanderers] the living have no control, for in forgetting the names they have lost the means of summoning or propitiating the spirits. (Colson, 1960, p. 376)

*Australian aboriginal spirits.* In Australian aboriginal cultures, the term *dreamtime* or *the dreaming* refers to a period of time that had a beginning but no foreseeable end. During dreamtime the natural environment had been created, including beings in the form of humans or animals responsible for establishing the local social order and its laws or rules of conduct. The dreamtime beings exist eternally and are joined by the souls of currently living people upon those people's deaths. In dreamtime belief, humans are part of nature, not fundamentally different than the mystic beings and animal species, all of which share a common life force.

> After death, especially if moral obligations remained outstanding, the incoporeal or immortal part of man which was destined to join the powers of the dreamtime might stay close at hand and manifest itself to kinsmen and others as a host or similar kind of being until, appeased through rituals, feasts and offerings, it was able to continue its journey into the dreamtime. The death of a man with malice or vindictiveness in his heart, with some score yet to pay, was a matter for great concern. His ghost would remain close to the living for some while, would annoy, hurt, and injure the living

until set at rest. The Aborigines were faced on the one hand with numbers of free-moving and self-willed powers, creative as well as destructive, of whom the beings of the dreamtime were prototypical, and on the other with the world of nature, a profusion of animals, plants, topographical features, and meteorological phenomena, each with its ordered modes. (Burridge, 1973, p. 75)

Further types of cultural belief about supernatural intervention in human affairs appear in Chapter 4, which directly addresses matters of causation.

## Soul

In the English language, the word *soul* identifies an inferred component of most folk psychologies. Perhaps the notion that death brings a complete end to a person's existence is such an unwelcome possibility—so incompatible with the urge to survive—that people are impelled to imagine some aspect of themselves that lives on after the body's demise. In addition, belief in a soul that endures after death can serve to explain certain puzzling events in people's lives.

Although the attributes assigned to the soul can differ from one belief system to another, in all cultures the soul represents a human being's spiritual essence. The following examples illustrate conceptions of *soul* in four cultures.

*Mayan soul.* The Mayan Indians in the highlands of southern Mexico believe that a person's soul (*ch-ulel*) is the major source of supernatural power. Three interrelated types of soul are associated with a person—the *ch-ulel* or immortal soul that will live on after death, the *ora* in the form of a burning candle in the sky that is extinguished by death, and the *canul* or animal-soul companion that disappears upon the person's passing away.

> The soul is placed in the body of an embryo by the ancestral gods. . . . While the *ch'ulel* is temporarily divisible into its [three] component parts as a function of various types of soul loss, it is considered eternal and indestructible. Only at the point of death does the soul leave the body . . . and eventually enter the pool of innate souls kept by the ancestors. (Vogt, 1965, p. 18)

Education, in the sense of a person's acquiring skills and discovering what the world is like, contributes to the maturing of the soul. The more knowledge a person acquires, the "hotter" and stronger the soul. As a result, wisdom and power are directly proportionate to the heat of the *ch'ulel*. People learn through the activities in which they engage, so that participation in activities is essential to the soul's development.

Mayan folk psychology identifies three major stages of soul evolution.

There is the child, who is referred to as *mu to xvul xch'ulel* (the soul has not yet arrived), the young person, whose soul has partly arrived, *vulem xa jutuk xch'ulel,* and the older person, whose soul has arrived, *vulem xa xch'ulel.* (King, 1999, p. 368)

Not only is an individual's well-being influenced by the state of his or her *ch'ulel,* but the welfare of the society is also affected.   People who know the most are believed to have the strongest souls; and by dint of their wisdom and strength of soul, they are capable of provoking either good or evil in the community (Modiano, 1974).

*Shinto soul.*   In the Shinto folk psychology that permeates Japanese culture, the core of human personality is the soul (*tama,* or *mitama* when the honorific *mi-* is prefixed).   However, the precise composition of this overall soul is a matter of debate.   One conception holds that the *tama* contains four aspects that operate under one controlling spirit where the forces generating the visible physical world—including the human body—differ from the forces that generate the unseen mental world (Herbert, 1967, p. 61).

The manifold ways that people behave can be explained by the combined interaction of these four factors of personality as each contributes in some fashion to individuals' development and behavior.

> The *ara-mitama* is variously defined as wild, raging, raw, the power destructive of what is evil and constructive of what is divine, a spirit empowered to rule with authority. . . . Man is not always pure, i.e. desireless, but can occasionally yield to temptations, [so] the soul has to oppose that trend and destroy desire; *ara-mitama* corresponds to that [corrective] action.
>
> The *nigi-mitama,* which is the counter part of the *ara-mitama,* is described as mild, quiet, refined, what gives peace, what makes adjustments to maintain harmony, a spirit empowered to lead to union and harmony, essence as opposed to manifestation.
>
> The *saki-mitama,* or *sachi-mitama,* is described as happy, flourishing, as what makes happy, what gives pure love, creation, a power that imparts blessings.
>
> The *kushi-mitama* . . . is variously described as wonderful, hidden and also hideous, the inside spirit, wisdom, invention, discovery, a spirit which causes mysterious transformations. (Herbert, 1967, pp. 61-62)

A further significant feature of Shinto folk belief is the relationship between a person's soul and the souls of all other Japanese.

> Shinto primarily sees man as a being-in-community and not as an individual. [He] is always being-in-becoming—never static.   He is not personified to the extent that he becomes easily distinguishable from his milieu; he is not individualized to the point where he might decide upon a course of life irrespective of others in his past, present, and future. (Spae, 1972, p. 30)

*Christian soul.* According to one Christian tradition, each person's soul is "created by God of nothing, immediately infused into the body (at birth) as the proper form thereof, by which man is, liveth, is sensible, moveth, understandeth, willeth, and is affected" (John Norton in Miller, 1963, p. 240). The human soul is conceived to be a unitary object, but an object which, like the Christian God, forms a trinity. This unified essence of each human is composed of a vegetative soul, a sensible soul, and a rational soul. The vegetative soul has the powers of nourishing and propagating, two characteristics that people share with the earth's plant life. The sensible soul has not only powers of nourishing and propagating but also additional equipment possessed by animals—external senses (sight, hearing, touch, smell, taste) and the internal senses of imagination, memory, emotions, and the musculature (*sinews*) that make motion possible. But it is the rational soul, the highest in the trinity, that distinguishes humans from the earth's other living things (Smith, 1959).

Following death, the human body disintegrates but the soul continues to exist in an invisible spirit form, transported to a place of eternal happiness (heaven) or torment (hell) as determined by God's judgment of the individual's worthiness during his or her lifetime. Therefore, a key purpose of people's conduct during their lifetime is to guard their purity of soul in order to enjoy a blissful spirit life after death.

*Hindu soul.* Hinduism, as practiced in south-central Asia, teaches that an eternal Cosmic Soul or Supreme Reality was the creator—and is still the controller—of the universe. At some point in the infinite past, this Supreme Power formed individual souls out of the Cosmic Soul, and placed those individual souls in such objects of the world as the bodies of humans and animals. Upon the death of a person or animal, the body decays but the soul lasts on, ready to be encased in a newly born body or object. This process of a soul occupying one body after another over the millennia is referred to as *metempsychosis* or *transmigration of the soul*. When a soul migrates, it carries with it consequences of the way the person who possessed it most recently conducted her or his life when on earth. For anyone who lived a moral life in keeping with the dictates of Hindu scriptures, his or her soul next inhabits a body that enjoys a better fate on earth than was enjoyed by the individual who recently had housed that soul. For people who have violated the dictates of the holy scriptures, their souls are transferred to bodies that will suffer a worse fate than did the previous owners. This influence that is carried from one body to another is called *karma* or *karman*, a term that literally means *deeds*. According to the principle of karma, the deeds that a person performs in daily life can carry either good or bad values. People accumulate the effects of their acts in the form of a moral-investment record. Thus, one's karma represents a progressive accounting ledger, with the total of bad deeds in one column subtracted from the total of good deeds in the other. As a result, a person's karma at any point in development can be envisioned as the algebraic sum of the effects of her or his good and bad deeds up to that time. The sum at the time of death determines the quality of life to be experienced by the body that the soul will next inhabit. In effect, Hindu folk psychology provides a logical way to support the concept of justice. Through the action of karma, people get out of life what they deserve. As they sow during one body's existence, so shall they reap during the life span of the body that their departed soul next occupies (Thomas, 1988).

We now leave the evident/inferred dimension of analysis to consider differences among people in how convincing they find the conceptions of reality that are typical of their culture.

## Degrees of Conviction

Cultural groups as a whole, as well as individuals within groups, can invest different degrees of confidence in their beliefs about what is real. Such degrees can be displayed on a scale ranging from the conviction that a thing *definitely exists* in the world beyond the person's mind to the conviction that a thing *definitely does not exist* except in people's imaginations.

| definitely exists | probably exists | possibly does or doesn't exist | probably doesn't exist | definitely doesn't exist |
|---|---|---|---|---|

The level of conviction about the true presence of things can vary from one thing to another. A Canadian Methodist may be thoroughly convinced of the reality of God but be highly skeptical about the existence of unidentified flying objects (UFOs) that are said to carry visitors from outer space. A Cuban college student may trust astrological predictions as true determinants of her fate, yet consider the atomic theory of matter to be a ludicrous product of some charlatan's imagination.

It is also the case that different proportions of people in a cultural group will hold different degrees of confidence in the reality of things. For example, Cho's (1986, pp. 193-194) survey of Korean villagers' attitudes about a spirit world revealed that many respondents subscribed to the center position on the above scale (possibly does or does not exist) by saying, "It is very hard to accept the existence of deity or to deny it." Hence, because they could not be sure about the matter, most villagers continued to perform rituals for appeasing spirits in case the fabled spirit world did indeed exist.

As a further example, 99 residents of New Delhi, India, who identified themselves as at least nominal Hindus, were asked whether study of the ancient scriptures, the Vedas, would influence people's lives during the next sojourn of their soul on earth. Twenty-eight percent of the participants believed Vedic study would produce karma to enhance an individual's fate in his or her next mundane existence (greater riches, a more saintly nature, greater intelligence). Another 35% said they could not properly estimate the influence of Vedic study on people's future lives, and 37% said they did not believe in the transmigration of the soul (Marek & Thomas, 1988).

In Buddhism, a spiritual essence of a person who dies will transmigrate, that is, will pass into the body of a newborn for another period of earthly existence. However, in Buddhism that essence is not a soul, because Gautama Siddhartha—the Buddha—rejected the notion of such an entity as the soul. Instead, the deceased's *vinyan* (*vinnana*)—meaning consciousness or stream of awareness—is what the newborn acquires. In order to reveal something of present-day Thai Buddhists' beliefs about transmigration, 116 followers of Theravada Buddhism were asked, "If a person dies of old age, does any part of the person live on in the future? If so, what part lives on?" (Marek & Marek, 1988, p. 222). In reply, over 80% of respondents said that something lives on. When asked what it was, 56% mentioned *vinyan* whereas 52% said it was a person's goodness or badness. Thirty-six percent said the person's reputation, bones, and material goods continue to exist, while 22% were unsure that there was such a thing as *vinyan* that would pass on. (The percentages total more than 100% because some respondents offered multiple answers.)

As noted briefly in Chapter 1, a Confucian worldview holds that people's accomplishments in life are chiefly the result of their own effort. The key to success is diligence rather than genetic endowment or environmental conditions. Confucius often made this point in his Analects.

> Study as if you were never to master it; as if in fear of losing it. . . . When strict with oneself, one rarely fails. . . . I do not instruct the uninterested; I do not help those who fail to try. (Ware, 1955, pp. 51, 53, 59)

In an interview survey among 175 adult adherents of Confucianism in Taiwan (71 university students and 104 people from the general population), two cases of pupils' school progress were described to interviewees who were asked what they thought was the main cause behind the pupils' levels of success—inherited ability, personal effort, or environmental conditions (quality of teaching, task difficulty). Over 87% of university students credited pupils' effort for their achievement in such fields as mathematics and foreign-language learning. In contrast, only 31% of the general-public sample attributed achievement to hard work, whereas 52% credited heredity and 28% the quality of teaching. (The percentage totals exceed 100% because some interviewees included more than one cause in their answers.) Thus, more university students than people from the general population expressed a traditional Confucian conviction (Lin & Thomas, 1988, pp. 252-253).

In summary, the extent to which members of a cultural group will subscribe to their folk psychology's beliefs about reality can vary from one type of belief to another.

## REALITY AND CULTURAL CHANGE

In Chapters 2 through 13, cultural change is viewed from two perspectives, which are referred to as sources and types. *Sources* identifies from whence a change originated: (a) from within the society itself, (b) from outside, or (c) from some combination of the two. *Types* refers to whether a change involves (1) a novel interpretation (worldview, theory) of an aspect of life, (2) a new technology, in the sense of innovative equipment or procedures for performing tasks, or (3) some combination of a new interpretation and new technology. The adoption of novel beliefs is at least partially motivated by—and serves as a response to—changes in such key conditions of the society as political control, economic planning, innovative technologies, population size and distribution, natural resources, climate and weather, and philosophical perspectives (including religion).

An example of one way that political and economic planning in a society may affect a people's folk psychology is found in the case of an ethnic group's cultural reality being altered by a national government's efforts to stimulate tourism. Tana Toraja (meaning Toraja Land) is an Indonesian ethnic region with a population of approximately 350,000 in the mountains of south-central Sulawesi (Celebes). During the 20th century, Torajans became famous in anthropological annals for their elaborate funerals and unusual burial cliffs. In 1974, the Indonesian government issued a national socioeconomic development plan that urged the expansion of the nation's tourist industry as a key source of income. Tana Toraja was chosen for inclusion in the plan, a choice that proved remarkably profitable. Whereas in 1973 only 422 foreigners had journeyed to the area, by 1994 more than 53,000 foreign tourists and 205,000 domestic tourists were annually visiting Toraja country.

A key feature of the tourism plan was the provision of guides who would direct visitors to interesting sites and describe Torajan history and culture, including the region's curious funeral practices. In the earliest days of the plan, the guides were individuals who, on their own initiative, accompanied visitors on trips through the villages. However, it soon became clear to tourism officials that the history and customs narrated by the volunteer guides were often inconsistent. Furthermore, the tales risked depicting Torajans as primitive pagans, whereas 80% were Christians. Therefore, the provincial government in 1985 decreed that only certified guides would be allowed to accompany tourists. Guides could earn certification by completing a training course in Torajan lore. One important purpose of the two-week course was to develop

> a uniform Torajan history and mythology to be presented to tourists, thus combating the perceived misrepresentations of Tana Toraja articulated by nonlocal guides. Moreover, for the workshop leaders, the wide regional diversity of Torajan origin myths was troubling: they feared tourists would hear conflicting stories and come to question Torajans' credibility. In essence, the workshop involved an active attempt to achieve consensus on the image of Torajans presented to outsiders. Ironically, what was intended to be a unified move against outside dominance provoked local dissent. The biggest issues debated at the workshop centered on whose version of Torajan history would become "official." Traditionally, each group of Torajan nobles bases its claims of high rank on descent from various heavenly ancestors who descended onto local mountaintops centuries ago. For the nobles present, it was important that their particular celestial forebears be incorporated into the official version of Torajan history told to tourists. (Adams, 1997, p. 316)

Thus, members of the workshop planning committee who came from different Tana Toraja localities not only wished to present a united front to the world, but they also sought to have their own traditional rendition of Torajan lore serve as *the correct* account. Several motives underlay the representatives' efforts. First, devising a unified history and mythology could enable Torajans, as one of Indonesia's minor ethnic groups, to produce an admirable public image of their culture and thereby raise the prestige of Tana Toraja in the eyes of other Indonesians. Second, a given locality's having its particular mythic history and monuments featured in the official account would mean continued substantiation of the high rank which that community's leaders enjoyed within Torajan society. Furthermore, the villages whose landmarks and customs were featured in an official account would have larger numbers of foreign visitors, thus increasing the income the villages received from tourism.

As it turned out, the final "official" interpretation of Torajan history was pieced together from the diverse versions urged on the planning committee by the most prestigious and persuasive nobles in attendance.

In summary, the official rendition of Tana Toraja history and culture that would henceforth be presented to the public was a *manufactured reality* that differed somewhat from the beliefs about reality that members of individual Torajan communities had acquired while growing up. This syncretic history would likely become the "true reality" that would be acquired as folk psychology by future generations of Torajans as a result of the official version being told over and over and, at some point, being cast in a published form for use in the schools.

# 3

# Knowing

*How do people come to know what they know?*

Questions about the nature of knowledge and about how knowledge is acquired are the province of the philosophical domain of *epistemology*. Different folk psychologies are often based on different epistemological assumptions. Consequently, folk psychologies do not all agree about (a) the process by which people derive knowledge, (b) the kinds of information or knowledge that can be obtained from different sources, and (c) the trustworthiness of those sources in the sense of how likely it is that such knowledge is valid or true. Each society's educational practices are products of cultural beliefs about these three issues.

The following discussion of such matters is organized under two headings: (1) knowledge processes and sources and (2) cultural change and the state of knowledge.

## KNOWLEDGE PROCESSES AND SOURCES

The sources of knowledge inspected in the following pages include (a) human nature, (b) personal experience, (c) models, (d) instruction, (e) dreams, (f) visions, (g) possession, and (h) fantasies.

### Human Nature (Innate Knowledge)

The issue of innate knowledge is reflected in the question: How much of what a person knows is inherent in the person's nature, and how much has been acquired through experience in the world? The term *innate knowledge* is not meant to imply that all inherent knowledge is available and in full working order at the time a child is born. Rather, *innate knowledge*, as used here, refers to thought processes, beliefs, and behavior that need not be learned but that become available for use at some time during the life span. In effect, different sorts of innate knowledge can appear at various stages of a person's development.

As the following discussion demonstrates, a distinction can be drawn between *knowing* (holding particular beliefs) and *capacity to know* (being capable of acquiring beliefs).

## Knowing

Some folk psychologies assume that certain sorts of knowledge are inborn. For example, ardent followers of Confucius accept the master's assertion that, although what most people know has been learned from experience and study, a few gifted individuals possess intrinsic knowledge.

> Those born with an understanding of the universe belong to the highest type of humanity. . . . [Thus], there may be some who create things without needing to acquire knowledge, but I am not of that type. After being taught much, I selected the best and followed it; I observed much and remembered it. This is knowledge of the second rank. (Ware, 1955, pp. 54, 107)

> I, for my part, am not one of those who have innate knowledge. I am simply one who loves the past and who is diligent in investigating it. (Waley, 1938, p. 127)

In a traducian version of Christian belief, the original sin of Adam and Eve in the Garden of Eden is passed down to all newborn children, so by dint of their inherited nature the young are prone to commit evil acts. Some theologians would also argue that children misbehave even though they intrinsically know better, that is, even though the contents of their consciences—the knowledge of what is good and what is evil—is innate. A practical implication of such a parental belief is that the task of child rearing requires that children's depraved nature be counteracted by instruction and punishment.

## Capacity to know

Most, if not all, folk psychologies assume that the capacity to gain knowledge improves gradually over the first two decades of life. The Western-type school, with its sequence of grade levels, is founded on such an assumption. Furthermore, in many cultures, increasing age is thought to bring increasing wisdom at a regular rate until death, so the advice of elders is held in high regard. Such a belief underlies the principle of filial piety that assumes such an important role in the Confucianism of China, Japan, and Korea. However, in recent times in North America and in certain European cultures, the elderly—those beyond age 60 or so—are generally considered intellectually less competent so that their opinions deserve to be disregarded.

The rites of passage from childhood to adulthood, found in most societies when the young reach an assumed "age of reason," reflect the cultural expectation that children's capacity to know has advanced to a level that equips them to assume adult roles, a level that includes understanding the content of the group's folk psychology. But it's not simply advancing age that entitles individuals to adult status. Instead, rites of passage to adulthood usually include activities designed to test aspirants' mental and physical qualifications for adulthood. Ways that cultures can differ in their views about when the young are ready to act adult are illustrated in the following pair of examples from Roman Catholic and Kwakiutl cultures.

*Christian confirmation.* In Roman Catholic and Greek Orthodox tradition, a succession of three holy ceremonies or sacraments symbolizes a believer's religious commitment. The first ceremony is baptism, which signifies a person's initial dedication to a Christian way of life. This dedication can be pledged by one's parents or by oneself, with the ceremony coming at any stage of life—early infancy through old age. The second sacrament is confirmation, administered by a bishop or his designated representative, which affirms

> —both on the part of the church and on the part of the candidate—a maturity in Christ. This means that it is no longer enough to be passively baptized and attendant at Mass; one must be actively engaged in the apostolate {wherein individuals] are strictly obliged to spread and defend the faith by word and by deed as true witnesses of Christ. (O'Malley, 1995, p. 17)

The third sacrament is the Eucharist, which involves church members participating in the holy mass by ingesting bread and wine that represent Jesus's flesh and blood, thereby symbolizing the member's communing with Christ.

Recently, much controversy has developed in Catholic culture about when, during a person's life, the second of the sacraments, confirmation, should take place. There have been marked differences in various Catholic dioceses about the age at which confirmation should be conferred, ranging from "about 7 years of age as the general practice of the Latin church" to ages 12, 16, or 18 in other places (O'Malley, 1995, p. 19). Church leaders in Rome in the early 1990s sought to regularize the age of confirmation throughout the Catholic world by proposing that the rite be delayed until the "age of discretion," which was often considered to be around the time of puberty. But Rome officials also offered American bishops the opportunity to designate an age they considered more appropriate for use in the United States. However, no more than a third of the bishops could agree on any age between 7 and 18 as "more appropriate." In response to the request from Rome, the U.S. National Conference of Bishops interpreted *age of discretion* in an elastic manner by recommending that confirmation be conferred around "the age of discretion, which is about the age of 7 and 18 years" (Duggan, 1993, p. 13). Critics of the bishops' lack of precision argued for rejecting certain ages. To illustrate, William O'Malley (a teacher at Fordham Preparatory School in Bronx, New York) wrote that the "age of discernment" has traditionally been thought to arrive around age 7, "based simply on the fact that at that age children begin personally to know they have done 'something wrong.'" However, O'Malley drew a distinction between (a) discerning that "some action is disapproved of by society and (b) internalizing the reasons why that action is dehumanizing and adopting [such an understanding] into one's personally reasoned moral code. Anyone who says reason 'clicks on' at age 7 has never taught high school" (O'Malley, 1995, p. 18). Besides rejecting year 7 as signaling a sufficient capacity to *know* in the sense that confirmation intends, O'Malley also rejected age 12.

> Children at 12 can surely make an act of faith in their parents, in nuns and priests, but they are incapable of a reasoned act of faith on the evidence of a personal understanding of the Gospel or of a rejection of the secular culture about them.  But this is what conversion means. . . . Those who advocate confirmation at age 12 are asking this kind of conversion of pre-pubescent children. (O'Malley, 1995, p. 18)

Thus, O'Malley would opt for delaying confirmation until the middle or late teens, when more maturity has produced greater "awareness that the Gospel is true and its truth internalized" (p. 19).

The typical indicator, other than age, of a candidate's readiness for confirmation has been the satisfactory completion of preparatory instruction, which may consist of lessons over a series of months or years. However, it is clear that there has been no established level of understanding church doctrine applied across dioceses, just as the "age of discernment" has also varied from place to place.

In view of the foregoing controversy, it's apparent that members of the Catholic clergy differ significantly among themselves about the capacity for knowing that the young display at successive age levels. And if we can assume that parishioners often accept their pastor's convictions about such matters—and that parishioners thereby include those convictions in their own belief systems—then there must be marked differences in the folk psychologies of different dioceses about when children are truly able to grasp the meaning of confirmation.

In contrast to the multiple ages for Catholic confirmation, the Jewish rite of passage to adulthood (bar mitzvah for boys, bat mitzvah for girls) is universally scheduled for age 13.

*Kwakiutl full tribal membership.* In traditional Kwakiutl Indian society on Canada's west coast, children are not full members of the tribe until they have successfully engaged in the Hah-Mah-Tsa initiation ritual. The young are permitted to face initiation at the time in adolescence that they are considered mature enough to bear the responsibilities of Kwakiutl adult status. The Hah-Mah-Tsa ceremony consists of two phases: (a) a four-day preparatory period during which the candidate is secluded in the forest to contemplate his worthiness for adult status and (b) the initiate's performing a series of public dramatizations in the form of chant-accompanied dances. This two-phase ritual period has already been preceded by years of parents' and tribe members' teaching the candidate the skills, knowledge, and attitudes that qualify an individual to be a true Kwakiutl. A youth is judged ready for the ceremony only after he has demonstrated that he will be a selfless (good) rather than selfish (bad) member of the community and that he can contribute to the tribe's welfare as a chanter, dancer, hunter, and fisherman.

The set of dance dramatizations that comprise the Hah-Mah-Tsa ritual signify stages of the initiate's earning full tribal status. In the first dance, he petitions the community for admission into their society and promises to abide by the requirements of membership. In the second chant-dance, he renounces selfishness. During the early phases of that performance, he is confronted by four malevolent characters representing four aspects of selfishness—the Grizzly Bear, the Thunderbird, the Killer Whale, and an unnamed specter. In the middle of the dance, the dour tone of the ritual changes into one of triumph of spirit over flesh, good over evil, as the four threatening creatures are transformed into supportive, benevolent patrons. Following this renunciation of evil, the village elders confer on the candidate a new esteemed name that he henceforth will bear, and he then performs the final dance that confirms his admission into the society (Johnston, 1982).

## Personal Experience

The term *personal experience* refers to people acquiring knowledge and skill from observing life and engaging in behavior without having been instructed in such matters. Some folk psychologies view direct experience as a more important source of knowledge than do others. This contrast is illustrated in Levy's description of child rearing practices in a Nepalese community and in a Tahitian village.

The Tahitian parents that Levy observed assumed that children learn to perform tasks chiefly by themselves, that is, by their independent direct experience, in keeping with the gradual maturational unfolding of their abilities. From a Tahitian perspective, no one teaches children very much.

> [Children] learn by watching and by playful trial and error that the adults often find amusing but sometimes annoying. . . . In a learning situation—as opposed to a simple direct command—to tell a child what to do (as opposed to the occasional what *not* to do) . . . is intrusive and taken as a sign of un-justified adult mood-driven irritability and impatience. (Levy, 1996, pp. 128-129)

In contrast to Tahitians, the Nepalese adults that Levy interviewed saw verbal instruction as a necessary vehicle for learning even the most basic behaviors, such as walking, eating, speaking, and bladder control. The ability to use and understand talk was thought to be an essential part of all training, a necessary condition of task mastery.

> In [Nepal] the untaught child would be incompetent not only in his or her physical skills but in his or her moral nature. As one man puts it, "Unless parents control and educate children, children will have bad characters." [Consequently,] the "natural man" is not only inadequate in his skills but morally problematic. In Tahiti, the child who learns by itself "naturally" achieves both task and moral competence. (Levy, 1996, p. 132)

Belief in the importance of direct experience is at the core of the psy-chology of such Marxist-based societies as the former Soviet Union, the People's Republic of China, and North Korea. The German social re-former Karl Marx (1818-1882) in the mid-19th century proposed a theory of societal development that would form the conceptual foundation of communistic societies in the Soviet Union and in a variety of other na-tions during most of the 20th century. He postulated that a society's style of producing and consuming goods and services determines the contents and functioning of people's minds. In other words, thinking does not initiate actions; instead, actions create thoughts. Thus, chil-dren's mental development consists of their internalizing the results of their transactions with their environment.

> The mode of production of material life [whether in a feudal, capitalistic, or socialistic political-economic system] conditions the social, political, and in-tellectual life process in general. It is not the consciousness of men that de-termines their existence, but, on the contrary, their social existence that determines their consciousness. (Marx, 1977, p. 389)

Mao Tse-tung, China's chief political leader and spokesman for com-munist psychology from the 1920s into the mid-1960s, taught that "who-ever wants to know a thing has no way of doing so except by coming into contact with it, that is, by living (practicing) in its environment. . . . If you want knowledge, you must take part in the practice of changing reality. . . . All genuine knowledge originates in direct experience" (Mao in Seyboldt, 1973, p. vii).

In some cultures people are expected to depend solely on direct experience for evidence of what is real and true. Consequently, one cannot accept information as true when it's received secondhand in the form of other people's oral or written accounts. "To know is to perceive directly with one's senses, and what one has not experienced or perceived directly, one does not know" (Watson & Goulet, 1992, p. 224). Thus, among the Orokaiva of Papua New Guinea, what is inside another person can never be known. "When questioned about what someone else is thinking or feeling, an Orokaiva will invariably answer, 'I don't know. It is his inside,' and no one, not even the anthropologist, can ever claim to know anything about it" (Iteanu, 1990, p. 41).

However, it is important to recognize that cultures can differ in how they define direct experience. For instance, the Dene Tha in the northwest of Alberta, Canada, not only accept immediate observations of "this world" as direct experience but also observations of the "other world" through dreams and visions, an extension of "direct experience" generally unacceptable in secular Western cultures. The knowledge-value of information received directly rather than indirectly by the Dene Tha is reflected in the way they speak of events reported as firsthand witness or as hearsay.

> A firsthand report includes the use of phrases like "I saw," "I heard," or "I know." A secondhand report includes verbal markers such as "it is said" or "this is what they say." It is not uncommon for a Dene Tha speaker to conclude with an expression such as *inla ghedih sehdih, edu edahdi, edu sián edahdi,* "this is what they said, he told me, I do not know, I myself do not know." Such continued reminders of the chain of transmission of secondhand knowledge serve to highlight the legitimacy of knowledge obtained at firsthand. (Watson & Goulet, 1992, p. 226)

## Models

Closely linked to direct experience is vicarious experience that guides individuals to copy other people's behavior. Acquiring knowledge vicariously consists of learning by observing other people's performance. Such experience is *formal* when it's part of a planned learning opportunity, as when a teacher assigns students to read a novel, view a videotape, or witness a court trial. Vicarious experience is *informal* when (a) people themselves choose what they will observe or (b) unexpected circumstances confront them with learning opportunities. For instance, a person may gain knowledge while glancing through a magazine in a physician's waiting room, chatting with a foreign visitor in a restaurant, or witnessing an auto accident.

All folk psychologies appear to include a large measure of modeling as a source of knowledge. In fact, most of the basic behaviors that typify a culture are acquired during childhood and adolescence by means of modeling. The term *basic behaviors* in the present context refers to actions that are performed by virtually all members of a cultural group and are performed frequently. Thus, the young have ample opportunity to witness and imitate such actions.

Perhaps the most obvious example of a basic behavior is language. Most of the vocabulary, syntax, grammar, and voice patterns that children acquire are not taught to them in a formal fashion. Instead, the young learn those things "naturally" by copying the people around them. Through imitation, the French child lends a distinctive nasal quality to certain words, the Spanish child trills r's, Polynesians insert glottal stops, the Chinese add tonal inflections, and children in certain African tribes learn to punctuate their speech with clicking sounds. Through modeling, children also adopt gestures and facial expressions that are meaningful to other members of their culture but not understood by outsiders.

Obviously, what people know as a result of modeling depends on the sorts of opportunities they have to observe behavior. For example, in Samoan Islands tradition, public matters have been debated and settled during meetings of the community council (*fono*) in an open, round council house consisting of a thatched roof supported on wooden posts. Villagers are welcome to sit outside the circle of posts and witness the lengthy deliberations of the chiefs (*matais*). In this living theater of government, Samoan youths learn how to conduct meetings and are simultaneously schooled in a variety of topics—effective public speaking, history, civics, and personal-social relations. For example, from witnessing the oratory of talking chiefs, the young discover that people are more convincing and gain admiration if they embroider their speech with poetic allusions to nature, legend, and custom (Thomas, 1987, p. 8).

In contrast to the Samoan case, the conduct of people belonging to occupational guilds and secret societies that are commonly found in cultures throughout the world is hidden from the general populace, so there is little chance for most people to copy the actions of members of such coteries. Likewise, people of one social class in any complex, stratified society usually lack opportunities to view the actions of the members of other class levels, opportunities necessary for copying the behaviors and the appearance that exemplify those levels—speech patterns, dress styles, gestures, skills, opinions, values, and topics of conversation. However, in the 20th century this limitation of opportunity was greatly reduced by the widespread dissemination of movies and television.

## Instruction

The term *instruction* is used here in the broad sense of directing people in how to learn and what to believe. The following paragraphs illustrate three of the many forms that instruction can assume—apprenticeship, schooling, and the study of learning materials.

## Apprenticeship

Apprenticeship involves an individual working alongside an expert in order to acquire the skills and understandings that contribute to success in the expert's field of endeavor. The apprentice learns from a combination of directly experiencing an event, copying the expert's actions, and attending to the expert's explanations of how to proceed. Apprenticeship is a more popular mode of learning in societies whose economic systems are dominated by agriculture, hunting, and cottage industries than in societies that are highly industrialized. Among peoples whose living depends chiefly on subsistence farming, herding, or fishing, children from an early age acquire their future vocations by toiling alongside their parents and older siblings. Economies in the early stages of mechanization typically feature a multitude of small crafts and business ventures to which youths can be attached as apprentices. Advanced industrial societies whose operation depends on workers with technological skills can still include apprentice training as a means of knowledge transfer, but only as a way of preparing workers for jobs involving no more than simple skills (janitors, waitresses, cashiers). For occupations requiring complex skills, employers expect workers to come with substantial general schooling and vocational training and then, in an on-the-job short-term apprenticeship, to acquire the knowledge and skills specific to the employer's particular line of work.

## Schooling

*Schooling*, as intended here, refers to an arrangement for acquiring knowledge that usually includes

- a preestablished body of information and skills that learners are expected to master (the *course of study* or *formal curriculum*),
- a particular time (school day, school year) and place (schoolhouse) for learners to gather and pursue their studies under the supervision of an authority (teacher, guru), and
- techniques of instruction that are believed to promote learners' progress (teaching methods and learning methods).

Cultures can differ significantly in the way they arrange these three sets of variables. Consider, for example, a type of Islamic school known in Indonesia as a *pesantren* (in Arab countries called a *madrasah*, in Malaysia a *pondok*, and in the Sudan a *khalwa*). Traditionally, the course of study has included memorizing passages of Islam's basic holy book (the Qur'an), wise sayings of the Prophet Mohammed (the Sunnah), Arabic language, Islamic history, and some religious law. The offerings of one pesantren have often differed from those of another, as governed by the preferences of the pesantren's instructors. Students of any age above early childhood may attend classes. They can enter and leave the school at any time during the year. Anyone who has attended such a school in the past and is reputedly well versed in Islamic lore can establish, and teach in, a new pesantren.

Schools similar to this Islamic institution have been organized by other religions as well—Buddhist *wat* schools in Thailand, Hindu *ashrams* in India, and Christian-missionary *faifeau* schools in the Pacific islands.

The colonializing activity of European nations between the 16th and mid-20th centuries wrought major changes in the form of schooling in all regions of the world beyond Europe. European explorers, armies and navies, and entrepreneurs carried to Asia, Africa, the Americas, and Oceania not only their business practices, but their religions and educational institutions as well. As a result, what came to be regarded as "proper schooling" by many of the colonizers' conquered peoples was an institution characterized by features beyond—or instead of—those found in traditional pesantrens, ashrams, and the like. The additional features included

- grade levels, with each grade in the schooling hierarchy intended for learners of a given age. The preestablished course of study for each grade is adjusted to the apparent abilities and experiential backgrounds of learners of the grade's age level.
- entrance requirements that applicants must fulfill before they are accepted for schooling.
- a curriculum consisting predominantly of secular rather than religious studies. The course of study typically includes (a) reading and writing the dominant language of the culture of the school's sponsors, (b) mathematics, (c) literature, (d) physical science, (e) social studies, (f) arts (drawing, painting, crafts, music, drama), (g) other languages, (h) vocational training, and (i) physical activities and sports.
- tests that determine (a) how well learners have mastered their studies and (b) whether the learners' achievement warrants their advancing to the next higher grade.
- a certificate attesting to learners' satisfactory command of the course of study over a sequence of grades (primary-school or secondary-

school diploma, college bachelor's degree, vocational-school credential).

Throughout the world, this European-style school has successfully competed against—and in most regions achieved greater prestige than—indigenous paths to knowledge.

Whereas the general form of the European model of schooling has been widely adopted throughout the world, specific characteristics of the model reflect traditional features of a society's folk psychology. This point is illustrated in Japanese schools. Under the newly installed Meiji regime in the 1870s and 1880s, the Japanese government, in a radical move toward modernizing Japanese society, adopted European-style schooling as found mainly in British, German, and American models. Whereas today that European structure continues to dominate Japanese education, certain schooling practices reflect a distinctive Japanese folk culture that emphasizes group identity in contrast to the individualism of European and North American societies. The group-welfare emphasis is widespread in Japanese culture. For instance, in criminal law, the primacy of the group's well-being over freedom of the individual permits Japanese police to search individuals' homes and persons in ways prohibited in the United States. The same strong concern for group solidarity and responsibility is expressed in Japanese schooling practices.

> Parents and teachers expect that public schools are the training grounds where children will learn how to "behave" in a community and conduct themselves in the wider democratic society. On a par with basic literacy and numeracy, group living is a central part of the Japanese elementary curriculum [which stresses] egalitarian participation, resolution of conflict by discussion and empathy for the other, commitment to the group, and willingness to transfer individual accomplishments to the group. (Le Tendre, 1999, p. 292)

The program of teaching social-living skills in Japan is divided into two main stages, the first in the elementary school (grades 1-6), the second in the middle school (grades 6-9). The elementary phase emphasizes (a) developing a sense of community and empathy for other people, (b) sharing resources and responsibilities equally, and (c) resolving conflicts and arriving at decisions in an egalitarian group. The middle-school phase emphasizes adjusting to a hierarchical social system in which individuals (1) assume different roles that involve different levels of power and responsibility and (2) strive to the utmost to perform their duties for the good of the group (Le Tendre, 1999, p. 293). A typical activity during both stages is that of cleaning and maintaining the school property in good order. Pupils perform the school's custodial duties, with teachers and administrators joining the workforce to demonstrate that everyone should contribute to the group's welfare by performing even menial tasks.

However influential the European model of schooling has been, at the outset of the 21$^{st}$ century there were people living in subsistence agricultural, fishing, and hunting societies who felt disenchanted with the imported version of schooling, so they returned to their traditional apprenticeship and modeling ways of knowing. An example from the mid-1990s is the village of Pere in the Manus Islands off the north coast of Papua New Guinea. A study by Demerath (1999) revealed that the difficulty—or impossibility—of village school graduates obtaining wage-paying employment in urban centers caused both parents and pupils to doubt the economic value of formal schooling. The realistic expectation that youths would remain in the village—pursuing traditional lifestyles—found the school building sinking into disrepair, teachers neglecting their duties, and parents taking little or no responsibility for fostering their children's school progress. Thus, the overwhelming proportion of what the Pere young learned came from their participating in traditional village life—acquiring conventional skills and beliefs by joining their elders at work, hearing tales of the past, and engaging in adventures with their peers. In effect, people simultaneously denigrated Western schooling and exalted their own culture heritage, which Demerath (1999, p. 192) interpreted as "villagers' collective perception of the constraints imposed on their lives by the world system of incommensurate differences [in status and opportunity] and their marginalized place within [the system]. . . . Pere villagers' valorization of 'traditional identity' and subsistence technology was a cultural response to preserve [their sense of] worth in this context."

## The study of learning materials

All literate societies have placed great faith in knowledge acquired through reading books and periodicals, so the phrase "knowledgeable person" is often considered synonymous with "well-read person." Consequently, a society that boasts a wide selection of reading materials and offers ready access to those materials on the part of the general public is typically held in higher esteem (more "developed" and more "modern") throughout the international community than are societies less blessed with reading fare.

Learning materials used in the educational efforts of newly literate societies include reading matter, oral histories, folklore, proverbs, and art products (drawings, carvings, sand paintings, music, drama, and dance).

*Reading matter.* It is apparent that much of the content of a society's reading matter is both (a) a result of the culture's folk psychology and (b) a propagator of the beliefs embedded in that psychology. In other words, the ideas espoused in widely read books and articles are usually the products of authors who are steeped in the culture's dominant worldview and reflect that view in their writing.  Those ideas are then urged on readers, thereby transmitting the beliefs from one generation to the next.

The significance of reading as a vehicle of cultural transmission is suggested by the observation that the effect of reading matter on perpetuating a people's folk psychology is in proportion to (a) the quantity of reading material available in a society and (b) the quantity of people who habitually read.  Because societies can differ markedly in both the amount of reading material available and in the extent and level of literacy in the population, the importance of reading for enculturation varies dramatically across societies.

Schoolbooks serve as important purveyors of folk psychologies by portraying life from the perspective of a culture's values.  To illustrate, a comparison of reading primers in Finnish and U.S. American elementary schools revealed that unobtrusive cultural characteristics were consistently implanted in stories.  For instance,

> Successful American heroes were idealized as independent and courageous individuals who stand out from the group, an image consistent with the romantic hero of American literature—particularly child heroes such as Tom Sawyer and Huckleberry Finn. . . . The successful Finnish hero, in contrast, was depicted as friendly, sensitive, and less likely to behave dominantly. This accords well with the Finnish stereotype that abjures boasting and elevates modesty as an ideal. (Hyönä et al., 1995, p. 293)

The authors of the study concluded that their results support the notion that

> the cultural ethos of a nation vigorously penetrates the content of its elementary school primers.  To the extent that these primers function as socialization agents, such tendencies appear to result in a hidden curriculum not even open to official central control.  To fully understand the effect of school materials to which children are exposed requires . . . knowing the value system that is part of the school's hidden curriculum. (Hyönä et al., 1995, p. 294)

A comparison of Japanese and U.S. American primers likewise revealed underlying differences in the folk psychologies of the two cultures.  American readers in the 1990s pictured children facing challenging complexities of life.  In contrast, Japanese primers portrayed the world as a safe, protected environment where people and nature lived in harmony.

> While the American reader presents difficulties children encounter and provides many examples of how children overcome their fears and their di-

lemmas, the Japanese reader seldom even acknowledges that children might have problems. . . . Whereas the inspirational messages that introduce the themes of units in American readers are frequently related to themes of adventure and invention, those introducing Japanese readers emphasize the close interrelationships between people, plants, and animals. (Gerbert, 1993, pp. 157-158)

Thus, the tenor of Japanese textbooks was in keeping with the well-known tendency in Japan to prolong the innocence and naiveté of childhood.

Like the Chinese, the Japanese have traditionally held the view that man's nature is inherently good, that human instincts can be trusted. . . . Today as yesterday, young children are accorded special indulgences in the home and are rarely subjected to physical punishment at the elementary school level. (Gerbert, 1993, p. 159)

The importance attributed to reading as a source of knowledge can vary from one folk psychology to another. Mao Tse-tung, despite having an extensive reading background himself, sought to dampen the Chinese people's faith in books by deprecating reading and by acclaiming learning derived from practical activity.

Nowadays, first, there are too many [school] classes; second, there are too many books. . . . Real understanding must be acquired gradually through experience at work. . . . We shouldn't read too many books. We should read Marxist books, but not too many of them either. . . . If you read too many books, they eventually petrify your mind. (Mao, 1974, p. 195)

*Oral histories and folklore.* Nonliterate peoples are obviously obliged to transmit knowledge orally, passing information from one person to another and from one generation to the next. Among the Australian Aborigines

All . . . technical skills, the arts of hunting and cooking, all nature's gifts, and observances of ritual and ceremonial, are made explicit, and kept intact in the social mind by the recital and dramatic portrayal of the creative and inventive activities of the *pulwaiya* [dreamtime beings, the characters of myth] by whose sanction they continue to exist and function. (McConnell, 1957, pp. 17-18)

Australian myths provided word maps of localities, told of the powers associated with the localities, encapsulated in words committed to memory most if not all of the data available to Aboriginal culture. . . . The religious leaders set themselves the interpretive task [of explaining what myths meant for the conduct of a particular person's life]. From [the religious elders] . . . the initiate learned not only the content of a myth but how to interpret it and so make it work for him. Further, in acting out the myth in a ritual situation, during initiation ceremonies for example, a man became himself a part of the myth, not only a representative of a dreamtime being, but, for the duration of the enactments, he became that dreamtime being itself. (Burridge, 1973, pp. 76-77)

It is also apparent that oral history is not limited to nonliterate societies, for members of literate societies also depend heavily on what people tell each other.

*Proverbs and aphorisms.* Nonliterate societies that count on people's memories as the medium for what should be learned often draw heavily on orally transmitted adages because of the concise manner in which adages convey ofttimes complex concepts. The motifs and forms of proverbial knowledge can vary from one folk psychology to another.

In the Lega society of the Congo,

the basic themes in the proverbs and aphorisms are death, sorcery, solidarity of the kinship group, continuity, respect for seniors, the idea of power, women, relationships between kinsmen, character traits, grandeur of the *bwami* [cultural] association, the moral qualities of initiates and seniors, and relationships between man and his environment. Motifs of fighting, quarreling, arguing, and verbosity are always dealt with pejoratively; they are ridiculed and criticized as wrongdoing. (Biebuyck, 1973, p. 55)

Proverbs in Legaland typically consist of two lines, with each line serving a particular function. A considerable knowledge of the culture is usually required to decipher proverbs' meanings. In the following adage, the first line establishes the symbolic identity of an entity (older person) and the second draws a conclusion about the first.

The senior [elder member of the society] is a turtle.
He was born for long distances. (Biebuyck, 1973, p. 55)

The meaning here is that seniors, however far they roam, always find kinfolk and compatible associates.

A proverb from the Ambo ethnic group of southwestern Angola teaches that it is hard to overcome an adversary by violent means or to break a bad habit: "Where *ngongo* trees have been cut down, there will always be sprouts coming up." (*Pali omiongo, ihapaefa oitutuma.*) Another aphorism teaches that a person should not be discouraged in the face of difficulties but, rather, should aggressively attack the problem: "To experiment or to try is preferable to inaction." (*Onhendabalo idule okumwena.*) (Estermann, 1976, p. 164)

*Art products.* Particularly in societies that lack a written language, artworks are apt to serve as learning materials. Second only to literature, songs are perhaps the most common art form from which people acquire information.

Native crafts also function as sources of knowledge. For instance, women in the Arapaho Indian tribes of North America's Great Plains have traditionally depicted tribal legends and spiritual beings in vegetable-dye paintings on buffalo-hide shields and in beaded designs on clothing, bags, and teepees (Waldman, 1988, p. 18).

Kwakiutl Indians on the Canadian Pacific coast have included totemic art as an important symbol of their worldview. Totemism, in its most general sense, refers to a symbolic connection that is assumed to exist between persons and objects. Those objects are most often animals. The totem poles of Kwakiutl culture are vertical tree logs carved in the semblance of one or more animals that a family or clan adopts as a guardian spirit. A family's particular totem animal is thought to exemplify personality traits that family members admire and, by means of the totem pole, are advertised as characteristics of the family itself—bravery, wisdom, cleverness, strength, or the like. The Kwakiutl entered into several kinds of relationships with the numerous species around them. The bulk of their meat diet was from the abundant resources of the sea and rivers —whales, seals, sea lions, codfish, halibut, herring, and salmon. The skins of smaller animals—such as beaver, mink, otter, martin, and fur seals— were converted into clothing and blankets.

## Dreams

Dreams consist of images that appear during sleep. In some cultures, dreams are widely regarded as valid sources of knowledge about the world, sufficiently convincing to serve as trusted guides to belief and behavior. In other cultures, the dreams of only certain individuals are thought to contain authentic information. And in still other places, dreams are not believed by the general populace to furnish reliable information about either the dreamer's own self or the surrounding world.

Not only may folk psychologies differ in regard to the truth value of dreams, but also in regard to the functions of dreams in people's lives.

### Dream functions

Dreams regarded as sources of knowledge may (a) prophesy the future, (b) guide decision making, and (c) reveal aspects of the universe.

*Prophesying.* Some dreams can be interpreted as intimations of various kinds of future phenomena, such as a person's proper occupation, the sex of an unborn child, imminent death, and good or bad fortune.

Among the Mayan Indians of Mexico, a shaman discovers his calling in life during a dream in which his soul (*ch'ulele*) is summoned before the gods who inform him that he must become a seer. Thus, through revelation rather than instruction a shaman acquires the supernatural insight that equips him to look into an ill person's soul and to restore the soul-loss that is responsible for the victim's suffering (King, 1999, p. 368).

In their interpretations of dreams, peoples can differ in the symbols they accept as portents of particular events. In Tikopia Island culture of the Solomon group east of Papua New Guinea,

> A woman dreams that she goes to the stream, fills her water bottles, and puts them in a basket on her back. It is believed that this indicates she will conceive and bear a girl-child. . . . Seremata, a young bachelor and expert fisherman, dreams on occasion that he sees a canoe approaching shore with some of his relatives in it. The canoe runs on a breaker, then swings and overturns—an accident that happens in real life. This he accepts as an indication that someone of his relatives will die, and he waits accordingly for the news. (Firth, 1967, p. 167)

Hunt (1989) has observed that in certain folk psychologies, the dreaded outcomes prophesied in dreams can be prevented by the dreamer recounting the event to other members of the group rather than keeping silent and thereby preserving the omen's force. In Seneca American Indian lore, a young woman dreamed that she was alone in a canoe, in the middle of a stream, without a paddle. She later told this dream to a shaman who invited her to meet with a number of other members of the tribe in a dream-guessing session. During the session, the group agreed that they could forestall the dream event from actually occurring by presenting the girl with a miniature canoe, complete with paddle (Wallace, 1958, p. 240).

*Guiding decision making.* In some cultures, people learn that they should heed the suggestions dreams offer about how to act. Among the Jivaro Indians living on the eastern slope of the Andes in Peru and Ecuador, men in search of shamanistic power attempt to make dream contact with the souls of ancient warriors (*ajutap*).

> *Ajutap* dreams typically have two parts: An initial vision of a terrifying beast or comet-like blast of light that the dreamer must confront and touch, followed by a second dream (sometimes separate from the first by a day or more) in which the *ajutap* presents himself to the dreamer in human form and tells him of his victory in battle. A man who receives such a vision is called "owner of a dream" or "one who has had a vision." His outward manner becomes forceful and self-assured since he knows that his enemies cannot kill him. (Brown, 1987, pp. 163-164)

Among the Raramuri of northern Mexico, God may arrive in a dream to offer special powers to a dreamer by displaying several light-colored pieces of paper. If the dreamer takes one or more papers, God will empower him or her to become a doctor, sorcerer, or both, or neither, depending on the colors of the papers the dreamer grabs. The role of doctor is the only position in the society that requires legitimization through a dream.

Every night, the souls of doctors join God and his assistants in watching over the other members of the community, preventing the Devil and his co-horts from hurting them. . . . If soul loss is indicated, the doctor concentrates his attention on locating the soul in his dreams on that or subsequent nights. The task is considered potentially quite arduous, requiring lengthy journeys through little known and often dangerous territories; as one man put it, it is like searching for a thief whose location is unknown. (Merrill, 1987, pp. 331-332)

An occasional folk psychology teaches that failing to heed the lessons that dreams offer can deprive a person of future access to dreams as a source of knowledge. According to one present-day shaman of the Hu-ichol Indian tradition in western Mexico,

If one doesn't do what a dream has directed him to do, one won't be able to dream well any more. That's why so many people don't know how to dream. . . . If a person . . . believes in the dream and follows the directions once the [shaman] explains it, . . . the gods will then send more dreams of this type because the person has now proven that he believes in the gods and obeys what he is told. (Valadez, 1986, p. 19).

*Revealing the universe.* In many cultures of Oceania, such as that of Tikopia, a person's soul (*mauuri* or *ora*) can wander away during a dream, visiting distant places and interacting with other mortals' souls and with beings of the spirit world. The dream images inform the sleeper of the wandering soul's adventures and thus ostensibly expand the dreamer's knowledge of both the visible and invisible world (Firth, 1967, pp. 334-337).

## Convincing Knowledge Sources

Cultures often vary in their conceptions of which sources of informa-tion provide true knowledge. As noted earlier, it is common in many cultures for people to believe as "true" those happenings told to them "second hand" by someone regarded as authoritative—a parent, teacher, theologian, scientist, philosopher, government official. But in other cul-tures, people learn to place greater faith in their own direct experi-ences—in what they personally see and hear. And because people directly witness images and events while asleep, such direct dream expe-riences may be judged *real* and *true,* because "seeing is believing" and "hearing is knowing." A case in point is the folk psychology of the Melpa people of the Western Highlands Province in Papua New Guinea. As is true throughout much of Melanesia, the Melpa accord truth value to direct experiences in both waking life and sleep. However, the overt appearance of things in dreams is not accepted as the real meaning. Therefore, dreams must be properly interpreted if their truth is to be grasped. So, to analyze a dream correctly, one must know the interpretation code.

> The first element of the code is to recognize that the truth may be the opposite of what is shown. Dreams that westerners would regard as wish fulfillments are interpreted as such also by the Melpa but always with the understanding that the meaning is [that] the wish will not be fulfilled. . . . In actuality there is more than one mode of dream-interpretation. One mode fixes upon a single feature which is held to be symbolic and extracts meaning from this; another mode takes the whole narrative and applies it to the dreamer's whole life situation—a *gestalt* as against an analytical method. (Strathern, 1989, p. 303)

Thus, in Melpa folk psychology dreams contain truth about the present, past, or future, but the truth is not obvious. Rather, it's hidden in symbolism, to be revealed only by applying the interpretation code.

In modern Western societies, dreams apparently are not believed by the general populace to offer reliable information about the world. Or, if dreams do reflect something significant at least about the dreamer, there is no way of knowing what that something is. However, certain proposals about dreams' meanings as offered by theorists from the "scientific community" have gradually been adopted by subgroups of the lay public, even though such beliefs are not held universally throughout the society. One example of a "scientific" explanation is Sigmund Freud's (1900/1953) assertion that dreams reflect wish-fulfilling activities of a person's unconscious mind, which works during sleep to solve problems from the dreamer's waking life. Another example is Carl Jung's contention that "Dreams are impartial, spontaneous products of the unconscious psyche . . . [that] show us the unvarnished natural truth," although often disguised in symbolic form (Jung in Hall & Nordby, 1973, p. 118).

Within the segment of the lay public of present-day Western societies that believes the images in dreams symbolize valid information, there seems to be no agreement about whether each symbol conveys the same knowledge for every dreamer or whether a symbol has a meaning unique to each dreamer's life. Freud contended that such an image as a tower or a bowl bore the same meaning for everyone (a tower representing the male sex organ and a bowl the female sex organ). But Jung suggested that symbols might be either universal or unique to individuals; and that dream images grew in diversity as, with the passing years, persons accumulate an increasingly abundant array of experiences and memories (Lazlo, 1993).

## Visions

Visions consist of images appearing spontaneously while a person is awake, without the person's conscious intention.

Although visions are expected to emerge spontaneously and not under an individual's control, people can take measures intended to encourage the occurrence of visions. In the past, throughout the Americas the ecstatic trance was nearly a universal rite. Eskimo shamans produced trances by the hypnotic rhythms of a drum. Plains Indians of North America sought visions by fasting, forced wakefulness, exposure to inclement weather, and self-inflicted pain. Most Indian tribes of the Great Plains have practiced the *vision quest* as an activity for eliciting information about a person's sacred name, personal guardian spirit, and other sorts of knowledge. A typical vision quest involves a youth going alone into the wild to engage in fasting and sacrifice that will stimulate visions. Such appearances are usually apparitions of animals and other natural phenomena that are expected to invest the seeker with spiritual power, suggest a new name the youth should adopt, and inspire the creation of sacred songs and forms of art. Upon returning home, the seeker may share the received visions with the tribe by reenacting the experience in new forms of dance-drama that subsequently may be blended into the tribal culture. In a similar fashion, Iroquois cultures of North America's eastern woodlands have included purification rites that require individuals at the time of puberty to engage in a vision quest in order to discover their sacred guardian and receive guidance in conducting their life (Brown, 1989, pp. 13, 15). If a shared vision is adopted by the group as part of its belief system, then the individual who received the vision will have helped enrich the group's folk psychology.

Among the Athapaskans of northern Alberta, Canada, children are encouraged to spend time wandering in the bush in the hope of meeting a spirit animal which may become the child's lifelong guardian and helper. Information about the encounter and the animal guardian are to be kept secret or else the bond between the person and the animal spirit will be broken. However, other members of the community may guess what sort of animal was met in the vision by their viewing the person's behavior, such as noting that the individual never eats a particular species of animal and always avoids certain sights and sounds.

> Someone with the eagle as a helper must not expose himself to the flash of a camera, which is likened to the glare of the eagle's eye. One who has the spider as helper avoids listening to a guitar or violin, whose strings are linked to the spider's thread. To defy these prohibitions is to risk one's power becoming too strong and turning against oneself. . . . Since it is through one's behavior that one reveals the identity of the animal helper, it

is through observation of each other's behavior that the identities of these helpers are inferred. (Goulet, 1996, p. 694)

According to Islamic lore, during Prophet Mohammed's adult life (7th century C.E.) he was periodically met in visions by the angel Gabriel who recited to Mohammed messages from God. Following these visitations, Mohammed dictated the recited messages to scribes (Watt, 1994, pp. 1-5). The resulting documents were later compiled to form the contents of the Islamic holy book, the Qur'an, considered by Muslims to be "the earthly reproduction of an uncreated and eternal heavenly original" (Rahman, 1994, p. 6).

In a variety of societies, visions have been intentionally induced by people's ingesting or inhaling substances that produce paranormal sights, sounds, and body sensations. Such is the case with the Navajo whose Native American Church focuses primarily on the use of the hallucinogenic peyote to engender apparitions and cure ailments (Brown, 1989, p. 25). The San Pedro cactus, still used in modern Peruvian folk medicine, has been a stimulator of ecstatic visions for centuries (*Mysteries of the Ancient Americas*, 1986, p. 300). As a further example, *kava*—a drink made from the pounded roots of a pepper shrub—is imbibed during Polynesian, Micronesian, and Melanesian rituals throughout the Pacific. Kava in substantial doses has a narcotic and hypnotic effect. Islanders often believe that kava inebriation brings them into communion with the gods and ancestors and thereby gives mortals access to potentially valuable knowledge.

> Unlike in contemporary Western theories of knowledge production, in Islanders' explanations for the origins and growth of an idea, the importance of inspiration far outweighs that of creativity. Clever people are those who control powerful means of inspiration, rather than those who are personally creative or talented. . . . Because Pacific people believe that knowledge can be inspired by kava inebriation, the drug is a typical ingredient of divination techniques. In Vanuatu, seers and mediums, called "clevers" (*kleva*) in local Pidgin English, often drink kava before divining the cause of someone's illness or the location of a lost pig. (Lebot, Merlin, & Lindstrom, 1992, pp. 154-155)

Although mental states generated by psychoactive drugs are thus viewed as sources of valuable knowledge in numerous cultures, in present-day Western European and North American secular cultures, visions produced by the use of psychedelic drugs are usually considered irrational hallucinations rather than trustworthy revelations of truth. Amazing visions reported by a person in an alcoholic stupor are not accepted as helpful insights into reality.

## Possession

The word *possession*, as used here, refers to a person's acquiring and expressing information as a result of being penetrated and controlled by a supernatural spirit. The possessed person serves as the vehicle that the invisible spirit requires for conveying messages to mortals. Hence, possessed persons are referred to as *mediums* because they link supernatural spirits to ordinary humans.

That possession is a source of knowledge is often asserted by the possessed. In Kefa—a village of around 250 residents in Zambia, East Africa—a healer named Vast Manda explained that

> I was first possessed by spirits more than 15 years ago and since then I have learned so many things and become wiser in my way of thinking than ever before—not only because I have grown older, but also because the *mizimu*—the spirits—have advised me. . . . I gain new knowledge and come to understand every good and bad thing about to happen in the village, in my family, and to myself. (Skjonsberg, 1989, p. 163)

A second example—this one from Newar society in Nepal's Kathmandu Valley—illustrates a form of possession often observed in Asian cultures. Clients may seek the aid of mediums for help with various sorts of problems, including physical and mental disorders, social difficulties, or simply vague distress and malaise. The medium—usually a woman of lower-class status—serves clients by summoning her personal possessing deity, which in Nepal is usually Hariti, the Buddhist goddess of smallpox who is said to be a spirit converted to Buddhism and to function as the guardian of children. This tutelary shade then addresses the client's problem through the medium. In many cases, clients' difficulties are attributed to "spoiling action" on the part of a witch, with the term *witch* applied to anyone who harms others through magic.

> The god who speaks through the medium's mouth may pronounce on the auspiciousness of certain times, may venture a diagnosis which makes use of Ayurvedic [ancient Hindu medical] concepts . . . [and may prescribe the application of] blessed and empowered powder, blessed and empowered water, brushing with a broom, and blowing [on the sufferer]. (Gellner, 1994, p. 31)

Knowledge-producing possession on a massive scale is illustrated by the Umbanda movement in Brazil. Umbanda is a syncretic religion combining elements of spiritism from France (in the 18th century), rituals from Africa, bits of Catholicism and of other major European and Asian religions, as well as some Brazilian inventions. From modest beginnings in the 1930s, Umbanda membership grew to between five and ten million followers by the late 1970s, plus thousands of nonmembers who occasionally availed themselves of the services of Umbanda mediums. In the vicinity of Rio de Janeiro by the latter decades of the 20th century, there were around 20,000 Umbanda cult centers (*centros espiritos*) with over two million practitioners (Brown, 1979, p. 276).

Umbanda's major rituals consist of sessions held in the evening two or three times a week at *centros*. The participants are divided into two groups—the ritual corps and the clients. Members of the ritual corps, who perform at the front of the auditorium, are uniformed personnel in charge of the ceremony. Those personnel include "the leader or *chefe*, the mediums, who are ranked according to their degree of spiritual preparation and ability to enact possession roles, and other individuals who are not mediums but have specific ritual duties" (Brown, 1979, p. 278). The clients—typically 30 to 50 individuals—sit on benches in the main section of the hall facing the ritual corps. Clients attend the sessions to obtain spiritual help in solving a variety of problems—illness, family disorder, unemployment, financial concerns, trouble with bureaucracies, and more. After the ritual corps performs introductory activities, including singing Umbanda hymns, clients line up to consult mediums.

Two defining features of Umbanda rituals are spirit possession and spirit consultation.

> Spirit possession is the most crucial aspect of Umbanda, since it provides visual evidence of the existence of spirits: benevolent spirits who dramatize their willingness and availability to help mankind by offering their services as curers and advisors, and malevolent or ignorant spirits who are revealed to be at work in the daily lives of ordinary men and women. (Brown, 1979, p. 279)

During a given session, mediums, and sometimes clients themselves, become possessed by spirits that send general messages and reveal information via the possessed individual. Then, at the time that each client consults a medium about the client's particular dilemma, the medium summons spirits to diagnose the problem and prescribe a cure. Depending on the nature of the client's problem, the assigned treatment may be a spiritual cleansing (which might include a ritual hug in which the negative fluids in the client's body are drawn into the medium's hands and from there shaken off with a snapping of the fingers), blessings, exorcisms, herbal remedies, rites to perform, or practical advice.

> The successful solution of the clients' personal difficulties and their feelings of being helped by *consultas* generates or strengthens belief in Umbanda's spiritual powers and forms the basis for continued interest and participation. As is commonly said, "O Umbandista entra pela porta do sofrimento" ("Umbandistas come to Umbanda through the door of suffering"). (Brown, 1979, p. 280)

O'Connell (1982) has proposed that possession typically occurs among marginal, subordinate, and underprivileged individuals who win recognition, improved status, and enhanced rights by exhibiting a condition of possession. Furthermore, he suggests that possession is most likely to occur in people who suffer stress due to their inability to meet their culture's role expectations. In support of this hypothesis, he cites the case of the Nguni peoples of southern Africa, and particularly the Xeside of the eastern Transkei. Known locally as *intwaso*, possession is considered an illness whose most common symptoms are heart palpitations, a sinking sensation in the stomach, listlessness, and a desire to be left alone—all as a result of fright and anxiety. The Xeside believe that the condition "may be cured through animal sacrifices to ancestors, but ideally the *intwaso* victim should become an initiate in a diviner's school and train to become a diviner *(isangoma)*" (O'Connell, 1982, p. 22). Studies of the onset of *intwaso* suggest that

> [Possession] can occur when an individual experiences failure in role performance. Hence, *intwaso* among women is associated with poor role performance in the domestic sphere, while *intwaso* among men is linked to poor role performance in the extradomestic sphere. Each case represents a conflict between individual performance and his or her culturally prescribed role. (O'Connell, 1982, p. 36)

## Fantasies

Fantasizing is a process of intentionally fashioning images or ideas while awake. It is an act of envisioning what *might be* rather than *what is*. For convenience of analysis, fantasies can be placed in two categories—*productive* and *idle*. Productive fantasies are imaginings that result in observable products. The products can be of many kinds—a drawing or painting, a new theory of the origin of the universe, an improved computer, a poem, an original interpretation of the Christian Bible or the Islamic Qur'an, a different system of cost accounting, a fresh strain of roses, a novel type of airplane, a unique musical composition, or thousands of other sorts of innovation. In contrast to productive fantasies are idle fantasies—ephemeral daydreams that may entertain, distract, or frighten the person who creates them, but which result in no perceptible product.

When *creativity* is defined as the process of originating something, of devising something novel or unique, then fantasizing qualifies as creative activity. As I see it, the creative process consists of a person rearranging one's memories—one's existing collection of beliefs—to form a novel pattern, resulting in something that did not exist before. Hence, one's new knowledge is fashioned out of one's existing store of beliefs.

When people use the adjective *creative* as a complimentary adjective, they rarely if ever mean that the product being judged is merely different from the usual. Rather, to be considered constructively creative, novelty must be joined by one or more other admirable characteristics, ones that may not be verbalized but, rather, may be only unconsciously or intuitively intended by the person who is offering the judgment. Two sorts of intended characteristics are the functional and the aesthetic. *Functional* refers to how well something carries out its proposed purpose. If a new style of electric can opener fails to open cans, it qualifies as "unusual" but not a "creative contribution." *Aesthetic* refers to how well a product meets people's standards of artistic desirability. A four-line verse that its author calls a sonnet will certainly be different from previous sonnets, but will not be judged by devotees of English literature as "creative" because even the verse's form is far outside the sonnet tradition.

What, then, is the relevance of this view of creativity for the analysis of folk psychologies? I would suggest that one important way folk psychologies can differ from each other is in the kinds of productive fantasies they value. The most respected kinds are encouraged and rewarded by a society, whereas kinds that are least valued are either ignored or discouraged. This point can be illustrated by the following examples that focus on functional and aesthetic effects of fantasizing.

### Functional standards

Cultures are not all alike in the extent to which they foster or accept deviations from tradition in modes of thought, including modes of thought that can result in technological innovations which may increase the efficiency of such functions as communication, transportation, people's work methods, information storage and retrieval, and more.

As one example, during the final decades of the 20th century there was a curious exchange of mutual envy between Japan and the United States. While the Americans were admiring the high scores that Japanese students earned on internationally administered science and mathematics tests, the Japanese were admiring Americans' technological creativity. In each nation, commentators attributed the other country's success (high test scores in Japan, technological creations in the United States) to its schooling practices and hoped that some of those practices would be adopted in their own society. Japanese critics complained that their education system, while excellent at teaching established knowledge, concentrated too exclusively on students' reproducing what their instructors taught and thereby failed to encourage productive fantasizing. American schools, in contrast, were seen as encouraging learners to debate issues and devise their own solutions to problems, thereby fostering creativity, particularly in science and technology. To support their charges, the Japanese noted that far more new developments in electronics and scientific theory originated in America and Western Europe than in East Asia. The complaints, in essence, were directed at an ostensible failure of Japanese schooling to prepare youths to develop novel technologies that would carry out functions in a more efficient fashion than did existing technologies.

Americans, on the other hand, criticized their own schools with failing to effectively teach established knowledge, so that steps were recommended for correcting this shortcoming, including the step of adopting Japanese curricula and instructional methods. Therefore, it was not a lack of creativity that worried the Americans but, rather, it was students' inadequate mastery of traditional knowledge ("Free Your Mind," 1999; Takahata, 1999; Todd & Shinzato, 1999).

Whereas the putative paucity of technological creativity in Japan is said to be the result of the neglect of fantasizing in the education system, the absence of technological invention among the Amish in North America is quite intentional. Amish Mennonites form a Protestant sect whose customs bearing on dress, technology, social relations, and religious doctrine seem frozen in time—suspended back in the 17th century at the time a Swiss Mennonite elder, Jakob Ammann, launched a revised version of Mennonite belief and practice. Today's Amish maintain agricultural communities in Canada and the United States, dress like 17th-century Swiss (plain black garb and the men bearded), and eschew telephones, electric lights, television, motorized transportation, and modern agricultural machinery. Amish children may attend public elementary schools but do not continue into high school. The rationale behind the Amish way of life is that the group's culture reached a condition of near perfection under Jakob Ammann, a condition that should not be tainted by innovation ("Amish," 1994).

### Aesthetic standards

The cross-cultural comparisons of fantasies' contribution to artworks offered in the following pages requires a preparatory introduction that explains the perspective toward aesthetic standards on which those comparisons are based. Hence, the first portion of this section is dedicated to explaining that perspective. The second portion then provides examples of aesthetic components of folk psychologies that distinguish one culture from another.

*A conception of creativity in art.* Each domain of artistic endeavor is typically identified by a label that implies particular characteristics that a work of art must incorporate in order to qualify for that label. Some labels are broad range, encompassing a diversity of more specific types of art. Broad-range labels include such classifiers as *painting, sculpture, tex-*

*tiles, poetry, dance, drama,* and *music.* The characteristics that an art product must display in order to belong in the *textiles* domain are obviously
different from those that warrant a product's being labeled *poetry.* Furthermore, within each broad domain, cultures often identify specific
types of art, with each type distinguished by certain features in addition
to those that define the broad domain. Those subclasses can be based on
different dimensions of art products. For example, in cultures derived
from European tradition, painting can be divided into subcategories of
media, of subject matter, and of style. Media can include *oil, watercolor,
acrylic, pastel,* and more. Subject matter can bear such labels as *still life,
portrait, landscape,* and *figure.* Styles can be designated *representational,
abstract, cubist, classical, impressionist,* and such.

It is thus the case that each type or form of art is defined by a set of
rules or aesthetic standards that designate what a work must possess if it
is to qualify as that type. I would then propose that creativity in art can
be of two main sorts. The first consists of a person's working strictly
within the rules to produce a novel variation of that art form. Novelty is
accomplished by artists devising unusual variations along a dimension
of their art form that is not restricted by the rules defining that form. For
instance, the rules governing the type of still-life painting labeled *cubism*
require that (a) the subject matter be restricted to inanimate objects
viewed at close range (in contrast to landscapes or seascapes seen from
afar) and (b) the pictured objects must be cast as stylized, overlapping
geometric forms. However, there are no rules restricting either the location of forms on the canvas or the colors used. Thus, an artist can
achieve novelty by inventing unusual relationships among geometric
spaces or unusual colors of objects and still be true to the definition of
that art form. In effect, the novel features of the art product are found in
dimensions of the work not restricted by its rules.

In the second sort of creativity, artists alter the rules enough to render
the work unusual, yet they still abide by most of the rules defining the
particular art form. In way of illustration, consider the career of the
Spanish artist Pablo Picasso. His early paintings would fit the label "realistic representational human portraiture"—with "realistic representational" meaning a nearly photographic depiction of a real-life person.
But as the years advanced, he gradually deviated from the traditional
conception of "realistic." During his "blue period," the complexions of
the people he portrayed were no longer the usual flesh shades; he had
altered the traditional rule about color so that everyone turned blue.
Soon he was no longer arranging the parts of the human body in the traditional pattern; instead, he separated the parts, placing them in various
locations on the canvas and coloring them extraordinary hues. Whereas

his work was still "representational human portraiture," the rule about "realistic" had been altered to fit his fantasies (Wertenbaker, 1974).

What, then, does the above conception of fantasy and creativity have to do with folk psychology? In response, I would propose that

- Cultural groups hold beliefs about (a) which characteristics (rules or aesthetic standards) typify different forms of art and (b) which forms are most acceptable and valued.
- The works of artists who create novelty within the restrictions set by the rules will be more readily accepted by members of the culture as legitimate variations of that particular art form than will the works that deviate from one or more of the traditional rules.
- As more artists adopt a new version of the rules that an innovator has introduced, a larger portion of the populace will be willing to accept and value works produced under those rules.
- Only when a substantial portion of the cultural group accepts a given type of art can that type be considered part of the group's folk psychology. More precisely, the greater the proportion of a culture's members that value an art form, the more that form deserves to be considered an element of folk culture.

*Aspects of creativity in typical art products.* The following cases suggest the role of fantasy in producing forms of art that became components of three cultures' folk psychologies.

On the Indonesian island of Java, the best-known type of folk art is batik, a form of textile dyeing developed prior to 1700, probably inspired by South India's painted cloths. The defining characteristics of batik are in its process and the appearance of the final product. The traditional process has consisted of the artist (a) drawing a penciled design on a sheet of cotton cloth, (b) using a small-spouted kettle to drip wax onto selected parts of the drawn design, (c) after the wax dries, dipping the cloth into a vat of dye, so that only the unwaxed areas are dyed, (d) melting the wax out of the cloth with hot water, (e) after the cloth dries, dripping wax onto undyed segments of the design, (f) dipping the cloth into a vat of dye of a different color, (g) melting the wax away, and (h) continuing this process for each color that is needed to complete the intended design. The oldest basic colors—regarded as classic—are indigo and brown, with undyed portions of the textile providing a third shade of creamy white. Early traditional designs—still popular—were formed with series of intertwined circlets, lozenges, lines, and dots (Rawson, 1994). During the 20th century, and particularly after Indonesians won political independence from Dutch colonial control in 1950, a remarkable diversity of colors and designs was introduced into batik art in Java and in the nearby nation of Malaysia. Designs included not only a host of abstract patterns, but also animals, supernatural beings, people, and events. Hence, at the outset of the 21$^{st}$ century, Indonesian folk culture offered a great variety of batik styles in women's ankle-length wrap-around skirts, men's shirts, wall hangings, and tablecloths. The abundance of designs was the result of (a) the nation's art community—with government support—encouraging inventiveness in all forms of graphic art and (b) the general public—along with foreign tourists—welcoming the innovations.

In Japan, from the mid-17$^{th}$ century well into the 20$^{th}$ century, *ukiyo-e* woodblock prints were among the most popular art forms. Even today, *ukiyo-e* prints continue to be treasured by art collectors throughout the world. Woodblock printing first entered Japanese folk culture during the Tokugawa era when the society's military class ruled the land with a heavy hand. Members of a prosperous, expanding middle class of merchants and artisans were not permitted a significant political role by the samurai rulers, so they spent their ample funds on extravagant "fleeting pleasures. . . . Their amusement tended to be frivolous and lighthearted, with emphasis on the sensual side of life" (Neuer, Libertson, & Yoshida, 1979, p. 23). The term *ukiyo-e*, meaning "the floating world," reflected the merrymakers' view of their existence—the belief that life was always in transition, always in motion, to be enjoyed as it flowed along. The era's woodblock prints, readily produced in large quantities, reflected the *ukiyo-e* theme of revelry and sexual indulgence by portraying scenes of courtesans and of actors from the kabuki theater. *Ukiyo-e* art was enthusiastically adopted into the society's folk culture, remaining an intimate part of Japanese life to the present day.

From its beginning, *ukiyo-e* art's defining attributes included (a) hand-carved wood blocks, (b) the hand-printing of the blocks on paper, either single sheets or pages in a book, (c) blackline drawings to which areas of color were added, and (d) daily-life subject matter, especially of an erotic—or at least a romantic—nature, usually featuring women. Within these defining rules, inventive artists over the centuries introduced novelty in terms of greater precision and detail in the drawings, new pigments (scarlet, yellow, green, vermilion), unusual perspectives (such as a bird's-eye view suggested by imported Dutch engravings), more diverse scenes from everyday life, alternative versions of feminine beauty, mica printing (pulverized mica glued onto the paper as a sparkling background for prints), and finer-quality paper. In effect, with the passing of time, the variety of art qualifying as *ukiyo-e* expanded as a result of successive artists' fantasies. That fantasizing as a way of knowing, was transmitted into folk culture by the public's eagerly embracing the increasingly diverse versions of *ukiyo-e* art (Neuer, Libertson, & Yoshida, 1979; Newland & Uhlenbeck, 1990).

A popular centuries-old type of Mexican drama is the masked dance, consisting of a public storytelling performance enacted by masked characters. The delimiting features of masked-dance art include (a) a story to tell, (b) dances that depict stages and the spirit of the story, (c) chants and/or instrumental music intended to convey the story's contents and moods, (d) masks worn by all or most of the participants, with the masks designed to portray the appearance and personality traits of the story's characters, (e) costumes suited to the characters' natures, and (f) amateur actors as the participants—village folk with a taste and talent for performing. A host of opportunities for fantasizing is available to mask-makers, musicians, and storytellers within the bounds of the mask-dance defining attributes. Consider, for instance, the range of options for types of stories and types of masks. Story types include religious themes (both precolonial—before the Spanish explorers arrived—and postcolonial Spanish Catholicism), folklore, actual historical incidents, ancestors' lives (enactments known as *viejos* [old men] and *viejitos* [little old men]), animal behavior, and festivals and rites (*Carnaval*). Types of masks include ones carved from wood, modeled in clay, fashioned from cloth or leather, cut from cardboard or tin, molded in rubber or wire mesh, cast in bronze, formed with wax or papier-mâché, painted in fantastic colors, and embellished with hair and beard. The depicted faces can be realistic or fanciful, ugly or beautiful, smiling, smirking, frowning, glaring, passive, sneering, and more.

> [In every community] there is usually at least one specialist responsible for providing local people with masks. This task rarely demands more than a fraction of the maker's time. Although the majority work as farmers throughout the year, mask-makers—like dancers—can have a wide range of other occupations. . . . Mask-makers are respected for their great wisdom. They know the storyline of every local dance, and which facial features to give each different character. (Lechuga & Sayer, 1994, p. 13)

In summary, every folk psychology includes conceptions of art forms that (a) are identified by defining characteristics and (b) provide opportunities for individuals to devise novel variations of a form within the boundaries delineated by the form's defining features. Individuals' fantasized alterations of an art form become part of the folk psychology to the extent that members of the cultural group adopt those alterations as acceptable versions of art. Cultures can differ markedly in the specific forms of art that are practiced and in the degree to which each form is valued.

## CULTURAL CHANGE AND THE STATE OF KNOWLEDGE

In recent centuries, the technological invention that potentially can exert the greatest influence on folk psychologies has been the electronic computer and its associated networks, particularly the Internet and World Wide Web. The power of the Internet to alter cultural beliefs derives from its ability to expose many millions of people to an immense variety of events and ideas they would otherwise never experience. The speed and breadth of the distribution of computers throughout the world has been unprecedented, far outpacing the dissemination of earlier communication media—printed materials (books, periodicals, newspapers), the mails, telegraph, telephone, and even radio and television. Linked to the issue of computers as modes of influence on people's beliefs is the matter of how much control is wielded over the availability of information. These matters are considered in the following paragraphs.

### Computers

The rapid advance of computers as a source of knowledge has derived from both the remarkable development of computers as machines and on the equally remarkable expansion of the storehouse of information that can be investigated via computer networks.

### Progress in computer technology

In the 1830s, the idea of a machine that would carry out computations assumed the form of a practical plan when an English inventor, Charles Babbage, envisioned a device he called The Analytical Engine. The inventor's machine would embody the principal elements found in present-day digital computers—a system (punched cards) for putting data into the machine and for taking out the results, a unit to carry out arithmetic computations, a memory unit for storing numbers, and a system for controlling the sequence of operations that needed to be performed. However, the machine-tool industry of Babbage's day was not equal to the task of fashioning the highly precise metal parts that his invention required, so a proper operating version of his analytical engine was never produced. Consequently, Babbage's plan lay neglected until the appearance of the first practical electromechanical computing machines appeared in the 1940s. A prominent example was the Harvard Mark I, completed in 1944, which used electrical switching elements to process data that had been entered into the machine on punched cards. To accommodate all of the switching equipment, the Mark I had to be 50 feet long and 8 feet high.

In the late 1940s, vacuum tubes replaced electrical relays, making computers 1,000 times faster than their pioneering predecessors. Then, in the 1960s transistors replaced vacuum tubes, rendering computers far more compact and faster than their forebears, capable of performing as many as 100,000 functions a second.

Since the 1970s, the development of faster and smaller computers that can perform a great variety of functions has progressed at an accelerating pace. By the end of the 20th century, millions of tiny transistors that formed electrical circuits could be built into a silicon chip the size of a child's thumbnail. On the average, each newly developed chip would double computer capacity every 18 months (Gates, 1995, p. 31). Consequently, a mainframe computer that filled a large room and cost a million dollars in the 1960s could be replaced in 2001 for a few hundred dollars by a desktop computer or a miniature handheld instrument.

Prior to the 1980s, most computers were of the mainframe variety, expensive bulky machines located in university computer centers, business offices, and government agencies. Their number throughout the world was quite limited. But with the invention of small, low-cost personal computers in the 1980s, ordinary citizens could have their own machine at home or in the office, so the sale of personal computers sped ahead at an extraordinary rate.

The pace at which computers were disseminated in the final years of the 20th century can be illustrated with the growth in numbers over the period 1985-2000. In 1985, an estimated 38.1 million computers were in use throughout the world. The total grew by 260% to 129.4 million in 1991, then to 257.2 million in 1995, and 535.9 million by 2000. However, the distribution by nations was very uneven, with the greatest number of users per capita in North America, Scandinavia, Britain, Australia, and New Zealand, while computer availability in Asia, South America, and Africa was very modest, indeed.

## Software and the Internet

Computers would be of little importance for enhancing people's knowledge if it were not for the access they provide to informative software and the Internet.

The term *informative software*, as intended here, means ideas about the world that are (a) entered into a computer's memory storage (hard disk) for retrieval at any time or (b) on a magnetized tape or disk placed temporarily in a computer to be searched for information. Examples of informative software contents are encyclopedias, songs, games, textbooks, novels, children's stories, cooking recipes, foreign-language lessons, and far more.

In contrast to informative software is *operating-instruction software* —directions given to the computer about how to carry out different functions, such as word processing, mathematical computations, the organization of data, drawing, music listening and composing, and the reproduction and editing of photographs and motion pictures.

Although informative software is of value in expanding people's beliefs about the world, the ability of such media to provide access to information is minuscule compared to the ability of the Internet. The Internet is a collection of interconnected computer networks maintained by governments, educational institutions, organizations, and commercial groups. The importance of the Internet as a potential influence on folk psychologies derives from its providing the largest compilation of information, ideas, and beliefs ever assembled. The World Wide Web, as the fastest growing part of the Internet, is a collection of millions of sources (*websites*) offering all manner of documents and media from all over the world. People find the Web's information by *going online*, that is, by connecting their own computers with the Internet via telephone lines and communication satellites.

Even with the enormous amount of information on the World Wide Web, the Web's significance in affecting the beliefs of the great majority of the world's peoples would be slight if only a small number of individuals had access to the Internet, that is, if only a limited number could *go online*. But such is not the case. During the 1980s and 1990s, the quantity of Internet users worldwide grew from a few thousand to an estimated 375 million. The Internet's greatest popularity has been in Europe and North America. Its use has been far less in South Asia, South America, and Africa. For example, by the outset of the 21$^{st}$ century, more than one-third of the world's 375 million users were in the United States. In 1995, less than 1% were in South Asia, where 23% of the world's people live. In Finland, 38% of the population were online, in the United Kingdom 26%, in Japan 20%, in Malaysia 3%, in Saudi Arabia 1.4%, in China 0.71%, and in India 0.5% (4.5 million people) (Hill, 2000). By 2000, the 10 countries with the largest number of Internet users were the United States with 135.7 million, Japan with 26.9 million, Germany 19.1 million, Britain 17.9 million, China 15.8 million, Canada 15.2 million, South Korea 14.8 million, Italy 11.6 million, Brazil 10.6 million, and France 9 million (Rubin, 2000).

Within any society, the likelihood that people's beliefs will be influenced by their access to the Internet varies by age, education, and gender. A report by the United Nations Development Programme showed that the typical Internet user was male, below age 35, had a university education and an income well above average, was urban-based, and spoke English (Hill, 2000, p. xxii).

From the vantage point of folk psychologies, implications suggested by the above sketch of Internet use are that the effect of the World Wide Web on people's belief systems will likely be greatest in these places:

- in advanced industrialized nations, particularly Europe and North America, Australia, New Zealand, Japan, South Korea, and Taiwan.
- among people with advanced education,
- among youths and young adults, and
- in cities rather than in rural areas.

Furthermore, folk beliefs that traditionally have been widely held within a culture will likely give way to more varied, individualistic beliefs as a result of the access to diverse ideas that the World Wide Web provides.

## Information Control

The advent of new communication media—such as computer networks, radio, television, and recent versions of print publications (newspapers, books, magazines, academic journals)—has brought to the fore questions about what implications those media hold for the public availability of different kinds of information. In particular, to what extent do the available forms of those media expand or limit the range of information open to the public?

Bagdikian (1990) has argued that, for most people in the United States, the sources of information about the nature of their world over the latter decades of the 20th century became increasingly restricted as mass communication media came under the control of fewer corporations. This trend produced what he referred to as a "private ministry of information." For example, by 1990 "twenty-three corporations [would] control most of the business in daily newspapers, magazines, television, books, and motion pictures," a number down from 46 in 1983 (Bagdikian in Gamson, Croteau, Hoynes, & Sasson, 1992, p. 374).

> Ideally, a media system suitable for a democracy ought to provide its readers with some coherent sense of the broader social forces that affect the conditions of their everyday lives. It is difficult to find anyone who would claim that media discourse in the United States even remotely approaches this ideal. The overwhelming conclusion is that the media generally operate in ways that promote apathy, cynicism, and quiescence rather than active citizenship and participation. . . . We walk around with media-generated images of the world, using them to construct meaning about political and social issues. The lens through which we receive these images is not neutral but evinces the power and point of view of the political and economic elites who operate and focus it. And the special genius of this system is to make the whole process seem so normal and natural that the very act of social construction is invisible. (Gamson, Croteau, Hoynes, & Sasson, 1992, pp. 373-374)

However, Bagdikian's complaints about international corporations controlling the ideas conveyed by newspapers, books, and television cannot be applied to the Internet and its World Wide Web. Up to the present time at least, no one has been able to control what is included on the Internet. Although some governments have attempted to limit the sorts of information that can be found on the World Wide Web, those efforts have been chiefly unsuccessful. This lack of control has both advantages and disadvantages. The principal advantage has been that people have available a great diversity of ideas to ponder, accept, or reject. But this freedom of access is accompanied by at least three disadvantages. First, there is no quality control over what goes on the Web. Truth and falsity have an equal chance of appearing on websites. Consequently, users need to apply their own tests of validity in judging what to believe and what to discard. Second, children whose judicious reasoning is yet undeveloped are not prepared to decide which information will lead to their constructive growth and which will do them harm. Therefore, some adult monitoring of children's use of the Internet appears warranted. Third, computers have been available chiefly to the more affluent socioeconomic classes in the more industrialized countries, and the principal language used on the Internet has been English. Consequently, a large portion of the world's peoples has not been able to take advantage of the Internet. However, in the opening years of the 21st century, the price of computers continued to decline, thereby making access to the World Wide Web more affordable; and new software enabled speakers of a great many of the world's languages to use the Internet in their own vernacular.

Despite the problems of certain cultural groups' inadequate access to the Internet, the World Wide Web is an exception to Bagdikian's charge that powerful corporations restrict the information from which people compose their belief systems.

# 4

# Cause

*Why do things happen as they do?*

Questions about *cause* are questions about the relationship (correlation) between two or more phenomena. When one thing changes, what happens to other things? And is the change in one thing the result of (caused by) the change in another thing, or is the simultaneous change in both things merely coincidental?

In this chapter, such questions as they bear on folk psychologies are inspected under two headings: (a) aspects of causality, and (b) cultural change and beliefs about cause.

## ASPECTS OF CAUSALITY

Diverse ways of viewing matters of cause include those of (a) *causal* versus *casual* correlations, (b) direct versus mediated cause, (c) methods of correcting causes, (d) time sequences, (e) multiple causation, (f) internal versus external causes, and (g) cross-cultural encounters.

### Causal Versus Casual Correlations

A significant consideration in understanding a folk psychology's explanation of why events happen as they do is found in the distinction between a proposed *causal* correlation and a *casual* or *coincidental* one. This distinction can be illustrated with an anecdote from the past about a retiree in a small Kansas town who spent his days sitting on a bench in front of the general store, reading the weekly newspaper and observing what occurred on Main Street. A correlation that particularly interested him was the relationship between the softness of the blacktop pavement on Main Street and the rate of infant mortality reported in the newspaper. The softer the pavement, the greater the number of infant deaths. So, to reduce infant mortality, he recommended that the city replace the blacktop with concrete paving which would not likely soften periodically. But critics of the retiree's proposal faulted him for mistaking casual for causal correlation.

So, when one variable changes systematically with changes in another variable, it doesn't necessarily mean that one of those variables is responsible for the other's behavior. The relationship can be the result of unknown factors. In the case of the Main Street pavement and infant deaths, the correlation between the two events may be the result of some other variable which, it can be argued, was the cause of each of the observed events. In the Kansas case, the dominant opinion in some societies would be that the direct cause of both events was atmospheric temperature which, they would say, was itself the result of more fundamental factors, such as the intensity of the sun's rays and the level of atmospheric humidity. Consequently, changing the pavement would not result in fewer infant deaths because the relationship between pavement and mortality was coincidental, not causal.

Since correlation itself does not necessarily tell anything about the cause of an event, what is required in order to establish cause is a line of logic that convincingly traces a cause-and-effect linkage between variables. Frequently in folk psychologies, adducing such an argument involves an assumption about the influence of unseen forces. Sometimes those forces are supernatural gods or ancestral spirits. Other times they are people's assumptions about the existence of some mental function (such as *conscience* to account for some types of behavior) or physical force (such as *gravity*, a concept adopted from scientific theory by the general populace to account for a particular relationship among objects in the universe). This matter of unseen causal forces is our next concern.

## Direct Versus Mediated Cause

A useful distinction can be drawn between *direct causes* of observed relationships and *mediated causes.*

### Direct cause

A direct cause is one in which an event is seen as immediately responsible for a subsequent event's occurrence. Statements of direct cause in folk psychologies are often expressed as maxims that identify which initial event produces a subsequent event. An example from cultures with a Judeo-Christian background is an assertion about a relationship between physical punishment and child behavior: "Spare the rod and spoil the child." Or, as a biblical injunction puts it, the frequency of physical punishment is correlated with the likelihood of a child's escaping a dire after-death existence.

> Withhold not correction from the child. Thou shalt beat him with the rod, and shalt deliver his soul from hell. (Holy Bible, 1930, Proverbs 23: 13-14)

Or, in a secular version from English folk tradition, "A wife, a dog, and a walnut tree—the harder you beat them, the better they be."

Therefore, in these cases and in the following examples, the second variable is considered to be the immediate, directly observable result of the first.

Among the Kwisi of southwestern Angola, sexual intercourse between a husband and his pregnant wife continues almost to the day of the birth, with the practice believed to "make the baby stronger" (Estermann, 1976, p. 28).

In northern Nigeria, Kagoro folk psychology links various types of misfortune with their particular direct causes:

> leprosy as the *nendyung* (automatic evil effects) of individual breach of some taboo, madness as the consequence of perjury on taking an oath, death in childbirth as the consequence of the wife's concealed adultery, and death in battle, hunting, or by other violence as unfortunate but normal, [the direct result of the visible act that caused the death]. (Smith, 1982, p. 7)

## Mediated cause

Many folk psychologies envision the relationship between events as mediated by intervening causal variables—often hidden—that link the two events. Whereas different belief systems may agree on the occurrence of the two events, they can disagree about the causal variables that connect the events. Two common conceptions of the linkages between an initial event and a subsequent event can be labeled *Type A* and *Type B*.

- *Type A*: (1) An initial event (2) motivates a supernatural spirit or force to (3) produce a subsequent event (a consequence or effect). For instance, a Jewish youth joins a satanic-worship cult, which angers the god Yahweh, who then plagues the youth with painful boils.
- *Type B* (1) An initial earthly event influences (2) an earthly mediator to (3) contact a supernatural spirit or force that (4) can produce a consequent event. As an example, the cattle belonging to tribe of herders have been wracked by disease, so the tribal leaders summon a shaman who performs a chant in which he solicits the aid of cosmic powers, which—if persuaded—can cure the cattle's malady.

In summary, the Type B causal chain includes an earthly mediator as one of the links, whereas the Type A chain does not. Usually the earthly agent in a Type B chain is a human, but in some cultures it's an animal.

*Type A: No human mediator.*  Assumed causal connections that involve no mortal mediator between an original event and a later event are common in many societies.

Tahitian culture in the southeast Pacific recognizes two general sorts of illness—(a) the kind that can be successfully treated with medications, surgery, and physical manipulation and (b) the kind that fail to respond to such direct therapy.  Among Tahitians, this second variety forms a broad class labeled *mai tupapau* (ghost sickness) in which disorders are believed to be the consequence of dead ancestors' displeasure at acts on the part of living members of the kindred.  "Mai tupapau is suspected whenever an illness or accident is unusual in its severity, course, circumstances, or resistance to standard therapies" (Clark, 1994, p. 220).

Sometimes it's not an active misdeed that causes supernatural forces to produce an unwanted outcome.  Instead, it's the neglect of an obligation.  For instance, in the Ecuadorian Indian village of Sucre—as in so many Christian communities—if people die without having been baptized, their souls will not go to heaven because their souls are still under the Devil's control.  Only when children are baptized and given a name do they deserve God's blessing and membership in Christian society.  Sucre lore also teaches that if the godparents (*padrinos*) of a newly baptized infant fail to eat and drink to excess during the baptismal breakfast, the child will not learn to walk or talk (Bourque, 1995).

An example of mediated-cause explanations is people's interpretations of why eating pork can result in serious illness and death.  Both Judaic and Islamic traditions ban pork as a food.  The Judaic Torah warns faithful Jews that

> The swine . . . is unclean unto you.  Of their flesh shall ye not eat, and of their carcass shall ye not touch. (Holy Bible, 1930, Leviticus 11: 7-8)

And the Islamic Qur'an informs Muslim readers that "You are forbidden (to eat) carrion, blood, and the flesh of swine" (Suhrawardy, 1941, p. 49).  The notion that there is something evil about pork as a food may have resulted from the fact that unrefrigerated pork does not keep well in a warm climate such as that of the eastern Mediterranean region.  Thus, in ancient times frequent illness befell people who included pork in their diet.  The belief that swine can be invested with evil spirits is also reflected in the biblical account of Jesus's removing devils from a pair of tormented humans and transferring the devils into a herd of swine (Holy Bible, 1930, Matthew, 8: 30-32).

In present-day industrialized societies, the informed public believes that becoming sick from eating pork is not the result of imaginary evil spirits but, rather, is the result of trichinosis, an illness caused by the larvae of a tiny worm that people have ingested while eating undercooked pork (Clayman, 1989, p. 1009). But even in cultures that attribute much illness to microorganisms, some people continue to avoid pork in the fear that there is something inherently evil in swine.

*Type B: Human intermediaries.* As illustrated in Chapter 1, in many cultures, selected individuals are believed to command skills for effecting the intervention of supernatural forces in human affairs. Such specialists are commonly referred to as priests, mediums, shamans, and witches. In some societies, only men are permitted to serve in the priestly capacity, as has been true in Roman Catholic and Episcopal traditions. In other places, only women can become mediums. Such is the case in Okinawa, where the position of priestess (*kaminchu*) is assumed only by females (Lebra, 1966). In still other societies, both men and women can qualify as intermediaries, as with the Ambo of Angola.

The task of a human mediator is to (a) identify the causes of events which seem unexplainable, (b) communicate with the supernatural forces that control life's events, and (c) apply remedial measures that are intended to correct, or at least to ameliorate, the unfortunate consequences that can result from the identified causes. Consider the role of the intermediary in one far-north Amerindian culture.

> [In the Eskimo's] arctic world of uncertainties, the central and all-important religious practitioner is the *angákut*, or shaman, [who] helps the people maintain the necessary delicate balance between this world of pragmatic necessities and the more subtle, but not less real world of spirits, souls, and graduated powers. The shaman is an intermediary between these multiple worlds, who can communicate, interpret, and indeed travel in mysterious flight through the worlds of Eskimo realities. The shaman's wisdom and special powers are critical to communal life and human survival. Through the shaman's familiarity with the spirit realms and through his ability to send out in ecstatic trance one of his souls, often called the "free soul," on a spiritual journey and quest, he is able to discern who among the people has broken the taboos causing the disappearance of the game. He is able to placate [the goddess] Sedna under the sea, or discover the cause of illness perhaps associated with "soul loss," or he may foretell future weather conditions and thus the appropriate time for travel. (Brown, 1989, pp. 7-8)

A culture's priesthood is sometimes structured as a hierarchy of levels, with the duties and powers of one level different from those of other levels. For example, among the Ambo of Angola, shamans known as *kimbandas* acquire their calling by means of a specific ancestor's spirit summoning them to the occupation of diviner. Individuals thus chosen are enrolled in the kimbanda order by a ritual requiring initiates to sacrifice a domestic animal, then drink its blood "and testify to the presence of the [ancestral] spirit by distress and powerful convulsions" (Estermann, 1976, p. 193). A different animal is used at each of the four levels of the kimbanda hierarchy—a rooster at the lowest level, a goat at level two, a dog at level three, an ox at level four. As individuals advance from one level to another, their power to summon supernatural forces, cure ailments, prophesy, and punish enemies increases.

Societies vary in the ways individuals acquire the priestly role. In the Pacific island culture of Okinawa, a woman achieves the status of a *kaminchu* through being chosen during a visitation from spirits known as *kami*. Women who reject this destined calling or who neglect to fulfill their ritual duties, are apt to be inflicted with a special sort of retribution (*taari*) that typically takes the form of psychosomatic disorders rendering the victim sick and weak, unable to carry out her normal activities, tormented with auditory and visual hallucinations, and troubled by distressing dreams. Such misfortunes may also be suffered by members of the shaman's family (Lebra, 1966, p. 37). Fear of punishment gives the priestess a potent reason to perform her duties diligently.

So far in our discussion, we have focused on human mediators who are expected to promote people's well-being. However, numerous cultures also include a class of individuals, generally referred to as witches or sorcerers, who are thought to generate misfortune and evil. The word *witchcraft* is an umbrella term used to account, in a general way, for undesired happenings whose apparent cause cannot otherwise be recognized or imagined.

> [Witchcraft] is a source of power not only to those who are active practitioners, but also to those who claim to be able to neutralize the witch singlehandedly or who join together with others to make him or her harmless. Because it is a craft practiced secretly by the solitary individual under the cloak of night, frequently suspect, but rarely talked about openly for fear of reprisal, fed by rumor and fears, frequently hinted at but rarely ascertained, it is a force exceedingly difficult to understand and to combat. (Skjonsberg, 1989, p. 166)

Grievous events in the lives of individuals—illness, death, loss of possessions, loss of a job—are more often attributed to witchcraft than are such widescale disasters as flood, drought, and earthquake. In particular cases of unwelcome events that fall within the broad realm of witchcraft, more specific causal conditions are typically cited, such as the responsible witch is identified, the witch's motive is estimated, and ways to counteract or thwart the witch are proposed.

In some societies, witchcraft accusations are political devices used to discredit people in positions of authority or to foil upstarts who are seen as a threat to the authorities currently in power. Rodman (1993) provides an example of charges of sorcery in the Pacific island state of Vanuatu (New Hebrides) arising during a time of political transition from colonial control (a British/French condominium government) to political independence. In traditional Vanuatu social structure, power and prestige were vested in a political elite—a class of chiefs securely ensconced in their positions. But the independence achieved in 1980 brought democratic-governance practices into conflict with the chieftain system. The chiefs sought to maintain and strengthen their authority by appealing to age-old custom (*kastom*), asserting that the new government should reflect the precolonial chieftain hierarchy. In opposition, commoners sought to gain a more equitable share of power than typically accompanies electoral politics and majority rule. The device used by the commoners to topple a high-ranking chief on the island of Ambae was to accuse him of sorcery—of intending to kill an elderly man by means of "poison talk" or "words in the wind." Thus, the accusers' tactic drew on the Vanuatuan folk belief in evil-intentioned magic as a causal agent. The sorcery allegation spread through the community in the form of rumor until it gained enough public credence to warrant a court trial in which the chief was found guilty and removed from his position of authority. As Rodman reflected on the incident, he concluded that

> The weight of the evidence suggests to me that much of the "poison talk" in postindependence Ambae was a discourse about local power and privilege. [The accused chief's] trial and political downfall are best understood as marker events, perhaps even turning points, in a clash between two rival coalitions on Ambae—one group finding a new support for the old political order in national-level rhetoric concerning kastom, the other resisting chiefly power and seeking new opportunities for wealth, power, and authority. Why would women and young men who aspire to be progressive local leaders use accusations of sorcery to challenge established authorities? . . . [Because] an accusation of sorcery can undermine a chief's authority in ways that more orthodox avenues of political competition cannot. (Rodman, 1993, p. 230)

*Type B: Animal mediation.* As already noted, sometimes revered animals are the functionaries believed to influence how events occur. In Kenya, members of the Luo clan living at Nyakach on the shores of Lake Victoria launched a campaign in 1989 to have a python snake named Omieri taken back from the capital city of Nairobi to Nyakach so it might die at home. The snake had received burns when someone set fire to its living area, so Omieri was taken to Nairobi for treatment. In Luo belief, the snake's comfort was linked to the tribe's well-being because Omieri was credited with the ability to ensure frequent rain and bountiful harvests. If Omieri were to die in Nairobi and be interred there, Nyakach would suffer a drought, leading to famine and economic loss for the Luo. As explained in *The Kenya Times* on August 26, 1989,

> Omieri was part of the village life, roaming the neighbourhood where children would stroke her with their hands and no harm came their way. . . .

She was a good snake. She would visit the village and then go back to the lake. And then there would be rain, a good harvest, and plenty of food. (Nyamongo, 1999, p. 258)

In the Bushman society of Angola, an animal mediator can affect an outcome even when the animal is no longer alive. If a hunter slays a large animal, the hunter does not take his catch directly into the village. Instead, he hides in the bush a short distance away. Eventually he coughs, which draws the attention of a companion who comes to converse with him.

"What are you doing here? Have you shot an arrow?" "Yes." "Did you hit the beast?" "Yes, it seems so, but I only saw the shaft fall." Then, when an absolute silence has been established in the encampment, [the hunter] enters. Nevertheless, he sleeps outside the hut that night, without cohabiting with his wife. If this rule were not observed, the beast would not stay dead. In the case of a small beast, the hunter restricts himself to lying on the ground and playing dead for a few moments. (Estermann, 1976, p. 11)

In Estermann's interpretation, the hunter's actions reflect belief in a power called *nyama*, an avenging force that a dead animal can evoke. By the hunter's cautious behavior, he seeks to avoid exciting the *nyama* which could directly punish him.

The folk psychology of the Kadara of northern Nigeria includes the belief that certain powerful repented witches can transform themselves into hyenas at night, while resuming their human shapes by day (Smith, 1982, p. 14).

*Varieties of natural and supernatural agents.* Causal forces can include both natural and paranormal ones. Important natural forces that are regarded as causes are envisioned conditions of nature, which is the first illustrated in the following discussion. Then there are paranormal forces, which can be of various kinds, including gods, animal phantasms, and spirits of dead ancestors.

*Conditions of nature.* The practice of geomancy is based on the conviction that events can be predicted through the analysis of geometric relationships. This is the belief that knowledgeable geomancers can divine how the directions of lines and the placement of spaces will influence people's lives by affecting such things as health, financial success, friendships, weather conditions, and more. The art of geomancy has been particularly influential in East Asian cultures for interpreting natural phenomena and establishing a harmonious balance between humans and their physical environment. As one example, in Chinese villages a *feng shui* practitioner (geomancer) is often hired upon the death of a family member to inspect the intended gravesite and, from examining the grave's location, to choose an auspicious day for the procession to the grave and for interring the corpse (Cooper, 1998, p. 387).

Geomancy often plays a key role in town planning and house construction. Kalland's (1996) description of the layout of a Japanese village (Shingu) reflects village planners' belief that the flow of vital energy (*ki* in Japanese, *ch'i* in Chinese) into the community is determined by the interaction of Taoism's complementary *yin* and *yang* forces along with the universe's five basic elements (wood, fire, earth, metal, water). Geomancers employ cosmological diagrams (mandalas) that reveal favorable and unfavorable relationships in directions and spaces. For example, in one version, two perpendicular lines cross at the center of a town or house layout.

> Evil forces flow along the northeast-southwest axis and auspicious ones along the northwest-southeast axis. By locating various religious objects in the dangerous *kimon* and *ura-kimon* directions, people seek to prevent evil natural forces from penetrating into the community while at the same time keeping the flow of good forces into the community along the other axis. (Kalland, 1996, pp. 30-31)

Astrology, similar to geomancy, involves beliefs about the effect of star and planet configurations on individuals' destinies and on the control of nature (when to plant crops; when to fish and hunt). Thus, people may confer with astrologers or consult published astrological predictions when faced with decisions about taking trips, investing money, changing jobs, marrying, and more.

*Intervening gods.* The folklore of many cultures is replete with descriptions of activists from the invisible spirit world who serve as the causal mediators between what seem to be correlated events. Here are several illustrations of such spirit powers and their modes of operation.

In the first example, a correlation is assumed between (a) the extent to which people abide by codes of acceptable behavior and (b) the ready availability of fish and sea mammals on which a particular Eskimo society depends.

> [Eskimos of the coastal arctic region believe] in an all-powerful goddess, half human and half fish, called Sedna or Takanaluk, who dwells in a great cave or pool under the sea wherein she keeps all the sea mammals, which she will release or withhold according to the degree to which the people observe or break the taboos, [that is, break the codes of appropriate behavior that have been established to maintain a balance of social relations within families and among larger social groups]. (Brown, 1989, p. 7)

Among the Kagoro of northern Nigeria, the sun is the icon of the creator-god, Onum, whose wife is represented by the moon. In Kagoro lore, an eclipse of the moon is explained as a quarrel between husband and wife during which Onum heaves a pot of porridge in her face (Smith, 1982, p. 11).

Two events that are conceived to be correlated in a causal fashion may consist of a viewable initial event (the cause) and a nonviewable consequent event (the effect). The mediator responsible for this connection is a god or spirit. Such is the case with earthly behaviors that are believed to result in rewards or punishments that the person's essence (the soul) experiences after the body's demise. For example, the Jainism derivative of Hindu tradition in India lists a series of sins (killing, lying, greed, hatred, slander, gossip, hypocrisy, illicit love affairs, and more) that can result in 82 kinds of dire consequences for a person's soul when that soul returns for another lifetime on earth following the end of the present lifespan. Such postponed consequences can include physical deformities, mental aberrations, bad dreams, lethargy, poor housing, general bad luck, or rebirth as a detested animal rather than as a human (Stevenson, 1971, pp. 130-139).

The Islamic Qur'an (*The Koran,* 1844) identifies consequences that ultimately result from both proper and improper behavior. Proper behavior, in the form of humans honoring and obeying God, leads to a life-after-death in a heavenly garden where there are

> Rivers of milk of which the taste never changes,
> Rivers of wine, a joy to those who drink,
> And rivers of honey, pure and clear. (Mohamed 15)[*]

Improper behavior, such as denying God and disobeying his commandments, results in life-after-death in hell, where the wicked will be clothed in a garment of fire.

> Over their heads will be poured out boiling water.
> With it will be scalded what is within their bodies as well as their skins.
> In addition, there will be maces of iron [to punish them].
> Every time they wish to get away from anguish,
> They will be forced back therein. (Hajj 19-22)

In contrast, some folk psychologies propose that certain observed events are not the causes of unperceivable later consequences but, rather, are the effects of conditions assumed to have occurred earlier. For example, in Okinawan culture, an act of murder is interpreted as an instance of two persons (both the victim and the murderer) being punished for having ancestors who were addicted to violence (Lebra, 1966, p. 39). This belief derives from the more general conviction that the sins of forebears will be paid for later by descendents being forced to suffer ill fortune. Likewise, the mediating gods will see to it that good things happen to the offspring of virtuous progenitors.

---

[*] References to the Qur'an identify the title of the chapter and the verse number of the cited passage.

*Animal phantasms.* Folk psychologies often include a belief in totemic animals whose characteristics and powers are attached to particular clans. Humans profit from this association both by bearing some measure of the totem's traits and by drawing on the aid of their totemic creatures in times of need. In some instances, the bond between humans and their totem has been regarded as so close that the two can assume each other's form. Members of Akar tribe of Nigeria have been believed by other clans to change themselves into leopards at will (Smith, 1982, p. 7).

Some cultural traditions teach that demons can appear in the guise of birds and wild animals to affect the fate of humans. According to Dassanetch lore in southwest Ethiopia, the appearance of certain wild animals foretells ill fortune for those who have seen the ominous beasts. However, the expected tragedy can be prevented by the performance of *ai faiset,* a ceremony that involves slaughtering a sheep or goat and allowing the blood of the carcass to drip over the bodies of members of the household. In Dassanetch folk psychology, blood frightens demons away (Almagor, 1978, p. 57).

*Ancestral spirits.* The religions of many cultures include ancestor worship as a cardinal practice. Such is the case among Confucianists of East Asia, the Azande of equatorial Africa, Blackfoot Indians of North America's Great Plains, the Iban of Borneo, the Lepcha of central Asia, the Pomo Indians of California, the Trumai of the MatoGrosso region of Brazil, and far more (Steadman, Palmer, & Tilley, 1996). In addition, the behavior of people in other cultures (in which ghosts, phantoms, and shades are assumed to play an important role in people's lives) suggests that such luminous beings are—as in religions with forthright ancestor worship—actually treated as spirits of dead ascendants. And in all such folk psychologies, a causal connection is assumed to exist between the living and the dead. Usually, it is imagined that the spirits can affect people's lives and/or alter conditions of the natural world. In many instances, it's also assumed that the behavior of the living can influence the spirits of the dead, particularly in affecting the departed forebears' feelings and attitudes. Offending the dead through insult or neglect can rebound on the living by the spirits failing to aid the living in time of need or by the spirits heaping troubles on mortal descendants. In contrast, honoring the dead through rituals and offerings enlists their aid in coping with life's problems. This reciprocal causal relationship between the quick and the dead is reflected in a variety of cultural practices. Among the Arunta of central Australia, during the period following a death

> No person must mention the name of the deceased . . . for fear of disturbing and annoying the man's spirit, which in ghost form, or as they call it, *Ulthana,* walks about. If the *Ulthana* hears his name, he comes to the conclusion that his relatives are not properly mourning for him [and]. . . he will come and trouble

them in their sleep, to show them that he's not pleased. (Spencer & Gillen, 1968, p. 498)

Among the Carib in the Guiana region of northeast South America, family members build fires around the grave of a departed relative "to purify it and to prevent the deceased from catching cold." In prehistoric times on the occasion of a burial, a slave or dog would be slain and put in the grave to care for the dead person (Rouse, 1963, p. 559).

The Iroquois of the North American eastern woodlands "both respect and fear the dead and therefore conduct a number of feasts for them" (St. John, 1989, p. 136).

In some cultures, such as that of the Kadara of Nigeria, dead ancestors are the necessary mediators between living humans and a powerful numinous being who, for the Kadara, is the creator-god Onum. The task of summoning the ancestral spirits so the living can communicate with Onum requires the use of five musical instruments——bullroarers, special flutes, and *dhupe* pods, which represent the ancestors' voices and movements, and the *ibini* drum and trumpets required for summoning the ancestral spirits. According to Kadara lore, the instruments were given to the original ancestors by Onum; over the succeeding generations, those instruments have passed to the present-day living descendants (Smith, 1982, p. 12).

The folk psychology of the Orokaiva of Papua New Guinea assigns dead ancestors no more than a modest role in affecting the affairs of the living. Spirits of the deceased never enter a village. Instead, they roam the bush, where they occasionally attack people but never kill them. When asked to do so, these shades of the departed may help hunters find game or may protect gardens and palm trees (Iteanu, 1990, p. 39).

*Auspicious conditions.* Not only may events depend on particular mediators to bring them to pass, but the conditions under which events take place may also affect the outcome. One of the most influential conditions is the mental state of shamans when they seek to divine the location of a lost object, diagnose a patient's illness, or predict the future. The desired psyche state for mystics among the Indians of the Americas has traditionally been achieved with the aid of such hallucinogens as *cohóba* snuff (made from the seeds of a tree related to the acacias and mimosas), tobacco, peyote cactus, and the Upper Amazonian jungle vine (*Banisteriopsis*) known in the Quechua language as *ayahuasca*—"vine of the soul." Still unexplained by botanists and cultural anthropologists is the puzzle of why American Indians

of all the peoples of the world, had been so fascinated with the effects on the mind of certain plants that they explored their territory for them and adopted perhaps 100 species into their religious practices. Yet in the Old World [of Europe and Asia], settled far longer by human beings and probably as rich in psychotropic flora as the New World, only a dozen or so such plants are known to have been used. (*Mysteries of the Ancient Americas*, 1986, p. 304)

Frequently hallucinogens form only part of the preparations soothsayers adopt to promote bright, insightful visions. Shamans among the Desna in South America's northern Andes must abstain from sex and eat only lightly on the days preceding an ecstatic trance session in which they psychically ascend to the Milky Way to convene with the supernatural Master of the hallucinogens, from whom they derive their spirit power (*Mysteries of the Ancient Americas*, 1986, p. 304).

Another propitious condition is that of client faith. In perhaps all cultures, needy people—in the form of clients—may turn to experts for help in curing ailments, making decisions, locating lost objects, or predicting the future. Experts include psychotherapists, priests, shamans, mystics, mediums, and the like. Typically, such healers and prognosticators contend that a proposed cure or prediction will succeed only to the extent of the client's faith that the nostrum or advice will indeed produce the desired outcome. Hence, clients of little faith are likely to be disappointed with the results of the consultation.

## A Natural/Supernatural Cause Typology

Somewhat different from the direct/indirect conception of causal beliefs is a natural/supernatural typology created by Murdock, Wilson, and Frederick (1978) from their analysis of theories of illness in cultures around the world. Although the focus of the authors' interest was illness, their typology could be adjusted to explain other sorts of events as well, such as personal losses (financial setback, disappearance of valuables, alienation of a lover) and widescale disasters (cyclone, earthquake, flood).

The researchers began by defining *illness, natural causes,* and *supernatural causes* as:

Illness: Any impairment of health serious enough to arouse concern, whether it be due to communicable disease, psychosomatic disturbance, organic failure, aggressive assault, or alleged accident or supernatural interference.

Natural cause: Any theory, scientific or popular, which accounts for the impairment of health as a physiological consequence of some experience of the victim in a manner that would not seem unreasonable to modern medical science.

Supernatural cause: Any theory which accounts for the impairment of health as the automatic consequence of some act or experience of the victim mediated by some putative impersonal causal relationship rather than by the intervention of a human or supernatural being. (Murdock, Wilson, & Frederick, 1978, pp. 450-451, 453)

The authors then examined theories of illness from 139 societies, past and present, in order to extract categories into which the theories could be meaningfully located. That process resulted in five types of natural theories and eight types of supernatural explanations. The following are the types, along with the names of representative cultures in which each has played a role (Murdock, Wilson, & Frederick, 1978, pp. 451-467):

## Natural causes of illness

- *Infection.* The victim's body is invaded by noxious microorganisms. *Representative cultures:* Japanese and the Nama Hottentot and Wodaabe Fulani in Africa.
- *Stress.* The victim is exposed to physical or psychological strain—overexertion, extended hunger or thirst, extreme heat and cold, worry, fear, and other emotional disorders that are the concerns of modern psychiatry. *Representative cultures:* Siamese in Thailand, Javanese in Indonesia Pawnee Indian in North America.
- *Organic deterioration.* Physical abilities decline as a result of advancing age, the failure of organs (heart, kidneys, liver), or serious inherited defects. *Representative cultures:* Not an important consideration in most folk theories but held widely among the folk of modern industrial societies.
- *Accident.* Physical injury not intentionally incurred nor caused by a supernatural agent. *Representative cultures:* Seldom do theories cite accident as a cause of illness; and even when mentioned, it is assigned a very minor role.
- *Overt human aggression.* One person injures another, typically during quarrels or in warfare. *Representative cultures:* Virtually universal in practice, though often not specified as causing illness.

## Supernatural causes of illness

The authors placed their eight supernatural theories in three classes representing mystical causation (4), animistic causation (2), and magical causation (2).

A *mystical theory* imputes a victim's illness to an assumed impersonal causal relationship rather than to a human or supernatural being. This is similar to *conditions of nature* listed earlier under kinds of supernatural agents.

- *Fate.* Personal bad luck, astrological influences, or an individual's predestined fortune or doom. *Representative cultures:* Egyptian, Turkish, Burmese, Vietnamese, Aztec.

- *Ominous sensations.* Experiencing strong sights, sounds, dreams, or feelings that are not merely symptoms of illness but are the direct causes. *Representative cultures:* Somewhat prominent in Pawnee Indian and Egyptian societies; a very minor consideration in 37 others.
- *Contagion.* Becoming ill from contact with a supposedly polluting substance or person. This is a mystical belief analogous to the natural theory of infection. *Representative cultures:* Evident in 49 of the 186 societies. The most common objects imagined to be pollutants are (a) a menstruating woman (more frequent in Africa) and (b) a dead body or objects associated with the deceased (more frequent in North America).
- *Mystical retribution.* Illness directly results from violating a taboo or moral edict. *Representative cultures:* Very important among the Thonga of southern Africa, the Mongo and Otoro of central Africa, and the Kaska of North America; less significant in another 34 societies.

An *animistic theory* attributes undesired outcomes to a personalized supernatural agent—soul, spirit, specter, god.

- *Temporary soul loss.* Whereas death is often assumed to involve a human's essence—the soul—leaving the body permanently, illness may be assumed to result from the soul temporarily departing. Curing the patient consists of locating and returning the soul. *Representative cultures:* A prominent cause among the Tenino Indians of Oregon, and a minor cause in 37 other cultures.
- *Sprit aggression.* Illness is due to "the direct hostile, arbitrary, or punitive action of some malevolent or affronted supernatural being. . . . It is reported as the predominant cause of illness in 78 of the sample societies, as an important secondary cause in 40, and as a rare or minor cause in 19" (Murdock, Wilson, & Frederick, 1978, p. 455). *Representative cultures:* A predominant cause in the Trobriand, Siuai, and Fiji islands of the Pacific, and among the Chricahua and Zuni tribes of North America, and Aztecs of Central America.

A *magical theory* blames illness on an "envious, affronted, or malicious human being who employs magical means to injure his victim" (Murdock, Wilson, & Frederick, 1978, p. 455).

- *Sorcery.* A human being uses magical techniques, independently or with the aid of a magician or shaman, to impair a victim's health. *Representative cultures:* Particularly important for Pawnee, Yurok, and Haida Indians of North America; and for the Jivaro, Amahuaca, and Lengua in South America.
- *Witchcraft.* The activity of a member of a particular class of human beings—witches—who wield special destructive power

aggressively to impair someone's health either voluntarily or involuntarily. *Representative cultures:* Rarely is witchcraft considered more than a subsidiary or minor cause of illness, but it does assume an important role in a few cultures, such as those of the Azandi and Tiv in Africa, and the Albanians and Kurds in the Mediterranean region.

In summary, folk psychology theories about the causes of illness —when categorized according to the Murdock, Wilson, and Frederick typology—display noteworthy cross-cultural differences. Furthermore, the typology can be extended to explain a variety of phenomena other than illness.

## Methods of Correcting Causes

The two main reasons people seek to understand causality are to avoid misfortune and, when trouble does occur, to remedy its cause. Folk psychologies abound in beliefs about proper remedial measures.

Among the Nyakyusa of Tanzania, such mishaps as illness and accident are thought to be punishment for kinship sin, that is, for an individual's failing to follow rules of correct conduct toward family members. To put matters right, the sinner must appease the ancestral spirits that are responsible for the punishment. This is accomplished by (a) henceforth abiding by kinship rules and (b) dedicating a prayer or an offering to the offended shades. A prayer consists of blowing a cloud of water from the mouth, then apologizing to the spirits. Offerings consist of a "a bull, a hen, or some beer, in the case of commoners; of a cow in the case of chiefs" (Wilson, 1960, p. 352).

Needham (1967), in his study of folk psychology among tribes in Malaysia, reported people's believing that thunderstorms are sent by a thunder-god as punishment for human misbehavior, including such sins as incest and mocking or laughing at animals. To appease the god and avoid death from flood or falling trees, it is necessary to offer a sacrifice, such as taking a few drops of blood drawn from one's leg, mixing the blood with a bit of water, and casting the mixture up into the gale. An alternative method of appeasing the thunder-god involves burning a tuft of hair from the head of the person who was guilty of incest or of mocking animals.

Scholars who specialize in the study of rituals have suggested that when people engage in activities whose outcome is unpredictable, difficult, or dangerous, they are apt to attribute the outcome of those events to supernatural agents who must be pacified by ceremonies. Consequently, activities whose outcomes seem under people's control usually are not attended by rites, whereas ones whose results are in doubt will frequently involve rituals. Brown and Van Bolt (1980) have illustrated this proposal with examples of hunting and agricultural activities among tribal groups in Brazil's Amazon basin and the adjacent Andes of Peru. Whereas the Desna, Amahuaca, Yagua, and Barama Caribs have no ceremonies associated with their gardening activities, they perform elaborate rituals in relation to hunting, which involves considerable risk and uncertainty. According to Brown and Van Bolt, one exception to this pattern is found among the Aguaruna Jivaro of Peru, who conduct ceremonies intended to influence the success of their root-crop agriculture, which consists mainly of growing manioc (cassava). Even though manioc is consumed by families at a great rate,

> available evidence suggests that gardens easily produce enough tubers to satisfy this demand and would even generate a surplus with little additional effort. Nevertheless, the Aguaruna themselves perceive manioc production as highly uncertain. They feel compelled to increase the chances of an adequate crop by using magical techniques to encourage plant growth and development. (Brown & Van Bolt, 1980, p. 187)

Their techniques include (a) establishing a harmonious relationship with the spirits that are in charge of gardening, (b) engendering propitious images through metaphors in songs, and (c) soliciting the animistic power of sacred stones. Because there is no verifiable scarcity or unpredictability of manioc production, Brown and Van Bolt estimate that the Aguaruna compulsion to perform magical gardening rites derives from an Aguaruna worldview—a folk psychology that sees life in general as a precarious venture.

An assumed cause of misfortune in many folk psychologies is the *evil eye*. Strangers, malformed individuals, and old women are the ones most often accused of causing other people's ill fate by glancing at them. Children are frequently considered the most vulnerable to evil-eye harm. In some societies, the power of the evil eye is regarded as involuntary, but more often it is thought to be an intentional expression of the glancer's envying the victim's prosperity or beauty. For example, Egyptian villagers believe that envy (*hasad*), by working through the agency of glance (*nazar*), can destroy or harm the objects or people against which it is directed (Ghosh, 1983). Protective measures against the evil eye vary among cultures. For example, among the Tamil of India, women commonly prepare a *kolam*—a colored-rice drawing on the doorstep of their house—to combat the effects of the Tamil version of the evil eye (*dhrishti* or *tirusti*). In Tamil culture, covetousness can be so strong that when the envious eye touches a desired object, it can affect the welfare of the object. The kolam protects the occupants of a house by acting like a net, a catcher of emotion-laden feelings, and a protective screen against the emotions cast out by those who pass by the doorway or who cross the threshold.

The evil eye is carried around by ghosts, demons, and bad spirits [which] are not necessarily wandering around in demon form outside of ourselves. Most of the time the demons are in you and me. Whenever you are just walking down the street and find yourself envious, jealous, full of *puramai*, or thinking of someone with evil intentions, your own evil eye can affect the person you are thinking of. It can directly affect that particular person's house, children, health, and everything that belongs to them. This force of emotion can be from your unconscious or conscious. You may not realize you are being jealous of someone. But that is why you need to protect others and yourself with the kolam. (Nagarajan, 1997, p. 50)

Kolams have traditionally consisted of colored rice-flour designs, with those made with dry-rice flour disappearing after a few hours and those drawn with a wet-rice-flour mixture lasting a few months. In recent times, kolams painted with acrylic colors have grown in popularity because they can last a year.

In an interview survey of 57 physicians in towns on the Texas/Mexico border, Martin, Richardson, and Acosta (1985) learned that Hispanic patients who attributed their ailments to folk-psychology causes blamed the evil eye (*mal de ojo*) for their maladies in nearly one-quarter of the reported cases. In contrast to the pacifying drugs and psychotherapy offered such patients by licensed physicians, the treatment applied by Hispanic folk curers (*curanderos*) consisted of rituals intended to counteract the power of the evil eye.

Folk belief among the Bariba of Benin in West Africa implies that witchery is an inborn trait rather than being caused either (a) by individuals voluntarily adopting witchcraft as a way of life or (b) by society guiding selected persons into witchcraft as a vocation or avocation. The notion that witchery is innate is supported by folk-psychology convictions about stigmata of infancy that signal the arrival in the world of a new witch baby. Five conditions believed to mark a neonate as an incipient witch are (a) babies born with teeth, (b) ones whose teeth first appear in the upper gums, (c) breech birth, (d) birth occurring at eight months, and (e) newborns who slide out of the womb on their stomach (Sargent, 1988, p. 80). Infants who display some combination of such signs, either at birth or during teething, have customarily been killed or abandoned. Although this solution to parents' inadvertently producing a witch has been outlawed by the Benin government, the practice is so embedded in Bariba folk psychology that it secretly continues in some households. The importance of parents recognizing the true indicators that a baby will be a witch is suggested by a case in which a child born with six fingers was killed as a witch by the father, "although an elderly midwife later remarked that the parents did not know the signs of witchcraft [because] six fingers actually indicates future prosperity, not danger" (Sargent, 1988, p. 81).

Human conditions regarded as regrettable in one culture can be considered desirable in another.  The Kagoro of Nigeria have traditionally believed that smallpox slays witches while sparing the innocent.  When smallpox appeared in neighboring tribes, elderly men and women who feared that witchcraft might emerge among members of their extended families would use primitive inoculation techniques to secretly infect their children and dependents.  The ones who died of the disease were judged to have been potential witches, while survivors were considered free from witchery (Smith, 1982, p. 7).

As a Western scientific perspective becomes increasingly widespread among the world's societies, scientific explanations of phenomena tend not to replace all established folk-psychology explanations.  Rather, they typically nestle somewhat uneasily beside traditional folk beliefs, producing people with a multifaceted version of cause.  This tendency is particularly noticeable in explanations of physical and psychological maladies and their treatments.  Queiroz (1984) illustrates such a phenomenon among the inhabitants of Iguape, a municipality in the rural area of an impoverished region of São Paulo state in Brazil. The people are descendants of the native Indian population and the first Portuguese settlers.  Outsiders call them *caiçara*, a derogatory term implying both poverty and cultural backwardness.  In Iguape *caiçara* folk psychology, there are three levels of causation for disease, with each level calling for a different sort of remedy.

> First, diseases can be caused by negative feelings from others (evil-eye, sorcery) or from within oneself (sadness, unsatisfied will, fright).  Second, they can be caused by an imbalance between the individual and his physical environment, as through the consumption of things considered too hot or too cold.  Finally, they can be caused by a deceased relative, by an evil spirit, or even by the will of God.  The first type of causation is sociopsychological, the second is natural, and the third is supernatural. (Queiroz, 1984, p. 63)

Western scientific explanations of disease fit into the second, natural-cause category, settled beside Iguape culture's traditional hot-cold theory—"a diffuse and uncodified form of knowledge derived from tradition and shared by the common people" (Queiroz, 1984, p. 63).  The hot-cold explanation is based on the belief that the body's welfare depends on a balanced combination of elements, most of them of a vegetable nature.  Imbalance is revealed by disease symptoms, with certain symptoms signifying that the disorder is of the cold variety and other symptoms signifying it's of the hot variety. Restoring balance in the case of cold maladies requires the administration of hot foods, hot medicines, and warmth.  Conversely, treating hot disorders calls for a diet of cold foods and medicines.

> Nowadays, the opinion that modern medicine is good and necessary for the welfare of everybody is practically unanimous among the population.  Almost all *caiçara* will tell you that microorganisms cause disease and that doctors and hospitals are more important in the control of serious disease than faith, religion, good food, rest, herbs, and home medicine. . . . [But] traditional natural medicine still thrives in certain limited circumstances where official [Western] medicine does not find it profitable to compete.  For many indispositions and minor illnesses, such as headache, bad digestion, constipation, and any disease that may be attributed to the malfunction of the liver, home medicine is always depended on. (Queiroz, 1984, p. 64)

## Time Sequences

Two aspects of time that can be important in folk psychologies are (a) the extent of time between events and (b) the timing of efforts to influence events.  I believe a case can reasonably be argued in support of the following propositions:

- Causal relations proposed in folk psychologies originated with a persuasive individual's proposal about causation as based on that individual's observations.
- The longer the time gap between two events, the more difficult it is to establish a causal connection between the two.  In other words, when two events are widely separated in time, it is hard to establish that the later event is a consequence of the earlier one.
- The more complex the time relations between events, the more elaborate the explanation of cause is likely to be.

### Origins of puzzling cause beliefs

Although the beginnings of folk beliefs about cause are often lost in the distant past, it seems reasonable to speculate that many such beliefs originated with someone's observing two events that were closely associated in time, then concluding that one event caused the other.  If the person proposing such a connection is a highly respected member of the community—a chieftain, seer, priest, shaman, or scientist—the belief is more likely to become part of the society's folk psychology than if the individual is either an ordinary citizen or is regarded as mentally deranged.  Such interpretations of coincidental events may have been the source of the following convictions about cause that are widespread in certain cultures.

Among tribes of southwestern Angola, a child's illness is often attributed to the young one's having been touched by the shadow of an eagle.

Furthermore, the Kwisi of Angola observe a sexual prohibition affecting the fathers of boys recently circumcised. Kwisi lore teaches that if a father engages in sexual relations during the time his circumcised son is recovering from the operation, the boy's wounds will fail to heal properly. (Estermann, 1976, pp. 26, 45)

The Jewish Talmud—which consists of legends, wise sayings, medical advice, ecclesiastical debates, and rules that enjoy the status of laws—includes such statements of causal relationships as

> A head long unwashed may be the cause of blindness; unwashed garments may lead to insanity; and an unbathed body may cause pocks.
> He who marries for money will not have good children, and he will have no profit from the money.
> He who hopes that his wife will die before him so that he may inherit her money will die himself and be survived by her.
> The glory of God rests only upon that home where there are children.
> (Cahn, 1962, pp. 275-301)

## Length of time

Because people's lives are filled with such a rich succession of events, the greater the time period between any two events, the more difficult it becomes to determine that the earlier of the pair is responsible for the later.

When a mother decisively instructs her daughter to wash the dishes, and the girl immediately obeys, it is easy to argue that the mother's firm order caused the dishes to be washed. But it is not so easy to recognize that a particular incident of sexual intercourse resulted in the birth of a child, because so many other things happened during the months between those two episodes. Perhaps some event other than the intercourse episode during those months was the cause. As a result, over the centuries different cultures have accepted different explanations of the cause of childbirth. For instance, consider the contrasting explanations of how sexual intercourse results in pregnancy as found in Trobriand Islands tradition and in present-day industrialized societies' folk culture.

Within many modern societies, the general public believes that copulation between a female and a male can result in a sperm cell from the male's ejected semen combining with an ovum cell within the female's womb to produce an integrated cell that will multiply many times throughout the next nine months to result in the birth of a baby. But such an explanation has not been part of the folk psychology in the Trobriand Islands of the South Pacific, where pregnancy is believed to result from one ancestral spirit inserting another ancestral spirit into the mother's womb. This action, according to folk belief, is most readily accomplished if the opening has been enlarged by intercourse, thereby explaining why women who have frequent intercourse become pregnant more often than those who do not (Malinowski, 1948, p. 236). Thus, both traditional Trobriand Islanders and typical Western Europeans agree that more frequent sexual intercourse results in more frequent pregnancies. However, the two societies' folk psychologies explain such a correlation by means of quite different conceptions of (a) the factors that participate as mediators to produce the correlation and (b) how those factors are linked in a causal chain.

## Complexity of time relations

The time periods involved in causal explanations vary in complexity from one folk psychology to another and from one aspect of life to another.

At first glance, the episode of the mother ordering her daughter to wash the dishes can appear quite simple. Yet a complete explanation of cause in this case can also require an understanding of other incidents in the past which, according to the particular folk psychology, produced the mother/daughter relationship. However, the explanation of cause in the dishwashing episode is still far simpler than the cultural explanation of many other phenomena.

Consider, for example, a Hindu belief that is also found in such derivatives of Hinduism as Buddhism, Jainism, and Sikhism. Hindu doctrine teaches that the fate an individual experiences during the present lifetime is a consequence of the individual's past behavior during earlier earthly existences when his or her soul inhabited a series of different bodies prior to the present one. In effect, Hindu belief holds that a person's current actions contribute to a kind of future moral bank account known as *karma*. Karma assumes the form of an algebraic sum of one's deeds in life—a sum comprised of bad deeds subtracted from good deeds. Upon the person's death, the accumulated *karma* is transferred along with the person's eternal soul into a new body. If the good deeds have surpassed the bad, then the accumulated positive karma will produce a happier existence in a future life on earth. If bad deeds have dominated, then the resulting negative karma will bring about a worse fate. Thus, an individual's well-being during the new lifetime in the new body is caused by that person's behavior during past lives on earth. Hence, Hindu folk psychology is founded on a belief in immanent justice—that people inevitably get the kind of life their past deeds have merited. The time sequence in a karmic-cause explanation is very complex, extending not only across multiple life spans but across thousands of deeds during each life span (Buhler, 1886; Renou, 1961).

Cultural traditions often dictate the time when attempts to influence events will be most effective. As observers of Hopi Indian ceremonies have sometimes remarked, rain dances performed near to the advent of the rainy season are more effective in producing showers than are rain dances held at other times of the year. Thus, people who are in charge of deciding when a ceremony should be conducted often select a time that experience has shown is likely to be propitious and will therefore support the folk belief as a valid interpretation of the way life operates.

## Multiple Causation

Questions about cause that have persisted over the centuries include: Can an event result from a single causal factor? Or, is every event the consequence of multiple causes? And if multiple factors are indeed responsible, can some of the factors wield more influence than others in producing the outcome?

Answering these queries has posed a demanding challenge for philosophers and lay persons alike. First, consider cause from the viewpoint of a sequence of historical events. Each happening can be interpreted not only as the result (effect) of previous events but also as the cause of happenings that will appear in the future. For instance, people may attribute a person's height to heredity. Thus, the person's potential height is seen as a quality inherited from parents, whose own height was determined by their parents, whose height was destined by their parents, and so on through an endless succession of ancestors. From such a historical-succession perspective, cause recedes infinitely back through time to some indeterminate beginning.

Next, consider cause as the result of either a single immediate factor or the convergence of multiple immediate factors. For instance, was a college student's low mathematics test score caused entirely by his having spent the previous night at a drinking party until the early hours of the morning? Or was his low score a result of a confluence of multiple factors, including a poor genetic aptitude for mathematics, inefficient study habits, an alcoholic hangover, lack of sleep, the distracting memory of his girlfriend's having left the previous night's party with another young man, and the noise of a gas-powered lawn mower outside the classroom window during the test session?

Thus, when accounting for the "why" behind events, people may attribute an event to a single cause, to a few, or to a multitude of factors.

In a comparison between folk-psychology interpretations of cause and so-called "scientific" interpretations, I believe folk explanations more frequently than scientific explanations cite a single factor—or a very limited few—as the reason something happened. Viewing events as the result of multiple factors is often reflected in scientists' statistical reports. For example, if they conclude from an experiment that "Thirty percent of the variance in the children's verbal patterns was accounted for by their parents' verbal patterns," then this leaves 70% of the variation in children's speech patterns to be accounted for by variables other than parental models. If a scientific study predicts an outcome that includes an error factor of 6%, the report is thereby implying that the study has accounted for 94% of the causes behind the expected outcome, with the remaining 6% apparently the result of unknown factors. As a further instance, the statistical procedure known as path analysis is designed to identify various routes through which causal factors travel to produce an event.

In contrast, folk psychologies appear more often to attribute events to single causes—failing to honor dead ancestors results in illness, conducting a special dance brings rain, and a stroke of good luck in a financial deal can result from a favorable relationship among the planets on a particular night. But folk psychologies may also posit a causal chain, in the sense of one event generating a subsequent event which leads to additional events. For instance, Toraja folk psychology in central Sulawesi (Celebes) teaches that prolonged emotional distress produces such physical and mental disorders as weight loss, insomnia, stomach and heart ailments, tuberculosis, and insanity that diminish a person's consciousness or awareness, leading the individual to commit offensive acts that cause other people emotional distress and a desire for revenge.

> Thus it is thought that hot, choked emotions may spread from person to person and so eventually come to jeopardize or destroy a community's unity, cohesion, and solidarity. Conversely, people believe that social or community conflicts often eventuate in or are accompanied by emotional and possibly physical disorder. (Hollan, 1992b, p. 47)

## Internal Versus External Causes

A common way of viewing attributions is in terms of whether the assumed causes of events in a person's life are within that person (inherited talents, self-control, diligence) or in the surrounding environment (other people's attitudes and actions, physical conditions, opportunities). Studies of such matters suggest that cultures often differ in their tendency to attribute events to internal rather than external variables.

A contrast in the attribution of causes underlying scholastic success was found in a study by Hess, Chang, and McDevitt (1987) that revealed cultural differences in beliefs about children's performance in mathematics. The researchers interviewed mothers and their sixth-grade children in the People's Republic of China and in Chinese American and Caucasian American groups in the United States. Mothers in China viewed lack of effort as the major cause of low performance. Chinese American mothers and pupils also cited lack of effort as important but assigned responsibility for academic achievement more evenly across various possible causes. Caucasian American mothers and pupils cited lack of effort less often than did respondents in the other two groups.

Yan and Gaier (1994) compared causal attributions for college success and failure among American and Asian students—358 undergraduates who took the Multidimensional-Multi-Attribution Causality Scale. All four groups (American, Chinese, Japanese, Korean) favored attributions for both success and failure in this order: effort, ability, task, luck. But Americans more often than Asians attributed academic success to ability. Students in the four Asian groups appeared more similar than different in accounting for academic performance.

Another facet of causal attributions is the phenomenon of self-serving bias—the tendency to take credit for success but to deny responsibility for failure. Chandler, Shama, Wolf, and Planchard (1981) asked 684 university students from India, Japan, South Africa, the United States, and Yugoslavia about their academic success and failure. The Japanese offered the most internal (accepting blame) causal ascriptions for failures and the least internal (taking credit) for successes. Indians were just the opposite.

## Cross-Cultural Encounters

Differences between cultures in causal-attribution customs often lead to problems of adjustment when people move from one society to another or when they encounter individuals from cultures unlike their own.

For instance, how does a student make the transition from a country where group solidarity is prized (Japan and China) to a context that prizes autonomy and devalues dependency (United States, England, Sweden)? Fujita, Ito, Abe, and Takeuchi (1991) observed that for the Japanese, conflicts often occur between preserving traditional Japanese values and adhering to the expected behavior patterns of American culture. Fujita et al. also discovered that children who have adapted well to the American behavior patterns may experience ridicule at home from their parents.

Yee (1984) identified four primary strategies that Asians are apt to adopt to deal with conflict, with all four emphasizing the avoidance of direct confrontation: endurance, look the other way, don't think too much, and activity. That these culturally ingrained orientations could serve to increase stress for Asians in an American setting is readily apparent. But such habits could also help immigrants bear the strain of culture shock, feelings of alienation, racism, powerlessness, and anxieties associated with falling short of achievement and success levels demanded by their cultural roots.

## CULTURAL CHANGE AND BELIEFS ABOUT CAUSE

As suggested in Chapter 2, changes in folk psychologies' conceptions of cause can result from the importation of beliefs from other societies or from contributions of unusually inventive individuals in the society itself. Such changes can involve either novel ways of interpreting familiar events or technological innovations that alter the way people act toward each other and toward their physical surroundings. How technical innovations can affect folk psychologies' notions of cause is clearly demonstrated in the ways people account for human physical maladies. As additional biological and psychological causes for people's ailments are discovered and disseminated throughout a society, existing folk beliefs in supernatural causes are increasingly replaced. An example from Delaware Indian history over the past three centuries illustrates such a process.

When the Delaware (Lenni Lenape) in the 18th century were ousted by white settlers and by Iroquois tribes from their homelands on the Atlantic seaboard, they moved west by gradual stages, with many of them forced in 1867 to settle on designated land in what is now Oklahoma. Throughout their travels, the Delaware maintained their traditional explanations of physical ailments and continued to practice long-standing treatment methods. The medical practitioners in Delaware culture were known as *ma-ta-en-noo*, tribal shamans functioning as medicine men. They attributed physical and psychological disorders—other than the most obvious cuts, bruises, and broken bones—to evil spirits. Diarrhea, vicious headaches, convulsions, delirium, and other maladies for which there was no visible cause were believed to be the result of evil introduced into a person's body by paranormal forces. It was often thought that a malicious sorcerer, operating from a distance, had infused a victim's body with poisons while the victim slept.

The two interrelated types of treatment for most illnesses were (a) the application of herbal medicines compounded from such plant products as corn silk, black walnut bark, elderberry flowers, and jimson weed and (b) supplicatory acts intended to appease invisible spirits and solicit their help. The following are examples of herbal remedies and the maladies they were expected to cure, as found in the practice of one mid-20th-century Delaware herbalist, Nora Thompson Dean (Indian name "Touching Leaves"), in northeastern Oklahoma (Weslager, 1973, pp. 62-70).

- Blackberry (*rubus*)—Tea is made from the crushed root to cure dysentery.
- Butler willow (*salix*)—When pressed on the gums, it firms the gums, such as after having a tooth removed.

- Elm (*ulmus americana*)—The liquid made from soaking the inner bark in water is taken to stop chills and coughing.
- Horse mint (*monarda*)—To cure headaches, soaked leaves are applied to the head as a compress, or else the liquid solution is drunk.
- Joe-Pye weed (*eupatorium*, also known as skunk weed, marsh milkweed, trumpet weed, and quillwort)—Crushed weed soaked in water produces a liquid applied to the face to improve the complexion.
- Persimmon (*diospyros virginiana*)—Warmed sap from twigs relieves earaches.
- Spurge (*euphorbia*)—Juice from a broken stem removes warts.

All animate and inanimate things in Nature were believed by the Delaware to be under the control of spirits that were placed within them by the Creator. The herbs used for medicines were thought to possess attributes given to them by their indwelling spirits. Consequently, the relationship of the herbalist to the herbs he or she gathered also had significant religious connotations, because the healing was the work of the spirits. (Weslager, 1973, p. 40)

In addition to using herbs for specific ailments, Delaware healers prayed to the Creator and to their individual guardian spirits for assistance in treating the sick.

Throughout the 20th century the popularity of traditional Indian healing practices declined under the influence of the dominant surrounding American version of European culture. In school, Indian children and youths learned scientific interpretations of disease—genetics, bacteriology, biochemistry, anatomy, and physiology. They were taught that the chemical components of herbs, rather than spirits which supposedly inhabited plant life, were the active agents that effected cures. The mass communication media—books, newspapers, magazines, radio, and television—also featured nonspirit explanations of illness. Furthermore, hospitals and medical doctors treated disorders from a modern-science perspective. As a consequence, even though vestiges of herbal medicine and its allied spirit-possession theory are still found in Indian communities, the use of traditional versions of Native American healing practices at the opening of the 21st century was very limited, indeed.

# 5

# Competence

*What constitutes competence, how are competencies identified, and what should be done about incompetence?*

The term *competence*, as used throughout this chapter, refers to how well people accomplish tasks. A distinction is sometimes drawn between *demonstrated competence* and *potential competence*. Judgments about demonstrated competence are based on observations of how well a person has performed some act. Judgments about potential competence are founded on estimates of how well someone could perform if the occasion demanded it and if the person "really tried." Such phrases as "He's an underachiever" or "I know she can do better than that" imply the belief that an individual's demonstrated achievement has not been an accurate indicator of that person's potential.

A variety of words other than *competence* are used in referring to people's potential or demonstrated performance—such words as *ability, aptitude, expertise, intelligence, proficiency, skill,* and *talent.*

Two ways that folk psychologies can differ are in (a) the nature of the competence associated with different roles in life and (b) cultural conceptions of incompetence, in the sense of what constitutes impairment. These matters, plus the effect of cultural change on people's competence, are the concern of this chapter.

## KINDS OF COMPETENCE

For the purpose of drawing cross-cultural comparisons, one convenient way to view competence is in how adequately people accomplish the activities that constitute the roles they assume in life. The word *role* in this context means a function in life that is composed of a particular set of repetitive activities. The role of *carpenter* is made up of the tasks carried out by people who follow the occupation of carpentry, the role of *husband* consists of the activities expected of a male spouse, and the role of *friend* is defined by the activities the folk psychology identifies as attributes of friendship. Thus, levels of competence are judged by how well people complete tasks that are identified with the various roles they play. One way that folk psychologies may differ is in the way task performance distinguishes between greater and lesser degrees of role competence. The following examples illustrate such differences in roles labeled *parent, child, spouse, leader,* and *communicator.*

## Parent

The term *competence*, when applied to parents, refers to how well parents perform the sorts of activities that are generally expected of fathers and mothers in a particular culture. Parental competence, in this sense of typical functions, is different than competence in terms of the influence parental behaviors have on children. In other words, the expected behaviors of parents may or may not represent—from an objective viewpoint—the most constructive ways to rear children so they will become happy and skilled, and will develop into productive adults.

As the following examples illustrate, the activities that compose parental roles not only may differ across societies, but they can also differ across social classes within a society.

### Differences across societies

The notion that parenthood at the outset of the 21st century was in a continuing state of transition is attested by studies in numerous societies.

Research into the background of parenthood in France reveals that a pervasive conception of mother and father roles in past centuries derived from Roman tradition as transmitted formally to French culture through Napoleonic law, which assigned a father absolute control over his children, his wife, and her property. But as the 19th century advanced into the 20th, and the industrial revolution progressively changed farmers into city-dwelling factory and office workers, fathers' rule over their offspring's behavior was gradually undermined.

> In the reduced urban families composed of father, mother, and children [forming nuclear families in contrast to earlier extended families], it was the mother who held the actual authority over the children [because the father was away at work], and it was the mother who had the educative function. In the 19th century society, parents were watched over by different institutions; the child was obliged to go to school, and the childhood "specialists" [who write about proper child rearing] appear. For the first time in the history of paternity, comes the idea that there may be "good" and "bad" fathers. (Delaisi de Parseval & Hurstel, 1987, pp. 67-68)

During the latter years of the 20th century, French conceptions of parenthood changed further, producing more varied types of acceptable mothers and fathers. Some mothers were employed outside the home, while others were not. There were more stepmothers and stepfathers as divorce and remarriage increased. And more fathers took over child-rearing tasks formerly borne only by mothers, particularly tasks of infant care. In effect, the variety of activities that qualified parents as competent was greater than ever before.

In Germany and Austria, the marked change in the labor force that occurred after World War II was accompanied by shifts in traditional folk-psychology notions of parental roles. The shifts were particularly affected by a dramatic increase in working mothers. By the mid-1980s, half of Germany's women ages 15 to 65 were employed; nearly half of them were mothers of children under age 18. In Austria, women made up 44% of the workforce, with one quarter of them with children under age 15. Thus, more than ever before, mothers added the wage-earner role to their traditional housekeeping and child-raising activities. At the same time, the notion of fathers taking responsibility for child care became increasingly common, especially within the population of young adults.

> In scientific research as well as in public discussion, the change in the father's role is being considered primarily with reference to the first years of the child's life. Until recently, fathers were almost exclusively seen as having an important role for older children, particularly their sons. . . . [In addition,] the meaning of the emotional father-child relationship has been emphasized more and more. Formerly, fathers' behaviors were primarily viewed under cognitive aspects [teaching children facts about the world] and with their modeling functions [providing an example of how to act]. Now, however, variables such as sensitivity and empathy are considered as relevant research material. (Nickel & Köcher, 1987, p. 108)

Thus, a new vision of the competent father was emerging in German-speaking cultures. However, the extent to which the general populace embrace this version of the "new father" as part of their folk psychology apparently has been less than the mass-communication media (popular books, periodicals, television) have suggested. In other words, the new and increasingly engaged father is more evident in the press than in the behavior of fathers (Nickel & Köcher, 1987, p. 108).

As Hwang (1987) explains, parenthood in Sweden since the 19th century has been affected in ways similar to those in other societies that have undergone structural changes, principally as a result of industrialization.

> The father's role as a trainer of the young was important in the agrarian society, where he passed on knowledge of farming, taught his children handi-

crafts, and taught them how to read and pray. By the middle of the 19th century, the family no longer functioned as a unit of production, that is, both the need to work together and the direct dependency on one another had diminished. A new type of family grew up—the middle-class and working-class families in the city—both of which had the father as the primary provider. Thus, the father left the family to work in the labor market (i.e., he left home), whereas the mother remained with the children and the household work. (Hwang, 1987, p. 117)

During the 20th century, and especially over recent decades, the Swedish government has provided strong encouragement for parents to assume nearly identical roles, with the encouragement assuming the form of financial support unprecedented in other nations. Like Swedish mothers, fathers can take parental leave during the infant's first year of life, with the initial nine months at nearly full pay. Fathers have the right to reduce their working time up to two hours per day until their child is age 8. Women have full opportunities to engage in work outside the home, and men are urged to spend time in child care and household tasks. Therefore, in terms of the government's family policies, parents are treated as equals. However, long-standing tradition is slow to yield, so changes in folk psychologies often lag behind official social-policy shifts, particularly among a society's older members. But ultimately, social pressure serves to alter the behavior of traditionalists.

Many Swedish fathers feel pressure from their spouses, friends, colleagues, and others to take more active interest in their children and, in this way, to share parental responsibility. . . . The knowledge that love develops through simple, everyday actions—such as feeding, comforting, bathing, and playing with the child—is gradually seeping into most fathers' consciousness. (Hwang, 1987, p. 136)

A salient feature of China's long social history is the division of parenting responsibilities between father and mother. In keeping with Confucian doctrine, fathers were charged with instructing and disciplining their offspring, whereas mothers were concerned with nurturing the young—being affectionate, kind, protective, and lenient, even indulgent. Fathers were expected to be unemotional in their relationships with their children, and particularly with a son who was expected to carry on the family traditions. Fathers were cautioned to be unemotional, not show anger when their children failed to behave as desired. Not only was it important to curb anger, but also to avoid inordinate displays of love, which could interfere with discipline and thereby produce a spoiled child.

A contradiction thus arose between the natural tendency of parents to love their children and the belief that parents had to refrain from loving them too much. The differentiation of parental roles into the strict father and the kind mother was one solution to this contradiction. The strict father played the role of the parent who, being the educational agent, had to observe that he and (especially) the mother did not drown the child with too much love. (Ho, 1987, p. 232)

Much of this separation of parental competencies continues in modern-day Chinese culture, whether observed in Hong Kong, Singapore, mainland China, or Taiwan. However, studies of Chinese family relations in recent decades have identified trends that are likely to progress into the future. One trend is for mothers to share decision-making authority that traditionally had been fathers' exclusive right. Mothers are also increasingly serving as disciplinary agents in the home. Fathers—and particularly those of the younger generations—are placing less emphasis on children respecting the elderly and more emphasis on children's right to express opinions, show self-respect, and be independent and creative. There is also some evidence that younger fathers are becoming more involved in child care, an involvement partially made necessary by more mothers taking employment outside the home (Ho, 1987, pp. 236-237).

## Differences across social-class levels

Within the upper classes of British society, a centuries-old practice that lingers today places young children in the care of a governess or nanny who is directly responsible for the care and training of boys and girls from their infancy into early and middle childhood. Mothers, and often fathers, would meet with their young offspring only for brief periods during the day. Between ages 7 and 10, boys would be sent off to boarding school, and girls would usually continue their education at home with a governess, concentrating on reading, music, art, French language, etiquette. Fathers' significant interaction with their sons occurred during vacation periods, increasing as the youths entered adolescence and could communicate with their fathers in a manly fashion. It was during this stage of boys' development that fathers would give advice about how males should conduct themselves in both social and occupational settings.

In the past, British working-class parents would directly assume the responsibility of raising their children, with the mother bearing the main burden of caring for and training both girls and boys during the first six or eight years of their lives. The father would be off working during the day, returning home in the evening when he might serve as disciplinarian, chastising recalcitrant offspring for their reported misdeeds. As boys approached adolescence, they would often be apprenticed to a tradesman, artisan, or factory manager to learn a vocation and begin earning a wage. Adolescent girls would continue to learn domestic skills from their mothers at home or be sent to the home of a well-to-do mid-dle- or upper-class family as a housemaid. In more recent times, since the advent of compulsory universal schooling that extends into the mid-dle years of adolescence, many of the learnings that working-class girls and boys formerly acquired at home or in apprenticeships have been taught in school. In other words, some of the competent parent's re-sponsibilities have been transferred to—or shared with—teachers.

Studies of British parents in recent decades suggest that behaviors tra-ditionally expected of mothers and fathers were changing at all social-class levels, with more mothers taking jobs outside the home and with more fathers helping with housekeeping and childrearing tasks than was true in the past (Jackson, 1987).

Rapid social change in the United States over the final four decades of the 20th century brought parenthood and family life to an unprece-dented condition. The trend was toward higher divorce rates, fewer children growing up in a two-parent family, more children born to un-wed mothers, and more women raising children without a male perma-nently in the home. Whereas these trends appeared at all levels of the socioeconomic ladder and within all ethnic groups, the incidence of mother-headed families was most pronounced among lower-class Afri-can Americans. Up until World War II, the two-parent nuclear family remained the dominant type for both whites and blacks. In 1940, only 10% of white families and 18% of black families were headed by females. These figures rose gradually between 1940 and 1960, then increased rapidly from the 1960s into the 1990s. The proportion of female-headed black families rose from 22% in 1960 to 28% in 1970, to 44% in 1990, and to 47% in 1998. At the same time, female-headed white families in-creased from 8% in 1960 to 12% in 1983, 13% in 1990, and 14% in 1998. Among families of Asian and Pacific Island heritage, the percentage of female-headed households in 1998 was 12%, among American Indians 24%, and among Hispanics 23% (Wilson & Neckerman, 1986, p. 234; U.S. Census Bureau, 1999, pp. 51-53, 62).

As the figures for African Americans suggest, the burden of parenting in lower-class black families was increasingly borne entirely—or almost entirely—by mothers, along with grandmothers and other female family members. Not only were fathers not available to supervise their children and serve as constructive role models, but in a great many cases they also failed to provide the financial support families require.

In 1986, our society crossed an important threshold. That year, for the first time in our nation's history, a majority of poor families were father-absent. Historically, for most poor children, poverty stemmed primarily from fa-thers being unemployed or receiving low wages. For most poor children today, poverty stems primarily from not having a father in the home.

In strict economic terms, this trend can be understood as paternal disinvestment: the growing refusal of fathers to spend their resources on their offspring. This trend helps to explain an apparent paradox. Public spending on children in the United States has never been higher. At the same time, child poverty is spreading and child well-being is declining. The explanation is that our rising public investment in children has been far outweighed by our private disinvestments, primarily paternal disinvestments. (Blankenhorn, 1995, pp. 43-44)

In looking to the future, David Popenoe estimates that the parenthood trend among lower-class African Americans is a harbinger of things to come for all of America's ethnic and social-class groups.

Black family life, then, appears to be a precursor of what family life is likely to become for the rest of the population. While African-American families undoubtedly face some stresses that are unique to them, they are instructively viewed as prematurely suffering the negative consequences of an American family environment that all groups share. (Popenoe, 1996, p. 26)

In summary, this changed vision of the competent (meaning the *acceptable* and *expected*) father and competent mother—as found in the folk psychology of present-day African-American lower-class males and females—may be the model of competent parenthood found in the folk psychology of much of the American population in the years ahead. If that trend does come to represent the society's dominant folk belief about parenting, then the traditional father competencies (other than that of furnishing sperm) must, by default, be assumed by other individuals and agencies—mothers, grandmothers, schools, churches, welfare bureaus, the police, the courts, and youth clubs.

## Child

Adults in every culture hold expectations for the physical, cognitive, and social behavior of children, including not only what sorts of competence are desired but also when during the period of development different abilities should appear. Such expectations are represented in folk psychologies that often differ from one culture to another.

By way of illustration, consider Joshi and MacLean's study (1997) of child-competency expectations held by a sample of suburban middle-class mothers of children under age 10 in England (70 mothers), India (50), and Japan (50). The mothers were given a list of 46 desired child behaviors and asked to indicate at what age a child should exhibit each type. The results showed that for the list of 46 as a whole, Japanese mothers expected mastery of the behaviors slightly earlier than the English mothers and markedly earlier than the Indian mothers. Such a result was in keeping with Kakar's observation that

An Indian mother is inclined towards a total indulgence of her infant's wishes and demands, whether these be related to feeding, cleaning, sleeping or being kept company. Moreover, she tends to extend this kind of mothering well beyond the time when the "infant" is ready for independent functioning in many areas. The Indian toddler takes his own time learning to control his bowels, and proceeds at his own pace to master other skills such as walking, talking, and dressing himself. (Kakar, 1978, p. 81)

In all three cultures, skill in self-care and rudimentary formal education was expected by middle childhood.

Ninety-six percent of the Japanese mothers and 84% of the English mothers expected competence by 4 to 6 years of age. Sixty-six percent of the Indian mothers expected competence by 6 to 8 years of age. It would appear that in all cultures mothers give prime importance to knowledge of numbers and the alphabet as well as basic skills related to bodily maintenance and cleanliness. (Joshi & MacLean, 1997, p. 225)

Within all three groups of mothers, a cluster of behaviors that relate to complying with adult commands, interacting constructively with peers, and using language adeptly were expected somewhat later, with the majority of mothers wishing children to command these skills during the years 6 to 8. Emotional control—including reactions to frustration and display of feelings—was expected even later.

In discussions of child development, psychologists have often focused on the autonomy that is both encouraged in and granted to children in North America and Europe. . . . [But] our data clearly reveal that, in England, there are areas for older children, such as travel between home and school, in which independence is not granted. . . . All Japanese mothers expect competence in this domain by 6 to 8 years of age. Fifty percent of Indian mothers expect competence by 6 to 8 years of age with an additional 42% expecting competence by 8 to 10 years of age. In contrast, only 3% of English mothers expect competence by 6 to 8 years of age, and the majority of English mothers (61%) do not expect competence in this domain until the age of 10 years or older. (Joshi & MacLean, 1997, p. 226)

## Spouse

The activities that conventionally comprise the roles of wife and husband are not identical across cultures. The following are versions of the wifely role in five societies.

In traditional Gusii communities of southwestern Kenya, when women marry they must leave their family and their familiar neighborhood to live thereafter on their husband's homestead. Without the support of their own relatives, they are obliged to be self-effacing and obedient in their relationships with authority figures in their husband's clan. Trouble results if young wives are self-assertive toward older males and females. To win acceptance, they must be respectful, do what they are bid, work hard, and avoid confrontations. Deviating from these role expectations invites punishment (LeVine, 1982).

Even stricter requirements for the competent wife continue to be imposed by the folk cultures of Muslims and Hindus in Bangladesh, northern India, and Pakistan, where a husband's honor depends to a great extent on his wife's protecting herself from the gaze of other men. Thus, in addition to assuming a subservient, respectful manner within the home—much like the behavior expected of the competent Gusii female spouse—the Muslim or Hindu wife must leave the house only when absolutely necessary. And while abroad, she is obliged to cover as much of her body as possible in loose garments—a practice known as *purdah* (veil). No more than her face—or preferably, only her eyes—will be exposed to public view. Even in the home, if any male relative (especially an older one) appears, the proper wife veils her head and face. Thus, the competent wife displays "shyness of demeanor, avoidance of eye-contact with males, avoidance of loud speech and laughter (particularly in the presence of or within earshot of males), and the limitation of conversation with non-family males to necessary work-connected topics" (Vatuk in Mandelbaum, 1988, p. 4). In contrast, the competent husband is free to move about the community and interact with anyone he chooses, so long as he does not become intimate with people of social-caste status below his own caste. He is responsible for providing the family's income, for making important family decisions, and for ensuring that his wife abides by the restrictions that her assigned role dictates.

Quite a different pattern of spousal competence obtained in the original matrilineal society of the Akan in southern Ghana, where inheritance and descent flowed through the female side of the family. Wives enjoyed considerable freedom, autonomy, and power as a result of the culture's sexual mores and the society's matrilineal structure. In the realm of sexual behaviors, Akans placed little value on female chastity, so that "lack of concern with female sexual virtue meant that women were not subjected to extensive regulation or kept isolated from men" (Smock, 1977, p. 176). Akan social structure did place men in dominant positions of political leadership (chief, subchief, headman, village council member). "Nevertheless, the determination of kinship connections through the female line of descent and the belonging of all children to the mother's family elevated women's importance and contributed to their sense of self-respect and dignity" (Smock, 1977, p. 176). Although traditional Akan spousal relations were somewhat eroded by British colonialism, which offered greater educational opportunities to males, even today gender relations continue to reflect vestiges of the matrilineal tradition.

Among the Inuit (Eskimos) of Arctic North America, spousal competence has been determined principally by the skill that individuals display in their work roles as judged by members of their own sex. Men's work has consisted principally of hunting, while women's work has been domestic—fashioning animal skins into garments, preparing food, caring for the young, and organizing a smoothly running household. "Women's tasks do not appear to be thought more onerous than men's, just different. Neither is the work of one more estimable than that of the other" (Guemple, 1995, p. 20).

In Sharp's (1995) analysis of long-established spousal roles in numerous North American Indian societies, he criticizes the dominance/submission interpretation of gender relationships that missionaries, settlers, and anthropologists of European heritage have imposed on Native American cultures since the earliest days of Westerners' penetration into Indian territories. According to a Eurocentric perspective, wives in most—if not all—traditional Indian cultures have been dominated and oppressed by husbands, rendered powerless by threats of punitive sanctions (social and physical) if they fail to abide by the dictates of their assigned subservient position. Sharp charges that such beliefs

> are too closely bound to the utopian discourse involved in the contemporary negotiation of Western political values and gender roles. In a more general sense, to utilize oppression . . . or dominance . . . to explain relations between genders is to presume that a terror model rather than a consensual model lies at the base of human cultural behavior. (Sharp, 1995, p. 48)

Sharp contends that members of the two genders have willingly adopted their roles by assuming that their physical abilities and emotional tendencies suit them to the division of labor that cultural tradition decrees. Thus, it is by consent rather than male oppression that separate spousal work assignments are adopted. According to such interpretation revisionists as Sharp, the putative Eurocentric misconception of gender relations derived partly from outside observers seeing only the public exercise of power in which males have usually played the part of leaders in community affairs. However, careful observation of family life reveals that power within the family has been exerted primarily by wives, and particularly by elderly women. Therefore, Ackerman, in her description of life among the Plateau Indians of northwest America (such tribes as the Salish, Kutenai, Sahaptin, Okanagon, Sanpoil, Flathead, and Nez Perce), concludes that gender roles

> though complementary, with little overlap existing in the work of men and women, failed to lead to a condition of male superiority. On the contrary, the genders were socially and economically equal. . . . Even though differential access of men and women to certain public roles existed, nevertheless,

that access was balanced, facilitating gender equality in traditional Plateau culture. (Ackerman, 1995, p. 78)

## Leader

The word *leader* is used here to mean someone responsible for guiding the activities of a group, particularly a group whose members form a nation, province, religious denomination, ethnic division, tribe, or clan. Not only can the leadership qualities commanded or implied by a folk psychology vary from one group to another, but they also can vary from time to time in the history of a particular group.

Tamadonfar's (1989) analysis of the qualities expected of leaders in Islamic states identifies three core requirements for leadership status—an intimate knowledge of Islam, a commitment to abiding by Islamic principles, and superior moral values. Over the centuries, a division of responsibilities developed between two sorts of leaders, caliphs and imams, with caliphs in charge of temporal affairs and imams in charge of religious matters. However, the fact that Islam is both a religion and a complete plan for a way of life, the caliph and imam roles have often overlapped. Individuals in the role of caliph have been responsible for directing the defense and maintenance of the Islamic state, settling legal disputes, punishing wrongdoers, providing troops to guard the frontiers, waging *jihad* (holy war) against any who refuse to accept Islam, organizing the collection of taxes, arranging the payment of salaries and the administration of public funds, and appointing officials. Competencies expected of imams include a sense of justice, flexibility, commitment, thoughtfulness, and detailed knowledge of the religion's dominant holy book, the Qur'an. In recent times, the duties of caliphs have often been assumed by leaders who bear such titles as president or prime minister.

A very different pattern of competencies is required for an individual to attain the status of social leader among the Orokaiva of Papua New Guinea. To deserve the appellation "big man" (*embo okose*) or "big woman" (*evuhu okose*), an individual must have a host of social relationships which have been acquired by participation in numerous rituals. Thus, the more rituals in which persons take part, the more relationships they accumulate (Iteanu, 1990).

Age and wealth are two important factors in determining who are considered competent to become leaders among the Dassanetch of southeast Ethiopia. The society is organized into generation sets, with people in the older sets accorded greater honor. When the Dassanetch elect individuals to the various formal political offices in their age-set system, they choose those who are known to be wealthy. The elected officials are then obligated to slaughter the number of livestock commensurate with the status of their office.  The higher the office, the more cattle, sheep, or goats to be sacrified (Almagor, 1978, pp. 56-57).

It is apparent that every society of substantial size or complexity has various sorts of leadership positions, with the qualities needed to fill these posts varying somewhat from one position to another.  This point can be illustrated with six kinds of leaders in the Maori segment of New Zealand's population during the middle decades of the 20th century, when the nation's population was around 2.5 million.  Maoris accounted for 7% of the total, while inhabitants of European heritage made up most of the remaining 93% (Winiata, 1967, p. 80).[*]  In traditional Maori culture, the leader accorded the highest status has been the *ariki*, who gains his position by dint of a royal ancestry.  The *ariki* is the paramount chief who heads clusters of tribes and subtribes.  His election to the position by the nobles is formalized by an elaborate ceremony.  The *ariki* symbolizes the maintenance of Maori tradition against the intrusion of European culture.

> [The *ariki's* method] is to refrain from active participation in [protest] movements, but rather to exercise a silent and passive, symbolic leadership. The strength of the *ariki* is in his isolation from the mundane affairs of the tribe, [but] his presence is necessary to add dignity to the proceedings, although he need not speak. (Winiata, 1967, p. 86)

The active burden of leadership is borne by the *kaumatua*, a tribal chief chosen because of his ancestry (descent from chiefs), advanced age (Maoris trust the wisdom of those with long experience), skills in oratory, memory for history, and knowledge of tradition, dedicatory incantations, and medical ritual.  "But it is the ability to speak at the gatherings for funerals and to welcome distinguished visitors that really takes the *kaumatua* to the fore.  Without this gift of expression, he is leader only in name" (Winiata, 1967, p. 87).

A third sort of leader is the *kuia*, the elderly wife of the *kaumatua*, responsible for arranging the catering and accommodations for visitors.  If her husband dies, the *kuia* ascends to his vacated position, bearing some of his authority and responsibilities, but aided in her public duties by other *kaumatua*.

Fourth is the *rangatahi*, a leader of such youth activities as pursued by athletic, musical, entertainment, and political groups.  A young person who aspires to the position of *rangatahi* is aided in his pursuit by kinship

---

[*] By 2001, the nation's estimated population was 3.85 million, with 14% of the inhabitants identified as of Maori ancestry, 77% European, 5% Pacific islander, and 4% Asian.  Most of the residents who registered as Maori were, in fact, of mixed Maori European heritage.

ties with the tribe that sponsors the activity and his skills of leadership in the particular activity involved.

Fifth, what is referred to as *the educated leader* is a position that evolved as the result of the immigration of European colonists (*Paheka*) that began in the early 19th century. The job of educated leader is one of negotiating between the Maori community and New Zealand's European cultural community. The educated leader is often the secretary, chairman, or clerk of Maori committees, charged with the task of writing petitions, composing land-transfer documents, and serving as translator between an *ariki* or *kaumatua* and members of the European populace. Fluency in both the Maori and English languages and knowledge of both cultures are basic requirements for the position.

A sixth type of leader is the *tohunga*, the traditional Maori faith healer, skilled in diagnosing and curing "Maori sickness" (*mate Maori*). *Mate Maori* is distinguished from *mate Paheka* (European sickness) that European-educated doctors are qualified to treat. In treating *mate Maori*, the *tohunga* first

> questions closely the patient and his immediate family to find the cause of the ailment. He examines dreams, for they tell the hidden cause of the trouble. Often this cause is a violation of a ritual prohibition. The *tohunga* recommends that the patient confess and apply for forgiveness. Many *tohungas* use apparatus such as intoxicating liquors, coins, water, and herbs as part of their healing programs. (Winiata, 1967, p. 96)

A contrast in beliefs about how leadership qualities are acquired is observed in the South Pacific islands. In Melanesian societies of the western Pacific, the position of chief is generally expected to be earned by a candidate's demonstrated skill in battle, social relations, economic ventures, occupational activities, oratory, and/or intellectual pursuits. On the other hand, leadership positions among Polynesian societies of the South Pacific's central and eastern regions more often pass through an ancestral royal line. Sons of chiefs—and sometimes daughters of chiefs—succeed their fathers in office. The apparent logic behind such a tradition is that the progeny of aristocratic parents acquire special talents for leadership by dint of their genetic endowment (biological superiority) and/or their being raised in a context that teaches leadership skills (environmental enrichment).

## Communicator

The kinds of language skills a person needs in order to be considered a competent communicator depend partly on individuals' ability to master language and partly on the composition and location of the particular society. This second factor—a society's composition and location—is of particular interest from the viewpoint of folk psychology. For most people in the United States, adeptly speaking, hearing, reading, and writing English is sufficient to qualify them as linguistically competent. The same is true in Australia and New Zealand. But fluency in a single language does not mark a person as a competent communicator in such multilingual cultures as those of China, India, Indonesia, Nigeria, or the evolving European Union. In Western Europe, a resident of France is best equipped to communicate efficiently with fellow Europeans if he or she speaks not only French, but German, English, Italian, and Spanish as well—and perhaps a Scandinavian tongue. In Singapore, where the officially recognized core language is Malay, it is even more important for the purpose of social competence that people are proficient in English, a Chinese dialect, and perhaps Tamil.

It is also the case that the style of expression considered proper for skilled communication is not the same in all cultures. For instance, Aoki (1990) has contrasted Western ways that people express their opinions with the ways that are acceptable in Japanese culture. He notes that in European and North American societies, a valued mode of verbal interaction is that of being assertive—a willingness to confront opposing views and to express one's feelings forthrightly during social encounters. In contrast, competent communication in Japanese tradition involves indirectness, requiring the listener to "read between the lines." Speakers keep their true attitudes to themselves, counting on listeners' ability to intuit speakers' masked thoughts.

> Japanese people, for this reason, have been considered less able than their European and American counterparts to state their opinions positively and unambiguously. Among observers of Japanese society, the tendency of the Japanese people to be "unable to give a clear yes or no, to lean toward indirectness and ambiguity, and to value harmony over their own opinions" [Ishii, 1987, p. 126] has been seen as a special characteristic of Japanese behavior as compared with European and North American behavior. (Niikura, 1999, p. 691)

Niikura (1999) sought to test this proposal with samples of white-collar workers from Japan and the United States and, in addition, to learn whether the version of the competent Japanese communicator also obtained in other Asian cultures—specifically those of Malaysia and the Philippines. Her investigation involved around 100 respondents in each country completing a 33-item questionnaire focusing on how people might express themselves in various social situations. The results confirmed the contrast between the hypothesized traditional Japanese and North American modes of competent communication. The results also showed that

Japanese, Malaysian, and Filipino respondents were similar in their respect for group solidarity and in the courtesy shown by junior members toward senior members, . . . [with] deference to the group valued in Japanese, Malaysian, and Filipino societies alike, as [a form of] positive cooperative behavior calculated to preserve harmony.  One might assume that the differences between the Asian and the U.S. perceptions of assertiveness in interpersonal relations and the conflicting views of how to maintain group harmony would be sources of misunderstanding and friction when such people interact. (Niikura, 1999, p. 697)

## CONCEPTIONS OF IMPAIRMENT

Folk psychologies can differ in (a) how they view handicaps as limitations on competence, (b) how impairments are categorized, and (c) what measures should be adopted to correct, or accommodate for, handicaps.

### Handicaps as Limitations on Competence

Marshall (1996) has distinguished between the concepts *impaired parts* and *impaired persons*.  People with impaired parts are ones whose ability to perform certain acts is either restricted or eliminated by a condition typically referred to as a *handicap*.  Nevertheless, such individuals can still participate constructively in society and lead satisfying personal lives.  In contrast, people who qualify as impaired persons are ones whose handicaps prevent them from adequately understanding their culture and engaging in their society's activities.

Marshall illustrates this *parts/persons* distinction with the culture of the Caroline Islands in the western Pacific.  He begins by proposing that Polynesian and Micronesian cultures emphasize the importance of the group rather than the individual.  "The person in these island communities exists not so much as an autonomous self (as in the West), but rather as part of a larger community of selves.  This group-oriented rather than individual-oriented view of the person presents a challenge to the concept of impairment that is widely used in the West"—the concept that individuals are impaired when they suffer any loss or abnormality of psychological, physiological, or anatomical structure or function (Marshall, 1996, p. 249).  Whereas in Western societies people who are lame or deaf or disfigured have traditionally been deemed impaired persons, in Polynesian and Micronesian societies those individuals who display an impaired part are not viewed as impaired persons if they can comprehend their cultural group's worldview—the group's folk psychology—and can participate in "the everyday web of social relationships, even if at a limited or reduced level" (Marshall, 1996, p. 250).

I argue that the evidence [from island societies] favors limiting the concept of impairment to those chronic or permanent conditions in which the self is socially isolated—in which the person either no longer wishes to be or no longer can be constructively enmeshed as an involved participant in community life . . . [so that] even serious physical impairment (e.g., paraplegia or blindness) is not necessarily a disability as long as the impaired person can construct new roles that permit active contributions to household and community life. . . . In these communities it is primarily various sorts of psychological or mental conditions that are disabling, and attention to psychological conditions leads directly to Caroline islanders' concepts of personhood. (Marshall, 1996, p. 250)

Islanders use the word *bush* (incompetent/crazy) in referring to individuals who are mentally retarded, behaviorally deviant, senile, or unable to talk about their thoughts and emotions. Such individuals are the members of island societies who qualify as impaired persons—truly incompetent.

## Categories of Impairment

Most folk psychologies—perhaps all—distinguish at least among broad categories of deviance. For instance, Malaysians identify two rough-hewn types of deviant behavior—one which is merely odd or strange (*aneh*) and another which is outright crazy (*gila*). Furthermore, all folk psychologies have words recognizing very obvious sorts of impairment, such as blindness, deafness, muteness, lameness, disfigurement, and marked mental retardation or derangement.

Furthermore, an increasing number of societies identify handicapping conditions that warrant official attention. One reason to specify impairments is to draw attention to conditions that require formal action to lighten the burden of the people so handicapped and/or to limit the trouble those individuals cause for "normal" members of society. The kinds of deviance officially recognized can differ significantly from one culture to another. By way of illustration, consider the cases of formally recognized impairments in China, Indonesia, and Britain.

By the 1980s, the four types of handicap mentioned in China's *Encyclopedia of Education* as warranting special educational attention were those of blindness, deafness, conspicuous mental retardation, and antisocial deviance ("Special Education," 1981-1982, pp. 49-52).

Until the 1980s, the Indonesian government-recognized impairments calling for official attention were the traditional kinds that had been recognized by Netherlands East Indies officials before Indonesia gained independence from Dutch colonial control in 1950. Those kinds were blindness, deafness, muteness, mental retardation, and physical disability. However, during the 1980s the official list of impairments meriting the attention of the education system expanded to include the cerebral palsied, the emotionally disturbed, the multiply handicapped, and the chronically ill (PPKSP, 1981, p. 1).

For Britain, Tomlinson (1982, p. 61) traced over nearly a century (1886-1981) the officially recognized types of persons who were thought to require special educational treatment for their impairments. She found that in 1886 there were only two statutory categories, both focusing on mental retardation, those of idiot and imbecile. By 1913, five more categories had been added—moral imbecile, mental defective (feeble-minded), blind, deaf, epileptic, and physically defective. In 1945, there were 12 categories, some incorporating more than one earlier designation (severely subnormal subsumed both idiot and imbecile), while other new varieties extended earlier categories (partially sighted was added to blind, and partially hearing added to deaf). By 1981, the official types numbered 14, with several more varieties suggested but not officially adopted. The 1981 list consisted of: child with learning difficulties (severe), child with learning difficulties (mild), blind, partially sighted, deaf, partially hearing, epileptic, maladjusted, disruptive, physically handicapped, speech defective, delicate, dyslexic, and autistic. Other suggested categories included: neuropathic child, inconsequential child, psychiatrically crippled child, and aphasic child. The percentage of children in the school-age population who could be diagnosed as fitting into at least one of these categories could be as large as 20% (Tomlinson, 1982, pp. 55-56).

Thus, as the foregoing cases demonstrate, not only do recognized types of impairment vary across cultures, but they also can change within a culture with the passing of time as (a) increasing amounts of scientific evidence distinguish more precisely among kinds of disability and (b) folk-psychology attitudes increasingly obligate the society to assume more public responsibility for aiding the handicapped.

In summary, greater efforts have been made since the late 19th century to alter the popular opinion that individuals who display impaired parts deserve to be stigmatized as impaired persons. Those efforts have consisted of measures designed to change the lives of "impaired persons" so they can perform competently and thus be considered socially nonimpaired. Such measures have included correcting people's handicaps.

## Correcting Impairments

Three ways of remedying faulty human parts are those of (a) directly repairing or replacing flawed organs, (b) providing medication that alleviates the effects of impairment, and (c) substituting a prosthetic device for the part that is either defective or missing.

Popular methods of repair include surgery, manipulation, and exercise. A surgeon may use bone grafts to correct lameness, may remove vision-blocking cataracts, or may transfer unblemished skin from the abdomen to repair facial scarring. An increasingly popular mode of surgical repair is that of transplanting a healthy organ from one person's body into the body of an individual whose organ has malfunctioned. A chiropractor may manipulate a patient's back in order to realign a twisted spine, and an orthodontist may manipulate teeth and jaw bones to correct faulty speech, painful chewing, or ugly appearance. A physiotherapist may prescribe an exercise and diet regimen to reduce gross obesity or strengthen weak muscles.

Medications are used for enabling people to operate productively by counteracting the effects of biochemical disorders of the body that impair normal functions. Analgesic pills relieve pain, atenolol reduces elevated blood pressure, and Ritalin controls the hyperactivity of children diagnosed as suffering from attention-deficit disorder. In East Asia, acupuncture is often used to effect cures for which chemical nostrums are employed in the West. In many cultures, rituals rather than medications are used to normalize people's mental and physical conditions. Agents conducting such rituals include psychiatrists, priests, faith healers, shamans, and medicine men.

Examples of popular prosthetic devices are eyeglasses, electronic hearing aids, crutches, false limbs, back braces, and wheelchairs.

## CULTURAL CHANGE AND COMPETENCE

One of the most important types of competence people need in order to make the most of their lives is that of communicating with other people. Particularly significant are the abilities to speak well, to understand others' speech and gestures, to read, and to write. In short, language skills are vital to human welfare. Three kinds of cultural change that can alter individuals' language competence are immigration, political transformation, and technological innovation.

### Immigration

Individuals who move from one society into another in which the dominant language is unfamiliar find themselves at a considerable disadvantage. Their language incompetence causes them to misunderstand what other people mean, and they often fail in their attempts to explain their own needs and intentions. Furthermore, because folk psychologies typically place so much emphasis on language fluency as an indicator of intelligence, a language-handicapped immigrant can appear dull-witted or obstinate.

## Political Change

A change in the governance of a nation or region can serve to reduce the communication competence of the populace. This occurs when new rulers impose on the society an unfamiliar language as the medium of communication for significant social interactions. The way such political change may affect language competence can be illustrated with shifts in political control of Indonesia between 1940 and 1950. For more than three centuries prior to 1942, Holland gradually gained hegemony over the Indonesian archipelago and governed the region as the Netherlands East Indies colony. When the Dutch first arrived, the islands' peoples were divided into hundreds of separate cultural groups speaking over 350 languages. One of the languages, known as Malay, served as a lingua franca, found principally in port cities, enabling members of different cultures to communicate with each other. Subsequently, under the Netherlands East Indies government, Dutch became the official language of government, commerce, and all schooling beyond the primary grades. Consequently, indigenous Indonesians who were linguistically most competent to deal with both the colonial officials and their fellow islanders were ones fluent in one or more regional language (such as Javanese, Sundanese, Batak, Achenese, and more), in Dutch, and in Malay.

When Japan entered World War II and captured Indonesia from the Dutch in early 1942, the Japanese military commanders intended to eliminate the use of Dutch and substitute Japanese as the official language of government, commerce, and schooling. However, because such a daunting task would necessarily be a long-term venture, Japanese authorities, as a temporary measure, outlawed Dutch and adopted Malay as the interim national language. Consequently, during the years of Japanese occupation, the most competent Indonesian communicators were those adept in (a) one or more regional tongues, (b) Malay, and (c) Japanese.

Subsequently, when the Japanese were defeated at the close of World War II, the Dutch sought to regain their colony. In response, Indonesian leaders resisted the returning Dutch, declared their independence in August 1945, and adopted Malay as the nation's official tongue, renaming it *Bahasa Indonesia* (Indonesian language). This act launched the Indonesian Revolution, during which indigenous patriots fought the Dutch military until independence was granted at the close of 1949. Thereafter, many older upper-class Indonesians continued to speak Dutch in their homes and offices. However, the Indonesians' post-revolution bitterness toward Holland, along with the fact that Dutch was not a very useful language for international communication, caused the new government to adopt English as the principal foreign language to be taught in schools. Consequently, over the last half of the 20th century, Indonesians who could be credited with substantial language competence were those fluent in Bahasa Indonesia, in one or more regional languages, and in English (Thomas, 1970).

## Technological Innovation

A recent invention that has wrought a dramatic change in people's access to information has been the computer Internet and its subsidiary World Wide Web. The Internet has required new communication skills of the millions who use it and has also increased the demands on non-English speakers. People who seek to locate information on the Internet must now be *computer literate*, adept at wending their way through the labyrinth of code words and software directions that computer use requires. In addition, by far the largest amount of information on the World Wide Web is in English. Thus, users who cannot read English are at a loss for comprehending most of the Web's contents.

To prepare children early in life to take advantage of the Internet, schools throughout the world—and particularly those in advanced industrial societies—increasingly include computer-literacy training in their curricula. However, there remain significant differences across societies in people's ability to access the Internet. The extent of those differences is reflected in the availability of computers in various countries. By the year 2000, the estimated number of computers per capita in representative nations was 580 per 1,000 inhabitants in the United States, 526 in Australia, 515 in Norway, 512 in Canada, 510 in Denmark, 505 in Finland, 509 in Sweden, 500 in New Zealand, and 441 in Great Britain. Less favored were such countries as Mexico (66 per 1,000), Russia (62), and China (11) (Brunner, 2000, p. 554).

The promise for greater access to the World Wide Web among non-English speakers appeared in 2001 when innovations in computer technology enabled individuals from many cultures whose native language was not English to communicate over the Internet in their own familiar tongue.

# 6

# Values

*What distinctions do people draw between beautiful and ugly, good and bad, desirable and undesirable, proper and improper, efficient and inefficient?*

One way to separate *facts* from *values* is to define facts as people's conceptions of what things exist and then to define values as beliefs about the desirability or quality of such things. Hence, statements of fact tell what exists, in what amount, and perhaps their relation to other facts. Statements of value tell whether something is good or bad, well done or poorly done, suitable or unsuitable. An example of a fact is the belief that different kinds of fish exist and each kind displays identifiable characteristics. An example of a value is the opinion that some kinds of fish are better than others.

Values can be divided into various types—aesthetic, functional, economic, social, and more.

Aesthetic values involve judgments from an artistic viewpoint. A flower garden may be described as "pleasingly arranged," a poem as having "a nicely turned metaphor," a dance performance as "delightfully innovative," and an office building as "ugly as sin."

Functional or technical values center on how efficiently something operates or on how well its parts coordinate—a speedy computer, a faulty water pump, a lazy workman, a stubborn mule.

Economic values concern how much profit or loss an investment yields. The purchase of a camel may be considered a "real bargain," a day spent hunting for a lost wallet is deemed "a complete waste of time," a winning lottery ticket is judged "a great return," and a bank savings account is criticized for yielding "too little interest."

137

Social values involve the quality of interactions among individuals and groups. Distinguishing between proper and improper social interactions is often referred to as a matter of moral, ethical, or social-convention values. Cultures can differ significantly in the social values that are typically reflected in formal laws and regulations as well as in unwritten customs and codes of conduct.

In the following pages, illustrative values found in different cultures are described under two headings—(a) types of values in folk psychologies and (b) values and cultural change.

## TYPES OF VALUES IN FOLK PSYCHOLOGIES

Folk psychologies can vary in the values they attribute to all aspects of life. However, in order to keep this chapter to a reasonable length and at the same time illustrate cross-cultural differences, the following description addresses only two kinds of values—aesthetic and social.

### An Aesthetic Value—Physical Attractiveness

The one aesthetic value chosen to illustrate differences among folk psychologies is that of people's physical appearance. The question becomes: Which human body shapes and facial features are the most attractive, which the least attractive, and why? An example of different answers to this question is found in the beliefs of North Americans and of Polynesian islanders regarding what constitutes the most desirable body weight and shape, especially among women. In North America, the cultural ideal is to be thin, whereas among South Pacific islanders the ideal is to be well filled out. In Tahitian tradition, girls of upper-class status were kept in special dormitories for weeks to be force-fed, then later paraded naked before the public to display their fattened and untanned bodies, admired by the populace and acclaimed by potential spouses (Oliver, 1989, p. 605).

Fatness is also highly valued in certain African societies where young women are isolated in "fattening huts" and fed high quantities of calorie-dense foods so they might attract a prestigious mate (Powers, 1996). In the Moorish society of Mauritania in northwest Africa, both fatness and buck teeth are signs of beauty.

> Women are subjected to *gavage*—that is, forced feeding, in order to gain weight. Fathers send daughters 10 or 11 years of age to live with herd-tending dependent *aznagui* who see to it that the girls gain weight . . . often by being tied to the ground, and, to expand their stomachs, given nothing but water for three days. Then they are crammed with milk, usually camel's milk. (Gerteiny, 1967, p. 72)

One study of college students' judgments of body shapes and sizes showed that Ugandan students rated fatter female and male figures as more attractive and healthier than British students did, thereby confirming the impression that thinness is favored in richer nations (Furnham & Baguma, 1994). Another study comparing the attitudes of Ghanaian and U.S. students produced similar results, with Ghanaian subjects judging larger body sizes as ideal. The American students were more likely than their Ghanaian counterparts to have dieted, with more U.S. females than males prone to diet (Cogan, Bhalla, Sefa-Dedeh, & Rothblum, 1996).

Societies also vary in the ways people seek to enhance their attractiveness. In cultures under strong European influence, people often decorate themselves with lip rouge, facial powder, suntan cream, finger rings, ear rings, and bracelets. In Polynesia, both men and women submit to tattooing. The larger the area of a man's body decorated, the greater the erotic appeal, since the indigenous method of tattooing is a painful process that can be borne by only the hardiest of men (Oliver, 1989, p. 605).

Analysts' efforts to account for why cultures differ in their standards of physical attractiveness have produced a number of proposals. One explanation suggests that there can be a link between a society's economic condition and people's social-class status. In societies in which food is hard to come by, people lower in the socioeconomic hierarchy are necessarily thin, whereas ones in the upper social classes can obtain all the food they desire. Hence, being fat becomes a symbol of high social status. For instance, fatness in Mauritania is a sign of wealth. Not only can the wealthy afford unlimited food, but they also are spared the burden of the hard physical labor that could keep their girth in check, so their avoirdupois is a sign of an enviable life of luxury. Thus, prior to the 20th century, most cultures considered corpulence a virtue to be pursued.

> During the 20th century, however, those attitudes have reversed in most developed countries. The most notable about-face has been among upper-class women. "You can never be too rich or too thin," declared the Duchess of Windsor in the 1930s, setting the standard for succeeding generations of socialites. (Powers, 1996, p. 16)

Another explanation attributes such cultural differences to the influence of religion. Banks (1992) reports that a review of the literature on eating habits reveals a long-standing relation between self-starvation and religious ideals in the Judeo-Christian tradition and suggests an association between contemporary anorexia nervosa and asceticism. However, asceticism is not a tradition limited to Western religion.

[In Hindu India] for nearly 3,000 years, ascetic yogis have struggled to liberate their spirits from the confines of human flesh. Swamis have buried themselves naked in snow or blazing sand, fasted until the meat melted off their bones. At worst, the body is a hindrance; at best, a moral battleground. . . . Asceticism is just as much the tradition of the West as of the East. Self-flagellating medieval monks and unsmiling Calvinist aldermen, celibate Shaker farmers and prudish Victorian old maids—our forerunners quite often displayed a horror of carnality. (Blank, 1996, p. 84)

Statistics on body-weight trends in the United States support the observation that people can subscribe to a cultural ideal yet engage in practices that conflict with that ideal. The U.S. Centers for Disease Control reported in 1980 that one-quarter of American adults were overweight. By 1991, that figure had risen to one-third of U.S. adults (Klein, 1994). Some observers have speculated that while people may view slim as desirable, if they live in a society featuring low-cost, tasty, high-caloric fast food, they may let appetite overrule the cultural ideal of thinness and thereby gain both weight and the guilt that can accompany the clash between a value and one's own behavior.

## Social Values

The social values in a folk psychology define the culture's conception of individuals' proper place in the society and of how people should treat each other. Of the many sorts of social values that may typify a culture, the two inspected in the following paragraphs concern status and morality.

### Social-status values

Throughout the following discussion, the term *social status* refers to the level of admiration that members of a society accord a person on the basis of attributes the person displays. Status levels form a hierarchy or vertical scale ranging from the highest admiration at the top to the lowest admiration at the bottom. A society typically has more than a single status scale, with each scale focusing on a particular attribute, such as wealth, lifestyle, education, beauty, occupation, service to society, religiosity, inventiveness (creativity), special skills, and more. Folk psychologies can vary in the attributes on which they base social status and in the composition of the resulting scales. This point can be illustrated with instances of status differences founded on material wealth, authority/power, and occupations.

*Material wealth.* The status people enjoy in different cultures can be influenced both by how people accumulate wealth and by what they do with the wealth they amass.

Among the Ron, a subsistence-farming people in central Nigeria, the society's folk psychology teaches that such valuable commodities as crops are owned by water spirits—invisible beings that furnish the water necessary for crops to flourish. Although it's agreed that those spirits are the proper owners of agricultural yield, the Ron still approve of people taking the water spirits' crops and converting them into wealth, but only if the wealth is then distributed throughout the community in the form of great feasts—food and drink for everyone. Thus, individuals among the Ron who are granted the highest status are ones who accumulate the most wealth and share it with the populace. In contrast, people who compile material goods and keep it solely for their own use are held in contempt, even accused of immorality. Although there are differences between richer and poorer Ron families in their material well-being, those differences are not extreme, because status depends so heavily on displays of generosity (Frank, 1995).

An interaction among social status, group solidarity, and productive exchange is demonstrated in the case of public gift-giving in rural Japan. Marshall (1985), in a study of life in the agricultural hamlet of Nohara in Japan's Aichi Prefecture, observed that, without exception, all 35 households in the hamlet gave a feast and useful accessories to the community on seven occasions during a family's lifetime:

> (1) the 42nd birthdays of male family members; (2) the 61st birthdays of male household members; (3) the 77th birthdays of male household members; (4) the marriages of male family members and female family members when the female's husband will become the household's successor; (5) the birth of the household head's or successor couple's first child; (6) the 50th wedding anniversary of a household couple; and (7) the construction of a new house by a member household in the hamlet. (Marshall, 1985, p. 169)

A month before an intended celebration, the head of the donor household provided the hamlet head enough funds to furnish a festive meal to which a representative of each household would be invited. If the sum was more than needed for the feast, then the remaining amount would take the form of a gift useful to the community as a whole—fluorescent lighting fixtures for the hamlet hall, electric fans, vacuum cleaners, cupboards for the hamlet-hall's collection of china, and the like.

These periodic events served three social functions. First, they promoted group solidarity by individual families entertaining their neighbors at an enjoyable feast and by their contributing items that made life in the hamlet more convenient. Second, the events furthered productive exchange by ensuring that people's surplus funds (beyond those needed for basic necessities) were distributed to others, an act that reduced the gap between rich and poor because the rich gave larger amounts and more expensive permanent items than did the less-affluent villagers.

Third, the gifts served to accentuate a donor family's rank in the social-status structure of the hamlet, with more generous gifts granting givers higher social status. This emphasis on social status in Nohara was interpreted as a reflection of the great significance accorded social rank in all branches of Japanese society.

The notion that a society's economic conditions can affect cultural conceptions of the wealth/prestige connection is demonstrated in Hatch's comparison of social-status beliefs in two farming communities, one on California's central coast and the other in New Zealand. When the Californians were asked to rank the area's farmers in terms of social status, they named as the most prestigious the farmers who owned the largest acreage and displayed the most expensive lifestyle. In effect, social status was based on wealth in terms both of property and of available spending money. In Hatch's opinion, his interviewees found that the task of distinguishing between farm families on the basis of affluence was easy, because the gap between the richest and poorest was so great.

In contrast to the simple wealth criterion used in California, the New Zealand farmers ranked their neighbors' social status by applying a combination of three factors—(a) farming ability, (b) cultivation or refinement, and (c) wealth. In regard to farming ability, Hatch observed wide differences among farmers in how efficiently they managed their crops and livestock. "The topic of who are good or bad farmers in the district, or in what respects a particular farmer is good or bad . . . is one of the first things [the local people] discuss when they comment on one another in private" (Hatch, 1987, p. 38). In social cultivation, families were ranked from the genteel to the rough. The genteel sent their children to prestigious boarding schools and deported themselves in a refined manner, whereas the "truly rough farmers are described as exhibiting the coarseness in appearance and behavior that one associates with manual workers in contexts like the pub" (Hatch, 1987, p. 39). In regard to wealth, New Zealanders assessed a family's acreage and gross income differently than did Californians. In New Zealand, the range of spendable income between efficient, large-acreage farmers and inefficient, small-acreage farmers was not nearly so great as in California because of the two locations' economic conditions. Large landowners in New Zealand typically carried heavy mortgages on their holdings, which reduced their net income. Furthermore, if they were not burdened with mortgages and thus enjoyed a high gross income, they were subject to income taxes which might take as much as 60% of their earnings, thereby markedly reducing their spendable funds. Thus, wealth, as a factor that combined with farming skill and social refinement to determine social status, was judged in terms of usable money, an amount that did not differ dramatically between large and small farming operations.

In the Sherpa culture of Tibet, there are no formal stratification distinctions as in India's Hindu caste structure. However, there are differences of wealth and status reflected in the concepts of *big people, middle people*, and *small people*. Big people are from the few families in the community that enjoy wealth and high status and thus form the top stratum of the social structure. On the bottom of the structure are the small people, members of a handful of very poor, propertyless families. Middle people make up the majority of the populace. They own property, are self-supporting, and identify themselves as "not-rich-not-poor" (Ortner, 1978, p. 101). Among Sherpas, there is widespread belief in demons who possess the least desirable of human characteristics—they are greedy, violent, anarchic, hungry, and always "attempting to corrupt others and subvert others' fragile good intentions [when those intentions] stand in the way of getting what one wants" (Ortner, 1978, p. 100). On the Sherpa social ladder, the "small people" who populate the lower rungs are seen as demonized—hungry, prone to steal and lie, sneaky, dirty, and likely to take unfair advantage of others.

> These views are supported by reincarnation theory, which says that these people were immoral in a previous existence; thus, one is somewhat justified in mistrusting them now. In fact, I never saw anybody give charity to the poor families of the village, or voluntarily do them a good turn. (Ortner, 1978, p. 101)

*Authority/power.* The word *power* refers to the extent of control a person or group wields over other people. The actual power relationship between two people (or two groups) is reflected in how—and the extent to which—Person *A's* (Group *A's*) behavior is influenced by the actions of Person *B* (Group *B*), and vice versa. If *B's* behavior remains unchanged by the actions of *A*, then *A* has no power over *B*.

The word *authority* refers to the power officially assigned to a position or role in a society. In other words, each lawfully recognized social position carries with it a statement or implication of the kind and degree of control the holder of that position wields over particular people, objects, or resources. The range of such authority differs from one position to another. The authority of a prime minister is obviously different from that of a police chief, secondary-school headmaster, shaman, trash collector, tenant farmer, father, or mother. Theoretically, a person's actual social power will be identical to the power authorized by that person's position. However, such may not be true in daily practice, since some individuals have personality characteristics and talents not in keeping with their authority. A weak-willed, intellectually limited king, who inherited his position from his powerful father, may not exert the control his position warrants if a strong-willed, clever adviser to the monarch becomes the proverbial "power behind the throne."

Each general social role (educational, political, military, religious, commercial, artistic, technological, philanthropic, and more) is organized as a status hierarchy, with some specific positions within that general role carrying greater prestige than others. In the realm of elective politics in the United States, the mayor of a small city is lower on the status scale than a state senator, while a state senator is lower than a member of the U.S. senate, who is lower than the nation's president. On a U.S. Army military-personnel scale, status advances through a sequence of ranks from that of private at the bottom, through corporal, sergeant, second lieutenant, first lieutenant, captain, major, lieutenant colonel, colonel, and finally to several levels of general at the top. In the Roman Catholic Church, the position of parish priest carries less authority and prestige than the post of bishop, which is less authoritative than that of archbishop, which carries less authority than cardinal. The ultimate authority at the apex of this religious hierarchy is the pope.

On authority/power scales, positions higher on a scale are officially assigned—or imply—control over greater numbers of people, more territory, and/or more resources than positions lower on the scale. In Catholic culture, the pope's decisions affect more people in more regions of the world than do decisions by cardinals or archbishops.

With the foregoing notion of authority/power hierarchies in mind, we now consider three examples of how such hierarchies may differ in folk psychologies around the world.

Among the Mandak of New Ireland in the southwestern Pacific, the most highly regarded authority system is based on the amounts and types of magic that individuals command. As in many other cultures, magical power for the Mandak takes the form of spells consisting of secret phrases and incantations designed to control objects and people—to make plants grow, to frighten animals away, to ward off disease, to heal the infirm, to harm enemies, and more. Spells typically require a specified sequence and number of utterances, with exact wording necessary to achieve the desired effect. Reversing the order of words or omitting a single word can cause magic power to fail. Adults compile a growing store of spells as the years advance, so that the older the person, the more spells he or she will own. "Because of the maturity requirement for employing some spells, people beyond their early sixties have the largest magic repertoires" and thus wield the greatest authority (Clay, 1986, p. 39).

In many societies, if not all, changing times can alter the characteristics that qualify an individual for a position of authority and power. Among the Tangu in northern Papua New Guinea, prior to the arrival of European colonial officials and missionaries, the individuals at the top of the authority ladder earned the role of 'big man' (*munika ruma* or 'community manager') by virtue of their skill as warriors, persuasive oratory in the village clubhouse, shrewdness in negotiating intertribal alliances, ability to produce valued products, special knowledge of ritual, advanced age, and the support of influential kin. However, as Europeans gained control over the region, increasing numbers of the Tangu became Christians, European material culture was introduced (tools, machines, modes of transportation and communication), and intertribal battles were forbidden. In this new social context, the traits expected of a big-man manager changed.

> Today, managers cannot rely on the unhesitating aid of kin or neighbours, nor can they exert influence through a clubhouse or count on their fighting skill and generalship. Instead, they are invited continually to maintain, prove, and demonstrate anew their ability to provide large quantities of foodstuffs for feasting exchanges. . . . For the Tangu, the value in producing foodstuffs for exchange, making artifacts, or having access to European manufactured goods lies in the way [those things] reflect skill, competence, shrewdness, cunning, wisdom, foresight, industry, and moral integrity. A mound of yams, or a fistful of feathers, or plaques of dogs' teeth, or a chest of European goods that did not directly reflect these qualities of their possessor would be pointless, of no value. (Burridge, 1969, pp. 38-39)

A different pattern of change appeared in the authority structure of Herero society in what is now the nation of Botswana in southern Africa. Prior to the arrival of Europeans in Herero territory during the 19th century, people lived in self-governing communities that had been founded by one extended family which, as time passed, was joined by other families. A person's position in the authority hierarchy was determined by two main factors—order of arrival in the community and a configuration of personality traits. The man who first settled his family in the location was considered the primary authority. People were obliged to do his will. Furthermore, as time passed, his position passed on to a close kin. However, whether others would willingly accept that kin as their leader (*omuhona*) depended on how well his behavior matched the Herero conception of proper chieftain behavior.

> First of all, he should not be too aggressive in his attempt to achieve the position. He should "go slowly to the symbols of high rank." The *omuhona* should also be scrupulous in his performance of his duties, lest the ancestors be angered and visit disaster upon the living. He must be fair in his adjudication of disputes and heed the advice of his counselors. He must not be overbearing nor seek greater authority than permitted, or his followers will simply pull up stakes and move elsewhere; and he will find himself a leader with no followers. (Vivelo, 1977, pp. 120-121)

However, during recent times a different criterion has replaced the traditional requirements for wielding control over villagers. In present-day Botswana, villages are no longer entirely self-governing. Instead, a national government with its bureaucracy determines who has authority over village affairs. In effect, the position of *omuhona* is defined by the overarching state. Consequently, the decisive factor in the appointment of a headman has become fluency in English, the language in which all official documents are written. No one with less than an upper-secondary-school diploma will be eligible, so that all but younger men are excluded because the middle-aged and elderly have had little or no formal schooling. The policy represents the central government's attempt to erode tribalism with its ethnic alliances that can fracture national unity. "By diverting attention from notions of descent to level of education, the government is emphasizing the importance of factors that are nationally determined and controlled at the expense of those that are locally defined" (Vivelo, 1977, p. 175).

*Occupational prestige.* Closely allied with authority status—but not identical to it—is the prestige associated with different vocations. Occupations can be seen as organized into general fields, with the specific occupations within each field accorded different levels of prestige. For instance, in the realm of medicine in North America, a brain surgeon is generally more highly regarded than a family medical doctor, who is accorded greater respect than a registered nurse; and the nurse is held in greater esteem than a midwife. It is also the case that one occupational field as a whole can be more prestigious than another. Within a folk psychology, the field of medicine may have higher status than the fields of education or law enforcement. The armed forces may be more highly regarded than the theater arts. Thus, the social status of a particular occupation would appear to be the product of interaction between (a) the status of the general field to which that occupation belongs and (b) the level of prestige of that occupation within its own field.

Researchers have often gathered information about folk opinions of occupational prestige by having respondents rank vocations by their social status. Such studies have suggested a high degree of consensus across societies about the relative prestige of occupations common to those societies. For example, during the 1950s and 1960s, a correlation of $r + .90$ or above was found in the ranking of comparable occupations by samples of residents in seven nations—Britain, Germany, Indonesia, Japan, New Zealand, Russia, and the United States. The occupations included those of physician, university professor, engineer, lawyer, head of a corporation or factory, military officer, schoolteacher, small-business operator, police officer, electrician, taxi driver, laborer, and others (Inkeles & Rossi, 1956; Thomas, 1962).

In attempting to account for such high agreement across cultures in occupations' status, analysts have suggested a number of explanations. One proposal has been that six factors found in all societies are accorded similar levels of value across societies, and people's judgments of those factors combine to determine the overall respect granted various vocational pursuits. The six factors can be conceived as dimensions, with each dimension serving as a scale for charting the social status of occupations.

> *Power dimension.* An occupation which represents greater power or control over larger numbers of people or over sources of greater wealth is accorded higher prestige than occupations which represent less power or control.
>
> *Financial-reward dimension.* An occupation which yields higher financial rewards is accorded higher prestige than one yielding lower rewards.
>
> *Crucial-role dimension.* An occupation which figures crucially in an individual's life at times of crisis (the physician at times of illness, the lawyer when a person is threatened with prison) is more prestigious than occupations that seldom or never play crucial roles.
>
> *Education dimension.* An occupation which demands more formal education will be accorded higher prestige than one which demands little education or training.
>
> *Mental-physical dimension.* An occupation which involves primarily mental-verbal activities is more prestigious than one involving physical work. (This might be labeled a white-collar versus blue-collar dimension.)
>
> *Service-to-society dimension.* An occupation which contributes more to the society's pursuit of its ideals is more prestigious than one that contributes less. (Thomas, 1962, p. 565)

Although there does appear to be considerable agreement among folk psychologies about the social status of certain occupations, there still may be occupational-prestige variations across societies as the result of conditions somewhat unique to different cultures. In way of illustration, consider the following examples.

In the landlocked countries of Switzerland and Transylvania, and in the Canadian provinces of Alberta and Ontario, the occupation of boat navigator is not accorded particularly great respect. However, throughout the Pacific islands, one of the abilities traditionally held in highest regard has been that of navigating oceangoing canoes over vast areas of ocean. Polynesian and Micronesian navigators accomplished remarkable feats of guiding their vessels to far-off islands by combining their observations of wind direction, cloud formation, patterns of ocean swells, sea currents, the location of the sun by day and stars by night, the roll and pitch of the boat, types of seabirds and fish encountered, and landmarks—at the place they were leaving and, when nearing the end of the voyage, at their destination. Navigators calculated their boat's speed by wind pressure, sea turbulence, amount and direction of ocean spray, and changes in the positions of sun and stars.

> The amounts of cumulative knowledge on which Island navigation was based constituted remarkable intellectual achievements—arguably the finest that any Oceanians ever achieved. Moreover, these systems of knowledge could be transmitted only orally, which attests to the mental abilities of the individuals who learned them, practiced them, and passed them along. (Oliver, 1989, p. 417)

Master navigators gained status not only by the complexity of their occupation, but by the crucial role their skill played in the survival of the society's members.

## Moral values

Moral values prescribe how people should treat each other. They may also define how people should act toward supernatural powers and the world of nature (animals, plant life, mountains, lakes, and the like).

*The nature of justice.* Recent decades have witnessed highly animated controversy among academicians over what principles should determine whether behavior is *just, fair,* or *proper.* Does morality or justice consist of (a) obeying secular laws, (b) treating everyone equally in terms of a social contract to which they agree, (c) abiding by the dictates of supernatural forces, (d) displaying compassion for others, or (e) maintaining societal equanimity.

*Obeying secular laws.* The Swiss developmental psychologist Jean Piaget (1948, p. 1) contended that "All morality consists in a system of rules, and the essence of all morality is to be sought for in the respect which the individual acquires for these rules." The rules may be in the form of written law or long-established, well-known custom. People who break the law deserve punishment, or at least rehabilitation, so they will henceforth obey the law. Or, if there is serious doubt about whether malefactors will abide by the law in the future, then their freedom of movement should be restricted, either by imprisonment, house arrest, or execution. In a strict application of this law-enforcement principle, the conditions under which people breach the law are not considered in determining their fate—"Commit the crime, you do the time." For instance, unconditional enforcement of the law appeared in Afghanistan after the fundamentalist Muslim Taliban (Students of Allah) sect took military control of the country in the late 1990s. The Taliban imposed such traditional Islamic punishments as cutting off the hands of thieves and stoning to death women found guilty of adultery.

> Since [the Prophet] Muhammad is believed to have said that music can distract a Muslim from Islam, listening to music is illegal. . . . In Qandahar, the

first major city the Taliban seized, which has since become their stronghold, a shop owner recalled: "Last week a man was caught listening to music. The Taliban police beat him badly, tied him up, hung his tape recorder around his neck and paraded him round the town in a jeep to show us what would happen to those who do not follow the law." (Willems, 1996, p. 6)

However, cultures often recognize mitigating conditions that affect the consequences a lawbreaker must face, and cultures can vary in what they accept as mitigating circumstances. In U.S. law, decisions about an individual's culpability in causing another's death are influenced by circumstances that differentiate among the legal categories of first-degree murder, second-degree murder, manslaughter, and more.

*Treating people equally.* An evenhanded-justice principle is reflected in the work of Lawrence Kohlberg (1976), who asserted that true justice consists of honoring universal rights for all people (equal justice) and of the overriding value of human life. In Kohlberg's interpretation of morality, simply obeying existing laws will not result in justice if those laws and their administration do not afford everyone equal treatment.

*Abiding by supernatural dictates.* A widespread conviction in many cultures is the belief that the highest level of morality consists of obeying the commandments of gods or spirits. Disaster in the form of illness, accident, loss of friendship, loss of personal goods, or a horrible life-after-death can be visited on people who fail to comply with the prescriptions of the supernatural powers.

As Rabbi Charles B. Chavel (1967, p. vii) explained, "The basic concept in the Jewish religion relating to practice is undoubtedly the *Mitzvah*, or the Commandment of the Lord. . . . To lead the highest type of Jewish life is possible only through observance of the mitzvoth. Whatever is conducive to that observance is held to be intrinsically good, and whatever obstructs it is held to be sinful, or intrinsically bad."

The Islamic Sunnah (Sayings of the Prophet Mohammed) reflects a similar concept of morality. "God saith, 'Oh, Man, only follow thou My laws and thou shalt become like unto Me'" (Suhrawardy, 1941, p. 82).

Christian doctrine not only implies a definition of morality like those of Judaism and Islam, but adds a further humanitarian requirement.

> And thou shalt love the Lord thy God with all thy heart, with all thy soul, with all thy mind, and with all thy strength; this is the first commandment. And the second is like this: Thou shalt love thy neighbor as thyself. (Holy Bible, 1930, Mark 12:30-31)

In the folk psychology of the indigenous peoples of Australia, morality is intimately concerned with luminous beings who inhabit *dreamtime*— that invisible place beyond the perceptible world to which a human's essence is expected to pass after death.

For the Aborigines sickness might be, but was more often not regarded as, simply physical illness. . . . Sickness tended to be regarded as a lapse from appropriate moral being. . . . For particular kinds of sickness there were prescribed medicines and techniques. Bleeding, binding, salves, packs, minor surgery, and amputation were among them. But behind every technique of alleviation or cure there was a feeling that it was the sick person's moral lapse that had to be cured rather than the physical symptoms; moral condition was generally regarded as more important than physical condition. The consequences of mere physical hurt or illness were relatively minor, but since moral lesion cannot exist in isolation, but must relate to others, the consequences reverberated to include all those who had had contact with the sick person. It was essential to try to find out all that had happened, and then to try to put the sick person's mind at rest. After death, especially if moral obligations remained outstanding, that incoporeal or immortal part or quotient of man which was destined to join the powers of the dreamtime might stay close at hand and manifest itself to kinsmen and others as a ghost or similar kind of being until, appeased through rituals, feasts and offerings, it was able to continue its journey into the dreamtime. The death of a man with malice or vindictiveness in his heart, with some score yet to pay, was a matter for great concern. His ghost would remain close to the living for some while, would annoy, hurt and injure the living until laid or set at rest. (Burridge, 1973, pp. 74-75)

*Displaying compassion.* A different foundation on which to base morality is a belief in the overriding importance of compassion, that is, basing moral decisions on empathizing with the plight of persons who have come into conflict with other people or with the law. Gilligan has argued that males and females ground their conceptions of moral matters on separate assumptions that derive from the different roles the two genders have traditionally been assigned in their societies. She proposed that in virtually all cultures, women's central activity has been in child care, whereas men have been charged with administering the society and its productive facilities. As a result, according to Gilligan (1982, p. 19), a woman's conception of morality that arises from caring for other people "centers around the understanding of responsibility and relationships, just as the [male's] conception of morality as fairness ties moral development to the understanding of rights and rules."

*Maintaining societal equanimity.* In some societies, the central moral concern is to preserve traditional patterns of rights and responsibilities among individuals and clans. For instance, the concept of justice among the Maring of Melanesia is not founded on a principle of supporting the law nor of showing compassion but, instead, on the need to protect the conventional system of interpersonal relations. Hence, the purpose of litigation is not to establish who is in the wrong or even if the law has been broken, but to restore the community's disrupted balance.

The crucial concept that Maring have drawn from their tradition and adapted to the [Westernized] trial situation is that of social balance or *kopla*; it is generally believed that justice is based on a restoration of equivalence between clans and persons. Accordingly, most trials begin with a pronouncement that its objective is to restore balance by "straightening" the matter. (LiPuma, 1994, pp. 154-155)

In LiPuma's interpretation, the motive behind Maring justice is the desire to protect individuals' and clans' ability to reproduce themselves and their way of life.

As men, women, pigs, and gardens were the essence of reproduction, any action that harmed them demanded violence, compensation, or both. Punishing an offending individual was not the purpose of compensation; the aim was and is to restore balance. Thus, a man convicted of homicide in 1978 was released two years later when his clansmen paid compensation. Most people viewed the jailing not as punishment, but as a means of forcing his clan to raise and render compensation. (LiPuma, 1994, p. 150)

*Differential application of values.* Frequently, moral standards are not applied equally to all people. In other words, the members of one social category are expected to abide by different moral values—or to be treated differently—than are members of other categories. As the following examples illustrate, categories receiving unequal treatment can be of various kinds, such as those of gender and of in-group/out-group.

*Gender morality.* A contrast between Mexican men and women in their standards of sexual behavior has been widely documented (Alegría, 1974; Coberly, 1980; Diaz-Guerrero, 1955; Hubbell, 1993). The idealized concept of the marital relationship stresses sexual fidelity to one's spouse on the part of both husband and wife. However, studies suggest that, especially in poorer rural and urban communities,

The reality is very often different. Young women marry hoping for a relationship characterized by trust and understanding. In contrast, young men expect marriage, after a courtship that imposes severe restraints, to provide license of sexual adventure. Typically they act on their expectations, and in time their wives are forced to accept "other women" as a permanent dimension of married life. An emotional disengagement then occurs, after which a wife turns to her children, female kin, and *comadres* for support. . . . If, in addition to being unfaithful, her husband is extremely physically abusive, a woman might be forced to leave him; otherwise [wives] tolerate flagrant infidelity almost indefinitely, so long as hope remains that their husbands will contribute to the maintenance of the family. The other factor, which from the woman's point of view is most conducive to remaining in the marriage, is the expectation that she [will] derive her social status from being a wife and her emotional gratification from motherhood. (LeVine, Correa, & Uribe, 1986, pp. 198-199)

This double standard of male and female sexual morals is obviously not limited to Mexican culture but has been a longtime feature of a great many societies. However, with the worldwide increase in women's levels of education—affording them a greater opportunity to become financially independent—and with more legally imposed equality for females, patterns of sexual morality between the sexes are moving toward a greater level of equality. What's been good for the gander in the past seems now to be good for the goose as well, and vice versa.

*Ingroup/outgroup morality.* The word *group* implies a boundary line encircling the individuals that belong to a group (insiders) and excluding those that don't belong (outsiders). Generic words that suggest the defining attributes of insiders include *family, clan, tribe, religious denomination, nation,* and *species.* Examples of terms that identify more precisely the membership of a group include *the Garcia family, the MacDonald clan, the Cheyenne, Episcopalians, Canadians,* and *humans.*

Often a culture's folk psychology defines—by outright declaration or by implication—how moral values should be applied differently to insiders than to outsiders.

Sometimes the difference between the recommended moral treatment of insiders and of outsiders is not stated as commandments but, rather, is embodied in the behavior of a respected leader. That behavior serves as a moral model to be copied by group members. An illustration is found in how God is portrayed in *The Book of Mormon*, exemplifying ways that Christians should be treated differently than non-Christians. Whereas God promises faithful Christians that they will receive such blessings as the ability to heal and work miracles and become fluent in many languages, he threatens nonbelievers with dire punishments.

> I will cut off thy horses out of the midst of thee, and I will destroy thy chariots; . . . and I will pluck up thy groves out of the midst of thee; so will I destroy thy cities. And I will execute vengeance and fury upon them, even as upon the heathen, as they have not heard. (*The Book of Mormon*, 1980, pp. 443, 521)

In the Middle Ages and thereafter, Gypsies—also known as Roma and Romany—migrated from northern India to Eastern Europe and Russia. Over the centuries, they gradually spread to other nations, all the while maintaining a remarkable amount of their own culture, despite their status as a minority within more dominant cultures. One noteworthy feature of Gypsy morality has been their applying different ethical standards within their own society than those they apply to the surrounding society. The matter of theft is a case in point. Roma ethics strictly forbid stealing from Gypsies.

If a gypsy is discovered having stolen anything from another gypsy, he is denounced publicly and is required to travel, eat, and even camp alone until he has repaid the injured party for what he had stolen . . . [and] he may also be required to work for an unlimited period of time without pay until he has repaid his debt to society. . . . [But] the gypsies' attitude toward theft from nongypsies [*gorgios*] may be quite a different story. Many groups of gypsies believe that to steal from a gorgio is not only not wrong, but highly commendable because of the courage and cleverness required to be successful. (Trigg, 1973, pp. 71-72)

The in-group/out-group application of morality is perhaps most blatantly demonstrated in times of war, when such virtues as honesty, bravery, affection, and self-sacrifice are expected to characterize the support one provides for one's in-group comrades. At the same time, the ethics of the in-group encourages its members to employ deceit, theft, physical/psychological torture, and murder in dealing with the enemy.

Whereas international conflicts pit one nation against another, communal conflicts involve neighbors as combatants. In Yugoslavia, ethnic and religious antagonisms have cast Serb against Albanian and Christian against Muslim; in India it's Hindu against Muslim; in Sri Lanka it's Singhalese against Tamil; and in Kalimantan (Borneo) it's native Dayak against immigrant Madurese. In addition to directly attacking members of what they conceive to be an enemy in their midst, ethnic and religious vigilantes destroy symbols of the enemy's presence. From Loizos' (1988) analysis of the periodic conflicts between Greeks and Turks on the Mediterranean island of Cyprus, he concluded that the underlying intent of unofficial militias is to maintain a distinct, single identity within the community.

These are very angry matters, which strike at segmented communal identities. It is essential in such matters that mosques and churches be destroyed, or desecrated, or converted to the place of worship of the other religion. Graveyards are dug up, the contents scattered, the gravestones defaced. Monuments to dead nationalist heroes are smashed, and street and village names rewritten in one and only one language. The idea is to wipe out all memory of the other group, to obliterate its traces, to rewrite past and present. (Loizos, 1988, p. 646)

## VALUES AND CULTURAL CHANGE

The apparent effect of cultural change on values relating to physical attractiveness and to gender roles can be illustrated with the cases of Pima Indians' increase in obesity and of middle-class Mexican women entering the labor market.

## Aesthetic Values—Body Weight and Shape

A variety of studies conducted in the United States have shown increases of obesity in the general population after World War II, and other studies have reported increases in dietary fat consumption during the same period. In one investigation, Price, Charles, Pettitt, and Knowler, (1993) reported a dramatic increase in obesity among Pima Indians that appears associated with greater exposure to Western customs and diet following 1945. Between 1965 and 1990 an examination was conduced of the body mass index (BMI = weight in kilograms/height squared in meters) of 1,128 male and 1,372 female Pima Indians aged 15 to 65 years who had been born between 1901 and 1964. The researchers found large increases in BMI among Pima Indian men and women in post-World War II birth cohorts (1945 and later).

> The parallel changes in body mass index, dietary fat, and exposure to Western culture following World War II suggest that culturally mediated changes in diet and level of physical activity associated with modern industrialized society may have led to the large increases in obesity in the Pima Indians and to smaller parallel changes observed worldwide in westernized countries. (Price, Charles, Pettitt, & Knowler, 1993, p. 473)

Apparently, Western values regarding a desirable diet and suitable exercise were altering traditional Pima beliefs about such matters.

## Social Values—Social Class and Gender

Two interlinked values subject to societal change concern social class and gender. To illustrate, Linda J. Hubbell has offered an example of such change in Mexico over the latter decades of the 20th century.

In traditional Mexican culture, middle-class status is distinguished from lower-class status in terms of occupation, wealth, and *cultura*. When Hubbell interviewed women in the city of Uruapan in the state of Michoacán, she learned that people in typical middle-class occupations included professionals, bureaucrats, teachers, some kinds of clerical workers, and owners of small farms or businesses. Manual labor was identified as lower-class work. However, such manual tasks as sewing and food preparation, as extensions of women's domestic duties, might be considered middle-class vocations. Evidence of wealth that qualified people for middle-class status included home ownership, the quality of home furnishings, estimates of current income, number of servants and cars, and children's educational opportunities. *Cultura* was reflected in people's values, level of education, literary or professional knowledge, and conformity to rules of proper behavior. "The middle class often believes that the lower class lacks these qualities essential to respectability" (Hubbell, 1993, p. 2).

Associated with such beliefs about social class are beliefs about gender. A conspicuous distinction drawn in traditional Mexican folk culture is between *machismo* (ideals about masculinity) and *marianisma* (ideals about femininity).

> Machismo, like ideals about middle class, concerns self-image and presentation of self. It includes the notion that a "real man" is one who can support his family. . . . Thus, a wife who works, either for wages or in her own business, constitutes a public admission that the husband cannot support her and their children without help. (Hubbell, 1993, p. 3)

In contrast, marianisma is a cultural ideal modeled on the Virgin Mary, who is portrayed as a mother sacrificing her own welfare for the sake of her children. Included in the marianisma image is the wife as "the most beautiful adornment of the home . . . a living testimony to [her husband's] manhood, wealth, and power" (Hernandez in Elmendorf, 1977, p. 148). Consequently, upper- and middle-class women "are socialized to believe that they are privileged to remain within this restricted sphere provided by their husbands, and must in return obey men and cater to all their needs and wishes" (Nash & Safa, 1980, p. 25).

The societal event that would challenge these values was the dire decline of the Mexican economy during the 1970s and 1980s. Confronted with rising expenses and potential loss of the husband's employment, middle-class families feared they would be forced into a lower-class lifestyle unless they could generate more income. One solution adopted by a significant number of families was that of married women accepting wage-paying work outside the home. This choice, so out of keeping with traditional folk psychology, was rendered bearable by means of stratagems designed to maintain values intact while permitting wives to engage in paid labor.

Hubbell's interviews with Uruapan women revealed a variety of devices working wives used to minimize the importance of their earnings and to maintain their husbands' established role as the family's provider. Wives' schemes included (a) avoiding talking at home about their work, (b) inconspicuously using part of their earnings to buy extra clothes and school supplies for the children, and (c) handing their husbands all—or at least a major part—of their earnings so the men would retain a dominant decision-making role.

> Husbands with working wives also have techniques for reinforcing their public image as the crucial income-earners, even though they are no longer sole providers. For example, many working women report that their spouses vehemently refuse to touch their wives' earnings. I construe this as a public claim that they do not need their wives' incomes in order to support their families. In such ways, couples rationalize the truth (that both incomes

are essential) to reduce the threat to the traditional male breadwinner image. (Hubbell, 1993, p. 7)

In conclusion, Hubbell's case of the Uruapan wives illustrates a phenomenon often observed in cultures during a time of rapid transition—values that fail to fit the society's changed reality tend to lag behind people's behavior that recognizes the new reality. In effect, people adopt rationales that enable them to bridge the gap between their changed behavior and their traditional values, rationales that continue in use until the values themselves catch up with the actual state of the world. The ultimate adoption of revised values often requires several generations, with youths more willing than their elders to revamp or reject traditional value commitments.

# 7

# Emotions

*Are the same types of feelings found in all cultures, does the importance of different emotions vary across cultures, and what sorts of situations are expected to elicit different types of affect?*

The words *emotion, feeling,* and *affect* are used here as synonyms for psychophysical conditions identified by such labels as *joy, anger, love, fear, happiness, shame,* and the like.

One of the issues about the emotional content of folk psychologies that has attracted the attention of researchers has been the question of whether the different recognized emotions are universal. In other words, are the same emotions found in all cultures? That question is the first issue addressed in the following pages. The second issue is the matter of how cultural teachings help fashion people's emotional reactions. The third is the matter of the connection between types of events and the emotions considered appropriate to those events. Finally, the chapter closes with an example of the relationship between emotions and cultural change.

## THE UNIVERSALITY OF EMOTIONS

The puzzle about the universality of emotions concerns whether (a) the emotions observed in one culture are found in all cultures, and thus are characteristic of humankind, or (b) emotions vary from one culture to another and thus are culturally constructed. Scheff's (1983) review of cross-cultural studies of emotional behavior led him to observe that

> Most universalists believe that the seat of emotions is in the center of the body, in the viscera. . . . Like Darwin, they see emotions as biological, genetically determined reactions that are universal in the human species. Most of those who take the culture-specific approach, on the other hand,

take the opposite position, that emotions occur in the mind and in the mind's reactions to the immediate environment, particularly the social environment. . . . According to the cultural-specific perspective, there is only one type of physical arousal, and this one type plays a role in all emotions. [So] the differences among the various emotions experienced—grief, fear, anger, shame, and so on—are not physiological but are caused by differences of *interpretation* of the same bodily arousal. In a context interpreted by self and/or others as one of danger . . . then autonomic arousal occurs and is usually interpreted as the feeling of fear. (Scheff, 1983, p. 335)

Scheff concludes that the evidence for the universality position is at least as strong as—"and probably stronger than"—the evidence for cultural specificity. What he believes may be the case is that such emotional responses as crying, smiling, startle, and disgust are fundamental and universal, whereas other more specific emotional displays may depend on culture. In effect, cultural traditions may determine the particular occasions on which *expressing* particular feelings is socially acceptable; hence, the culture governs the form those displays assume. However, the notion that the same general sorts of situations elicit the same types of feelings in different cultures has been supported by several investigations. From a summary of studies in which respondents from European, North American, and Japanese cultures were asked to link different situations with the kinds of emotions those situations would generate, Mesquita, Frijda, and Scherer (1997, p. 270) concluded that

> In all cultures, the important [types of eliciting events] were: good and bad news, continuation of or problems with relationships (e.g., pleasure from contact with friends, feeling rejected, fear of quarrels), temporary meetings (e.g., meeting one's friend for dinner), separation (e.g., journey), permanent separation, birth and death, pleasure (e.g., sex, music), interaction with strangers, and success and failure in achievement situations. The categories that were needed to describe the [emotion-producing] events for each particular emotion [anger, sadness, fear, happiness] were, to a large extent, also similar across cultures. Thus, there is evidence that particular emotions are cross-culturally elicited by similar antecedent [situations].

Another investigation involved students from Canada (57 French speakers, 54 English speakers), El Salvador (42), and the United States (62) answering questions about what they believed makes a person happy. The answers from all four cultural groups stressed family relationships, pursuing and reaching valued goals, and a positive attitude toward self as important, thereby suggesting a similarity of attitudes across the cultures. However, in describing conditions that affect a positive attitude toward life and self, Salvadoran participants more often referred to religious values and sociopolitical conditions, whereas North Americans more often mentioned hedonistic factors (enjoying activities) and personal power (Chiasson, Dubé, & Blondin, 1996).

Part of the difficulty in settling the universal/culture-specific issue comes from differences among cultures in the way emotions are labeled and described. The problem is further confounded when labels imply the sources of various emotions. This point is illustrated in Hollan's (1992b) analysis of how emotion terms among the Toraja of central Sulawesi (Celebes) often derive from the root *penaa* (breath).

> Someone with a "large breath" (*kapua penaanna*) feels healthy, energetic, and proud; someone with a "choked breath" (*pusa' penaanna*) feels dizzy, confused, bewildered, and so on. Under normal circumstances, one is cool (*masakke*) and one's breath unchoked, so that one feels alert, conscious (*mengkilala*), and aware of the implications of one's actions. In contrast to states of cool awareness are those emotions like anger, frustration, intense grief, drunkenness, or possession, in which one's breath becomes hot *malassu penaanna*) and choked. Under such circumstances, one becomes confused, dizzy, and no longer conscious or aware of one's actions. (Hollan, 1992b, p. 46)

A variety of other studies have been conducted to answer the universal/culture-specific question. The nature of such investigations and conclusions reached can be illustrated with examples of the emotions known in the English language as *grief, romantic love, familial love, romantic jealousy,* and *anger.*

## Grief

A useful distinction can be drawn between *grief* and *mourning.* Grief is the reaction a person experiences after the loss of a valued friend, particularly such feelings as anxiety, fear, despair, sadness, anger, and guilt. Mourning is the behavior a particular culture identifies as appropriate following a death (Sanders, 1989).

Consider, for example, how grief is expressed in different cultures on the death of a loved one. A literature survey of mourning practices in 73 ethnic groups revealed that 72 displayed crying as a prominent reaction to bereavement (Rosenblatt, Walsh, & Jackson, 1976, pp. 15-18). Only one group—the Balinese—rarely appeared to cry as an act of mourning. Thus, the survey's authors judged that there is much similarity among peoples' emotional reactions to death, with the tendency to weep probably innate. In slightly over half of the societies studied, adult females cried more often than adult males; in the remaining societies, no distinction appeared between women and men in the amount of weeping.  The differences between the two clusters appeared to be determined by learned cultural traditions rather than genetic inheritance.

In the 72 groups, the manner and extent of crying varied significantly from one culture to another, with the particular crying patterns apparently passed from one generation to the next by the young imitating their elders.  Among the Thonga of South Africa, following the burial of a revered member of the tribe, a lament would begin with women shouting loudly and throwing themselves on the ground.  Their wailing started on a very high note and gradually lowered in tone (Junod, 1927, p. 143).

Among the Huron Indians of North America, the death of a relative was traditionally mourned by women wailing for weeks, especially before daybreak, with their grief expressed in a diminished fashion for as long as a year.  During their period of bereavement, they refused to "adorn themselves or bathe or anoint themselves, had disheveled hair, and observed a sullen silence" (Tooker, 1964, p. 133).

In Ifugao culture in the Philippines, a female relative of the deceased would arrive on the scene to wail, usually with her blanket over her head, and her keening would often be joined by the other women relatives present.  Some of them might scratch their faces in despair.  Men would not wail but occasionally would slash their bodies with bolos, particularly if it was a child of theirs who had died (Barton, 1946, p. 147).

In the controversy about whether there are culture-specific emotions, a folk ailment commonly known as *susto* in Hispanic communities has sometimes been cited as a variety of affect unique to Hispanic culture.  From the perspective of the person suffering the disorder, susto is experienced as soul loss due to magical fright.  But from the viewpoint of anthropologists studying the phenomenon, susto has been variously interpreted as "a hysterical anxiety state, a result of the inability to live up to social role expectations, or as a biomedical link between hostility and hypoglycemia" (Houghton & Boersma, 1988, p. 145).  However, Houghton and Boersma have compiled evidence to support their proposal that susto is not an emotion unique to Hispanics but, instead, is a particular case of the general loss-grief linkage found not only among Hispanics but also among Anglo-Americans and peoples of other societies around the world. The authors argue that typical symptoms of susto are the same as those found in other cultures among persons who suffer loss that precipitates grieving. The symptoms include "nervousness, depression, fears of nervous breakdown, a sense of panic, 'peculiar' thoughts, nightmares, trembling, loss of appetite, loss of weight, reduced working energy, and fatigue" (Parkes in Houghton & Boersma, 1988, p. 146).  Loss-incidents that cause people to grieve can be of various kinds— death, marital infidelity, desertion, a friend's rejection, being dismissed from a valued position, financial setback, and more. Although in the Americas the incidence of susto is greater among women than among men, Houghton and Boersma (1988, p. 149) estimate that the disorder is not a sick-role that women consciously choose in order to win sympathy but, rather, "is a natural result of the Latin American female's more frequent experience with grief. A person with susto is usually treated by folk curers *(curanderos)* with either ethno-pharmacological remedies or religious rites. Pharmacological treatments include suppositories and oral unguents supplemented by potions and mouth washes made with vegetable substances (Signorini, 1982, p. 315).

## Romantic Love

Historians and anthropologists in Western societies have for some time promoted the belief that the notion of romantic, passionate love is a European contribution to world culture—a notion created in the Middle Ages in Europe, embellished during the Renaissance, and sustained into modern times. However, some evolutionary-oriented anthropologists and psychologists have recently explored the possibility that romantic love is a universal emotion, common throughout humankind. In an effort to cast light on this controversy, Jankowiak and Fischer (1992) surveyed information from 166 societies around the world to discover evidence of romantic love in those societies' folk beliefs. To guide their investigation, the authors defined romantic love as "an intense attraction that involves the idealization of the other [person], within an erotic context, with the expectation of enduring for some time into the future" (Jankowiak & Fischer, 1992, p. 150). They distinguished romantic love from the "companionship phase of love (sometimes referred to as attachment) which is characterized by the growth of a more peaceful, comfortable, and fulfilling relationship [that] is a strong and enduring affection built upon long-term association" (Jankowiak & Fischer, 1992, p. 150). The materials they analyzed included historical accounts, ethnographies, and such cultural products as legends, ceremonies, stories, songs, and dances. The indicators they adopted for assessing the presence of romantic love in a culture included

1. accounts depicting personal anguish and longing;
2. the use of love songs or folklore that highlight the motivations behind romantic involvement;
3. elopement due to mutual affection;
4. native accounts affirming the existence of passionate love; and
5. the ethnographer's affirmation that romantic love is present.
   (Jankowiak & Fischer, 1992, p. 152)

By applying these criteria, the researchers were able to code each of the studied societies as having either (a) love present or (b) love absent. Their results showed that romantic love appeared in 88.5% (147) of the 166 societies, with the percentages in different regions of the world ranging from 76.9% in subsaharan Africa to 95.7% in Western Europe and the Mediterranean.

> The fact that we are able to document the occurrence of romantic love in 88.5% of the sampled cultures stands in direct contradiction to the popular idea that romantic love is essentially limited to or the product of Western culture. Moreover, it suggests that romantic love constitutes a human universal, or at the least a near-universal. (Jankowiak & Fischer, 1992, p. 154)

## Familial Love

In contrast to romantic love is the affection that members of a nuclear or extended family are expected to feel for each other. The way such affection is expected to be expressed can vary among cultures.

During research in the Samoan Islands, Eleanor Gerber was puzzled by Samoan informants telling her that fathers severely beat their children in a spirit of love (*alofa*). The explanation she received for this ostensive "tough love" was that

> Fathers and children are closely identified, and the behavior of children reflects almost directly on the reputation of the parents. . . . Because of this close identification, fathers stand to be shamed if their children misbehave. They must teach them right from wrong, but children, especially young children, learn only with the incentive of pain. Concerned fathers, who worry about their children's capacity to shame them and wish to make their children good people, therefore beat them. (Gerber, 1985, p. 131)

Notions about what constitutes *family* and how family members should express their care for each other can lead to cultural misunderstandings when people from different cultures interact. This point is illustrated in an experience described by Dahl (1999) from his study of Malagasy culture on the island of Madagascar off the east coast of Africa. Twenty Malagasy families resided in a school compound that was supervised by a Western missionary family. The missionaries were considered by the Malagasy residents to be the compound inhabitants' *father and mother*. As the dry season advanced, the Malagasy residents suffered from a lack of drinking water. The missionary family had foreseen such an event and had prepared for it by constructing a cistern to collect water that ran off the roof during the rainy season. The Malagasy families sought to cope with the water emergency by sending their children to fetch water from the cistern. But the missionaries refused—"*Anay io*" ("The water is ours, not yours"). The Malagasy were shocked that their Western "parents" denied them such a vital commodity as water. Dahl (1999, p. 87) deduced that the conflict resulted from the two sides bringing the following contrasting cultural meanings to the confrontation.

> *Westerner interpretation:* The Malagasy does not respect our property. He is stealing. He has no individual pride. He is a beggar. He is short-sighted. He has not foreseen and prepared to meet the difficulties that may show up in advance.

> *Malagasy interpretation:* The Westerner has no concern for the extended family. He is not a good "father and mother." He shows no solidarity. He is selfish and arrogant, which is very bad. He does not respect the "good relationship."

## Romantic Jealousy

Jealousy, according to one definition, is "a state aroused by a perceived threat to a valued relationship or position and motivates behavior aimed at countering the threat" (Daly & Wilson in Buss, 2000, p. 29). Such a broad definition can embrace a variety of relationships, including those between siblings, colleagues, employees, teammates, parents, lovers, and more. *Romantic jealousy*—perhaps the most common kind—involves a perceived threat to a relationship with a sexual partner.

A distinction is sometimes drawn between jealousy and envy, with jealousy conceived as "fear of losing an important relationship with another person to a rival" and envy as a feeling that occurs "when a person lacks what another has and either desires it or wishes that the other did not have it" (Parrott, 1991, p. 4). In other words,

> Envy implies covetousness, malice, and ill-will directed at someone who has what you lack; jealousy, in contrast, implies the fear of losing to a rival a valuable partner that you already have. (Buss, 2000, p. 30)

Sharpsteen (1991) proposes that jealousy is a *blended emotion*, meaning a form of affect compounded of multiple emotions, "all directed toward the same object, but aroused by various and often conflicting aspects of the object or situation" (Arnold in Sharpsteen, 1991, p. 36). In the case of jealousy, the blend's components are fear, anger, and sadness. Thus, romantic jealousy involves fear, anger, and sadness at the prospect of losing a loved one.

The two sorts of evidence on which people judge the existence and intensity of someone else's jealousy are (a) inferences drawn from observing that someone else's behavior and (b) ways the someone else says he or she would feel and act in hypothetical social situations. The hypothetical situations are usually in the form of anecdotes or videotaped episodes depicting the loved one giving attention to—and/or receiving attention from—a person whom the jealous individual views as a rival. Studies designed to discover cross-cultural differences in romantic jealousy have used both direct observation and hypothetical descriptions for collecting data.

As in the case of other forms of emotion, frequent debate often occurs over whether romantic jealousy is innate—imbedded in one's genetic endowment—or learned. One answer apparently shared among many who study such matters is that "Although the capacity to experience jealousy is inherited, that capacity is actualized through social structures. Jealousy requires a particular culture to give it life—the wherefore for its expression and usefulness" (Hupka, 1991, p. 255). Hence, we could expect romantic jealousy to be found in all human groups, but folk psychologies would differ in the sorts of situations believed to warrant romantic jealousy, the emotional intensity elicited under various conditions, and the kinds of behavior expected from jealous people.

A social-structure interpretation proposes that as societies have evolved, each has provided different ways of organizing relationships among people, with those ways resulting in different views of romantic jealousy. In effect, various social structures give rise to different needs, goals, and values. For example, a society in which the nuclear family is the key unit of parents' sexual satisfaction, childrearing duties, and economic security will offer jealousy-evoking situations that differ from those of a society in which responsibilities for child-rearing and economic security rest in the broader community and sexual satisfaction is available from a wide range of partners. Hence, in the nuclear-family society, a husband's sexual infidelity poses a greater threat to the wife's economic security than infidelity does in a community-focused culture. Consequently, the nuclear-family society is expected to produce greater jealousy on the part of the wife. For cultures in which ownership and the control of most matters is vested in males (paternalistic cultures), a female's infidelity is interpreted by husbands as a major blow to the male sense of mastery and honor. Hence, cuckolded males become the target of derision and are expected to be fiercely jealous.

> A male member of the Kabyle tribe of Algeria is socialized to defend, as a categorical imperative, the honor of the family, the good name and renown of the ancestral lineage; and his own respectability, glory, and esteem. If the Kabyle's honor is impugned through, say, the illicit sexual relations of his wife, he is expected to disdain the deepest feelings for his spouse and kill the wife who has sullied the aforementioned cherished absolutes. Driven by the love of honor, he jealously guards it against

infractions with a vengeance difficult to comprehend in societies with other values. (Hupka, 1991, pp. 264-265)

Societies can also differ in the extent to which they consider jealousy on the part of husbands and wives to be equally warranted. Numerous cultures have maintained what is referred to as a *double standard* for marital infidelity. In Greek culture, if a wife has an affair with another man, her husband is dubbed a *keratas*, "the worst insult for a Greek man—a shameful epithet with connotations of weakness and inadequacy. . . . While for the wife it is socially acceptable to tolerate her unfaithful husband, it is not socially acceptable for a man to tolerate his unfaithful wife and if he does, he is ridiculed as behaving in an unmanly manner" (Buss, 2000, p. 52). Thus, it is considered more natural in Greece for a husband to be jealous of his wife than for a wife to be jealous of her husband.

In many places, the notion that marriage should be based on—or at least should include as an important component—the sexual attraction of romantic love is not viewed as an important requirement. Consequently, marriages are founded on other considerations—financial gain, economic security, ensuring a family's social status, providing progeny, increasing one's influence, and the like. Such societies as those of China, Japan, and Korea in which parents or go-betweens traditionally have decided whom a person will wed are examples of cultures that have not based marriage on romantic love. In those settings, feeling jealous over sexual affairs outside of marriage is not as likely to occur as it is in places that hold romantic love as a core element of marriage—unless, of course, the liaison outside of wedlock threatens a family's reputation or spouse's economic security, social status, and ability to produce offspring.

Romantic jealousy can be analyzed according to several of its components, such as individuals (a) feeling that their affection has been betrayed, (b) expressing aggression, (c) being emotionally devastated, and (d) seeking emotional support. The patterning of such components can vary across cultures. Bryson (1991) investigated combinations of such components by creating a questionnaire about people's reactions to jealousy-eliciting situations and administering the questionnaire to nearly 100 male and 100 female university students in each of five nations: France, Germany, Italy, the Netherlands, and the United States. The results of students' responses to jealousy-evoking situations showed significant differences across nations.

As an overall summary, one may characterize each national group in terms of its most extreme profile features: It appears that, when jealous, the French get mad, the Dutch get sad, the Germans would rather not fight about it, the Italians don't want to talk about it, and the Americans are concerned about what their friends will think. (Bryson, 1991, p. 191)

## Anger

The term *anger,* as used here, refers to a strong sense of displeasure and belligerence occasioned by a person's feeling frustrated, insulted, or wronged.  Anger is generally considered a universal emotion, found among all peoples, but its mode of expression can vary from one culture to another and from one individual to another.  Not only can ways of venting anger differ across cultures, but cultural traditions concerning which situations are accepted as warranting particular expressions of anger can vary as well.  For instance, among the Utku Inuits of northern Canada, displays of anger have been permitted only on rare occasions, such as in fury vented on a person who is being ostracized for seriously violating social custom and on sled dogs who misbehave (Mesquita, Frijda, & Scherer, 1997, p. 365).

As a contrasting example, Shokeid's (1982) study of Jews from Morocco, who had settled in two villages in Israel, demonstrated that the immigrants' habit of rude verbal and physical aggression appeared more frequently in their dealings with relatives than in their interactions with other villagers or outsiders.  The Moroccan Jews' reputation of being vituperative and short-tempered had preceded them to Israel, so their habit of verbally firing insults at those who crossed them was no surprise.  However, the sorts of people on whom they heaped the greatest abuse often astonished Israelis who were from other national backgrounds.  The Moroccan origins of such a style of social interaction was not apparent.  Some observers speculated that it derived from a long history of Jews in Morocco suffering discrimination, so their aggression served as a form of social protest.  Others viewed such aggression as a device for besting competitors in economic and political encounters. Whatever its source, the immigrants' mode of venting anger was a well-known feature of their culture.  But what Shokeid found most curious was the contrast in the frequency and intensity of verbal aggression toward relatives compared to aggression toward nonrelatives—that is, toward villagers from other families or toward outsiders who entered the village on business.  Contrary to the expectation that, in a spirit of familial affection and solidarity, villagers would be politer to, and more tolerant of, members of their own family than nonrelatives, observations of social behavior suggested just the opposite.  Brothers, sisters, spouses, cousins, and in-laws were the most frequent targets of angry outbursts. Expressions of anger toward outsiders were fewer and more subdued.

> The Moroccan immigrants that I observed seem to have been highly selective in their targets for both verbal and physical aggression.  Under similar circumstances of dispute and provocation, they more frequently and more violently attacked those individuals with whom they were involved in a web of social ties. . . . Disputes between neighbors from

different families were frequently far milder than those between neighbors from the same family group. (Shokeid, 1982, pp. 272, 276)

In seeking to account for this apparent anomaly, Shokeid proffered two explanations. The first was that there are more opportunities for conflicts between relatives who live in proximity than between individuals who are unrelated, because the relatives interact with each other more frequently and under more emotionally charged circumstances. The second explanation was that Moroccan Jewish folk psychology included a belief that the greater the closeness of a relationship, the greater the license to express anger without the danger of suffering regrettable long-term consequences. Such a belief was supported by the cultural conviction that verbal aggression is

> natural, a sign of purity of motives and sentiments. This attitude was expressed in statements such as: "Dirty mouth—clean heart," "He who has evil in his mouth does not have evil in his heart," "I scream but I don't keep a grudge." (Shokeid, 1982, p. 275)

Frequently, after having shouted out their protest during an argument, the antagonists would calm down and start home or "engage, often good-humoredly, in discussion on another issue" (Shokeid, 1982, p. 275). Or else, a few days following an altercation between family members, the one who had initiated the dispute might invite his adversary to a feast, and their earlier antagonism would be forgotten. The immigrants' folk psychology thus appeared to view the right to abuse relatives as a symbol of affection and family unity—as the privilege to offend the ones you love, and doing so with impunity.

In the culture of the Kaluli tribe of Papua New Guinea, expressions of anger are not only considered normal but also are respected as symbols of the openly angry individual's strength of personality.

> A man's temper, or 'tendency to get angry,' is a major feature by which Kaluli judge his character and assess the degree to which he is a force to be reckoned with. It represents the vigor with which he will stand up for or pursue his interest vis-à-vis others, and the likelihood that he will retaliate for wrong or injury. Anger is an affect that is both feared and admired. The vigor or personal energy a person is expected to have is broadly exemplified in an emotional style I have characterized as volatile, expressively passionate. . . . Rage, grief, dismay, embarrassment, fear, and compassion may be openly and often dramatically expressed. (Schieffelin, 1985, p. 173)

Whereas anger is an acceptable, normal emotion in some folk psychologies, in others anger is not tolerated. For instance, at the core of the Buddhist religion is the conviction that human life is plagued with suffering and sorrow.

Birth is painful, in old age we suffer from various illnesses and from realizing that death is near, and through our "100-year lifespan" we experience continual physical and mental distress—loss of limb, the death of a friend, a broken marriage, and more. We suffer from wanting things and not obtaining them. To those who say they have experienced joy in their lives, the Buddha explained that even moments of joy are cause for sorrow because we know the moment is fleeting and will soon be over. (Marek, 1988, p. 98)

Consequently, the proper goal of life is to diminish—indeed, to eliminate—all emotion, both negative and positive, and thereby achieve the peaceful state of nothingness known as *nirvana*. High among the feelings to be purged from the personality is anger, identified by Sherlock (1997) as one of the *three fires* (along with greed and delusion) that must be extinguished if people are to achieve nirvana. Anger is viewed by Buddhists as a form of suffering, because the angry individual suffers as well as his or her victims (Leifer, 1999). The Dalai-Lama (1998), as a modern-day Buddhist sage, advised his followers to be patient with others, even enemies. By feeling respect and gratitude for an enemy, Buddhists develop patience, avoid anger, and increase compassion, thus producing favorable conditions for progressing along the path toward enlightenment. Three cultures influenced by Hinduism and Buddhism are those of the Indonesian islands of Java, Bali, and Sulawesi (Celebes), where people learn to hide anger and dismay behind a facade of calm composure and equanimity that minimizes interpersonal conflict (Geertz, 1960).

## LEARNING EMOTIONAL RESPONSES

Schieffelin (1985, p. 169) has proposed that children learn that "how people feel in a particular situation is not only supposed to be 'natural,' given the situation, but it is also socially expected, or even socially required." Thus, in every society, the *how* and *when* to express feelings is taught by example, instruction, and the administration of reward and punishment from the time of infancy. Not only may the approved elicitor-expression linkages vary from one society to another, but the links may differ from one age period to another. For example, among the Kipsigis people of Kenya's western highlands, infants who cry from physical or emotional distress are immediately comforted by their mothers.

The idea of leaving a baby to cry in order not to "spoil" it would be seen as bizarre, and the American practices of letting babies or toddlers cry for long periods at night in order to break them of the habit of getting up was strongly disapproved by Kipsigis observers. (Harkness & Super, 1995, pp. 25-26)

However, by later childhood, crying is highly condemned by the Kipsigis, especially at the time of circumcision for boys and clitoridectomy for girls (puberty rites of passage). At that period of life, crying children bring disgrace on themselves and their family.

A study by Harris (1989) of Dutch, English, and Nepalese children showed that in all three countries children between ages 5 and 14 followed a highly similar pattern of development in recognizing various emotions. The younger children were adept at identifying feelings that could be revealed by distinctive facial or posture cues—*fear, happiness, sadness, anger,* and *shyness.* Then, beyond age 7, children could also cite situations that evoked emotions which had no obvious expressive display—*pride, jealousy, gratitude, worry, relief, guilt,* and *excitement.* However, the Nepalese participants differed from their European agemates in the life situations described as elicitors of various emotions. Specifically, the themes reflected in the examples offered by children in the remote Nepalese village featured

> the burdens and anxieties of agricultural labor . . . ; the pleasures associated with certain special foods or treats in an otherwise bland diet of rice or maize and lentils . . . ; [and] the proximity of serious illness, poverty, and death. . . . By comparison, the European children . . . inhabited a more protected world of toys, pets, and school. (Harris, 1989, p. 84)

Events generally considered disgusting can either be condemned and punished or else regarded as unfortunately necessary because they promote some greater good. In effect, children are taught to tolerate certain offensive situations, but their toleration can be accompanied by a feeling of marked discomfort. An example is a disgusting healing practice of the Yurok Indian tribe in Northern California.

> What are the causes of child neuroses (bad temper, lack of appetite, nightmares, delinquency, etc.) in Yurok culture? Yurok children are supposed to be able, after dark, to see the "wise people," a race of small beings which preceded the human race. If a child sees a member of this race, he develops a neurosis, and if he is not cured he eventually dies. (Erikson, 1987, pp. 384-385)

For treatment, the child is taken to a tribal shaman who presses her face tightly against the child's abdomen and sucks the "pain" from above the child's navel.

> These "pains," the somatic "causes" of illness (although they, in turn, can be caused by bad wishes), are visualized as a kind of slimy, bloody materialization. . . . Having swallowed two or three "pains," [the shaman] . . . puts four fingers into her throat, vomits slime into a basket, . . . and spits the child's "pain" into her hands. Then, as she dances, she makes the

"pain" disappear . . . until she feels that all the "pains" have been taken out of the child. (Erikson, 1987, p. 386)

Cultures also vary in the labels they attach to emotions. The feelings associated with what seem to be equivalent terms in different languages can actually vary from one culture to another. Such is the case with the emotional state and the interpretation allied with the English-language label *love* as compared with the ostensibly equivalent French *amour*, German *liebe*, and Indonesian *cinta*. These terms may not all imply exactly the same emotional experience in different cultures. Even within a single society, such labels as *love, fear, joy, guilt,* and *distrust* are not conceived precisely the same way by all members of the society, because each person has constructed his or her emotional state and interpretation from a different set of instrumental-learning, didactic-instruction, identification, and modeling events.

In summary, children learn from their society how they should label and interpret their feelings. But less clear is the process of how a given culture determines which kinds of events should generate which emotions. And least apparent is how—or even if—patterns of culture affect neural receptors and emotional states (Lewis & Saarni, 1985, pp. 3-10).

## EVENT AND EMOTION CONNECTIONS

As noted earlier, variations are often found as to the sorts of events that are expected to elicit displays of emotion. Among North American Indians, Apaches are considered "by nature" a people who like to laugh, particularly at people finding themselves in an embarrassing or ridiculous position. Outbursts of laughter are rarely restrained unless there is the risk of hurting someone's feelings or there are strangers around (Goodwin, 1942/1969, p. 556).

Cultures are also characterized by the dominance of certain emotions. An example is the prominent place of shame (*haka'ika*) or embarrassment in the Marquesas Island culture of the southeastern Pacific. All sorts of situations that would not cause shame in other cultures will bring on shame or "stage fright" in the Marquesas as well as in a variety of other Polynesian societies. Furthermore, the social function of shame can vary with the stage of life.

> Shame emerges in childhood, for Marquesans, out of a less valued and less differentiated "fear" (*ha'ameta'u*). The "shame" of the young may paralyze action when they are subjected to disapproval. With adults, "shame" is expected to function more as a guidepost to situations to be minimized or avoided. (Kirkpatrick, 1985 p. 110)

Shame is also an omnipresent emotion among Egypt's 'Awlad Ali Bedouins. A primary concern of the 'Awlad Ali is to protect their autonomy and honor, so the slightest threat to their sense of self-sufficiency excites a strong feeling of shame (*hasham*).

Just as shame dominates the emotional life of Marquesans and the 'Awlad Ali, so anger (*liget*) is the focal emotion among the Ilongot of the Philippines. In their respective societies, these key types of feeling

> were talked about frequently; constant attention was drawn to situations relevant to those emotions; and the organization of social life was geared to steering those emotions in socially acceptable directions, either by avoiding them or by giving them shape in a socially acceptable manner. (Mesquita, Frijda, & Scherer, 1997, p. 269)

Differences in the socialization of girls and boys can account for differences in how females and males experience emotion-laden events, and those differences can vary across cultures. In a study conducted in India and in England, preschool and early-primary-school children in the two countries listened to a series of stories in which a central character feigned an emotion. The task of the children was to identify whether the expressed emotion was real or only appeared genuine. The Indian preschool girls proved more adept than either the English girls or the Indian and English boys at distinguishing between real and feigned emotion. By way of explanation, the authors suggested that girls in India are more often restricted to the home setting than are boys so that girls experience many more situations in which children are expected to show appropriate behavior toward adults.

> A greater emphasis is placed on deference and decorum in the socialization of girls than of boys. . . . [Because] the ability to conceal inappropriate emotion from significant others (i.e., to "be polite") is culturally valued, then it is not surprising that girls achieve this understanding at an earlier age than boys, given the pressure on them to conform. (Joshi & MacLean, 1994, p. 1380)

In both the Indian and English samples, the children's justifications for their answers led the authors to conclude that it was not a heightened sense of empathy that motivated children's close attention to adults' expressed emotion but, rather, the driving force was their desire to avoid "being smacked or scolded by adults, with the Indian children making many more references than the English children to physical punishment" (Joshi & MacLean, 1994, p. 1380). As might be expected, the ability to differentiate between real and feigned affect increased with age among both Indian and English girls and boys.

Misunderstandings can result from the fact that a label identifying a widely recognized emotional state within one culture may not be easily translated into the language of another culture and thus may not be comprehended by members of the other culture. An example is the emotional condition commonly expressed with a single word in certain Pacific island cultures but not adequately conveyed by any term in English-speaking societies. That word is *musu* in the Samoan Islands and *nguch* in the Ifaluk Atoll (Gerber, 1985; Lutz, 1985; Thomas, 1987). The emotional quality of *musu* or *nguch* can only be approximated among English-language speakers by an admixture of such terms as bored, irritable, not up to it, kind of sick, distressed, fed up, and dissatisfied. In islanders' tradition, feeling *musu* is an acceptable reason for getting up late in the morning, being absent from school or work, or avoiding routine responsibilities. In an islander's home culture

> One's musu is a sufficient explanation; it is never questioned by others or justified by the person who experiences it. The self-attribution of musu serves, then, as a mechanism by which a person can avoid a burdensome situation while at the same time not having to admit to the existence of unacceptable feelings. (Gerber, 1985, p. 129)

However, problems arise when islanders move into other societies where pleading *musu* or *nguch* is of no avail—societies in which people are responsible for meeting their obligations despite feeling irritable and out of sorts.

## EMOTIONS AND CULTURAL CHANGE

Although the types of occasions that are expected to generate feelings may seldom if ever change in a culture, the acceptable ways of venting those feelings sometimes do change. The expression of anger is a case in point. Anger is usually, if not always, a feeling that moves an individual or group to punish another individual or group. In some instances, the anger is no stronger than mild irritation and disapproval. In others, it's intense fury. The sorts of punishment regarded as acceptable for expressing anger vary not only by the nature of the precipitating deed but also by cultural tradition. Within North American folk culture, some deeds warrant no more than a critical retort on the part of the person who feels victimized—as when another driver takes one's own intended parking space or when a waitress spills coffee on one's pants. Other deeds call for more aversive consequences—a stiff monetary fine or jail time for a driver who, under the influence of alcohol, has caused an auto accident. And people convicted of murder can be imprisoned or executed by hanging, a firing squad, or lethal injection. But in other cultures, these same types of behavior may be seen as deserving somewhat different expressions of anger.

Consider, now, one familiar kind of corporal punishment that has been changing at different times in different cultures. That kind is whipping, spanking, or beating unruly schoolchildren with a switch or cane. The tradition, known in Britain and its former colonies as *caning*, has been gradually abandoned over the decades in a variety of societies as their folk psychologies have grown increasingly sensitive to the physical and mental well-being and "rights" of the young. Newell (1972, pp. 9-19) has reported that the use of such punishment in schools was outlawed by Poland as early as 1783, by Holland in the 1850s, France in 1887, Finland in 1890, Norway in 1935, Sweden in 1958, and Denmark in 1968. Following World War II, Israel and Japan, along with the Soviet Union and its satellite countries of Eastern Europe, denied teachers the right to wield the cane. In contrast, corporal punishment by school personnel was still being permitted in Australia, Canada, New Zealand, South Africa, certain school districts of the United States, and a variety of other countries. Not until 1986 did the British Parliament outlaw caning in public schools, and only in 1998 was the ban extended to private schools. In mid-2000 an English court case involving a man repeatedly caning his 9-year-old stepson sparked the government to alter an 1861 law that provided parents the right to cane children as a means of "reasonable chastisement." The law was amended to bar parents from spanking their offspring with anything but their hands. Also banned was the practice of smacking a child's head, eyes, or ears (Gazlay, 2000).

# 8

# Humor

*What conditions and events are thought to be amusing or laughable, and why?*

For humor to qualify as an aspect of folk psychology, humor need not be created by laypersons. Indeed, most jokes, gibes, and caricatures are the products of specialists—jesters, clowns, pranksters, comics, harlequins, comedians, jokers, mimes, mummers, and cartoonists. So the characteristic that qualifies humor as a feature of folk psychology is the widespread enjoyment of humor by the general public.

Exactly what it is that members of a culture regard as humorous seems to be among the more difficult aspects of culture for outsiders to understand, because catching the point of a joke so often requires cultural information that's been left unstated. If people are to be amused, they must fill in the unstated information from a store of knowledge they share with fellow members of their society. Consider these three examples of one-liners from U.S. American culture.

Other than that, Mrs. Lincoln, how did you like the play?
People who live in glass houses should dress in the dark.
That was no ladle, that was my knife.

To appreciate the first of these, the listener must (a) recognize which Mrs. Lincoln is being addressed, (b) know the circumstances under which Abraham Lincoln was assassinated, and (c) tolerate the sort of irony that is referred to in American culture as *sick humor*.

To appreciate the second example, the listener must (a) already know the aphorism "People who live in glass houses should never throw rocks" and (b) enjoy being fooled by an unforeseen, yet logical, twist of the aphorism at the end.

The third example makes no sense unless the listener is acquainted with (a) English-language punning and (b) the following specimen of traditional vaudeville repartee:

Who was that lady I saw you with last night?
That was no lady, that was my wife.

Thus, the listener must first be able to catch the point of the original "Who was that lady . . ." joke, and then appreciate the alliteration (consonance) of *lady* with *ladle* and the rhyming of *wife* with *knife*, as well as to recognize that ladle and knife are both kitchen implements. A person from a non-English-speaking culture might retell the Who-was-that-lady joke but inadvertently substitute *woman* for *lady*, failing to recognize that those two words connote different meanings for knowledgeable native speakers of English. Such a substitution not only alters the point of the joke but alters it in a way that diminishes the amusement that the joke is designed to provide.

The purpose of this chapter is to offer examples of humor that can be properly understood only in relation to the folk psychologies of the concerned cultures. The examples include references to eight interrelated kinds of humor that are defined as follows:

**The unexpected.** An anecdote can begin with an introduction which, in people's cultural experience, will lead to an anticipated conclusion. However, in the midst of the narration, the expected conclusion is replaced by a different ending which, although reasonable, was not predicted. For example, "Hickory, dickory, dock, two mice ran up the clock; the clock struck one but the other one got away." People who are amused by such wit are perhaps laughing at themselves for having been misled.

**The double meaning.** Sometimes getting the point of a joke depends on understanding multiple meanings attached to words, as in the answer to this riddle: "Question—What do lawyers do when they die? Answer—They lie still."

**The ridiculous.** People or animals behaving in ways that are out of character with the norms of the culture are often the source of amusement. But what sort of behavior is worthy of laughter and what sort is not can vary from one culture to another. Furthermore, cultures can differ in their customs regarding the conditions under which unusual antics are considered humorous rather than in bad taste. Making sport of drunkenness may be amusing in a stage drama but may be censurable in a hospital emergency room.

**The forbidden.** Allied to the ridiculous is behavior that violates cultural norms but is permitted under certain circumstances. Clowning that serves as social criticism or pokes fun at people in positions of authority or honor may be allowed in particular settings, possibly because it's believed to serve as a social safety valve, helping release antagonism which otherwise might be vented in more disruptive ways.

*The analogically apt.*  An analogy consists of a comparison of objects or events on the basis of their having one or more characteristics in common. Laughter may be evoked by such comparisons as "Her Easter bonnet looked like an overcooked, three-egg omelet."  Or "President Clinton's second inaugural address was about as thrilling as a four-day camping trip in the parking lot of an abandoned auto-parts store" (Durst, 1997, p. 14).

*The exaggerated.* People may be amused by a description that is far out of proportion to what they customarily recognize as reasonable. For instance, "I was attacked by a mosquito the size of a stealth bomber." Or "This cat's a world-class speed eater.  Within less than a minute she can consume a half-bucket of sardines, 19 bonbons, four pounds of cheese crackers, a flagon of imported champagne, and a laptop computer."

*The ironic.* Irony involves using words in a way that suggests the opposite of what the words customarily mean.  "I just *loved* changing three flat tires during the snowstorm." Or "After he failed the lie-detector test for the third time, they began calling him George Washington."

*The parodied.*  A parody is an impersonator's imitation of someone's behavior, with the imitation drawing attention to—and often exaggerating—the subject's distinguishing features in a fashion intended to amuse.  The features can include physical mannerisms, facial expressions, vocabulary, grammar, opinions, favorite topics of conversation, voice quality, and mode of dress.

Cultures can differ from each other in the forms that humor assumes and the functions that humor is intended to serve.  The following examples illustrate (a) kinds of humor in different cultures and (b) effects of cultural change on the popularity of types of humor.

## EXAMPLES OF FOLK HUMOR

Two vantage points from which to analyze folk humor are those of (a) humor's forms and (b) humor's functions.

### Forms of Humor

Humor can be conveyed many ways, with certain forms more popular in one society than in another.  Forms include (a) a written or oral story, anecdote, verse, joke, riddle; (b) drama—a one-act or three-act play, monologue, dialogue, pantomime, dance, puppetry, musical comedy; (c) cartoon—single panel, series of panels, booklet, motion picture; and (d) music—a song or instrumental composition.

Some forms of humor are specific to—or at least closely associated with—a particular culture, such as circus clowns in Europe and America,

Punch and Judy puppetry in Italy, pantomimes in France, mummers at Christmastime in England and Northern Ireland, buffoons in Javanese shadow-puppet plays, female jesters at weddings on the Pacific island of Rotuma, masked jokers in the Chinese opera, comic *réog* quartets of Indonesia, and stand-up monologists on American television.

Certain types of jokes, riddles, stories, or verse forms can be unique to a culture. Two types from English-speaking societies are the oxymoron and the limerick. An oxymoron is a meaningful expression that amuses by its being composed of seemingly contradictory terms, as in *open secret, working vacation, pretty ugly, extinct life, small crowd, good grief, resident alien, skinny broad,* and a food market called "Little Giant Superette."

A limerick is a five-line verse in a traditional meter and rhyme scheme whose content is intended to be funny.

> An amorous gourmand named Tate
> Took a girl on an 8 o'clock date,
> But I cannot relate
> What this fellow named Tate
> And his tête-á-tête ate at 8:08.

Whereas a small quantity of lasting limericks—including the one about Tate—are refined enough for general circulation, the greatest number that endure are dedicated to risqué, pornographic, or scatological subject matter that appeals to the segment of the English-speaking public that is amused by the lewd. In the opinion of the editor of the 1,700 bawdy verses appearing in the book *The Limerick,*

> the clean limerick has never been of the slightest real interest to anyone since the end of its brief fad in the 1860's. Nor has this fad ever been successfully revived by the periodic advertising contests, exciting amateur versifiers to hack together clean limericks by the tens of thousands. (Legman, 1969, p. vii)

## Functions of Humor

Roles played by humor in people's lives include those of (a) therapy, (b) political subversion, (c) self-deprecation, (d) mockery, (e) censure, (f) amusement by dint of incongruity, (g) one-upmanship, and (h) stereotype exploitation.

### Therapy

In Saposnik's analysis of Jewish humor, he contends that

> Jewish comedy has historically been therapeutic as well as defensive. A shield against the world, it is also an outlet for aggressions, neuroses, anger, ill will, and just plain annoyance. Telling a joke, like a story, allows for objectivity, a placing of emotions outside the self to be shared by all. . . .

Jewish comics have a desperate need to communicate, to tell someone else their troubles, to ensure that . . . they are not alone in the world. The hurt begins in the frustration that is Jewish history: exile, dispersion, wandering, living on the margin, walking the tightrope between an unrealized heaven and an unfulfilled earth. The hurt begins in youth and may last a lifetime, but it is often submerged, kept to oneself, suppressed. (Saposnik, 1998, p. 311)

During and following World War II, sardonic jests about the treatment of Jews under the Nazi regime included the following pair.

Achtung! Achtung! No smoking in zer gas chambers.
Did you hear about the new German micro-wave oven? It seats 25. (Wilde, 1978, p. 89)

To vent some of the hurt and resentment at their societal plight, Native North Americans make sport of the images of Indians and their culture perpetuated by the dominantly white-European American society.

Being Indian is . . .
Watching John Wayne whip 50 of your kind with a single-shot pistol and a rusty pocketknife on the late show.
Having at least a dozen missionaries from 12 different faiths trying to save your heathen soul every year.
Having a Christian missionary tell you it is wrong to believe in more than one Divine Being, then listen to him tell you about God, Jesus Christ, the Holy Ghost, the Virgin Mary, St. Joseph, St. Patrick, St. Christopher, St. Francis, etc., etc.
"Graduating" from a reservation high school and not being able to read an 8th grade English book from your white urban friends' school.
Meeting at least two dozen anthropologists before you're 21.
Feeling that Grey Wolf, Thunder Chief, Smoke Walker are more beautiful names than Smith, Jones, Brown, or Johnson. (Lincoln, 1993, pp. 315-317)

## Political subversion

From ancient times, humor has been used by people of subservient status to express their anger toward their rulers. During the Tokugawa era in Japan (1600-1868), a rapidly expanding merchant class adopted humor to express its dissatisfaction with life under the samurai government.

The laws of Tokugawa's shoguns centered upon Chinese-derived Confucian traditions that placed restrictive doctrines upon many forms of social behavior. As an escape from this moralizing ideology, the masses turned to literature, and joke books were produced that gave voice to the merchants' intent to subvert rulers' decrees. (Dodge, 1996, p. 57)

Populations ruled by an oppressive regime often circulate anecdotes that ridicule the policies and practices of the government by portraying its personnel as dolts.  In the 1970s, this riddle was popular in Czechoslovakia.

Why do Czech militiamen go round in groups of three?
One can read, one can write, and the other is keeping an eye on the two intellectuals. (Davies, 1990, p. 81)

## Self-deprecation

A type of self-denigrating humor often observed among colonized peoples consists of a dialogue in which a member of the indigenous culture displays an inept command of the language of the colonial power.  A typical scene involves an exchange between an actor playing the role of a colonial official interviewing a native member of the culture who has learned a few stock phrases of the colonizers' language but fails to understand when those expressions are suitable.

Official: "I need to ask you a few questions.  First, what is your full name?"
Young man: "Very well, thank you."
Official:  "No, I mean, what do you call yourself?"
Young man: "I hope your wife is in good health."
Official:  "I have no wife."
Young man: "I am happy to hear that."
Official: "Look, just tell me your name."
Young man:  "Yes, that is a shame."

In such cases, the object of the ridicule is not the colonial power but, rather, the individual who is distinctly disadvantaged in the situation—the local person who is obliged to communicate in a medium over which he or she has little command.   Thus, an audience of indigenous individuals who themselves have no more than a flawed understanding of the foreign tongue are laughing at their own cultural plight.  "The implied criticism is turned inwardly to a collective self rather than outwardly to some authority, as is more commonly the case in comedy sketches" (Sinavaiana, 1992, p. 210).

In Russia during the final decades of the Soviet Union (1970- 1990), a spate of denigrating ethnic jokes—"perhaps better classified as invective than humor"— were being circulated about Ukrainians, Georgians, and Chukchis (Scherr, 1998, p. 495).   At the time, Ukrainians and peoples of other minority cultures were pressing for statehood, and the bitter humor seemed to reveal Russians' antagonism toward such minorities.  However, according to Emil Draitser's (1998) interpretation, the Chukchi japes were ultimately not about the Chukchi at all but had arisen in the

1970s largely "as a vehicle for political humor and later evolved into self-deprecatory jokes in which the Chukchi are stand-ins for the Russians themselves" (Scherr, 1998, p. 496).

## Mockery

Humor in all of its forms is frequently used to ridicule or caricature people or events. The humorist's intent can be to

- expose human frailties (self-exaltation, self-righteousness, self-deception, greed, pride, envy, dishonesty),
- mock deviations from social convention, or
- make sport of people who are famous or in positions of authority.

An example of mockery is the clowning performed by transvestites in the Lusi-Kaliai society of the northwest coast of New Britain Island in the southwest Pacific. During ceremonial activities, women dress as men to burlesque male behavior, including that of warriors, village chiefs, guitar-strumming youths, and drunks. The mimics achieve their comic effect through exaggeration, ridicule, and the incongruity of females posing as males. They also parody the actions of outsiders, such as the actions of overweight, arrogant white men and "self-important politicians who wear shoes, socks, and dark glasses and jingle keys in their pocket" (Counts & Counts, 1992, p. 91).

Mockery is sometimes risky business, since there is the possibility that an authority who is being burlesqued will later retaliate against the clown. Cultures can vary in their methods of coping with this danger. In Samoan tradition, the lead actor in a skit is the principal critic in lampooning persons of authority, such as talking chiefs, political leaders, pastors, teachers, or celebrities. The man in the role of lead actor is easily recognized, for he appears as a personified ghost in women's garb. Hence, his status is indeterminate—neither person nor shade, neither woman nor man. Such an uncertain identity absolves him of any blame for insults he delivers. As additional protection, he may from time to time step out of the role of clown

> to comment on the stage action as though a mere observer or to interact directly with the audience. Such a singular breaking of the dramatic frame serves ostensibly to distinguish the actor's real-life identity from that of the stage persona, who is purportedly animated by a possessing ghost. (Sinavaiana, 1992, p. 196)

## Censure

Jesting can also serve as public exposure of disapproved behavior. Such humor can have one light-hearted goal (amusing the crowd) and the four serious goals of

- informing the audience of behavior to avoid,
- warning people that even if they escape official sanctions for their unacceptable acts, they still invite the embarrassment and blame resulting from a public exposé of their foibles,
- avenging misconduct, and
- enabling jesters to escape the charge of slander by attiring their attacks in the guise of frivolous fun.

Macintyre (1992) found instances of both gentle and harsh censorious humor on Tubetube Island in Papua New Guinea's Milne Bay Province. An example of gentle rebuke was a pantomime performed by three women during a going-away party honoring Macintyre on the eve of her departure from Tubetube. The spontaneous drama took the form of a husband being caught by his wife in a sexual liaison with another woman, culminating in the wife's dragging the husband off in a highly distressed state. The scene was a comic rendition of an actual episode that had occurred in that village not long before, with the three participants in the original incident among the members of the audience witnessing the burlesque.

Harsh censure among the Tubetube involved a rarely used type of jesting called *kiyo*, whose purpose was to express public disapproval and exact both revenge and compensation for wrongdoing. In one case, the *kiyo* was performed by the kinsfolk of a dead woman whose now-widowed husband remarried before completing the customary mortuary exchanges for her death. "His offense was twofold—he insulted his wife and her kin by failing to observe mourning taboos, and the debts associated with a lengthy marriage were not settled" (Macintyre, 1992, p. 139). The humorous part of the *kiyo* appeared during the first of the *kiyo's* two stages, when the kinsfolk marched to the malefactor's house, shouting uproariously. But the second stage, involving a verbal duel, was deadly serious. The kin demanded compensation in the form of pigs and other valuables; in response, the widower's village defenders argued back, seeking to keep the compensation as low as possible.

> If the offended [kin] at any stage believed that the villagers were not readily going to give sufficient compensation, they reverted to the shaming, humorous mode—or threatened to do so. This threat of further public humiliation ensured that demands were met. (Macintyre, 1992, p. 139)

## Amusement by dint of incongruity

Laughter is often occasioned by incongruity, such as a mismatch between an event and the emotion it evokes. Consider this incident reported by anthropologist Elizabeth Marshall Thomas (1959), who studied the San (Bushmen) of the Kalahari Desert in southwest Africa. She reported that on one occasion when the Bushmen with whom she traveled needed meat for their meal, they shot a springbok they spotted in a field. The bullet hit the animal in the stomach, causing it to jump and kick wildly before dying. The San, greatly amused by such antics, laughed and leaped about, imitating the springbok's vaulting and bounding, a reaction in contrast to the anthropologist's own pity for the beast's plight. Following the incident, the San remained in good spirits, apparently delighted with the entertainment the springbok had furnished. The anthropologist judged that such an unsympathetic response resulted from San culture's lack of emotional identification with animals.

> The San . . . do not regard animals as sentient beings; the springbok's kicking in his agony appears to them funny because in their view the animal *pretends* to suffer pain like a human being, though [the San believe the springbok] is incapable of such feelings. (Koestler, 1994, p. 687)

So it is that what seems incongruently funny from the perspective of one culture's folk psychology may not be considered funny at all from the vantage point of another belief system.

A different sort of amusing incongruity is behavior that far exceeds the normal. An instance is that of mortuary feasting among the North Mekeo people of central Papua New Guinea. Extreme sadness at the death of a loved one is expressed among the Mekeo by the immediate blood relatives feeling unable to carry out their customary life roles. Despondent, they no longer work or fulfill routine duties, so their spouses and other relations serve as substitute laborers who temporarily bear the mourners' responsibilities. Finally, the mourning period is terminated by means of a ritual that causes great amusement for the grieving family members, thereby transporting them back into their normal life activities. The ritual is a burlesque mortuary feast (*ipani*) in which the laborers request food for the services they have rendered, and the grieving hosts respond by providing enormous quantities of staples and delicacies that the laborers are to consume. As the laborers gorge themselves, their abdomens begin to swell,

> and many make a show of intentionally extending their bellies outward and grabbing and massaging them so they will hold even more food. Soon, however, the laborers' gesticulations, facial expressions, and body contortions start to reveal momentary signs of growing satiation and physical

discomfort. Still, the laborers call out for more, more, and more food. It is this exaggerated eating and greed on the part of the laborers that constitutes the essential point of humor for the [blood relatives] watching. Although the [blood relatives] remain in death and sadness and are expected to cry and grieve rather than laugh, the vision of their overeating spouses and affines involuntarily elicits from them laughter, mirth, and in their terms, "happiness" (*engama*). And just as the laborers punctuate their greedy demands for more and more food with groans and gestures reflecting their sated conditions, the [blood relatives] occasionally interrupt their own belly laughs and near-hysterical derision to shout further commands in sham outrage. (Mosko, 1992, pp. 111-112)

## One-upmanship

People often use joking as a stratagem for verbally besting a rival. Such humor is known in American parlance as *one-upmanship* or *put-down*.

In North America, a formal version of the put-down is known as the *roast*, a public ceremony during which friends and acquaintances of a famous person amuse the audience with insulting, satirical gibes about the famous guest's appearance, mannerisms, interests, habits, and accomplishments.

In many cultures, members of one group use put-down humor to belittle the region or traits of another group, as in this German riddle about the low-lying territory of Ostfriesland.

> Why do seagulls fly upside-down in Ostfriesland?
> So they don't have to see the wretched place. (Krögersonn, 1977)

Or consider this quip by offered to me by a Montanan who intended to put down the neighboring North Dakotans through reference to the defeat of Colonel George Custer's U.S. Army troops by Indian tribes in Montana territory in 1876.

> Custer, addressing his troops on the eve of the battle at the Little Bighorn River: "Men, I have bad news and good news. The bad news is that tomorrow we are all going to be massacred. The good news is that we won't have to go back to North Dakota."

The following example from the Murik society on the north coast of Papua New Guinea illustrates a put-down exchange in the form of an implied analogy that can be understood only by those acquainted with Murik culture's double meanings for *betel nut* and *bush*. As Barlow (1992, p. 71) explains, "Two betel nuts and a betel pepper, representing male genitalia, are often offered by a female joking partner, who says, 'Eat and be happy.'" The word *bush* literally means the *forest* where betel nuts are gathered, but *bush* is also slang for female genitalia.

> First woman: "You don't give me even one betel nut."

Second woman: "There's betel nut. You go look for it. Lots of it in the bush."
First woman: "Ahh, too hard to pull it out. You pull it out and give it to me."
Second woman: 'So! You don't know how to get it out? You must do it
    yourself.' (Barlow, 1992, p. 71)

Thus, whereas the bandy between two women is ostensibly about gathering betel nuts in the forest, the pair are actually indulging in an obscene exchange about each other's generosity ("You don't give me even one betel nut," "You pull it out and give it to me") and sexual prowess ("go look for it,""do it yourself").

> The first woman plays the role of supplicant, challenging her partner to be generous. The second woman responds by mocking her partner's lack of initiative and know-how. The use of sexuality as a metaphor for resourcefulness is drawn from the context of a secret [women's society] ritual . . . [in which young women learn to respond to verbal attacks through] initiative, risk taking, and self-assertion rather than conformity or obedience. (Barlow, 1992, p. 71)

## Stereotype exploitation

A practice found in all societies is that of attributing distinguishing traits to members of an ethnic, religious, national, social-class, occupational, educational, or recreational group. All folk psychologies include ethnic and religious stereotypes. The way psychologies differ is in the sorts of characteristics attributed to different groups.

When the European Union was being formed, a wag in a sardonic mood drew on people's acquaintance with popular national stereotypes to propose that everyone within the union would soon display an identical personality composed of (a) the kindheartedness of the Germans, (b) the flexibility of the Dutch, (c) the culinary skills of the British, (d) the openhandedness of the Scotch, (e) the sobriety of the Irish, and (f) the humility of the French.

In time of war, populations are especially prone to denigrate their enemies in the form of humor. British sociologist Christie Davies (1990, pp. 178-179) has proposed that people are apt to believe that all members of a religious or ethnic group display the traits reported in any widely publicized incident that has involved only some members of that group. For example, in 1940-1941 an Italian army of more than a quarter million men was destroyed in North Africa by an Allied force of 30,000 who took 130,000 prisoners, including numerous generals. This event led to a rash of jokes picturing all Italians as reluctant warriors.

> How do you train Italians to be soldiers?
> First teach them to raise their hands above their heads.

> The Italian army has a new battle flag—a white cross on a white background.

> For sale: 10,000 genuine Italian rifles. Cheap. Never been fired. (Davies, 1990, pp. 174-175)

During and after World War II, German militarism under the Nazi regime was likewise ridiculed. The director of a holiday recreation site was described as greeting a newly arrived group of vacationers with:

> Good morning, happy holidaymakers. Please line up in twos. You will then march to the dining room. From there you will march to the swimming pool. From there you will march to the Dance Hall, and from there you will march through Belgium, France, and Holland. (Irwin, 1972, p. 106)

One of the commonest forms of ethnic humor in many societies depicts certain cultural groups as stupid. In the United States during the early decades of the 20th century, an entire genre of jokes about "dumb Irish cops" was widely disseminated, picturing the "Irish policeman as an ethnically distinctive and unqualified, uneducated, and unskilled political appointee who exercised petty but personal coercive authority" (Esar, 1978, p. 234).

In Davies's opinion, ethnic jokes that portray members of a cultural group as stupid

> indicate who is at the center of a culture and who is at the edge, and that the culture of the butts of the jokes is subordinate to and derivative from that of the joke-tellers. Ethnic jokes about stupidity are also jokes told at the expense of groups seen as static and unenterprising by those who see themselves as dynamic and competitive. In an open society, the jokes indicate the existence of a known and established cultural and economic pecking order of ethnic groups regardless of official rhetoric about equality or pluralism. The butts of the jokes may be liked or disliked, but they are not esteemed. (Davies, 1990, p. 322)

## HUMOR AND CULTURAL CHANGE

The popularity of different kinds of folk humor can vary with the times. Jokes, cartoons, or songs about ethnic and religious groups are particularly sensitive to shifts in the political and social climate of the day. Such humor typically stereotypes—and often belittles—the group at which it's aimed.

During the final decades of the 20th century, U.S. American society was engaged in a cultural shift that included attitudes toward ethnic humor. Whereas jokes about ethnic, religious, gender, and sexual-preference groups had traditionally been popular in the United States, minority-group social pressures that began most noticeably in the 1960s and accelerated into the 1980s charged that people who indulged in ethnic humor were being insensitive to the feelings of members of the groups that were the target of wisecracks. A growing number of institutions—schools, colleges, business firms, social clubs, government agencies—adopted either formal or informal policies condemning ethnic and religious jokes, with sanctions often applied to individuals who failed to abide by the policies.

> When the civil rights movement was in early bloom, public ethnic and racial humor in many places went through a period of heightened disapprobation. This attitude, whether affected or genuine, bespoke the belief that verbal respect between races was a part of the solution to the mass of problems the movement was confronting. It was not hip to sound like a bigot, even in jest. I can remember a time when the telling of a racial joke in a room of young people would make disapproving heads turn. (Doloff, 1998, p. 11)

Consequently, as one observer put it, "In many American circles an ethnic joke is ten degrees more evil than adultery and even worse than smoking" (Mitchell, 1991, p. 43).

At the same time, critics of the move to eliminate ethnic and religious wit adopted the term *political correctness* as a label intended to disparage attempts to curtail freedom of speech. Consequently, by the 1990s some reversal of the anti-ethnic-joke trend had risen, often in the semblance of societal maturity. As a result, verbalized prejudice—particularly in the public entertainment field—appeared again to be more acceptable.

> [This new movement's rationale], offered only condescendingly and infrequently by its professional practitioners, is that we are all so socially evolved and sophisticated these days that we can enjoy some laughs at one another's expense without meaning or taking offense. Moreover, it's argued, derisive racial and ethnic stereotypes can also be used in self-referential and self-mocking ways so as to actually ridicule and devitalize the misperceptions that have created them. (Doloff, 1998, p. 11)

Thus, animated public debate about the propriety of ethnic, religious, gender, and sexual-orientation humor was widespread. On one side were accusers condemning ethnic humor as socially destructive.

> I suspect that there are a lot of people . . . who relate to racial and ethnic humor in the old-fashioned way—as a method of indirectly venting hostility and encoding prejudices more succinctly in their minds. When they laugh at a racial joke, they are not laughing because a nasty old stereotype is being deconstructed, but because the stereotype affirms or coincides with their own ill-formed antagonistic feelings and fears of other races. [Legitimizing such stereotypes by their] casual use in the media makes many people simply more comfortable with them. . . . There are kids out there who are

learning their initial racial attitudes and vocabularies from such humor. (Doloff, 1998, p. 11)

On the other side were defenders claiming that the ethnic gibe and risqué humor in general defuses tensions by serving as a release for intergroup animosities, educates by exposing ethnic stereotypes, and undermines prejudices by showing how ridiculous they are.

> Today's puritans are a drag on our culture, impeding frank talk about race, sex, class, and sexuality, and deadening our public wit at the same time. It's no coincidence that in the 1980s, before multiculturalism killed racial jokes, productive discussions of race were more common. . . . The major problem with ethnic humor—that it is often deployed by the powerful against the powerless—is best answered not by silencing the powerful [heterosexual, male whites] . . . but by unleashing the humorous abilities of the powerless. Allowing ethnic humor means that blacks are allowed to make fun of whites, gays are allowed to make fun of straights, and women are allowed to make fun of men. (Segal, 1992, pp. 9-10)

In sum, at the outset of the 21$^{st}$ century, the status of ethnic, religious, sexual-preference, and gender humor in American folk culture was in a state of transition.

# 9

# Self and Not-Self

*How do people distinguish between one's-self and not-one's-self?*

The central conviction on which this chapter is founded is that everyone—or at least everyone beyond the earliest years of childhood—has a concept of *self*, a sense of "who *I* am" in contrast to "who *they* are." The *they* can be parts of one's own body, other people, other animate beings (apes, dogs, cats, birds, salamanders), and the world's inanimate objects (necklaces, firearms, houses, clothing, a plot of land). In effect, as people grow up, they discriminate between *self* and *not-self*. For the purposes of this book, such a self/not-self distinction is important because folk psychologies do not all agree about what one's self includes and what constitutes not-self.

Among theorists operating within European and North American tradition, there is a kernel of agreement about the meaning of *self*, but not all of them define the concept in quite the same way.

More than a century ago, the Harvard University philosopher-psychologist William James (1961) suggested that the *self* could profitably be viewed from two vantage points which he called the "I" and the "me" of self. The "me" component—defined as "the sum total of all a person can call his"—includes three constituents of the self-as-known: (a) all material characteristics (body, possessions), (b) all social characteristics (relations with others, roles played), and (c) all spiritual characteristics (consciousness, thoughts, psychological mechanisms) "that identify the self as a unique configuration of personal attributes" (Damon & Hart, 1988, p. 5). When questioned carefully, a person can usually describe much of what comprises the "me" facet of self-as-known. But the "I" portion is far more elusive, since the "I" is the self-as-the-knower, consisting of four kinds of awareness not easily cast into words—awareness of one's influence over life events, of the unique quality of one's life experiences, of one's personal continuity over time, and of one's own awareness.

Other theorists have defined self differently. Arthur Combs and Donald Snygg (1959, p. 124) proposed that the *phenomenal self* "is not a mere conglomeration or addition of isolated concepts of the self, but a patterned interrelationship or Gestalt of all these. It is the individual as he seems from his own vantage point."

Gordon Allport (1961, p. 110) described the self as a "kind of core in our being. And yet it is not a constant core. Sometimes the core expands and seems to take command of all our behavior and consciousness; sometimes it seems to go completely offstage, leaving us with no awareness whatsoever of self."

Michael Lewis (1990, p. 279) equated *self* with *identity*, which is "mostly cognitive—a set of beliefs about oneself that we refer to as a 'self-schema.' Identity, for the mature human, refers to our beliefs about ourselves, including consciousness and our similarity to and difference from other humans and nonhumans around us." Achieving identity "allows the organism to determine who it is and where it belongs."

Although many theorists have considered the self to be entirely conscious, Earl Kelley included unconscious functions as well.

> The self consists of an organization of accumulated experience over a whole lifetime. It is easy to see, therefore, that a great deal of the self has been relegated to the unconscious, or has been "forgotten." This does not mean that these early experiences have been lost. It merely means that they cannot readily be brought into consciousness. (Kelley, 1962, p. 9)

All of the foregoing conceptions of self are products of scholars functioning from a modern-day, Western European/American worldview. However, the analysis of folk psychologies reveals that such a perspective toward self is not universal throughout the world. As a Princeton University anthropologist, Clifford Geertz, has proposed,

> The Western conception of the person as a bounded, unique, more or less integrated motivational and cognitive universe, a dynamic center of awareness, emotion, judgment, and action organized into a distinctive whole and set contrastively both against other such wholes and against its social and natural background, is, however incorrigible it may seem to us, a rather peculiar idea within the context of the world's cultures. (Geertz, 1995, p. 29)

Thus, notions of self can vary from one culture to another. In this chapter, ways that people conceptualize self in different societies are first analyzed along two dimensions, those of (a) psychological identification and (b) stereotypical roles versus individualism. Then the presentation of self in different cultures is discussed, followed by examples of the relationship between cultural change and the self.

## PSYCHOLOGICAL IDENTIFICATION

As demonstrated by examples throughout this chapter, one obvious way that one folk psychology's notions of self differ from another's is in the features of the world that are believed to compose the self. This approach to analyzing the concept of self can be explained in terms of psychological identification. Such identification is the process by which someone envisions aspects of the environment—parts of one's own body, other people, other animate beings, inanimate objects, events—as being intimately bound within that individual's personhood. Perhaps the most obvious indicator of whether, and to what degree, an individual identifies with an object or event is the emotion experienced in response to what happens to that object or event. For instance, a mother learns that a child at school has won a prize for academic excellence. The degree of pleasure with which the mother greets such news suggests the extent to which she identifies with the child. If the winner is her own daughter, the mother will likely be delighted, since the child—through the process of identification—is part of the mother's self. But if the prizewinner is a stranger, the mother will probably be emotionally unmoved since she doesn't identify with that child; in effect, the strange child is not included in the mother's sense of self.

Two important dimensions of such identification are (a) the target objects or events which people consider—either consciously or unconsciously—as being part of their self and (b) the strength of identification as reflected in the intensity of emotion experienced upon learning of the target object's fate or well-being. A person's target objects can be of many kinds—one's family members, friends, pets, favorite restaurant, ethnic group, gender, political party, cherished clothing, religion, hometown, nation, college, admired movie star, and far more. The strength of identification with a target object can vary from high to low. This two-dimensional conception of identification is pictured in Figure 9-1 for a hypothetical 20-year-old youth in western Canada.

The few aspects of life included in the diagram are ones chosen to illustrate different strengths of the youth's identifications—his (a) own body and its state of health, (b) parents and siblings, (c) best friend, (d) the college he attends, (e) the province of British Columbia, (f) Canada, (g) the Grizzlies basketball team, (h) the welfare of gray whales, (i) the women's-rights movement, and (j) the campaign to save the Brazilian rain forests.

Aspects of life experienced as the most significant parts of the youth's self (William James's "me" or self-as-known) are located toward the left end of the "targets of identification" scale, with the estimated strength or significance of aspects symbolized by the greater height of their shaded region. Aspects experienced as of least importance in the youth's sense of self are located toward the right end of the scale as indicated by their diminished shaded area. Thus, from the perspective of the diagram, one's self-as-known consists of a graduated scale extending from aspects of life that are extremely important in one's sense of self to those that are of very little importance. Events affecting the welfare of the aspects toward the left end of the scale generate strong emotion—with joy, pride, and relief experienced for events that promote the aspects' well-being, whereas despair, guilt, and anger are experienced for events that endanger the aspects' welfare.

Figure 9-1

**An Identification Model of the Self**

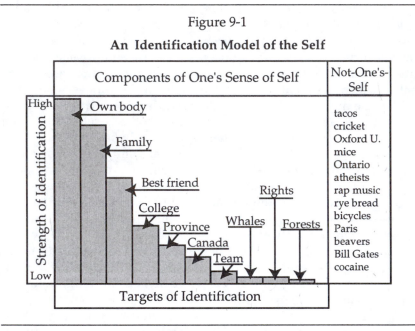

In summary, from the viewpoint of Figure 9-1, one's sense of self consists of a collection of aspects of life with which one identifies; and the strength of identification varies among the different aspects. The less a person identifies with an aspect (signified by the weaker the emotion generated), the more that aspect is felt as being *not-one's-self*. The millions of objects, people, and events to which a person is emotionally indifferent (as suggested by the 13 items in the right column) qualify as entirely *not-one's-self*.

## Cultures and Components of the Self

The things with which people most strongly identify, and thereby include in their sense of self, can be affected by culturewide values. Thus, the most prominent components of self in one culture often differ from those most prominent in another, as suggested in the following examples of groups and objects with which people identify.

## Groups

As noted in Chapter 1, in every culture each person is a member of various groups that can differ in their defining attributes—physical features, ideals, values, habits. Everyone incorporates into his or her *self* selected attributes of each group of which he or she is a member, with some of those characteristics assuming a more prominent role than others in the person's sense of self.

One of the most significant groups in perhaps all cultures is that of ancestors. A person's identification with forebears can be signaled in a variety of ways, including bearing a family name (an individual's last name in Western cultures and first name in Chinese and Korean traditions). The identification is usually closest with one's parents, particular one's father. Many cultures have followed the tradition of assigning sons names that identify their fathers—Rolf Stevenson (Swedish: Rolf, son of Steven), Jock MacDonald (Scottish: Jock, son of Donald), Isaac ben Aben (Jewish: Isaac, son of Aben), Sean O'Brien (Irish: Sean, descendant of Brien). People's identification with ancestors is also reflected in their treasuring objects inherited from relatives, dedicating offerings and prayers to departed progenitors, and performing rites that symbolize the continued existence of ancestors in descendants' current lives.

An example of such rites is the periodic *ohuma* ritual of the Kadara of northern Nigeria, a performance that features public dancing by young men wearing costumes donned in secret to represent masked versions of ancestors. Prior to a performance, the dancers drink special potions "prepared by their lineage priests which ensure that the personality of the dancer will be replaced by the returned ancestral spirit" which the ceremony depicts (Smith, 1982, p. 10). The music accompanying the dancers is provided by five types of folk instruments, the

> *Ininimi*, [a kind of] bullroarer; *ibini*, the special drum required to recall the dead; *ahusha*, the death flutes covered with cobwebs that make strange wailing sounds; *ahupe*, the gourds with holes that whistle weirdly; and *uyige*, or *tholi*, the open-ended bird-bone flute that emits a rasping sound. On the successive comings and goings of these ancestral spirits, their movements and utterances are signaled by [the instruments], all of which are rigorously concealed from women and noninitiates [preadolescent boys] in the *ebe* hut or lineage shrine. (Smith, 1982, p. 10)

## Places

One way that the significance of place in persons' conceptions of self may be demonstrated is in the age-old practice of including one's locality in one's name, as in Ponce de Leon (Spanish: Ponce from Lion Province).

According to Crocker (1977), in Bororo societies of Brazil's north-central Mato Grosso the two most significant cultural elements included in people's identities are their ancestry and the location in which they reside, with location becoming the stronger of these two determinants. The importance of place in Bororo tradition gains much of its strength from the fact that Bororo villages are quite isolated, not only from the broader Brazilian society but from each other as well. Rarely does any-one move out of the village and rarely do newcomers enter, so that "residence . . . has overcome blood as the basic mode of determining social identity" (Crocker, 1977, p. 130).

Personal, inherited songs have served as key components of self among the Chemehuevis Indians of the southwestern United States. These melodic epics—bearing such names as *Deer Song, Mountain Sheep Song,* and *Salt Song*—provided

> an oral map of his territory. Also the song described the hunter's equipment and the way in which these accoutrements moved in response to the swift and rhythmic movements of his body; and along with the character and "feel" of the land it conveyed a poignant sympathy for the animal hunted and a sense of the relationship between the hunter and the hunted. From the songs and from the Chemehuevis' attitude toward them one learns that the connection between a man, his song, and his [land] was sacred and un-breakable, and that the animal he pursued was included in this sacred unity. (Laird, 1976, p. 10)

## Objects and actions

Throughout Polynesia, as in many parts of the world, plots of land—and particularly land inherited from one's forebears—is one of the most highly valued components of people's sense of self. For instance, Howard's (1990, p. 265) description of life on the Fijian island of Rotuma focuses on the frequency and emotional intensity of altercations over real estate.

> Being associated with one's ancestors, land is at the very heart of one's sense of identity. To deny people's claims to land is to threaten the very core of their social essence and, by implication, their social worth . . . [so] it is no wonder that disputes over land become passionate.

Among the North American Plains Indians,

> Through the rigors and sacrificial elements of [strenuous dances and painful physical feats] individual participants often receive powers through vision

experiences, and the larger community gathered in support of the dancers participates [through identification] in the sacred powers thus generated. (Brown, 1989, p. 17)

Other symbols of self are tools of one's trade that form an intimate part of one's appearance of self.  The Mongolian horseman treasures his mount, the French classic-car restorer adores his auto, and the Japanese baseball player identifies with his favorite glove and bat.  In the Tobi Island culture of the Micronesian region of the Pacific Ocean, a man's adze is a public symbol of his masculinity.

> Reflecting its great utility as an all-purpose tool for everything from opening coconuts to building canoes, an adze is a very powerful symbol of masculinity.  Long hours are spent sharpening it, and a work-bound Tobian man would no more think of leaving his house without his adze on his shoulder than an American executive would set off without a briefcase. (Black, 1985, p. 259)

In such a manner, the symbols of one's vocation become elements of one's public identity.  The tools and the manner of talking about one's work—the nomenclature of one's occupation—help signify "who I am."

The most expansive concept of self is perhaps found in the worldview of the Navajos of New Mexico and Arizona, where

> The human personality is a whole with every facet [of the universe], interrelated both within itself and in relationship to the totality of phenomena seen and unseen.  Within this interrelated totality, everything exists in two parts, the good and bad, the positive and negative, or the elements of male and female; they complement each other and belong together. (Brown, 1989, p. 23)

## STEREOTYPICAL ROLES VERSUS INDIVIDUALISM

Another way of viewing the self in addition to the identification perspective is that of a *stereotypical-role/individualism* dimension.

---

stereotypical role                                                    individualism

### Stereotypical Roles

Some societies maintain a strict and broadly encompassing social-stratification system wherein a person is born into—and destined to remain in—a particular role within the system.  To a great extent, that assigned role defines the nature of a person's self.  The classic example of such a society is the Hindu caste system as practiced in India and on the Indonesian island of Bali.

Geertz pictures the Balinese as adopting a conception of self that features the position each individual occupies in the society's Hindu social order that was imported from India many centuries ago. Within the traditional Hindu caste system, people inherit their social roles via their parents' positions in the society, and they are obliged to remain in their inherited position throughout their lives. Geertz likens Balinese society to a drama played over and over according to an established script that defines the relationships among the characters and specifies how each character must act. Deviations from the script are unacceptable. Thus, uniqueness of self, so often lauded in European and North American cultures, is discouraged in Balinese tradition.

> There is in Bali a persistent and systematic attempt to stylize all aspects of personal expression to the point where anything idiosyncratic, anything characteristic of the individual merely because he is who he is physically, psychologically, or biographically, is muted in favor of his assigned place in the continuing and, so it is thought, never-changing pageant that is Balinese life. (Geertz, 1973, p. 62)

In this pageant, only the dramatis personae—the characters of the play and not the actors as individuals—are significant and endure. One's *self* is simply decreed by the role one is assigned by dint of inheritance. Hence, self is not achieved by virtue of such personal attributes as one's appearance, innovative intellect, or aesthetic taste. In short, the Balinese conception of self concentrates on the roles people are allotted and on the beliefs and values dictated by those roles.

In people's task of devising a self-identity, there are certain advantages to being raised in societies that urge individuals to fit defined roles and accept the group's beliefs.

> The interiorization of culture allows an almost effortless identity construction, . . . providing a system of meanings and values that automatically give them a satisfactory cohesion. The more individuals identify with the group, the more they emerge with a typical social personality common to all members of the group. . . . [In ideologically monolithic cultures,] members participate most profoundly in a culture that tends to be systematic and coherent, to occupy the ideological space without competition, and to be accepted without reservations because it is considered as originating in the transcendent and absolute truth. Communion in this type of culture tends to render useless, or to greatly reduce, the individual negotiations required by identity dynamics because the difficult management of the relationships with themselves and the environment has been taken care of by the group. This strong feeling of security reinforces an almost fusional identification to the social group. . . . It is therefore in these societies that the possibility for members to "individualize" themselves is reduced to a minimum. . . , [and people] are unlikely to be frustrated by the gap between their actual roles

and imaginary roles, unlike what happens in the West, especially in key moments like adolescence, with the well-known difficulties that this produces. (Camilleri & Malewska-Peyre, 1997, pp. 51-52)

## Individualism

At the opposite end of the scale from the stereotypical-role extreme are societies in which a broad diversity of selves is not only tolerated but even encouraged. In such individualistic societies, persons viewed as eccentric are cherished, so long as they don't violate others' rights.

From the standpoint of a person's constructing a satisfying self, individualistic societies have the advantage of providing multiple options from which to choose, thereby serving the desires of persons whose talents, appearance, and felt needs do not neatly match a monolithic culture's single personality model. For example, commentators on the attitudes within societies sometimes suggest that such peoples as the Dutch and Danes are more tolerant of individuals' unusual appearance and behavior than are Egyptians or Iranians.

## Collectivist/Individualist Dimension

Very similar to the stereotypical-role/individualism scale is a collectivist/individualist continuum that researchers often use in describing cultures.

---

collectivistic culture          individualistic culture

When people are asked to portray themselves, members of complex, individualistic societies more often refer to, and focus attention on, their private self (personal accomplishments and possessions), whereas members of simpler, collectivist societies more frequently mention their group identity (affection for others, obligations to the in-group). Furthermore, in collectivist cultures, social interaction is marked by a display of politeness and harmony rather than confrontation, debate, and disagreement.

On a collectivist/individualist scale, Fijian folk psychology belongs near the collectivist end.

> Individualism is loathed and discouraged for the sake of group solidarity and harmony. Few alternatives are available. Individual desires and wants are thus constrained, though everyone's basic needs are satisfied within the social and cultural framework of the kin group. (Ravuvu in Becker, 1995, p. 17)

Analysts of culture have frequently contrasted Western (European origins) and Eastern (East Asian origins) conceptions of self. A typical European or North American is expected to display an individualistic self which has resulted from an introspective search to discover "who I am as an individual." In contrast, a typical Japanese, Chinese, or Korean is expected to exhibit a collectivist, interdependent self.

> According to any number of ethnographic accounts, Japanese culture does not favor any such introspective quest [as that expected in the West] but stresses, instead, attention to the demands of others and surrender to social conventions. . . . As a consequence of the cultural significance of conformity and social obligation, it has often been argued that the Japanese must then have selves that are merged into a shared communal identity. (Lindholm, 1997, p. 405)

What is apparently the most thorough documentation of such a collectivist, social, interdependent self is provided by Marcus and Kitayama (1991). The authors' compilation of studies of self conceptions in societies around the world suggest that collectivist views of self are dominant in many Asian, African, Latin American, Pacific Island, and even certain southern European cultures. As explained by Lindholm (1997), Marcus and Kitayama have proposed that interdependent

> Chinese and Japanese do not feel or express anger or other strong emotions since they are concerned with fitting in and accommodating themselves with others. Chinese and Japanese and other interdependent people therefore are said to carefully arrange discourse so as to avoid giving offense or causing conflict. But if they have extinguished their capacity to feel anger or other antisocial emotions, why make the effort or organize conversation and interaction in such a formal fashion? (Lindholm, 1997, pp. 412-413)

Consequently, Lindholm (1997) has suggested that it's important to distinguish between a person's (a) private sense of self and (b) publicly displayed evidence of self, that is, one's *self-representation*. In Lindholm's opinion, people's public representations of self are strongly influenced by social conditions that affect how people learn to get along with each other and still satisfy their own needs. He suggests that members of East Asian "interdependent" communities have traditionally lived in close contact with each other, leading to carefully formalized interactions in order to maintain the surface calm necessary for preserving social relationships.

> Where "interdependent" individuals must continually interact with one another in their household and in densely packed face-to-face communities, Americans have the enviable capacity to simply retreat from interaction—simply pack up and move away. This does not necessarily mean they have different selves, only that the actual historical and cultural circumstances permit them a degree of physical and psychological distancing from others in a "culture of avoidance" that is less possible for their Asian counterparts, who must rely on formal etiquette to maintain the boundaries of

potential conflictual social worlds while protecting the psychic spaces of individuals. (Lindholm, 1997, pp. 413-414)

However, Hollan (1992a, p. 283) has objected to the practice of drawing sharp distinctions between so-called collectivistic and individualistic societies in people's conceptions of self, "because researchers often contrast simplified and idealized cultural conceptions of the self rather than comparing descriptive accounts of subjective experience." In support of his objection, Hollan conducted "nondirective" interviews with Torajans in Sulawesi (Celebes) and with Americans in the United States. Hollan's interviews with individuals' about their *sense of self* convinced him that "one can find evidence, *in some contexts*, of an independent, autonomous self among the 'sociocentric' Toraja of Indonesia and of an interdependent, relational self among 'egocentric' Americans in the United States" (Hollan, 1992a, p. 294). Thus, from Hollan's perspective, each person's self-concept can be seen as derived from two principal sources—the culture's value system and one's own particular values. We might then expect some commonality among individuals in the kind and strength of their identifications that come from cultural teachings and social pressures. But we also might expect individual deviations from these general tendencies as a result of each person's particular needs and life experiences.

## THE PRESENTATION OF SELF

The word *personality* derives from the Latin *persona,* meaning an actor's mask. Hence, in this sense, *personality* can be seen as the facade an individual presents to the world to represent "the self that I want people to believe I am." Folk cultures can differ in the approval they accord to various devices people use in their presentation of self. The three aspects of self-presentation illustrated in the following examples are those of appearance, social behavior, and names.

### Exhibited Physical Appearance

In all cultures, people meddle with their natural appearance so as to alter the image they present to the world. This penchant for humans to adorn their bodies accounts for a variety of societies' vocational specialists (cosmeticians, hairstylists, clothing manufacturers, tattoo artists, skin surgeons, bodybuilders) whose services attract the public to spend vast amounts of time and money.

The particular aspects of appearance and behavior interpreted as significant indicators of people's self-identity can vary from one culture to another. This point is stressed in Pollock's (1995) comparison of the use of masks in Western cultures, in the culture of the Kulina Amerindians of

Brazil's western Amazon region, and among the Kwakiutl Indians of North America's northwest coast.

> The mask works by concealing or modifying those signs of identity which conventionally display the actor, and by presenting new values . . . [ones] that represent the transformed person or an entirely new identity. (Pollock, 1995, p. 582)

Pollack proposes that in cultures rooted in European tradition, the most common mask of merrymakers at parties and of robbers who relieve victims of their valuables is an eyehole mask covering only the upper portion of the face in order to shade the eye-area from recognition. This tradition, in Pollock's opinion, is based on the belief that people's characters are most readily revealed by their eyes. Such phrases as "the eyes are windows to the soul" and "you can't trust a person who has shifty eyes" are cited as evidence of that belief. In contrast to Western tradition, Pollack describes identity masking in Kulina culture where, he contends, the key to identity is thought to be in people's speech rather than in their appearance. Among the Kulina, a person's ostensive self is revealed in what that individual says and how he or she says it. Thus, Kalina masks—the personas that people choose to exhibit publicly—are words and styles of oral delivery rather than facial coverings or body adornments. For example, in the *tokorime* healing ceremony, the mask that shamans adopt to transform themselves into mystical beings is not a facial disguise but, rather, is

> *song*, the special songs of the spirit animals represented [in the ceremony]. These songs present both the sounds and imagery that characterize the animal. During the ritual, shamans emerge from the forest, singing in the voice of the spirit they represent; village members hear the shamans singing as they dance into the village, and [the villagers] shout out the name of the animal spirit, or jokingly make the sounds characteristic of the animal—the grunting of peccaries or the call of a particular bird. The effect is entirely aural, a rich complex of songs and sounds in which style and imagery combine to signal the transformation of shamans into spirits, and in which the transformed identity of the shamans is expressed. (Pollock, 1995, p. 587)

Unlike the Kalina, the Kwakiutl create elaborate head and body coverings in the images of revered animals in order to alter the wearers' identity. In Kwakiutl lore, tribal clans' original ancestors were animals who shed their skins and emerged as humans, bestowing the totemic animal names that continue to identify the clans today—bear, wolf, seal, and the like. During ceremonies, the Kwakiutl transform their appearance in order to recapture the identity of their ancestors by donning masks in the guise of their clan's animal forebears. In addition, many Kwakiutl masks open to reveal a second mask underneath. The person was, in effect, a series of layers. . . . The outer layer displayed one's public identity, the public 'person,' while the innermost core was one's 'soul' or spiritual identity. The mask associated with one's [totemic animal] name displayed a form of one's identity. (Pollack, 1995, p. 584)

## Exhibited Social Behavior

When people witness an incident of social behavior, they often speak of the event in either one of two ways. The first way is to evaluate the act itself—"That was a generous thing to do" or "That was a mean trick." The second way is to interpret the act as an indicator of a character trait of the actor—"That's a generous woman" or "He's a mean-spirited kid."

In interactions between people from different cultures, the distinction between these two ways of viewing social behavior is important for two reasons. First, two folk psychologies can differ in the kinds of self-characteristics they hold as admirable and the kinds they condemn as deplorable. Thus, social behavior approved in one culture may not be approved in the other. And if a single incident is accepted as representing an observed actor's true and abiding self rather than as a somewhat unique event, the observer will identify the actor as "that kind of person" rather than see the event as merely "that kind of act"—an act that cannot be understood without information about the multiple conditions that combined to produce it. I believe that people often regard single instances of social behavior on the part of persons from other cultures as indicators of those persons' enduring traits. When such inferred traits are ones approved in one's own culture, the observed persons are regarded favorably. When the traits are disapproved in one's own culture, the persons are viewed with suspicion and dislike.

The following examples illustrate traits of persons' public selves that may differ from one folk psychology to another.

A much-debated issue over the centuries has been the question of whether there is such a thing as *national character*. Do the people of one nation exhibit a shared public self that differs from the shared public self displayed by people of another nation? Or is the idea of national character merely a fiction, the perpetuation of stereotypes and prejudices that have no basis in fact? Alex Inkeles (1997) sought to settle this issue by interviewing—and administering personality tests to—a sampling of Germans, Russians, and U.S. Americans. His analysis of the resulting data convinced him that there were, indeed, personality traits common to members of a nation that distinguished them from members of other nations. Inkeles proposed that a people's public displays of self were manifestations of underlying personality traits, and those traits were a product of "the unique social, economic, and political conditions existing in any country, rather than as products of race or as innate national traits. As such they are mutable, subject to change and in some respects to control and planned development" (Inkeles, 1997, p. 133). In other words, a population's putative national character, according to Inkeles, is a learned, cultural creation rather than a biological necessity.

To support his proposal, Inkeles first collected evidence from Germans immediately following World War II. He concluded that the two dominant components of German national character during the 1930s and 1940s were (a) an emotional, idealistic, active, romantic element and (b) an orderly, hardworking, hierarchy-preoccupied, methodological, submissive, gregarious, materialistic factor (p. 132).

> Changes in these distinctive patterns cannot ordinarily be effected by a direct assault on the patterns themselves, but must come from changes in the political and socioeconomic situation which gave rise to them. To proceed by direct assault on the values of an entire nation is to ensure only unstable, fleeting, surface results, and may, because of the induced conflict between new values and an old social system, introduce strains and tensions which can have serious unintended consequences in the form of new outbreaks of social unrest and communal upheaval. (Inkeles, 1997, p. 133)

Inkeles did not assume that every German had precisely the same public display of self or underlying character traits. But though he recognized significant individual personality differences among citizens, he still contended that certain traits were held in common to form a *modal personality*, meaning a pattern of personality features widespread in the population. He also suggested that there might be more than one modal pattern in a nation, reflecting differences among subgroups, such as ethnic, social-class, or religious factions.

In contrast to the German national character that Inkeles abstracted from his data, he identified a Russian national character from the in-depth study of 329 individuals who had fled from the Soviet Union for political reasons or to enjoy a better standard of living. Personality traits that appeared to be frequent among these Russians included needs for affiliation and dependence (security), free acceptance of their own basic dispositions (oral gratification, sex, aggression, dependence), a conflict between polarities (trust versus mistrust, optimism versus pessimism, faith versus despair), high self-esteem, high emotional expressiveness, and grandiose planning without attention to necessary details. That this personality profile may not apply to all Russians should be apparent, since the sample of informants was small and consisted of refugees rather than permanent residents of the former Soviet Union. Thus, this particular trait pattern is best seen as a modal personality for a specific class of Russians at a given time in history.

Inkeles's study of Americans led him to conclude that a traditional modal national character included beliefs in self-reliance, independence (freedom to act), initiative, persistence, cooperative action (working in groups), trusting others, a sense of efficacy (in contrast to fatalism), optimism, openness to new experience (progressivism), equality, and anti-authoritarianism. These values, Inkeles asserted, are traditional ones carried over from the early days of the republic. However, they are not immutable. Three changes in this American folk personality that Inkeles identified during recent decades include (a) greater tolerance of ethnic, religious, and sexual diversity, (b) an erosion of confidence in political institutions, and (c) a decline in the ethic of hard work, temperance, and frugality.

## Names

In many cultures—perhaps all—the names that people are given, or that they adopt, are frequently intended to imply attributes of those individuals' public selves. Among Jews, Christians, and Muslims alike, such appellations as Moses, David, and Solomon are assumed to suggest that modern-day bearers of those names include in their personalities admirable traits of their original name-holders. Likewise, among Christians the name Mary is linked to the revered mother of Jesus or perhaps to a respected forebear in a present-day Mary's ancestral line. Not only is the name Mohammed the most popular male forename among Muslims, but also apparently is the most frequent in all cultures combined.

Titles appended to individuals' original names, usually during adulthood, are meant to suggest some characteristic of the name holder, with the title often becoming an intimate part of—or substitute for—the individual's original name. *Christ*, meaning *savior*, is such a term. And *Buddha*, meaning *the enlightened one*, is far better known than the famous religious leader's actual name, Gautama Siddhartha.

Sometimes the virtue that parents hope their offspring will embody is directly stated as the child's name—Chastity, Victoria, Purity, Verity, Noble, Courage. And among the North American Plains Indians, during the pubertal rite when youths would go into the wilderness to endure austerities, their task during this vision quest included viewing sights and hearing sounds from which they would gain the name they would bear the rest of their life—Running Wolf, Brown Rabbit, Swift Stream, Sitting Bull, Buffalo Slayer. Or else a name acquired in later childhood, youth, or adulthood would signify a notable characteristic of the bearer—Tall Elk, Crippled Deer.

In the Bororo culture of Brazil, acquiring a name not only signifies that its bearer has a social identity, but the act of assigning a name is also what generates the person's soul and makes the individual human.

> When the Bororo infant seems to have survived the dangers of the first six to ten months of life, the name-giving ceremony takes place. Up to this point the child's death would have had no social implications whatsoever; its corpse would have been enterred privately by its parents in the same manner used to bury domestic animals. But, given a name, the infant possesses a persona or, in Bororo idiom, a soul (*aroe*) which constitutes an identity that, should he die, requires a complete funeral. (Crocker, 1977, pp. 131-132)

The identification of the name with the person in some cultures is so strong that the name itself is assumed to produce the effect it implies. Among Marshall Islanders in the north-central Pacific, people of high rank have been given names incorporating the word for sky or heaven (*lan*), intended to signal the bearers' deified status.

> Chiefly babies were named soon after birth; born sacrosanct, their power increased throughout life and even into death. Sacred sobriquets still exist, and their mere mention, whether the bearers are alive or dead, could evoke reactions of fear. Not only did royal namebearers maintain extraordinary control of supernatural power, recitation of a praenomen could invoke those powers from afar and cause harm to common people on earth. (Carucci, 1984, p. 143)

Judeo-Christian-Islamic tradition teaches that persons who utter the name of God or revered prophets (Jesus, Mohammed) in jest or anger ("saying the Lord's name in vain") invite disaster. Hence the injunction against using sacred names as curse words.

## SELF AND CULTURAL CHANGE

As the ethnic and religious composition of societies becomes increasingly diverse, folk psychologies appear to move from collectivist toward individualized conceptions of self. During recent decades, the process of societal diversification has accelerated as technological advances in communication and transportation have improved people's ability to learn about other cultures and to move easily from one society to another. Consequently, within modernizing societies, greater varieties of belief and behavior become available. As the diversity of cultural options increases, the society—in order to maintain peace and amity—becomes more tolerant of people choosing among options. Consequently, the *selves* found in such a society become more individualistic.

Although societal tolerance for multiple types of self enables a person to more easily construct a self suited to his or her felt needs, such freedom is accompanied by the problem of individuals maintaining a secure identity.

Modern societies create and reinforce a crisis of meanings, because social mobility brings individuals into contact with different or conflicting values that constantly test the unity of meanings on which they live. Furthermore, the cultural system having changed, individuals must themselves reestablish this unity [of meanings]. . . . The process is difficult and the results obtained more fragile, because they are less backed by social confirmation. Given the possibilities of social mobility and the intense competition in all aspects of Western societies, the self-image of individuals is constantly being threatened more than in traditional groups. (Camilleri & Malewska-Peyre, 1997, p. 54)

When people move from one culture into another, their original ethnic, national, and religious identity is at risk, with the risk in proportion to the degree of difference between the contending cultures. This has been demonstrated in a study comparing individuals' cultural identities among (a) immigrants to France from the Maghreb countries (Algeria, Libya, Morocco, Tunisia), Portugal, and Spain and (b) immigrants to the United States from Poland (Malewska-Peyre & Zaleska, 1980). Adolescent children of second-generation Polish immigrants in America had an easier time establishing their identities (because Polish culture shared much in common with American culture) than did adolescents from immigrant families in France (because the Muslim worldview in North Africa was so different from either French Christian or French-secular folk psychology).

Second generation migrant adolescents tended to share the values of their French peers rather than those of their parents. This was particularly significant for the young girls from Maghreb countries. In their own ethnic group, the male occupies a dominant position, while the woman is deprived of independence. On witnessing the apparent equality between men and women in France, the North African girls became aware of their low status. They are, more than boys, confronted with the problem of whether to maintain their religious and ethnic identity. For these young people, the main problem consists in reconciling their parents' traditional values and their [own] participation in the cultural community of their peers. This is sometimes impossible. (Camilleri & Malewska-Peyre, 1997, p. 55)

Thus, conflict between generations in a family is exacerbated when parents bring habits and attitudes from their original culture into the new setting while their children are adopting beliefs, behaviors, and a sense of self typical of the youths in the dominant culture that surrounds them. Cardes's (1983) study of Hispanic immigrant families in Florida revealed that

[Immigrant] mothers who are isolated within their homes because of child-bearing responsibilities, language difficulties, and traditional concepts of women's all-encompassing maternal functions often find it particularly difficult to adapt to the larger, predominantly Anglo society. In their role as "culture bearers" for the family, their relative lag in acculturation to the world outside the home can lead to severe marital and parent-child conflicts. (Chilman, 1993, p. 159)

An immigrant's sense of self can also be challenged by conditions in the new host society that urge role changes on family members. This problem has been illustrated in Gold's study of Vietnamese refugees in the United States. Even if the newcomers had held respected diplomas or well-paying, white-collar jobs in Vietnam, when coming to the United States most of them were obliged to take work as "laborers or operators, or in service occupations such as electronics assembly worker, driver, factory worker, clerk, janitor, or food handler . . . [jobs that are often] poorly paid, part-time, seasonal, or without [fringe] benefits" (Gold, 1993, p. 308). The move from one society to another may also result in a role reversal that places family members in an unaccustomed relationship that affects their self-concepts. This often occurs for the roles of husband and wife,

> with the wife taking on the breadwinner role as well as some of the status and power that accompanies it. This may be because women's jobs, such as house cleaner, hotel maid (a major source of employment for female refugees in San Francisco), and food service worker, are much more readily available than the male-oriented unskilled occupations that the men seek. In other cases, the mother becomes breadwinner as she supports the family by working in a menial job while the father attempts to find professional employment. (Gold, 1993, p. 309)

Social conditions in the host nation during different time periods can also influence the *sense-of-self* problem faced by immigrants. For example, in the United States, social change during the 20th century effected a shift in many immigrants' conception of what constitutes a proper self-concept, that is, what constitutes the ethnic identity to which they should aspire. During the first quarter of the century, the Americanization movement was in full force. Immigrants were all expected to shed the cultural accoutrements they had brought from the "old country" and to don the beliefs and behaviors of the culturally homogenized "real American." As President Woodrow Wilson told foreign-born citizens in 1915,

> You cannot become Americans if you think of yourselves in groups. A man who thinks of himself as belonging to a particular national group in America has not yet become an American. (Shaw, 1924, p. 115)

This task of shedding the old in favor of the new was far easier for some ethnic groups than for others. The transformation for people from the British Isles was relatively simple, since so much of the "real American" self was modeled on Britishers' home culture—language, the law, family structure, roles, and more. Immigrants from China, Yugoslavia, Egypt, Norway, the Sudan, and many other nations faced far greater difficulty acquiring "real-American" personalities. To become truly acceptable in America, the newcomers had to change many of their attitudes and behaviors. When they could not readily accomplish this feat, their sense of self suffered. Consider, for example, a second-generation Filipina's description of her father's experience as a newly arrived child in the 1930s.

> Being an immigrant was a source of shame for my dad. He remembers being in elementary school, speaking broken English, and having his classmates tease him for not speaking as everyone else did. Whenever he was accused of being from the Philippines, he would absolutely deny it, and say that he was born in Hawaii. Because he was teased so often and stereotyped, things associated with the Philippines came to denote something degrading in my dad's opinion. Being Filipino and speaking Tagalog were sources of ridicule for him, and he came to resent those parts of him. (Revilla, 1997, p. 101)

However, the final quarter of the 20th century was a period of significant change in the identity that a growing number of people from ethnic minorities in North America viewed as desirable. This change began most notably during the rebellious social movements of the 1960s and accelerated into the decades that followed. No longer was America touted as a nation that produced a single variety of American self. Instead, the analogies of *mixed salad* and *mosaic* replaced *melting pot* to reflect the multicultural composition of American society. Many members of ethnic groups now sought to establish an identity that included of a large measure of the indigenous culture of the "old country" melded with features of present-day American life. However, efforts to define what constitutes a proper ethnic identity for people who trace their ancestry to a given nation have been fraught with difficulty. The efforts of Filipino Americans are a case in point. Three components that Filipino-American activists have sought to incorporate into a proper Filipino ethnic identity have been particular conceptions of physical appearance, sexual orientation, and language skill. The description of what a typical Filipino looks like has led to conflict because Filipinos can differ markedly from each other in appearance, especially if individuals are products of marriages between parents of different ethnic stock. The proposal that the sexual orientation of a true Filipino is heterosexual has been criticized by gay members of the Filipino community (Mangaoang, 1994, p. 39). The matter of defining the language skills required in a proper Filipino identity has proven difficult because (a) there are different languages spoken in different regions of the Philippines and (b) Filipino Americans who do not speak one of those languages resent being considered inferior Filipino Americans. Even the question of whether to call themselves *Pilipino* or *Filipino* remains unsettled, with *Pilipino* more popular in California and *Filipino* more common in the Pacific Northwest and Hawaii (Revilla, 1997, p. 106).

In summary, the matter of ethnic identity in the folk psychologies of North America's ethnic groups is currently in a state of change, accompanied by a good deal of conflict among subgroups of American society regarding which sort of ethnic identity Americans should embrace.

# 10

# Rites and Rituals

*What purposes do cultural ceremonies serve?*

Folk psychologies, as cultural patterns of thought and belief, can be reflected in rites and rituals. The initial, major portion of this chapter offers examples of functions performed by such observances. The final short segment of the chapter concerns the effect of cultural change on rituals. Throughout the chapter, the terms *rites* and *rituals* are treated as synonyms.

## FUNCTIONS OF RITES AND RITUALS

Cultural rituals can have a variety of purposes, including those of (a) soliciting the aid of supernatural powers in times of need, (b) appeasing sensitive mystical beings, (c) establishing individuals' cultural identity, (d) promoting group solidarity, (e) enforcing group boundaries, (f) signifying key life events, (g) maintaining social-exchange traditions, (h) settling disputes, and (i) rationalizing puzzling events. A further function of some rituals is that of (j) doing harm. Ways of carrying out these functions can vary from one culture to another.

### Solicit the Aid of the Supernatural

Rites are often conducted to attract the good will and support of transcendental powers—gods, angels, ancestral spirits, ghosts, shades, and the like. This aid-seeking function is intimately linked to the matters of cause discussed in Chapter 4. When people are unable to offer easily observed, mundane reasons for why an event has occurred, they are apt to cite unseen forces as the direct cause or as entities that can influence the cause. Many forms of rituals may be used for summoning such forces and requesting their help.

The following three examples of diverse forms that such rites can assume are drawn from the cultures of Great Plains Indians in North America, Korean villages, and a Christian church service that could be found in virtually any part of the world.

Once a year—at the time berries ripened in the Colorado and Wyoming prairies—Arapaho Indians would conduct an elaborate Sun Dance as an appeal to the powers of the universe to renew nature and ensure future tribal prosperity. The dance was a test of endurance for the fasting male participants, who performed around a sacred tree trunk in the center of a large enclosure of poles and greenery, their dance accompanied by drumming and singing. The rite apparently originated with the Sioux and became known among the Cheyenne as the New Life Lodge and among the Poncas as the Mystery Dance (Waldman, 1988, pp. 19, 193).

In Korea, the *byolsin-gut* ritual is a seasonal community activity passed down from ancient times. Its purpose is to invoke the aid of the gods to ensure agricultural and human fertility in the coming year. During the daylong event, a village shaman welcomes the descent of the deities Tangun or King Suro by reciting age-old myths. Then most of the day features boisterous play that includes acrobats, masked dancers, and peasant music. The festivities reach their high point in an ecstatic orgy marked by chaotic behavior produced by participants' feeling possessed by mystic forces that release them from the rules of decorum of normal life (Kim, 1982, p. 61).

A common practice in Christian churches is a prayer that is part of every church service. Parishioners gather at an appointed hour Sunday morning or any other designated time to listen to the denomination's minister or priest recite scripture from the Bible, deliver a sermon designed to teach the meaning of scriptural passages for the conduct of people's lives, and pray to God. The prayer is spoken aloud by the minister or priest, with the members of the audience expressing their agreement with the supplication by bowing their heads and periodically uttering "amen" in chorus. The typical prayer includes (a) recognition of God's power and wisdom and (b) appeals for God's aid in solving problems that the faithful face in their lives. A supplication need not be offered in a place of worship but, rather, is more often an individual appeal for help in other settings. Such is the case when a student writes the initials JMJ in the upper corner of an examination paper as a plea to the Holy Family (Jesus, Mary, Joseph) for aid with the test questions. It is also an individual plea for success when a baseball player crosses himself as he steps to the plate for his turn at bat.

Close kin of rituals are *spells* in the form of words that are assumed to have magical powers, either in their own right or as devices for enlisting the assistance of supernatural forces. In China, past and present, there has been widespread belief in spells known as *shen,* employed for driving away ghosts and demons, and spells called *gwei,* for beckoning the powers of heaven and earth. Spells cast as magic formulae written on slips of paper can be purchased by ordinary citizens from Chinese paper shops, although they are bought far more often by mediums, diviners, priests, and nuns who specialize in calling on paranormal forces to remove obstacles along life's path. Spells can be used for influencing events both large and small.

> To tame the gods of the weather and to bring fertility to the land, to drive back armies and frighten off tigers, as well as to guide the spirits of the dead through the afterworld. In addition, [spells serve] to keep out the mosquitoes, to cure headaches, to stop rats chewing at clothes, and to keep away burglars. (Bloomfield, 1983, pp. 91-92)

## Appease Sensitive Mystical Beings

People often conduct rites to mollify paranormal spirits who, it is imagined, have been offended either by neglect or by people's having engaged in forbidden acts. And just to make sure that the spirits continually feel revered by their earthly subjects, rites may be performed periodically even when not needed for undoing a current spate of ill fortune. An instance of this variety of ritual is the *pambin tullal* rite of the Nayar caste in the central Kerala region of South India. Traditionally, the Nayars have been military and landholding folk who worship serpent deities believed to inhabit the serpent grove which is part of a family's property. Displeasing the deities by destroying, violating, or neglecting the sacred grove can incur a serpent curse. Acts of violation that anger the deities include felling trees, removing soil, damaging hallowed stones, or permitting a menstruating woman or a low-caste individual to enter the grove. All of the kinfolk, whether or not they live nearby, are collectively held responsible for such violations, so all may suffer for the acts.

> The deities are benevolent gods who must be taken care of and given their due, in return for which they will take care of the family. But, like many other Hindu deities, serpent deities have a volatile, dual nature. When offended, they can become dangerous and actively malevolent, and offenses against them are relatively easy to commit. . . . A serpent curse affects family prosperity—usually by causing childlessness, child deaths, lack of marriage proposals or job opportunities. More rarely, the curse results in leprosy and other skin diseases. *Pambin tullal* can be offered in response to particular problems but generally is performed every few years as a general preventative to the curse of the deities and to maintain overall well-being of the kin group. (Neff, 1987, pp. 63-64)

The ritual is not conducted by the Nayars themselves but, rather, is performed on their behalf by hired members of the relatively low-status Pullavar caste whose occupational specializations are those of astrologers, medicine men, priests, and singers in snake groves. The Pullavars command unique powers by virtue of their caste profession. The *pambin tullal* ceremony is a complex event carried out in the serpent grove for one or more nights, beginning at sunset and finishing just before daybreak. Throughout the ritual, Pullavar experts draw mystic figures across the ground in colored powders, offer food and incense to the deities, pray, sing, and perform frenzied dances.

Cultural tradition among the Bellona Islanders of the southwest Pacific has required close attention to placating the fearsome god Tehainga'atua by dedicating rituals to him. Tehainga'atua is portrayed as a repulsive noumenal being who eats raw human flesh and practices incestuous sex. He can wreak widespread disaster through his ability to control the violent forces of nature. As a result of his vindictive character, the powerful Tehainga-'atua is prone to kill people and visit catastrophe on a community if not treated with great respect. However, his destructive bent can also be used to advantage during a battle. Before Bellonese warriors set out on a raid, they can conduct a ritual in a secret setting in the bush to enlist Tehainga'atua's help. The ritual involves identifying who should be killed and by whom. Then, according to folk belief, "the god would steal the victim's *ma'unga* [the essence of self] and in this way make him die" (Monberg, 1991, p. 55).

## Establish Cultural Identity

As explained in Chapter 9, every person's *sense of self*—a sense of identity or of "Who I am"—derives at least partly from the culture in which that person's experiences are embedded. Each individual's language, values, educational activities, occupational and recreational pursuits, attitudes toward other people, and uses of technology are to a great degree cultural acquisitions. Rituals are among the important devices for blending cultural characteristics into people's sense of identity.

In North African societies, the pubescent initiation rite for girls often includes snipping away pieces of genitalia (clitoridectomy and labiadectomy) to eliminate the erotic pleasure gained from sexual intercourse. This practice ostensibly serves several purposes—identifies females as members of that particular culture, removes a motive for women to engage in premarital and extramarital sex, dramatically emphasizes femaleness by symbolically excising external "male" genitalia, and maintains male dominance over the society. For example, in certain Kpelle tribal regions of Liberia,

By removing the primary source of physical pleasure, sexual relations are culturalized, separated from mere biology. Since men are viewed as the masters of culture in Kpelle [tribal] ethno-ideology, and since intercourse is a male prerogative in this polygamous society, the surgery in effect symbolizes women's submission to men, even though it is women who perform the actual operation. (Erchak, 1992, p. 71)

Among people who study cultures, two questions about cultural identity not yet answered to everyone's satisfaction are these: Does the essence of one's cultural identity reside in one's beliefs, one's behavior, or in some combination of belief and behavior? And do some cultures place the essence of identity more in belief than in behavior, or vice versa? In response to these queries, Tooker (1992) has argued that in Western cultures, religious identity is based on doctrinal beliefs while ethnic identity is founded on innate characteristics (physical appearance) and traits acquired very early in life. Tooker labels such a process of identity formation *interiorization*. In contrast are cultures in which a person's observable behavior is considered the essence of identity, thereby producing an *exteriorized* version of a group's nature. Tooker cites the Akha culture in the highlands of Burma (Myanmar) as an instance of exteriorization of ethno-religious identity. In way of illustration, she describes the case of an Akha wife who gave birth to twins, an event which, according to Akha tradition, is a terrible disaster.

This calamity brings great impurity and danger to both the family and the village as a whole, danger which must be eliminated through elaborate purification ceremonies. Numerous sacrifices are required; animals and resources are needed. After the infanticide, the parents of the twins left the village to live briefly in the forest as tradition prescribed. They did not, however, have enough funds or animals to perform the expensive set of sacrifices and spirit chantings that would allow them to come back to live within the village boundaries. (Tooker, 1992, p. 799)

The couple's solution to their plight was to move to a Christian settlement where they "took on" Christianity and began to act like Christians, abandoning Akha animistic rites and adopting Christian rituals. But before long, wealthy relatives lent them the funds and animals needed for the cleansing ceremonies, so the couple could "reconvert" to Akha ethno-religious custom and return to their village. Tooker observed that—in this case as well as in others—the transition from one ethno-religious identity to another was made with no apparent anxiety about basic cultural convictions. Absent was the sort of conflict of beliefs that would bother members of societies in which identity was strongly interiorized. For the Akha, a shift in identity simply entailed displaying the behaviors typical of the new culture into which they had moved.

Some rituals are not in the form of periodic festivals or special occasions. Rather, they appear as daily life patterns that embody cultural identity. Clark (1994) offers an example from the Tahitian island of Tahaa in the southeast Pacific's Society Islands. France has held the islands since the mid-19th century as a "colony" and recently as a semi-independent "territory," with no prospect of the French government ever relinquishing control of the region. Over the years, an undercurrent of the indigenous people's resentment of their French masters has coursed through island society. Today, this sense of alienation continues in habits designed to maintain the locals' Polynesian (*Maohi*) cultural/ethnic identity through their using Tahitian language, modes of dress, hygiene, diet, and medical nostrums on occasions not requiring the imported French culture. Whereas Tahitians wear Western garb when attending the island's Protestant church, both men and women, when relaxing at home and visiting friends or going to dance rehearsal, don the traditional wrap-around, knee-length skirt (*pareu*) and often the head garland (*hei*) that signify their continued allegiance to *maa Tahiti* ("Tahitian custom" or "the Tahitian way"). From precolonial times to the present, Tahitians have been fastidious about bathing. When not engaged in dirty work—farming, repairing equipment—they have insisted on keeping a clean body and clean clothes. In addition, Tahitians have been known for their generosity and sharing, a key requirement in their traditional communal lifestyle. In modern times, Tahitians distinguish themselves from their French masters by using the phrase *sale Farani* (dirty Frenchman) to denigrate what they consider two objectionable traits attributed of the French—careless physical hygiene and stinginess. In diet, Tahitians also distinguish imported foods from those inherited from their ancestors. While Tahitians do avail themselves of items perceived to be French (dairy products, beef, dry foods, canned goods, potatoes, rice, bread, sugar), they often prefer traditional meals of fish, roast pig, taro, breadfruit, cassava, bananas, mangoes, and papaya. In medical matters, *Maohi* culture is also differentiated from French culture.

> When faced with a health crisis, Tahitians may treat themselves at home with *raau Tahiti* (Tahitian medicine), *raau tinito* (Chinese medicine), or *raau farani* (French medicine). Alternatively, they may consult a *tahua* (a specialist in Tahitian medicine; often *tahua* have special spiritual powers that aid their healing efforts), attend the government clinic, or consult with a private practitioner of cosmopolitan medicine. (Clark, 1994, p. 220)

If a Tahitian nostrum (a mixture of ingredients whose combination is usually kept secret) fails to achieve the desired results, the patient may turn to a Western-style clinic. But the two treatment systems must be separated from each other if an unfavorable outcome is to be avoided. "Every one of my collaborators told me either that one must take a purgative before commencing a course of French medicine or that one must wait three days before beginning the French medicine, if one had been taking Tahitian medicine first" (Clark, 1994, p. 220).

In summary, Clark (1994, p. 221) proposes that "When a Maohi dons a pareu, sits down to a meal of maa Tahiti, practices scrupulous hygiene (and contrasts it with French habits), consults a tahua, or asks an aunt for a preparation of raau Tahiti, he or she is embodying, through action and experience, Maohi ethnicity."

## Promote Group Solidarity

A significant function of cultural identity is that of fostering group unity. Because members of a society share so many cultural-identity characteristics in common, they tend to feel most confident and comfortable in the company of "our kind of folks."

One ritual practice for furthering group identity is the recounting of historical incidents and myths that become cultural property held in common by members of the group. For example, Jews' cultural ties are strengthened when they all learn about Moses leading his people out of Egypt, Noah building an ark, Jonah being swallowed by a whale, and Job's faith being tested by his suffering continuing misfortune. In like manner, Christians are linked together at Christmastime by the tale of Jesus's birth and at Easter by the story of his crucifixion. The sense of being Greek is strengthened by the Greek populace recalling Homer's tales. The feeling of being American is enhanced by people's learning the myths of George Washington felling a cherry tree and of the young Abraham Lincoln trudging through the snow to borrow books he would read beside the fireplace in his family's log cabin.

An example of a genre of story deriving from a particular historical incident is the cannibal myth shared among Shoshoni Indian tribes in the western United States. The following is one present-day version of the myth that goes back to the occasion of the 1863 Ruby Valley Treaty, when soldiers of the Second Cavalry, California Volunteers, "pacified" the Shoshoni, convincing them to sign an agreement with the American government that deprived them of land and the freedom of movement that the Shoshoni had traditionally enjoyed.

> The Treaty of 1863 made in Ruby Valley . . . was signed by our principal chiefs and headsmen. . . . So it was that the white people and the representatives of the United States Government put out the word that they were anxious to meet with the chiefs and the people of the Western Shoshoni Indian Nation for the purpose of signing the Treaty. . . . So when the Indians had all gathered, the solders grabbed the rifles and killed an Indian which they had previously captured. . . . They cut the Indian up and put him in a huge iron pot . . . and cooked him and then the soldiers aimed their rifles at

the heads of the people and forced the people to eat some of this human flesh. (Temoke in Clemmer, 1996, p. 214)

An array of similar myths portraying whites as cannibals continue to be circulated among the Shoshoni, with the tales retold and embellished by speakers at tribal gatherings and by elderly family members to entertain the young during winter evenings at home. Clemmer (1996) interprets the persistent cannibal-whitemen myths as a device that (a) separates "we" (the Shoshoni) from "they" (the dominant white American citizenry), (b) elevates Shoshoni character above that of their despised white oppressors, and (c) unites diverse Shoshoni tribes into a consolidated ethnocultural and political force.

Another sort of oratory that contributes to group identity is the historical narrative that reemphasizes the form and legitimacy of a social system and of the system's role players. An example is the Samoan *fa'alupega*. It consists of a description of the hierarchy and the history of chieftain titles for a Samoan locality. When visitors appeared in a village or when important ceremonies were conducted, the local talking chief would speak to the audience, reviewing the magnitude of the honorific titles borne by the attending chiefs. The narration would begin with a description of the most prestigious titleholder, along with a recounting of his most revered possessions. Then came descriptions of the supporting chiefs and their titles in descending order, followed by an accounting of the chiefs' spokesmen—their "talking chiefs." The frequent repetition of this chieftain hierarchy enabled members of Samoa's oral culture to keep in mind an accurate picture of the power and privilege structure of their society (Thomas, 1987, pp. 26-27).

## Enforce Group Boundaries

Sometimes the principal function of a ritual is to enhance the feeling of importance of members of an in-group by the ritual's exclusionary nature. Therefore, the underlying purpose of the ritual is to prevent outsiders from participating in, or even discovering, the in-group's activities. Gregor (1979) proposes that this is the prime purpose of many of the men's secret brotherhoods found around the world, brotherhoods that "draw their primary significance not from whom they include, but from whom they exclude" (p. 250). He illustrates the exclusionary character of rituals by an example from Mehinaku Indian culture of the northern Mato Grosso in Brazil's tropical rainforest.

The typical Mehinaku village is circular. Large, extended-family residences form the outer periphery that encompasses a central plaza. A small house in the plaza serves as both a temple and social club, but it's exclusively for men. Every man in the village is automatically a member of the club by virtue of his sex. No women are ever allowed to enter the building or to witness any events associated with it.

> Here the men assemble to engage in idle conversation while they work on arrow baskets and other crafts. Here too they play the sacred flutes representing a spirit called *Kowka*. Unless the men play the flutes and drink manioc [cassava] porridge in the name of the spirit, *Kowka* will become angry and "take away" some of the villagers' "souls" (literally shadows, *lyeweku*). The representations of other spirits, in the form of masks, bullroarers, and costumes, are slung from the rafters of the men's house. (Gregor, 1979, p. 253)

The lore surrounding Kowka and the events that transpire in the men's house are tightly kept secrets. All that women know about the rituals are the consequences they themselves can suffer if they either enter or peek into the house or if they witness the trio of musicians who periodically play the sacred flutes to the rhythm of a simple stamped dance step. (The flutes are wooden instruments, about three feet long, that sound like bassoons in a Western orchestra. The center musician—"master of the songs"—carries the melody, accompanied by the two subsidiary musicians, one on his left and the other on his right. Women must never learn the identity of the flutists.) What women can expect if they violate the men's-house prohibitions is to be gang raped. Hence, when walking in the plaza, women stay clear of the men's house and avert their eyes so they will not offend Kowka who, the men say, "would kill us if a woman came in here" (Gregor, 1979, p. 254).

Gregor (1979, p. 256) points out that the secrets the men so closely guard are really of no practical import, so that "a village girl who managed to slip unseen into the men's house would certainly be disappointed." (Gist's [1940] survey of American fraternal orders showed that candidates are often disappointed to discover that the only things secret about such clubs are their initiation rituals.)

Then why the secrecy? In Gregor's analysis, secrets—even secrets of no real consequence—have the power of differentiating one group from another. Hence, the secrecy of the Mehinaku men's society serves to mark the barrier between the sexes and emphasize men's domination of women by excluding women from ostensibly powerful sacred knowledge. In this way, Mehinaku men's rites "provide the men with a stage for dramatizing their position within the society" (Gregor, 1979, p. 259).

## Signify Key Life Events

Among the most common ceremonies found in cultures throughout the world are initiation rituals that signify a person's passing from one social status to another.

The passage may be from one stage of human development to another, as in Protestant Christians' rites of

- infant baptism, in which parents of the newborn dedicate the child to a Christian way of life,
- church membership around the time of puberty, when budding youths declare their own informed intention to guide their lives by Christian doctrine,
- marriage, with its lifelong commitment to a mate, and
- a funeral ceremony at the time of death, when the departed is entrusted to the Lord's care.

Ways that such events may differ across cultures can be illustrated with instances of adolescent initiation rites and of funeral rituals.

## Initiation rites

Sometimes a ceremony serves both to symbolize advancement toward maturity and entrance into a select club or association. Such rituals that mark boys' and girls' passage from childhood to adult status are practiced in an estimated one-quarter of the world's societies. The ceremony can assume many forms.

Traditional practices of the Mandan Indians of North Dakota have included an annual Okipa ceremony in the late spring or summer during which youths fasted for days; had their chests, backs, and legs slashed; and were raised toward the roof of a ceremonial lodge in rawhide thongs and ropes. By bearing such torture, they sought to prove their manhood and generate trance-like states in which visions seemed particularly vivid and meaningful (Waldman, 1988, p. 124).

The Nootka Indian tribe on the northwest coast of North America included among its gods the Wolf Spirits. Around the time of puberty, all Nootka boys were obliged to undergo an ordeal in which they were kidnapped for days by men dressed as wolves and taught wolf songs and dances. Finally, they were rescued in a make-believe battle and freed from the Wolf Spirits by a special dance (Waldman, 1988, p. 162).

Among the Maasai of Kenya and Tanzania, tradition dictates that pubescent boys' ritual circumcision be followed by a period of transition to manhood during which the young initiates are obligated to kill small decorative birds which are cleaned and mounted on a wooden rack that each youth wears as a headdress. Throughout the months of passage to manhood, the lad also lets his hair grow and wears a dirty black robe infused with fat, the same sort of apparel worn by women who have just given birth.

> He adorns himself with two swirls of copper wire, usually worn by women, at the ears, a necklace of blue beads, and a headband of reeds. He must

wear sandals made of skin, rather than the usual rubber-tire variety. The initiate must have no contact with metal weapons, so he carries a wooden club and a bow and arrows [used for slaying birds]. His fingers, first the left hand, then the right, are adorned with small skin rings, gifts from girls as signs of friendship. (Galaty, 1998, p. 227)

At the end of the initiation period, the youth shaves and trades his ragged robes for bright, clean, red ones. The wire earpieces are replaced with colorful beaded earrings, and the wooden armaments are discarded in favor of an iron sword and spear. Finally, the rack of birds is stored behind his mother's bed.

Galaty (1998) interprets the youth's headrack of delicate birds as symbolizing the immaturity of the childhood that each initiate leaves behind when he enters manhood and is entitled to wear a warrior's headdress featuring a lion's mane and ostrich feathers. In the boys' headracks "of birds skinned and mounted, we also see an iconic replica of the initiates' symbolic death [children] and rebirth [as adults] in the experience of circumcision" (Galaty, 1998, p. 227).

Some initiation rituals are not created and supervised by adults but are invented and directed by the young. Alves (1993) studied 9- and 10-year-old boys in Lisbon, Portugal, who organized activities symbolizing their desired departure from childhood and from adult controls—activities that included rampages, acts of daring, and narratives that bore all the marks of rites of passage.

## Funeral rites

The obvious final event of a person's earthly existence is death, which is accompanied by funeral rites. The amazing diversity of ceremonies associated with dying appears in Metcalf and Huntington's (1991, p. 24) observation that

> Corpses are burned or buried, with or without animal or human sacrifice; they are preserved by smoking, embalming, or pickling; they are eaten—raw, cooked, or rotten; they are ritually exposed as carrion or simply abandoned; or they are dismembered and treated in a variety of these ways. Funerals are the occasion for avoiding people or holding parties, for fighting or having sexual orgies, for weeping or laughing, in a thousand different combinations.

The nature of present-day funerals is the result of a variety of factors, including religious traditions, costs, the diminished availability of burial sites as the result of population growth, and concern for maintaining the environment. Throughout the industrialized world, formal burial in a coffin, as a long-established religious practice, continues as the preferred method of internment, despite the increasing costs involved. Eighty-seven percent of the deceased in France, 80% in the United States, and 96% in Spain are placed in graves or family vaults. In Mexico and Russia, cremation is popular "because ashes are easy to move to safety in times of political upheaval and graves are often robbed" ('World's Way of Death," 1998, p. 95). In Japan, because of the shortage of land and its high cost, cremation is nearly universal.

The typical North American mortuary rite, which features preparing the deceased for public viewing, is considered quite odd by members of most cultures. The process involves what Jessica Mitford mocked in *The American Way of Death* (1963, p. 54) as the newly deceased's being "sprayed, sliced, pierced, pickled, trussed, trimmed, creamed, waxed, painted, rouged, and neatly dressed . . . transformed from a common corpse into a Beautiful Memory Picture. . . . In no part of the world but in North America [are such embalming and restorative-art procedures] widely used." (See also Mitford, 1998.)

Not only are there diverse forms of funerals, but funerary rituals can serve more functions than just signaling the end of a life on earth. One additional role is that of providing for the expression of grief at the loss of a friend. Consequently, weeping in sorrow is a frequent element of the mourning process in many societies, but the time when weeping is expected or allowed can differ across cultures. For instance, in eastern Zambia, no one is permitted to cry before the deceased has been washed and dressed and the village headman notified. After those requirements have been fulfilled, women mourners are told to cry in an area set aside for them in the newly departed's home (Skjonsberg, 1989, p. 174).

In Africa, among the Bushmen of Angola, villagers wail and lament as long as the body of the deceased is unburied—a period of four days for an adult and two for a child. Children are buried inside the family's hut, but adults are buried outside with their head pointing east. The death of an adult signals the time that the family should move to a new site. Men cast green branches on the grave; women and children mark their heads with a bit of charcoal, toss charcoal on the grave, and utter the ritual words

"Accept this offering. We are going farther into the forest. We will meet you there!" (Estermann, 1976, p. 10)

Not far from Bushman territory in Angola, mourning among the Kwepe is a brief affair. In former times, it lasted but a single day. More recently it has extended for three days. Upon an individual's death, the people present, with no expression of grief, truss up the corpse's arms and legs so the deceased can be buried in the traditional squatting position. The dead person's belongings are then removed from his or her hut, and the hut is burned to the ground. On the third day, relatives and friends share wine and take turns drawing a few puffs on a long pipe in remembrance of the departed (Estermann, 1976, p. 45).

In only a few places, such as the Indonesian island of Java and among the Kwepe of Angola, is weeping rare or absent. The Javanese value an evenness of feelings from which highs and lows of emotion are removed. Peoples' appearance of tranquility results partly from a pervasive fatalism and absence of fear of dying which is accompanied by a conviction that death is a peaceful condition, empty of desire and striving. Such an attitude likely hearkens back a millennium or more to the strong Buddhist/Hindu influence in Java and on the adjacent island of Bali where children learn to hide sorrow behind a facade of calm composure and equanimity that minimizes interpersonal conflict (Geertz, 1960). The dominant culture in Bali teaches that one should not cry during mourning, but in practice the Balinese weep as much as members of other cultures (Scheff, 1983).

Funerals may also provide for the passage of the deceased from mundane mortality to a spiritual existence in a life after death. This threshold period between earthly life and the ultimate acceptance of the soul in a spirit world—a period referred to as *liminality*—can vary from one culture to another in the length of time involved and in the activities in which living friends and relatives engage. On the Southeast Asia island of Borneo, tribal groups maintain a custom of secondary burial. Not only is a body buried shortly after death; but months or years later when the flesh has disintegrated, the bones are exhumed and another funeral ceremony memorializes their reburial, with that second ceremony accompanied by great feasting. During the time between the primary and secondary burials, the soul of the deceased is expected to have traveled from the world of the living to spirits' eternal resting place (Hertz, 1960).

The main purpose of elaborate funeral rites among the Nyakyusa of Tanzania is to drive the dead person away from the living relatives' dreams and imagination, because frequent dreams of the deceased are feared to portend the dreamer's own death. Dreamers also fear that ancestral spirits will come to punish them for sins, for breaches of kinship duties—especially for the head of a family failing to use his inherited wealth for the benefit of his dependents or for young people failing to respect their elders (Wilson, 1960, p. 351).

Another function of mortuary rites is to establish inheritance—the transfer of possessions, titles, roles, responsibilities, and rights from the deceased to the living. This function is perhaps most obviously demonstrated in the rites attending the death of a tribal chieftain or monarch. Over past centuries in Thailand, the elaborate ceremony on the occasion of a king's death has featured the successor to the throne conspicuously honoring the departed and accepting the responsibility to carry on the traditions of the recent monarch. The elaborateness of the ceremony has been intended not only to convince other pretenders to the throne of the futility of their ambitions but also to impress the country's regions that the power of the central authority remains undiminished upon the king's demise (Metcalf & Huntington, 1991, p. 140).

Linked to the function of establishing inheritance is that of affirming a society's hierarchical structure and of locating people's place in that structure. For example, in the South Pacific nation of Tonga

> At funerals one can see how the various elements of society fit together, and especially how hierarchical principles of status and rank pervade life and death. Funerals can also make statements of political reality, indicate the elevation of certain lineages over others, and suggest what elements of the stratified social system the family wishes to bring to the attention of the public. (Keppler, 1993, p. 476)

## Maintain Social-Exchange Traditions

According to social-exchange theory, anytime someone does something good or bad to—or for—someone else, the recipient of the act is obliged to respond in a particular manner. Sometimes this principle of *just deserts* assumes the guise of a ceremony.

Various sorts of commodities can be involved in social exchanges, with some sorts more typical of one culture than of another. This point can be demonstrated with the examples of *kulas, potlatches,* dinner invitations, thanksgiving prayers, and revenge.

### The kula

*Kula* is an elaborate system of social exchange conducted through a network of communities located on an extensive ring of islands off the coast of Papua New Guinea. The exchanges involve food, shell-bead necklaces, and armshells whose distribution earns honor and fame for the givers. The system has consisted of travelers from one community visiting other communities and islands to offer shell objects that bear graded titles of veneration on the basis of their aesthetic quality and exchange history. Shell necklaces are passed around the ring in a clockwise direction while armshells move counterclockwise. The greater the renown of the kula objects that a person owned and then gave away, the greater the esteem in which that person was held. Both the consumable (food) and nonconsumable (seashell ornaments) items have performed a variety of exchange functions: (a) enhanced a giver's reputation for generosity, (b) extended the giver's social relationships and fame beyond the local community, (c) obligated receivers to reciprocate with gifts in the future, thereby enriching the original giver's collection of valued objects,

(d) increased the giver's political influence, and (e) acquired honor and political power for the giver's home community (Munn, 1986).

## The potlatch

*Potlatch* is a traditional ritual practiced by Indian tribes living along the northwest coast of North America, such tribes as the Kwakiutl in British Columbia, the Nootka on Vancouver Island, and the Tlingit in Alaska. A typical potlatch consists of a public ceremony in which a person of great wealth—usually a clan chief—gives away enormous quantities of goods, including food, wood carvings, blankets, baskets, furs, and personal items.

A brief description of Tlingit potlatch practices can illustrate the preparations made for such rituals and the social-exchange functions potlatches perform. In the past, the eight occasions in Tlingit society that warranted a potlatch were those of passing authority from a deceased chief to a successor, building a longhouse, carving a hat, presenting a Chilkat blanket, unveiling a heraldic screen, dedicating a totem pole, removing shame for misbehavior, and formally introducing a chief's staff (Tollefson, 1995).

Preparations for a potlatch could be very elaborate. Typically, the clan chief would invite the members of his council of advisers to a feast a year before the intended potlatch in order to announce his plan to host the event. This early notice gave ample time for people to prepare—to compile the list of guests from other clans, to invite the guests, to collect the goods that will be given away, and to practice the chants and dances that accompany the ceremony. Often the chief would first quietly distribute his wealth to the well-to-do people of the village, then wait for several months when those gifts had to be returned with interest, thereby increasing the largesse he could bestow on the guests who would attend the potlatch.

In return for the chief's potlatch generosity, he would receive (a) validation of his authority to rule the clan, (b) power over political rivals, (c) evaluation and verification of the clan's right to resources, (d) the opportunity to bestow titles, (e) the establishment or reaffirmation of alliances with other clans whose leaders have been invited to participate in the ritual, (f) the resolution of interclan disputes, (g) the social removal of shame, and (h) the maintenance of regional stability through distributing wealth to rival clans as an expression of both respect and friendship (Tollefson, 1995).

## The dining invitation

All cultures include customs that can qualify as minor, informal social-exchange ceremonies. Examples are ways of welcoming guests, of introducing a newcomer to a group, of greeting a friend, of conducting a business meeting, of celebrating birthdays and holidays, and of responding to an invitation to dine. The example of a dining engagement in present-day North American society can illustrate social-exchange aspects of such a custom.

A person who accepts a dinner invitation from a typical American family incurs an obligation to offer something in exchange for the dinner engagement. What that something will be depends on certain features of the giver and the receiver. If host and guest are both adults of similar financial means and social position (or are two families of similar status), then what may be expected in return is (a) a gift the guest brings to the dinner (a bouquet of flowers, a bottle of wine, a toy for the host's child) and/or (b) at a later time the guest invites the host to a dinner or other event of equal quality. Guests also can appropriately send a thank-you note or else phone their appreciation to the host a day or so after the dinner. But different age and socioeconomic relationships between host and guest can alter what is properly given in return for the meal. A 16-year-old boy, invited to dine with his girlfriend's parents, is obliged simply to offer the parents and the girl his sincere thanks for the invitation. And if a wealthy family entertains a family of meager means, the wealthy family will expect no more than an expression of appreciation. However, the less-affluent recipients—motivated by pride—may feel that thanking their host is not enough, so they may invite the host family to dinner (perhaps at a restaurant) or may send a gift.

Misunderstandings about what sort of exchange is appropriate in response to a kindness often arise when the givers and receivers are from different cultural backgrounds, since the customs bearing on such events can vary markedly across cultures.

## The thanksgiving prayer

A ritual found in many societies is a prayer expressing thanks to the controllers of the universe for blessings received.

In Christian tradition, expressions of gratitude to God can take the form of a family's saying grace at mealtime, an individual's praying at bedtime, or a minister's publicly giving thanks on behalf of the faithful during Sunday morning worship service. And a football player may kneel and bow a moment after making a touchdown in recognition of the divine aid he believes contributed to his feat.

Devout Muslims, during five daily prayer sessions, honor Allah and express appreciation for the good fortune they enjoy.

Gratitude and fear seem to be motives behind people's prayers of thanksgiving. First, people who recognize that they are not in full control of their own destinies often believe that divine forces are heavily involved in determining their fate. Thus, when good things happen, proper courtesy requires that the divine forces be credited for their benevolence. Second, people may fear that jealous, vengeful spirits will be offended if not appropriately honored. Hence, it is prudent to thank those godly beings for their generosity, thereby encouraging the bestowal of additional blessings in the future.

## Revenge

Revenge is a form of social exchange that involves an individual or group retaliating against what is believed to be the source of a misdeed. Injuries that call for revenge can be of many kinds—death of a relative or compatriot, physical harm, loss of property, loss of employment, insults, damaged reputation, or the disparagement of one's family, religion, ethnic group, or nation. Not only do customs relating to vengeance vary across cultures, but in some societies revenge becomes ritualized, assuming a set ceremonial form. Such has been the case in numerous preliterate communities in which there is an absence of law or a breakdown of legal procedures. Offenses suffered by one clan at the hands of another results in a feud, frequently a *blood feud* in which members of the offended clan seek to maim or kill members of the group blamed for the original offense. However, there are often ritualized ways of ending a feud without continued bloodshed. For instance, in the Trobriand Islands of Melanesia and among the Nuer of the Sudan, revenge more often takes the form of payment (blood money) rather than reciprocal killing ("Feud," 1994).

## Settle Disputes

Cultures can employ a variety of rituals for adjudicating interpersonal conflicts. A wide range of methods for settling disputes, extending from peaceful negotiation to warfare, are practiced among the world's cultures. Frequently, the customary method adopted by a group varies with the particular type of dispute. For example, a peaceful treaty may be negotiated between parties on one occasion, a court case will be used on another occasion, and violence (a duel between individuals, a bombing attack between nations) will be favored under other circumstances. The following examples demonstrate diverse conflict-resolution rituals in several folk psychologies.

In numerous Christian Protestant religious denominations, issues are settled by the majority vote of group members. However, such denominations as Roman Catholicism vest the right to resolve controversies in the order's authority hierarchy—in priests, bishops, cardinals, and the pope. In such systems, the higher an individual's position on the authority ladder, the greater that individual's power to make decisions. In contrast, Quakers reject both voting and authoritative dictate as a proper means for settling disputes. Without a priestly hierarchy, Quaker culture requires that group discussion and negotiations must continue until all members agree or else dissenters are willing to "stand aside."

> What is particularly interesting about the consensus method is that it respects the presence of conflict and allows for the full airing of differences. It also depends on a disciplined spiritual maturity of members of the community, a common acceptance of collective inward illumination of the group, and great skill in intellectual discernment and interpersonal and intergroup communication. (Boulding, 2000, p. 99)

Three mechanisms that foster the peaceful settlement of disagreements in the Rotuma Island society of the South Pacific are people's belief in immanent justice, in mediation, and in *faksoro*. First, a widespread conviction among Rotumans is that justice is immanent—that justice is built into the very nature of the universe. Consequently, wrongdoers eventually get what they deserve—their just deserts—in the form of ill fortune, even though at the moment it might appear that they are getting away with misconduct. Second, the wisdom and influence that respected elders and honored chiefs possess can be trusted for arbitrating disputes, so that violence will not be necessary for adjudicating conflicts. The third ritualized device is *faksoro*—offering a sincere public apology for transgression.

> By construing apologies as honorable, persons who have offended others can gain compensatory status for admission of wrongdoing. That acceptance of such apologies, given the proper circumstances, is virtually mandatory makes them especially effective as strategies for ending disputes. (Howard, 1990, p. 286)

Whenever a government expands its rule to encompass formerly independent cultural groups, imported agencies and their rituals arrive to contend with traditional modes of resolving conflicts. One way this competition between cultural practices may work out is illustrated with the case of the Dou Donggo, an ethnic group located on the eastern end of the island of Sumbawa in the Indonesian archipelago. During the process of the Indonesian government's extending its control over the peoples of Sumbawa, a police force and formal court system became available for settling disagreements within Dou Donggo society. However, as Peter Just (1991) reports, the police and courts are rarely if ever called on to deal with social conflicts.

> In part this is a matter of community solidarity, but it is also the result of pragmatic considerations, for to involve outsiders is to relinquish a share of control over the outcome of a dispute: bribes could become a factor and there is far less assurance that the outcome of a legal proceeding left to strangers to resolve will be as sensitive to local needs as one resolved by people who have to continue living together as neighbors. (Just, 1991, p. 109)

Rather than depend on an intrusive national government's agencies, the Dou Donggo much prefer the long-established cultural practice of trusting conflict resolution to highly regarded elders (*doumatuatua*) who hold no official position of authority but qualify for their role of arbiters as a result of long experience that has resulted in wisdom and moral rectitude.

> Most of the work of a *doumatuatua*, and much of the authority that attaches to him, does not derive from performances in formal gatherings. . . . [The] great part of conflict resolution in a village like Doro Ntika takes place in the consensus-building processes of gossip among friends and neighbors and in whispered intrigues among the disputant's kinsmen and allies. It is here, in the interstices of formal process, that a *doumatuatua* operates most effectively, and it is in these matters that he is most likely to be called upon for help. In many ways, then, a person becomes a *doumatuatua* not so much by the delivery of opinions in formal legal settings, but by being asked to negotiate a brideprice, or muster arguments in a land dispute, or lend his good offices to the termination of a betrothal, or intercede more immediately in preventing a dispute from erupting into violence. (Just, 1991, p. 112)

## Rationalize Perplexing Events

The role of some ceremonies is to furnish an explanation for happenings whose causes are either puzzling or socially unacceptable. An example of such a role is the folk-psychology explanation of children's inexplicable deaths in rural Tlaxcala, Mexico, where a child's mysterious demise may be attributed to attacks by bloodsucking witches. To render a witchcraft interpretation publicly convincing, members of a dead child's family can stage a ritual to persuade members of the community that witchery was indeed responsible for the death. Roberts and Nutini (1988, p. 408), when reporting 47 such witchcraft events in the Tlaxcala region, proposed that the rituals were staged exercises in deception "in the sense of . . . a characteristic arrangement or situation that deceives or deludes with or without calculated intent." Each of the staged events was a quickly planned public narration designed to satisfy

> groups of people who already believed in the existence of bloodsucking witchcraft that something like the following sequence actually occurred: (1)

the witch transforms herself or himself into an animal, leaving his or her legs in the fireplace; (2) the witch locates a suitable infant; (3) the witch enters the house, sometimes as a small insect; (4) within the house the witch returns to her or his human form; (5) the witch sucks the blood of the infant, usually attacking the upper part of the infant's body; and (6) the witch leaves the house or scene either in human or animal form, depending on the situation. (Roberts & Nutini, 1988, p. 410)

The apparent motive behind such staged deception was to save the child's family from censure for having neglected or abused the child.

While it is probable that many of the infant victims died from some such natural cause as crib death, suffocation as a result of negligence or infanticide probably occurred. In one or two cases there seems to have been village gossip insinuating that infanticide was the cause of death, but with every such event a potentiality for damaging gossip was present. Any voiced suspicion carried implications of harm for a family in the small worlds of these villages. (Roberts & Nutini, 1988, p. 411)

## Do Damage

People can suffer harm from certain cultural ceremonies. Sometimes the harm is intended by those who impose the rites, even though the rites are portrayed as beneficial. Other times the harm is inadvertent. The following examples concern female circumcision, seclusion for boys, and child marriage.

### Female circumcision

An example of a procedure that results in a mixture of intentional and unintentional damage is female circumcision, an event mentioned earlier in this chapter as a device for establishing cultural identity. The circumcision operation comes in three forms. The first is Sunna (meaning *tradition* in Arabic) which involves surgically removing the prepuce or tip of the clitoris from a female's sexual equipment. The second, clitoridectomy, consists of cutting out the entire clitoris and the labia. The third, and most extreme, is infibulation, which leaves the victim with only a tiny passage for expelling urine since the vagina is sewn up as part of the procedure.

Female circumcision (or, as critics label it, *female genital mutilation*) is chiefly considered a rite of passage from childhood to adulthood. The ritual has a long history, apparently originating in northeast Africa as an indigenous religious observance and subsequently adopted in African Muslim societies even though female circumcision lacks Islamic roots. Today, there are an estimated 100 million circumcised women in the world, with 2 million more added each year. The rite is most widely performed in Africa, where it appears in at least 26 of 43 nations. Surveys in the early 1990s revealed that 97% of women in Egypt have been circumcised, 90% in Sudan, 94.5% in Eritrea, 93.7% in Mali, nearly 100% in Somalia and Djibouti, and 43.4% in the Central African Republic (Chelala, 1998; Tynan, 1997). In Kenya, over 75% of adolescent girls and 100% of women over age 50 have been subjected to the rite (Chelala, 1998). The same tradition is also occasionally found in Java, Sulawesi (Celebes), Malaysia, Ecuador, and Peru. Although most girls are circumcised around age 7 or 8, in some African cultures the ritual is performed on infants and in other cultures on young adult women (Rushwan, 1995).

Circumcision is criticized for producing two types of harm, one unplanned and the other intentional. The unplanned harm consists of physical damage, because the surgery is usually performed by village women who have no medical training and do the cutting with an unsterile razor blade, kitchen knife, sharp stone, broken glass, or scissors. For the circumcised girls, the procedure can result in extremely unfavorable physical outcomes—shock, loss of blood, tetanus, blood poisoning (septicemia), inability to pass urine, severe anemia, abscesses, ulcers, dermoid cysts, urinary tract infections, blood clots that prevent menstrual blood from escaping, infertility, and death (Ford, 1995; Rushwan, 1995).

The planned harm takes the form of females being forced to undergo circumcision to prevent them from enjoying sexual intercourse. Circumcision is endorsed by husbands who contend that wives who fail to derive pleasure from intercourse are less likely to engage in liaisons with other men. The intent to eliminate women's sexual satisfaction is a key reason for circumcision's popularity in African Muslim communities, since the practice is compatible with Islamic tradition that restricts females' exposure to males, as represented in the requirement that women, when in public, cover all parts of the body except the eyes or face.

## Male seclusion

An instance of unintentional harm deriving from a ritual is the practice of male pubertal seclusion by 10 Indian tribes in Alto Xingu, central Brazil. The seclusion, which can last from several months to three years, is a rite intended to promote a boy's social, psychological, and physical maturing as he passes into adulthood. The period away from normal social contacts is marked by numerous taboos to protect a vulnerable youth from a multitude of evil forces. An investigation of the effects of seclusion on adolescent boys' well-being revealed that 24 out of 133 secluded boys (ages 11 to 20)

> showed symptoms of intoxication, with seven of them dying in the acute phase, whereas the other 17 developed peripheral neropathy. The mortality rate among males was 6.6 times higher than among females. Our findings

suggest that the high risk of death associated with male pubertal seclusion results from the use of some native plants in infusions or ointments in the rite's purification process. (Pinto & Baruzzi, 1991, p. 821)

## Child marriage

Although the marriage of young girls—some in their infancy—is illegal in India, hundreds of secret weddings are still performed in the nation's most tradition-bound regions. If the bride is near puberty or beyond, she goes immediately to live with the groom's family, where she is obliged to serve members of that family in whatever ways they choose. But if the bride is much younger, she returns to her own home until she reaches puberty. Child marriages continue because they are mutually convenient for the two families; the bride's parents need not support her for very long, and the groom's family acquires an unpaid servant and sometimes a dowry ("Child Marriages," 1994).

## Summary

As the foregoing examples demonstrate, rites and rituals can serve a variety of functions within a society. But as the passing of time brings technological advances and greater communication among peoples, revisions can influence the forms and functions of cultural ceremonies, as the following cases show.

## RITUALS AND CULTURAL CHANGE

Processes of cultural change as they relate to rituals can be demonstrated with female circumcision, funerals, and credit cards.

### Female Circumcision

The way the practice of female circumcision responds to cultural change can usefully be viewed through the lens of conflict theory, which portrays events as confrontations between opposing forces. One set of forces that seeks to retain the circumcision rite contends against another set that would alter or eliminate the rite.

A formidable range of factors combine to defend circumcision rituals. Men who hope to maintain their historical domination of women can favor circumcision as a device for sustaining their control. In this endeavor, they may enlist the support of religious lore that ostensibly represents God's or Nature's will. In a survey conducted in the Sudan in 1993, more than 50% of male respondents asserted that female circumcision is a Muslim religious requirement (Rushwan, 1995). Men's favoring circumcision is further supported by folklore, such as the belief that a man will turn impotent or die if his penis touches a clitoris ("Female Circumcision," 1997, p. 2).

Women who themselves have been circumcised often reason that their own experience is also suitable for their female offspring. In the Sudan survey, 41% of the women interviewed approved of the ritual "because it promotes cleanliness, increases a girl's chances for marriage, improves fertility, protects virginity, and prevents immorality" (Rushwan, 1995, p. 17). In a girl's passing from childhood to adulthood, circumcision may also be seen as a device ridding females of a lingering masculinity. Thus, in cultures that interpret the clitoris as an undeveloped penis, a woman who still has her clitoris intact can be considered somewhat bisexual and a bad marriage risk.

The forces arrayed against circumcision include medical, human rights, feminist, and educational organizations as well as legislatures. The World Health Organization and the United Nation's Children's Fund, along with a variety of medical associations, have attacked the practice through (a) information distributed via mass-communication media, (b) medical clinics, (c) foreign-aid programs, and (d) the political lobbying of legislators. Activists from the growing feminist movements in North America and Europe have recruited women in developing nations to press for the abolition of female circumcision. As a result of such efforts, the governments of Egypt, Kenya, Senegal, and Togo have outlawed the practice. However, the rite is so embedded in culture that simply passing a law proscribing the custom has failed to stop it. Circumcision has gone underground. This means that trained medical personnel who earlier had legally performed circumcision have now abandoned the practice that henceforth will be continued surreptitiously by untrained women in unsanitary settings. Or, as in Kenya, despite the law's banning circumcision, some medical personnel secretly continue to perform it in order to augment their regular income ("Medicalization of FGM," 1999).

A strategy for retaining the passage-to-adulthood feature of the circumcision rite while avoiding any physical mutilation is found in an innovative substitute introduced in Kenya in 1996. The plan, known as *Ntanira Na Mugambo* or "circumcision through words," is an alternative to traditional female circumcision. It's a joint creation of the Kenyan Maendeleo Ya Wanawake Organisation and the Program for Appropriate Technology in Health (PATH), a nonprofit, international organization whose aim is to improve the health of women and children in developing countries.

> [Ntanira Na Mugambo] consists of a week of seclusion, where the girls are taught basic anatomy and physiology, sexual and reproductive health, hygiene, gender issues, respect for adults, development of self-esteem, and

how to deal with peer pressure. Because the girls want recognition, during the final day of celebration they receive a certificate, presents, are granted special wishes, and become the center of attention in the community.

The program also has a "family life" educational component in the schools, community outreach activities, and a "male motivation" component aimed at young men. After the men receive their training, where they are taught the negative effects of female genital mutilation for women's health and quality of life, they have to commit themselves not to require that their future wives be circumcised. These approaches are complemented by the education of the girls' mothers, fathers, aunts, and godmothers on the advantages of the new approach. (Chelala, 1998, p. 126)

In effect, the intent of the strategy's sponsors has been to alter the form of the adolescent-rite-of-passage component of the participants' folk psychology.

## Funerals

In recent decades, several types of cultural change have conspired to alter traditional funerary practices in a variety of societies. The types have included a diminution of religious belief, the intrusion of foreign cultural practices, and technological innovations.

The decline of Christian church membership in Germany during the latter decades of the 20th century was accompanied by an increasing number of secular funerals (25% in Berlin, 10% in the country at large). Downey has portrayed the typical nature of secular funerals as follows:

> Family and friends have assembled in a chapel on cemetery grounds. They hear not a hymn but a piece of classical music. Then a man rises and walks to the podium. He is dressed not in an ecclesiastical robe, but in a business suit, and his first words are not "In the name of the Father and of the Son and of the Holy Ghost," but "we are assembled to remember a life which has come to an end." He reads poetry, perhaps German classics, or something folksy. He may set forth Marxist ideals, although that occurs less and less often these days. He recalls the life of the deceased. More secular music follows as the family makes it way to the grave. (Downey, 1998, p. 358)

A similar decline in traditional funerals among Catholics in the U.S. state of Delaware motivated Bishop Michael A. Saltarelli to issue a paper titled "The Need to Promote the Consistent Use of Catholic Funeral Rites." The paper was a combined plea and warning to parishioners after nearly 24% of burials at Catholic cemeteries in recent months had failed to include a funeral mass ("Delaware Diocese," 1999, p. 4).

Since the 1980s, Korean funeral customs have been changing at an increasing pace, apparently as the result of industrialization, urbanization, and the influence of Western culture, including Christianity. Whereas in Korean tradition funeral ceremonies have been held in the mourners' homes and then the deceased is buried, in recent times more ceremonies have been conducted in mortuaries and the corpse cremated (Lee, 1996).

Computer technology began to alter funeral arrangements in North America during the 1990s as the Internet started offering services traditionally furnished by funeral parlors in the deceased's home town. As a result, the funeral director at the local mortuary was being replaced by websites that could guide grievers through funeral planning (Cremation Specialists at www.cremation.com), set up a virtual memorial for $14 (www.HeavenlyDoor.com), and post eternal obituaries for computer users to read (Comarow, Cohen, & Mulrine, 1999).

Appalled by the high prices that his parishioners were being charged for caskets and mortuary services, a Catholic priest in Arizona established a World Wide Web site (www.xroads.com/funerals) that revealed the actual costs to morticians for the contents of funeral services (Bryce, 1996, p. 5).

To care for the funerary needs of increasingly multicultural societies, the largest funeral company in North America—Service Corporation International—placed representatives in cities to conduct their business out of minivans that carried sample cremation urns, a catalogue of caskets, and other funeral accessories. A representative would meet with the bereaved in their home to help plan each step of the funeral, adjusting the nature of the ceremony and its supplies to the financial and cultural needs of the particular family ("Frugal Funerals," 1996).

As a consequence of such cultural changes as the above, folk beliefs about the proper conduct of mortuary practices were undergoing revision in numerous societies.

## Credit Cards

Cultural change may produce new markers of passage from one life stage to another. In the following case, legislation (a new law) precipitated by a technological advance (computer networks) furnished youths a new symbol of adult status. Poniewozik (1998) observed that a recent Child Online Protection Act in the United States required proof of computer users' adult status before they would be permitted to open "adult-level" (pornographic) sites on the World Wide Web. The act provided that a credit card would be accepted as proof of adult status. Thus, possessing a credit card could now be seen as a symbol of passing from adolescence to adulthood, because the cardholder not only could access pornography but also could borrow money without a cosigner.

# 11

# Time and the Life Span

*What is the nature of historical time and of the human life span?*

Conceptions of historical time and of the human life span can vary from one culture to another, with those variations bearing important implications for how people think about life and for how they behave. The following discussion begins with alternative versions of historical time, continues with varied conceptions of the life span, and closes with an example of the effect of cultural change on notions of time and the life span.

## VERSIONS OF HISTORICAL TIME

In cultures that trace their roots to Europe (typically referred to as *Western cultures*), historical time is conceived to be linear, portrayed as a straight, unbroken line extending from the past into the future. In secular versions of this linear model, the question of exactly when time began in the past and when it will end in the future remains unanswered. The relatively recent *big bang* theory of the creation of the cosmos has been gradually entering the folk psychology of scientifically informed cultures. According to the theory, the physical universe began more than 10,000,000,000 years ago when the cosmos's primordial compressed state reached a condition of high temperature and density that suddenly exploded into the matter that has evolved to compose all things that exist today. However, in some religious traditions, historical time is estimated to have begun several thousand years ago, with the end of time predicted to occur during a specified period in the future. The Suidas teachings found in the Tuscany region of Italy propose that the universe and its contents were created over a six-thousand-year period, and will continue for six thousand years more (Gaskell, 1981, p. 184). In certain religions, such as Buddhism, time's beginning and end are judged to be indeterminate—a mystery remaining unsolved (Marek, 1988, p. 84).

The folk psychologies of still other cultures depict historical time in ways quite different from that of a continuous straight line. North American Indians have traditionally subscribed to a concept of time and process "universally understood not in the Western linear manner, but in terms of the circle—that is, cyclical and reciprocal. The seasons of nature, the span of life, human or nonhuman, are understood in a cyclical manner and are reexpressed formally in architectural styles reflecting the cosmos and through a rich variety of ritual or ceremonial forms and acts" (Brown, 1989, p. 4).

The Aztecs and Mayans of Central America held such a cyclical view, vestiges of which are still observed today in some Mexican Indian cultures. Originally, two calendars functioned in parallel to guide the conduct of life. One calendar cast the solar year into 18 months, each 20 days long, with 5 unnamed days added to make 365. The solar years were then grouped into 52-year units, comparable to the Western calendar's centuries. The second calendar, whose year contained 260 days, was used for divining the fate people could expect in matters of birth, marriage, and other important decisions.

> Just as the world was created, destroyed, and recreated time and again, so smaller units of time repeated themselves. The year and every new cycle began with the lighting of fires in the temples and even on the hearth, for the end of one and beginning of another was a time of uncertainty. The most fearful period was the end of one 52-year cycle, for the Aztec believed that if the present world era was to come to a cataclysmic end, it would happen then. (*Mysteries of the Ancient Americas*, 1986, p. 291)

An undulating sort of cyclical time is recognized by adherents of China's Taoism (The Way) who subscribe to a widely accepted interpretation of the line in Lao tzu's (604-531 B.C.E.) *Tao Te Ching* that reads "Turning back is how the way moves" (Lau, 1963, p. 25). The interpretation holds that all things undergo a process of cyclical change that results from the interaction of Taoism's complementary forces of Yin (the passive female principle) and Yang (the dynamic male principle). When either Yin or Yang goes to extremes, the other one takes control, thereby resulting in continuous life cycles.

> What is weak inevitably develops into something strong, but when this process of development reaches its limit, the opposite process of decline sets in and what is strong once again becomes something weak, and decline reaches its lowest limit only to give way once more to development. Thus, there is an endless cycle of development and decline. (Lau, 1963, p. 25)

However, when Cooper (1998) studied Chinese culture in Dongyang County, Zhejiang Province, he learned that people celebrate their birthday by eating "longevity noodles" (wheat or rice noodles containing two eggs). The belief that noodles are a longevity food is explained by the noodles' length, implying that Dongyang Chinese may conceive of time in terms similar to Western metaphysics—by the metaphor of distance measured along a continuous cylinder extending from the present into the future and leaving the past behind.

Another way of gauging historical time, especially popular in nonliterate cultures, is in terms of significant events. What people recall about the past is located, not in relation to hours or days or years, but in relation to important happenings—marriages, births, deaths, changes of residence, trips, people's visits, changes of employment, financial gain or loss, fire, flood, drought, earthquake, and the like. Leach (1961) has suggested that among such event markers are those that signify passage from one stage of life to another, drawing attention to the "psychologically unpleasant experience" of time's irreversibility, thereby serving as a measure of mortal time. The most important of those events in Chinese village culture are birth, marriage, the family dividing (in families with more than one son, when additional sons leave the parents' home to start separate families), and death (Cooper, 1998).

In cultures that conceive of time in terms of events, the sorts of occasions that define longer periods usually differ from those that mark shorter periods. This point is illustrated in Eickelman's (1977) description of time concepts among the Bni Battu, a herding and agricultural people living in the Tadla Plain on the western foothills of the Middle Atlas mountains in Morroco. A year's time is divided into the four seasons, with summer and winter the most prominent markers, for they determine where and when herding and farming activities take place. Spring and autumn are seen as transition periods. A week is divided into market days, with particular markets held on different days. A day is seen as

> punctuated by the five daily prayers obligatory to all Muslims, but not always practiced. Their performance is calibrated to the position of the sun. These are the prayers of dawn, mid-day, late afternoon, sunset, and a final "supper" prayer. In town, these prayers are fully integrated into the rhythm of social life; the opening and closing of shops and other daily activities are often regulated by them. In the countryside, the timing of the prayers is fully known by men, although [the prayers] are performed by few persons. The daily prayers are seen as related to each other but are not seen as orderly divisions of time that can be used for counting. Instead, they are concrete experiences. (Eickelman, 1977, p. 44)

Other specific events which can be conceived of as sequential but not spaced evenly across linear time are such happenings of personal significance as particular individuals' birth, leaving the community, marriage, acquiring a new home, death, and the like. Time, in this sense, is not identical for everyone in the culture since different persons experience such memorable moments at different linear times. Although the Bni Battu are somewhat aware of the Julian solar calendar and the Muslim lunar calendar, people's daily lives are rarely guided by such formal concepts of time. Rather, daily life is conceived temporally "in terms of irregular, island-like concrete experiences" (Eickelman, 1977, p. 44)

In an event-time system, no time has passed if nothing is happening. A person sitting idly under a tree is not "wasting time," for no event of consequence is occurring. As Hall (1959) found in his study of Pueblo Indians, events begin when they begin and no sooner. He learned that a ceremonial dance does not start at a particular time but, rather, "It starts when 'things' are ready." Hence, time is not "an external standard that can interfere with events to trigger them into action. On the contrary, it is the events that trigger the actions to be taken" (Dahl, 1999, pp. 48-49).

A kind of simultaneous time—in which olden days exist at the present time—is recognized in some folk psychologies. Among Australian Aborigines and some tribes in Papua New Guinea, rituals featuring chants and enactments reminiscent of the past are performed to reestablish the past in the present. Such ceremonies "memorialize the past through myth, narrative, and names. Ritual commemorates these memories and recreates the past, especially ancestral movement through and creation of the landscape and various spatially anchored events" (Silverman, 1997, p. 115).

The Upper Skagit Indians in the state of Washington divided historical time into two periods, a remote time when the world was different and a recent time. During the first period, which Collins refers to as the myth era,

> animals were much larger than they are now. Beasts like the dog and raven were as large as human beings, spoke, and in general behaved like humans. The topography was entirely different; there were no mountains, and rivers ran in courses different from their present ones. (Collins, 1974, p. 211)

The first historical period was subsequently transformed into the second, present-day era by a benevolent tribal hero and his brothers—Knife, Fire, and a third brother who associated with a trio of guardian spirits, Raven, Mink, and Coyote.

## Status as It Relates to Event Sequence

Another aspect of time that can be part of folk psychologies is the status accorded events in relation to when they occurred. As an illustration, North American Indian tradition generally proposes that (a) in the original creation of the occupants of the universe, animals appeared before humans, and (b) whatever appears earlier is superior to whatever appears later. Thus, animals are thought to enjoy a certain superiority over people, and the respect accorded certain animals derives at least partly from this belief. Analysts of Indian traditions have also suggested that this sequence-of-appearance principle, when applied to human generations, accounts for the high respect shown to the aged in Native American societies (Brown, 1989, p. 71).

## THE HUMAN LIFE SPAN

Folk psychologies do not all agree about how to determine when an individual's life begins and when it ends or what stages a person passes through during a lifetime. This disagreement more often concerns a person's ethereal essence (soul, spirit, or psyche) than the person's body (soma).

## The Body

The body's most obvious life span starts with birth, when the newborn exits from the mother's womb and begins to breathe. However, folk psychologies increasingly move the body's beginning to a point in time before birth. In "scientifically informed cultures" that point is the moment a sperm cell from the father joins an ovum in the mother to produce an integrated cell that will multiply at a rapid rate until the infant's birth around nine months later.

In most cultures, the body's sojourn on earth ends with physical death, as signaled by the heart's ceasing to beat; but there are varied beliefs about what should be done with the remains. In Hindu practice, the body is cremated and the ashes cast into a river or sea, thereby returning the body to the original elements from which all matter in the universe is ostensibly composed—fire, air, earth, and water. In Judeo-Christian-Islamic tradition, when a person is buried or cremated, it's customary to think of the body of the deceased being converted back into earth, as reflected in the oft-uttered funeral benediction implying a life-and-death cycle: "Ashes to ashes, dust to dust."

Ijaw folk psychology in Africa's Niger Delta teaches that mortals pass through a cycle in which dead ancestors can be reborn as children who come into the world with supernatural powers derived from a spirit world populated by ancestors. The young not only can communicate with the spirits but also can return to the spirit world by dying (Leis, 1982).

Successive stages of life in some cultures are likened to phenomena of nature, such as the advance of the seasons. In Sucre, an Ecuadorian Indian community, a parallel between the development of people and of crops is manifested in the use of plant imagery to explain human reproduction and growth. The parallel is also seen in periodic festivals, including the Easter celebration (Bourque, 1995, p. 75). Other cultures compare the human lifetime to animals' life phases. For instance, the Dassanetch of southwest Ethiopia equate a youth's achieving manhood and setting up his own household with the behavior of bees when a hive becomes packed and a portion of the residents leave in a swarm to establish their own colony in a different location (Almagor, 1985).

People who ponder the pattern of the body's decline over the life span are challenged to account for why humans fail to remain youthful as the years of adulthood advance. In the folk psychology of Bororo society in the Mato Grozzo region of Brazil, the essence of a person's strength or vitality is *raka*, which is carried in the blood. A person's *raka* exists in a finite amount that can never be increased but gradually diminishes with the passing of time. The progressive loss of *raka* is revealed in the symptoms of aging—reduced strength, wrinkling of the skin, stooped posture, and more.

> Copulation is responsible for most loss of *raka*, but failure to observe dietary and other restrictions during pregnancy, birth, initiation, funerals, and other periods of ritual danger can also diminish a person's limited stock of *raka*. On the other hand, *raka* can be sustained—individuals can stay young— through careful observance of all dietary and other restrictions, by sexual continence, and especially through the consumption of certain game animals, fish, and plants. (Crocker, 1977, p. 131)

## The Spiritual Essence

There is marked variation across cultures in beliefs about the length of life of the soul or numinous self.

Members of modern industrial societies who subscribe to a secular folk psychology accept the belief that each individual not only has a body but also an invisible *mind* (a thinking and remembering capacity). However, they deny—or seriously doubt—that anyone has a soul, particularly a soul that endures after visible death. Thus, to adherents of secular belief systems, the issue of when one's soul begins and when it ends is mere fantasy, not worth discussing. But for proponents of religious persuasions, the issue is intensely important.

Judeo-Christian-Islamic lore holds that at some time while an unborn child is in the mother's womb, God infuses a soul into the fetus. Exactly when this occurs is a matter of continuing debate. In Islamic tradition, as reported in the Sunnah (Sayings of the Prophet Mohammed), the soul is encased in the body 120 days after conception.

> Every one of you is made [into a fertilized ovum] which stays there in the womb of his mother for 40 days. Then he is made into a clot of congealed blood for another 40 days, then into a lump for 40 days. Then God sends an Angel to put a soul into him, and the Angel issues four words [foretelling] his earnings, his death, his deeds, and whether man is going to be happy or miserable. (Munzudi in Almunzri, 1977, p. 488)

Whereas a person's human spiritual core in Judeo-Christian-Islamic belief is created about the same time as the body, when the body expires, that core—the soul—lives on in an invisible condition. All souls, however, do not experience the same destiny after the death of the body. Through the grace of God, some souls spend eternity in heaven, while others enter hell or an indeterminate state called limbo (Thomas, 1985).

Hindu dogma contends that each person's spiritual essence began at some unspecified moment in the infinite past when individual souls separated out of the master Cosmic Soul to be placed in an earthly body. That soul may thereafter leave the initial body upon that body's demise, only to be encased in another body for the period of that new physique's tenure on earth, then into a further succession of bodies—human, animal, or inanimate—until the personal soul attains final release through the person's leading a perfect life, allowing the soul to merge once more into the Cosmic Soul (Buhler, 1886, pp. 492-495).

In Confucianism, both physical and spiritual life begins at conception in the form of potentials that are gradually activated over the years following birth. Physical life normally ends seven or eight decades later with the death of the body, but the spirit lives on for an indeterminate period to be honored ceremonially by those family members and friends still alive on earth (Chen, 1963).

In Japan's Shinto tradition, a person's potential for godlike qualities is inherited from the ancestral line that extends back to the earliest deities. However, the life of the individual person begins with conception. As in Confucianism, the spiritual self will continue to exist for an indefinite period after the body's decay. At death, a person's soul (*tama*) can assume any of a number of forms, even appearing as a ghost, a monster, or a shining ball moving through the night air. Souls of those who died violently "are particularly restless, they could be dangerous to the living unless placated by food and purification" (Spae, 1972, p. 37). Such appeasement of souls is a sacred duty, especially during the 49 days following death when the departed one's spirit is thought to linger within the house before leaving for a place of comfort. Some Shinto authorities claim that the soul returns to the gods a year after death (Herbert, 1967,

p. 67), while others propose that 33 years after death the soul may become a revered spirit—a *kami*—and thereby enter the ultimate stage of happiness during which it blesses and protects family members who are still living (Spae, 1972, p. 38).

As is true in many cultures, the Luo people of Kenya see death simply as a rite of passage within an eternal life span. When persons die, they are not separated from their clan but merely transformed from physical beings into spiritual ones that still belong to the same clan (Nyamongo, 1999).

An envisioned death-and-birth cycle among the Dene Tha (an Athapaskan subpopulation in northern Alberta, Canada) proposes that the soul of a dead person can enter the womb of a woman so as to be born again in a sex of the soul's choice. The Dene Tha accept several sorts of evidence as proof of such reincarnation—evidence that includes (a) a mother-to-be or a father-to-be telling of a dream about their expected infant being the reincarnation of someone now deceased, (b) people recognizing that an infant's appearance or personality resembles that of somebody who died, (c) someone's vision of a dead person roaming public places or private homes in search of a woman's body to inhabit, (d) a child's displaying the affections and aversions of someone now dead, (e) an older child or adult, in a waking state, recalling events of past lives, and (f) birthmarks similar to those on someone now deceased (Goulet, 1996, p. 695).

In summary, beliefs about the lifetime of the noncorporeal self vary markedly from one folk psychology to another.

## CULTURAL CHANGE AND CONCEPTS OF TIME

Beliefs about what constitutes time and the human life span are often altered by religious or philosophical conversion. When such conversion is widespread in a community, rather than limited to one or two individuals, the newly adopted perspective qualifies as a component of the community's folk psychology. Sometimes the introduction of a novel notion of time completely obliterates a culture's original conception. Or in other cases, the converts are able to accommodate both the old and new versions, thereby producing a syncretic interpretation that will often dismay and distress the agents who introduced the innovation—such agents as missionaries, political activists, teachers, shamans, and social scientists.

Laird (1976, p. 44) reports that in the days before Europeans invaded the territory of the Chemehuevis Indians in the southwestern United States, historical time had been circular, reflected in the arrival and departure of the seasons in an endlessly repeated pattern. However, in the latter decades of the 19th century, with the arrival of settlers and the U.S.

government's asserting its authority over the indigenous peoples, time suddenly became linear. One version of this intrusion took the form of the Ghost Dance, carried into Chemehuevis territory by tribes from the north. The dance and its accompanying lyrics preached of an impending doom, warning that the world soon would be destroyed by fire. Only those individuals who had actively participated in the ceremony would survive, "dancing on top of the flames until the time of renewal should come. This suggests a strong Mormon influence upon those responsible for bringing the Ghost Dance south" (Laird, 1976, p. 44.

Among many of the Chemehuevis, conceptions of the lifespan were also altered by the European invasion. Laird (1976, p. 247), in commenting on the inability of Christian missionaries to completely erase traditional Indian religious concepts and practices, observed that "In recent times the Catholic church has developed a happy faculty for coexisting with those symbols of an earlier belief which it cannot assimilate—as in the Pueblos, where the same men attend ceremonies in both church and kiva." This coexistence included merging a Christian view of the soul's journey after death with the existing view of the Native Americans. For instance, the traditional Chemehuevis version of that journey pictured the shade of the deceased traveling far north to Spirit Land, where the crops are always abundant and clans are distinguished by the color of the corn they possess. Such a belief could easily be united with the less precise Christian portrayal of how a soul arrives in heaven (Laird, 1976, p. 40).

# 12

# Gender and Sex

*In what ways are females and males alike and different, and what sorts of sexual activities do they practice?*

All folk psychologies identify likenesses and differences between males and females in terms of both sex and gender. Throughout the following discussion, *sex* is defined by the physiological differences between males and females. The term *sexual behavior* refers to ways people attempt to satisfy their sexual urges. *Gender* is defined by the traits attributed to each of the sexes, traits that decree the roles in life considered proper for males and for females. Whereas a person's sex is determined principally—if not entirely—by genetic inheritance, gender is a product of people's opinions. Gender, in effect, is a social construction—an agreement among members of a society about the social and psychological traits that distinguish males from females. That agreement can differ from one culture to another. In the following pages, cultural conceptions of gender are described under two headings: (a) gender variations across folk psychologies and (b) gender and cultural change. Those two topics are followed by cultural beliefs regarding (c) people's sexual orientation, (d) their sexual behavior, and (e) the effect of cultural change on sexual orientation and behavior.

## GENDER VARIATIONS ACROSS FOLK PSYCHOLOGIES

Four interrelated ways that folk psychologies can differ in their conceptions of gender are in conceptions of female and male (a) traits, (b) roles, (c) status and power, and (d) behavior expectations.

## Gender Traits

In all societies certain important personality characteristics attributed to women differ from those attributed to men. Furthermore, there is considerable agreement across societies about what many of those traits may be, as illustrated in a study of *pancultural gender stereotypes* in 25 nations, including ones from Europe, Asia, Africa, Oceania, and the Americas (Williams, Satterwhite, & Best, 1999). To obtain respondents' notions of female and male traits, researchers asked women and men college students in each country to judge which adjectives out of a list of 300 described females, which described males, and which could describe both females or males. The 25 traits most often assigned to females across the 25 countries were: affected, affectionate, anxious, attractive, charming, complaining, curious, dependent, dreamy, emotional, fearful, feminine, fussy, meek, mild, sensitive, sexy, shy, soft-hearted, submissive, superstitious, talkative, timid, weak, and whiny. The 25 traits most often associated with males were: active, adventurous, aggressive, ambitious, autocratic, coarse, courageous, cruel, daring, dominant, energetic, enterprising, forceful, independent, inventive, logical, masculine, progressive, robust, rude, self-confident, stern, strong, tough, and unemotional. Whereas there was considerable agreement across the 25 societies in people's opinions about gender-related personality characteristics, the emphasis given to each trait often differed from one country to another.

Other studies of perceived gender traits in a variety of societies have characterized women as retiring and emotional, compassionate, lacking physical strength and stamina, followers rather than leaders, intellectually inferior to men, making decisions through intuition rather than logical reasoning, and often changing their minds. Males, compared to females, have been portrayed as more aggressive and outspoken, more intelligent, more logical, more objective in their judgments, more resolute in their decisions, and blessed with greater initiative, physical strength, and stamina. (Tong, 1998). Consequently, some critics of such stereotyping have suggested that

> women are treated as if they are governed by their bodies and men as if they are ruled by their minds. . . . Where men think, women feel. The man is the head of the family, the woman the heart. (Jamieson, 1994, p. 53)

The traits assigned to the genders are often rooted in long-established religious doctrine and pictured as decreed by God. For example, passages of the Jewish Bible (the Old Testament of the Christian Bible) depict women as fearful and timid (Isaiah 19:16; Jeremiah 50:37, 51:30*).

---

* Each biblical citation identifies the name of the book, the chapter number, and (following the colon) the verse number.

Catholic tradition glorifies Jesus's mother Mary as being chaste, virtuous, compassionate, passive, nurturing, and particularly dedicated to child care—a model to be emulated by females young and old. The fundamental source of doctrine in Islamic societies is the Qur'an, which portrays women as innately inferior to men in strength, intellectual ability, and logical judgment. Therefore, "Men shall have pre-eminence over women, because of those advantages wherein God hath caused the one of them to excel the other" (*Koran*, 1844, p. 64). However, this does not mean that women are devoid of power. In Islamic doctrine, women's inherent sexual attractiveness can readily take advantage of men's inherently strong sexual drive, so men can experience uncontrollable sex urges if not protected from women's wiles. This captious view of females, sometimes referred to as the Dangerous Woman Syndrome, is also found in a variety of cultures outside of Islam (Derné, 1995).

## Gender Roles

The term *gender roles* refers to the culturally dictated tasks or functions that males and females are expected to perform. Role expectations are part of a society's folk psychology.

Derné's (1995) study of family life among upper-middle-class Hindus in Benaras, India, identifies consistent roles for wives and husbands. When a woman marries, she and her husband are expected to live with her husband's parents. She is obliged to free her mother-in-law from housekeeping chores, to obey her mother-in-law's commands, to bear child-rearing responsibilities, and to remain at home unless given permission to go out. If the wife does leave the home, she is to be accompanied by a family member in order to prevent her from talking to men and to protect her from strangers who might endanger her. A proper Hindu wife always obeys her husband without question or complaint. In contrast, the husband's role consists of earning the family's living, making all important decisions (often with the aid of his parents and siblings), and entertaining himself as he chooses.

In accounting for the prevalence of such role assignments, Derné contrasts the bases for action of middle-class Hindu men and white, middle-class North American men.

> The Hindu men I interviewed largely—but not wholly—share an informal commonsense understanding of what motivates individual action. This distinctive *social framework for understanding action* is different from the dominant framework of American men . . . who usually see actions as depending on the choices of autonomous individuals. [In contrast,] Hindu men understand individual actions as determined by the social group to which the individual belongs. . . . Hindu men fundamentally distrust any individual action unrestrained by caste and family. (Derné, 1997, p. vii)

According to Derné, the secure place that gender-role distinctions continue to hold in Indian folk belief is not simply a function of tradition. Rather, men actively support the distinctions out of self-interest, out of the belief that such role assignments "help maintain male privilege by making women docile, obedient servants in their husbands' families" (Derné, 1997, p. 16).

In traditional Islamic societies, the life of a woman is expected to center on fulfilling her husband's needs, carrying out his commands, and tending his children. The proper Islamic woman need not attend school nor should she work outside the home. To prevent men other than her husband from being sexually tempted by her seductive appearance, the typical woman is confined most of the time to her home and, when outside the home, is required to cover as much of her body as possible, including the wearing of a scarf or hood (*hejab*) over her head and a veil to conceal her face.

Virtually all folk psychologies' conceptions of occupations distinguish among women's work, men's work, and work considered equally appropriate for both genders. For instance, among residents of Huaili village in North China, "Women are described by villagers as better suited for the close care of cotton plants and for picking cotton; men are viewed as especially valuable for the planting and harvesting of grain" (Judd, 1994, p. 42). Furthermore, in Huaili, as in most of the world's cultures, "men rarely contributed to domestic labor [meal preparation, housekeeping, child care], and many found the idea that they might do so laughable" (Judd, 1994, p. 44).

The Nuer of southeastern Sudan, whose villages are located along the Nile River and its tributaries, maintain a rigid division of occupational specialization between men and women. Men herd cattle, fish, and hunt. Women are not permitted to take cattle to grazing lands. Instead, they must milk the family's animals twice a day, tend gardens, prepare meals, maintain the home, and care for children (Bonvillain, 1998, pp. 64-65).

However, other societies are more egalitarian in their occupational assignments. Among the Navajo in the U.S. Southwest, men have worked more often in house building, agriculture, and caring for cattle and horses, while women have tended sheep and goats and done the family's weaving, cleaning, cooking, and child rearing. But these have not been rigid role assignments.

> Indeed, it was common for women or men to perform any task, or for tasks to be carried out by women and men together. Most ceremonial practitioners were male, but women could also become practitioners. As for political roles, which became important on the reservation, they were once held predominantly by men but, recently, have been taken on by women as well. There are also indications that before the reservation pe-

riod, some women went to war along with men and that those who were successful warriors became war chiefs. (Stone, 1997, p. 126)

The way different roles are assigned to males and females sometimes results from a society's attempt to accommodate separate belief systems that have been adopted at different periods of the society's history. For instance, in modern times, Korean rural villagers continue to practice an ancient indigenous folk religion that endures compatibly with more recent Confucian beliefs "because its emphasis on the power of the dead person's spirits can be the common ground with the ancestor worship ceremonies which are the core of Confucian rituals" (Cho, 1986, pp. 185-186). Responsibility for perpetuating these parallel forms of religion are divided between the genders. In relation to the Confucian tradition of filial obligation, men conduct formal worship ceremonies (*chesa*) honoring their direct ancestors. Women, operating from the indigenous folk psychology perspective, conduct rituals for spirits excluded from the Confucian family ceremonies.

> While a man provides the backbone of family relationships by performing *chesa*, a woman counterbalances the spiritual structure by pleasing neglected ancestral spirits in order to prevent unpredicted family misfortune. (Cho, 1986, p. 190)

In keeping with this division of labor, most Korean shamans who are charged with negotiating between mortals and the neglected spirit world are women.

Subcultures within a society sometimes differ in their conceptions of proper role assignments. For example, Stephen reported that among rural women in Brazil the gender roles in household decisionmaking and the titling of land and of houses to women varied by ethnic group.

> Women of Italian, Polish, and German descent stated that men dominated household decision-making and that only sons inherited land and agricultural machinery. Women of Portuguese-Brazilian descent stated that they had received land from their parents and felt they had a more equal say in household decision-making. (Stephen, 1997, p. 212)

## Gender Status and Power

The word *status* means the level of respect or prestige accorded a person or a type of person by members of the particular society. Status is closely linked to power, when *power* is defined as the ability to influence the behavior of others. Two dimensions of power are authority and influence. *Authority* is the power prescribed by the culture and is represented in customs and laws that are part of the folk psychology. *Influence* is the power that derives from an individual's own abilities, skills, charisma, or similar personal characteristics.

Status can be general or else specific to selected aspects of life. A general status attribution observed in many folk psychologies is a belief in male superiority and female inferiority. Males are thought to be more competent overall and more deserving of respect and praise than females, so men are invested with greater authority than women. However, in other folk psychologies the status attributed to each gender depends on the specific facet of life under consideration.

Societies can differ in the width of the status gap between males and females. An extreme gap is illustrated by the extent of male dominance among Yanomamo villagers who inhabit the Amazon River border between Brazil and Venezuela. The highest prestige among the Yanomamo is accorded victorious warriors—males who defeat their rivals in frequent raids between villages, with the raids aimed at killing as many inhabitants as possible and capturing young women to serve as wives in the attackers' polygynous society. Being a successful warrior is a principal consideration in elevating a man to the position of village leader. Prestige also accrues to men who contract multiple marriages, particularly with daughters of prominent fathers in neighboring villages. For women, marriage emphasizes their low social standing. When they wed, they move to their husband's village, thereby "isolating them from their own kin, stranding them in unfamiliar communities and depriving them of any emotional support in the event of conflicts in their new households" (Bonvillain, 1998, p. 78). As wives, they can look forward to frequent beatings and sexual assault. Their status is further diminished by customs governing Yanomamo economic life. All direct production of subsistence goods through farming, hunting, and fishing are carried out by men. Women's contributions to family life are limited to meal preparation, housekeeping, and child care—activities judged less vital for the family's welfare.

In contrast to the marked status discrepancy between males and females in Yanomamo society are the more similar social positions of men and women among the Navajo. Traditional Navajo social structure has been *matrilineal* (the ancestral line is traced through the wife's side of the family), and *matrilocal* (the husband comes to live with the wife's clan or family). In matrilineal cultures, authority and power are often divided somewhat equally between the sexes. Both women and men can independently own such property as livestock, and both participate in work assignments and in decisions about family matters. The respected status of Navajo women in the past is suggested by records from early Catholic missions reporting that in cases of murder, the murderer was required to pay compensation to the victim's family—three or four horses for a male victim, five or more horses if the victim was female.

According to Reichard (1950, p. 29), Navajo "ritual teachings stress male and female as a basic form of symbolism; the notion is that only by pairing can any entity be complete."

> Although egalitarian gender relations among the Navajo have persisted, recent economic transformations have altered productive roles and contributions of women and men to their households. . . . Families who continue to focus on sheepherding and farming tend to live in traditional [extended matrilocal arrangements]; those engaged in wage work tend to split off into nuclear [small family] units. (Bonvillain, 1998, p. 60)

Frequently the characteristics envisioned as proper for one gender are displayed by certain members of the opposite sex, so that the folk psychology's portrayal of gender-suited traits may be somewhat at odds with reality. For instance, in the folk tradition of Blackfoot Indians living in Montana and in the Canadian province of Alberta, such attributes as boldness, aggressiveness, and a drive to amass property and social power are considered ideal traits for men. Hence, women who display those characteristics are called "manly hearted." The fact that such women are not unusual in Blackfoot society is suggested by a 1939 study revealing that about one-third of elderly (over age 60) North Piegan women qualified as manly hearted. They owned property, were effective managers and workers,

> forthright and assertive in public, in their homes, and as sexual partners, and were active in religious rituals. Blackfoot men claim they want women to be submissive, docile, and quiet—that is, women should be pposite in character to the ideal man—but in fact, the manly-hearted woman is admired as well as feared by both men and women. (Kehoe, 1995, p. 115)

Therefore, in the analysis of cultures, a useful distinction can be drawn between the kind of gender status and power in a society's folk psychology and the status and power reflected in daily social intercourse. An illustrative case is that of male-female relations in an Upper Burma (Upper Myanmar) village described by Spiro (1997). Whereas in the formal, folk-psychology version of village society men enjoy superior status in virtually all realms of life, in certain realms—such as that of the family—women are actually in greater control.

> The wife holds the purse strings—as is true in most of Southeast Asia. If the husband needs or wants spending money, he must ask his wife for it. As the men view it, the women hold the purse strings because a man expects his wife to assume the financial responsibility in their marriage. The women, however, view this arrangement as a mark of the husband's dependency on the wife. Men, so the women claim, are irresponsible—somewhat like children; were it not for the wife's control of the

family income, the husband would squander the family resources on other women, gambling, and drink. (Spiro, 1997, p. 17)

In addition, the wife often controls other important aspects of her husband's life—what he wears, the food he eats, the friends he brings home, and where he spends his time away from home. However, in order to maintain the cultural conviction that husbands' authority is supreme, wives' dominance in such matters is necessarily subtle. There thus exists the anomaly of (a) a folk-psychology belief in males' general superiority and (b) women's actual superior status in selected domains of life. To explain this discrepancy, Spiro proposed that

> Because of their subordination to and dependence on females in the domestic domain, many males, according to my argument, form the belief that in some important respects they are inferior to females. Since this belief thwarts their wish to believe in [general] male superiority, it is a threat to their self-esteem and consequently arouses narcissistic anxiety. Hence, even though in some critical respects the Ideology of the Superior Male is false, the males are highly motivated to believe it is true by a powerful wish to believe that it is so. (Spiro, 1997, p. 142)

However, performing a role does not necessarily mean that the individual filling the role enjoys the status and power that the role's social position seems to imply. For example, research among Filipino families focusing on two indicators of status and power revealed that even though 92% of wives were in charge of family finances, their husbands—especially in urban settings—had a greater share in deciding how the money was spent. Furthermore, most wives asked their husbands' permission to go out with friends (92%), lend money to relatives (91%), and buy clothes and personal items (63%) (Bautista, 1977). The form of Bautista's study did not make clear the extent to which wives' deferring to husbands actually reflected less power on the wives' part or represented only a semblance of docility dictated by Filipino folk psychology's image of male superiority.

In another Philippine study (Contado, 1981), interviews with husbands and wives among barrio families in eastern Samar concerned task/role allocations and decisionmaking. The results suggested that wives tended to assert more influence than husbands in joint-decision situations, thereby offering support to Spiro's interpretation of gender-power conditions among village families in Burma.

In summary, people's verbal assessments of status and power may not accurately represent status and power in daily personal-social relations. Thus, folk psychology in the form of verbal opinion is not necessarily identical to folk psychology in practice.

## Behavior Expectations

Cultural beliefs about gender traits and roles lead to particular expectations about how females and males will behave. Those expectations then help determine why people may treat girls and boys differently.

In Mixtecan Indian villages of Mexico, the local folk psychology's gender distinctions are reflected in different child-rearing practices that result in different behavior of boys and girls.

> In many of the observations, we encountered the sequence where a mother requests something of a daughter and repeats the request, but each time the request is repeated, it tends to get stronger and stronger until the daughter complies. The pattern with a son is very different in that, in general, the son either complies after being asked a few times or else worms his way out entirely. . . . Girls are expected to be more deferent to adults than are boys. This is certainly, at least in part, preparation for adult roles, but it also reflects the somewhat earlier and stricter obedience training for girls [who are obliged to help their mothers with household tasks]. (Romney & Romney, 1963, p. 70)

A study of child rearing in an Okinawan village also revealed a difference between the expectations for boys and for girls.

> Girls assume caretaking of young siblings earlier and more seriously than boys. A 6-year-old girl may be entrusted with a younger sibling during a whole afternoon. A boy, looking after a younger child, is more likely to abandon or neglect his charge than a girl. . . . Inevitably the girls find themselves with the greater or entire portion of this duty, for the boys either simply refuse or evade assuming their share. This shirking of duty is partly supported by the mother, who, by her failure to enforce assignments, displays passive acceptance or approval of the boys' actions. A girl, however, invites censure not only from her mother but also from other girls for similar actions. (Maretski & Maretski, 1963, p. 619)

Such differential handling of males and females may significantly influence personality development. A survey of the treatment of boys and girls in U.S. schools suggested that teachers' low expectations for female students discouraged girls from participating in class activities, particularly in mathematics, science, computer, and physical education classes. Such negative behavior also encouraged girls to avoid or drop classes in which they felt patronized or devalued. The researchers concluded that such treatment sends gender-specific messages that foster low self-esteem, low self-confidence, and low future aspirations. Consequently, girls learn to depend on teachers and others for guidance and answers rather than depending on themselves. Throughout these negative lessons endured by girls, boys bask in positive attention. Boys learn to become more autonomous and more curious about the world, willing to discover answers for themselves and develop their own abilities. As girls' self-esteem decreases, they are likely to believe that their lack of ability has caused their inadequacies, whereas boys blame lack of effort for their failures. Teachers and students alike come to view girls as incapable (noncompetitive = feminine) and boys as able (competitive = masculine), especially in sports and physical activities, thus reinforcing societal messages passed down in traditional folk belief (American Aassociation of University Women, 1992; Jenkins & Bainer, 1990).

That folk-psychology views can be acquired early in children's lives has also been suggested by studies in North America showing that young children of both genders

> expect girls to be more successful in school and more well-behaved than boys; girls are more concerned than boys with pleasing others, following classroom rules, and being good; students consider reading, artistic and social skills to be feminine but athletic, mathematical, spatial, and mechanical skills to be masculine; boys and girls believe it is more important to do well in subjects associated with their own sex. (Bank, 1985, p. 4879)

## GENDER AND CULTURAL CHANGE

Over the last six decades of the 20th century, two historic events effected significant changes in Americans' beliefs about gender traits and roles. The first event was World War II, which witnessed a large number of women—formerly housewives—taking employment in defense industries and filling positions left vacant by men drawn into the armed forces.

The second event was the feminist movement. Although the most intense version of the movement appeared in North America and Western Europe, the movement's reach was worldwide (Jelen, 1990).

Today's feminism traces its roots back at least two centuries to Mary Wollstonecraft's 1792 *A Vindication of the Rights of Women* (1975) and to the 19th century women's suffrage movement. However, the highly visible recent American feminist efforts are barely four decades old, starting in the 1960s and accelerating into the 1970s and 1980s. According to Bonnie Watkins and Nina Rothchild,

> The modern American women's movement seemed to emerge spontaneously in the 1960s. It began at kitchen tables and in company cafeterias, at PTA meetings and in legislative hearing rooms. It happened in the lives of individual women who responded to the messages of the early days: the personal is political, sisterhood is powerful. (Watkins & Rothchild, 1996, p. xv)

In North America, the efforts of feminist activists have started to effect changes in the views the populace holds about females' traits, roles, and behavior. In other words, the gender content of American folk psychology has been undergoing revision. Evidence of that change comes from several sources.

First, consider the public's answers to this gender-role question asked by Gallup pollsters in 1937 and 1969: "Do you approve of a married woman earning money in business or industry if she has a husband capable of supporting her?" In 1937, only 18% answered *yes*; by 1969, 55% said *yes*. By 1972, about 68% approved of married women working, and by 1982 the proportion reached 75%. Interviewees were also asked a second question: "Would you vote for a woman for President if she qualified in every respect?" In 1937, only around 30% of respondents answered *yes*, with fewer men than women approving of a woman as president. By 1975, 80% of both men and women answered *yes*. (Duncan & McRae, 1978, pp. 3-5; Bianchi & Spain, 1986, p. 238).

Next, note the increase in the percentage of women in the American workforce after 1950. In 1950, 3.9% of the nation's women worked outside the home. By 1960, the proportion was 37.7% and in 1970, 43.3%. By 1980, more than half (51.5%) the population of women were in the workforce; by 1985 the number had risen to 54.5% (Rix, 1988, p. 127). Many of the women in the workforce by 1998 were mothers with children under age 18, with the proportion of working mothers positively correlated with their levels of formal education—58.4% of mothers with high-school diplomas were employed compared to 66.5% with bachelor degrees and 73.6% with graduate or professional degrees ("Moms in the Work Force" 2000).

In the early 1990s, public-opinion pollsters questioned a broad sample of American women about which personality traits they associated with females. Traits the respondents were asked to judge were three that historically had been considered female characteristics (caring, self-sacrificing, traditional) and three typically attributed to males (independent, ambitious, competitive). The results showed that nearly all women (99%) regarded *caring* a female trait. Whereas the majority felt *self-sacrificing* applied to them, more mothers (82%) than nonmothers (66%) did so; and about a third of the interviewees wondered whether self-sacrificing was a positive trait. When asked whether *traditional* applied to them, 72% of the interviewees agreed that it did, and 80% of all respondents felt it was a positive quality. When asked about the once exclusively male descriptors, the women displayed a marked shift from tradition. Most (89%) saw themselves as independent, 81% as ambitious, and 62% as competitive. The assumption that each new generation of females was adopting more traits traditionally associated with males was supported by the fact that younger women more often than older ones (a) saw themselves as independent, ambitious, and competitive and (b) doubted that self-sacrifice is a valued quality (Henry, 1994, pp. 57-58).

In sum, Americans' beliefs about women's traits and proper roles were in a state of transition during the closing decades of the 20th century. Those changes were accompanied by *cultural lag*, meaning that the treatment of women in the marketplace failed to keep pace with people's verbalized attitudes. This lack of synchrony between expressed folk psychology and women's experiences in daily life drew criticism from observers who sought to have American society achieve a truly egalitarian relationship between the genders in roles, responsibilities, and rewards.

> We, as a society, have embarked on a road toward equality between the sexes to which there is no turning back. If we want a productive labor force of female and male workers, but also value the family, work hours must be flexible, day care available and affordable, and work within the home equitably divided [between women and men]. Until there is widespread recognition that day care, equal wages, and housework are not just "women's issues" but are much broader family issues affecting all persons, the balancing act women are engaged in currently will be just that—a fragile juggling always subject to breaking down. (Bianchi & Spain, 1986, p. 244)

## SEXUAL ORIENTATION

The term *sexual orientation* is used here to mean people's preferences for the partners with whom they engage in sexual intercourse, or at least those whom they sense to be sexually arousing. It seems likely that the concern societies have held about sex-partner preferences extends well back into prehistoric times. That concern has been reflected in customs and formal laws which accord greater approval to some kinds of sex partners and sexual acts than to other kinds. Attitudes about sexual orientation are thus part of a society's folk psychology.

Over the centuries, the diversity of sex partners has included (a) persons of the opposite sex (heterosexuality), (b) persons of one's same sex (homosexuality), (c) persons of both sexes (bisexuality), (d) one's own self (masturbation), (e) various kinds of inanimate objects (assisted masturbation), and (f) animals of different sorts (bestiality). Which of these types have been acceptable, and the degree of each type's acceptability, has differed from one culture to another and from one era to another within the same culture. An example of culturally based moral strictures against certain types of sexual partners is found in the Torah—Judaism's basic set of holy books that form the early section of the Christian Old Testament. Such beliefs are also honored in Islamic tradition. For instance, the Torah condemns engaging in sexual intercourse with a person of one's own sex, with animals, or with a menstruating woman (Maimonides in Thomas, 1997, p. 181).

Societies have also distinguished between acceptable and unacceptable sexual partners on the basis of individuals' social status. Each of the following conditions has been approved in some societies and condemned in others: (a) formally married partners having sexual relations outside their marriage (extramarital sex), (b) sexual relations between a common-law husband and wife, (c) sexual relations prior to marriage (premarital sex), (d) one partner paying the other for sexual services (prostitution), (e) one partner forcing the other to engage in intercourse (rape), (f) one partner being an adult and the other a child (pedophilia), and (g) one partner lawfully having a diversity of other permanent partners within the bonds of marriage (polygamy) or outside of marriage (polyamory). Whereas incest (sexual intercourse with a close relative) appears universally condemned (except for rare cases of royal marriages in ancient Egypt and in precolonial Hawaii) and heterosexuality universally approved, the remaining forms of relationship have been permitted in some societies and proscribed in others.

The diversity of cultural attitudes about—and practices of—one of the most frequently studied sexual orientations (homosexuality) is illustrated by the following examples.

From their survey of documentary evidence, Callender and Kochems (1983) concluded that in the past, 113 native North American societies recognized a further gender category beyond female and male, with the third category reserved for homosexuals and bisexuals, a class often referred to as *berdache* or *two-spirit*. *Berdache* has been defined in various ways, including (a) a category of male humans who fill an established social status other than that of man or woman (Blackwood, 1984) and (b) a category of both male and female humans who behave and dress like the opposite sex (Angelino & Shedd, 1955). The provision of such a third sex or gender has existed particularly in California, the Great Basin, and parts of the Plains and Prairies, less often in the Southwest and Pacific Northwest, and least frequently in the Arctic, Subarctic, and East.

> [Individuals of third-gender status] generally were viewed as special people who fulfilled roles that conferred social prestige. They were respected for their practical skills and spiritual knowledge. They were everywhere understood to be a group distinct from women and men regardless of the fact that they resembled females and males biologically. (Bonvillain, 1998, p. 188)

A further example of a "third sex" is the *muxe* role in Zapotec culture of the southern Mexican state of Oaxaca. *Muxe* are persons who appear to be predominantly male but display certain feminine characteristics. Although seen as different from ordinary males, they are not discriminated against in their societies and are often credited with unusual intellectual talent that leads to success in academic pursuits and a variety of respected occupations. That a boy's nature is bent toward *muxe* status may show up as early as age 3 or 4, and often around the time of puberty, in his preference for girls' play activities (dolls, housekeeping, dressing up in female garb) and in his imitating his mother more often than his father. Zapotecans consider the *muxe* role to be inborn, so a mother whose *muxe* son is teased by other boys is likely to caution, "Leave him alone. God made him that way" (Chiñas, 1995, p. 294).

Another sort of "third sex" is that of the Hijras of India, a class of people on the lowest levels of India's traditional caste system. Hijras form a religious community of men who dress and behave like women and whose culture centers on the adoration of Bahauchara Mata, who is one version of the mother goddess worshipped throughout India. Among Hijra rites is one in which members undergo ritual surgery in which their genitals are removed so that they more closely simulate female physiology. They are required to display feminine behavior—wear their hair long, adorn themselves in female clothing and accessories, behave modestly, assume a woman's postures when dancing, and adopt a passive role in sexual encounters.

> Through their identification with the mother goddess and the female creative power she embodies, Hijras have a special place in Indian culture and society. As neither men nor women, themselves unable to create life, they function as an institutionalized alternative gender role of ritual performers, and this is the basis of their traditional occupation. They perform after the birth of a child, traditionally a male child—these days, sometimes a female child—and also at weddings, both occasions that have an obvious connection to fertility. (Nanda, 1997, p. 82)

Their public performances can be outrageous, as they lift their skirts to expose their mutilated genitals and hurl well-practiced verbal abuse at viewers who insult them, a ruse effective for extorting money from their audiences. Some analysts of Hijra culture suggest that, even though Hijras engage in sexual acts with men, they are not truly homosexual, since they have been transformed into a third sex and therefore do not qualify as males engaging in sex acts with males.

The rationale underlying the widespread practice of male same-sex relations in Papua New Guinea and the Melanesian islands of the South Pacific is the belief that homosexual relations between an older male and a boy are necessary for a youth to attain true manhood. Members of those societies contend that "boys do not become physically mature as a result of natural processes. Growth and attainment of physiological maturation is contingent on the cultural process of initiation, and this entails insemination [with the boy ingesting the man's semen] because it is semen which ensures growth and development" (Kelly, 1976, p. 38).

The conception of homosexuality that permeates traditional Brazilian folk psychology is intimately associated with the culture's distinction between masculinity and femininity, a distinction strongly emphasized in child-rearing practices. Males are expected to play a dominant, controlling role in all aspects of life and females to be submissive and obedient to the males' desires and directives. This contrast between male *actividade* and female *passividade* is reflected in people's sexual behavior, with the male *(homen)* expected to be the active penetrator and the female *(mulher)* the passive receiver. Consequently, in judgments of individuals' masculinity and femininity, the question of who penetrates and who receives is of greater significance than whether a sexual encounter involves a partner of the same or of the opposite sex.

> A *homen* who enters into a sexual relationship with another male does not necessarily sacrifice his *masculinidade*, so long as he performs the culturally perceived active, masculine role during sexual intercourse and conducts himself as a male within society. A *mulher* who conforms to her properly passive, feminine sexual and social role will not jeopardize her essential *feminidade* simply by virtue of occasional (or even ongoing) sexual interactions with other biological females. (Parker, 1995, p. 244)

Thus, in same-sex engagements, a man who plays the active role is not labeled *homosexual* nor is a woman who assumes the passive role. This viewpoint obviously differs from the dominant conception of homosexuality in Europe and North America, where gays and lesbians are dubbed *homosexual* no matter which role—active or passive—they assume in their sexual encounters.

Another contrast between European and traditional Brazilian views is the Brazilians' "playful" sexual experimentation in later childhood and adolescence.

> Among *rapazes* [boys or young men], same-sex play and exploration is almost institutionalized through games such as *troca-troca* (turn-taking), in which two (or more) boys take turns, each inserting his penis in his partner's anus. It is perhaps even more obvious in the expression "Homem, para ser homem, tem que dar primeiro"—A man, to be a man, first has to give (in receptive anal intercourse)—often used by older boys seeking to *comer* [engage] their slightly younger playmates. And while such practices are perhaps less explicit among groups of *moças* [girls or young women], early sexual play with same-sex partners is cited nearly as frequently by female informants as by males. (Parker, 1995, pp. 245-246)

However, such experimentation usually does not portend an adult life of same-sex encounters or of general social behavior that exemplifies masculinity and femininity. Typically, the demanding Brazilian training regimen in masculine and feminine social roles during childhood ensures that males and females adopt their proper active and passive behavior as adults, in both the bed and the society at large.

## SEXUAL BEHAVIOR

Cultures have also differed in the acceptability of different sorts of sexual behavior, parts of the body involved, and equipment used. In some societies, civil or religious laws have proscribed such practices as fellatio, cunnilingus, and sodomy as "unnatural acts," whereas other societies have accepted any acts experienced as satisfying by participants who are "consenting adults."

A sense of the diversity of accepted sexual behaviors across cultures is suggested by the following examples.

Tahitian and Trobriand children's playing at copulation and genital manipulation at an early age has been viewed with indulgent amusement and even encouraged by their elders. Before puberty, girls could be introduced to copulation by older males, and boys might engage in intercourse as soon as they could manage an erection. During their teens and early adulthood, both sexes might pursue assignations with various partners. However, once they were married, women—and to a great extent men as well—would limit their sexual encounters to their mate (Oliver, 1989).

Customary sexual behavior among the Gusii of Kenya is markedly different. Masturbation is severely punished. Homosexuality is viewed as an abomination and thus rarely if ever found in Gusii society. However, boys around the age of puberty may be expected to test their incipient sexual prowess by engaging in intercourse with a goat or cow, an act for which the punishment is light, "as it is assumed that the youth is attempting to find out if he is potent in a rather harmless way" (LeVine, 1974, p. 324). Among adults, heterosexual relations within one's clan are forbidden. Marriage is always between a male and female from different clans—clans that typically are bitter enemies. And the sex act between husband and wife seems to reflect this interclan animosity. A wife is required to dislike coitus and to resist her husband's advances. Consequently, the husband is obliged to force himself on her, and she is expected to suffer during the encounter.

> The conception of coitus as an act in which a man overcomes the resistance of a woman and causes her pain is not limited to the wedding night; it continues to be important in marital relations. . . . The wife does not take an active role in the foreplay or coitus and will not remove her clothes herself if she has not already done so for sleeping. Most importantly, it is universally reported that wives cry during coitus, moaning quietly, "You're hurting me, you bad man" and other admonitions. Gusii men find this practice sexually arousing. (LeVine, 1974, p. 316)

It's a matter of male honor for a newly married man to engage in intercourse with his wife as many times as possible. "When a bride is unable to walk on the day following the wedding night, the young men consider the groom 'a real man' and he is able to boast of his exploits, particularly the fact that he made her cry" (LeVine, 1974, p. 315).

One question that interests researchers is why societies may differ in the typical sexual behavior of their members. That is, to what extent are cross-cultural differences in sexual behavior explained by peoples' biological natures and to what extent by the customs of their culture? In response, Oliver writes that

> There is no evidence I know of indicating that Oceania's numerous "racially" distinctive populations differed from one another, genetically, with respect to the strength, duration, periodicity, and so forth, of their respective members' sexual needs. Yet, there is perhaps no domain of their behavior encompassing wider variations, from society to society, in the *cultural* ways those needs were satisfied. Some of the variations may have resulted, directly or indirectly, from natural environmental factors (such as diseases that debilitated physical energies in general and sexual vitality in particular). . . . On the other hand, most of that variability can only be attributed to other, more specifically *cultural* "causes"—but in most instances causes too remote in time to reconstruct. (Oliver, 1989, p. 590)

Oliver has illustrated this diversity by contrasting (a) the early and open sexual conduct of Tahitians in the southeast Pacific and Trobriand Islanders in the southwest Pacific with (b) the much restrained sexuality of the Mae Enga in the New Guinea Highlands and of the Manus in the southwest Pacific's Admiralty Islands.

## CULTURAL CHANGE AND SEXUAL ORIENTATION

A marked cultural change of the late 20th century, found especially in Europe and North America, was a shift in folk-psychology conceptions of proper—or at least acceptable—forms of sexual behavior and sexual partners. Traditionally, the sole culturally approved sexual act consisted of a male and female married couple engaging in intercourse that involved the male's inserting his penis into the female's vagina. The use of any other phalanx-like object or receptive orifice in a sexual act was condemned in religious doctrine and became the source of criminal laws whose breach could be punished by imprisonment and/or fines, with the violations always accompanied by social stigma. As for sexual partners, social custom and the law limited them to husband and wife. Premarital coitus was proscribed, and detected adultery led not only to public censure and disgrace but to legal sanctions. Individuals convicted of homosexual encounters could be imprisoned, as illustrated in the case of British playwright Oscar Wilde who, in 1898, wrote *The Ballad of Reading Gaol* after serving a two-year prison term for his love affair with the son of the Marquis of Queensbury.

During the 20$^{th}$ century—and most dramatically after 1960—long-established tradition came under attack, with the last four decades of the century witnessing vitriolic conflicts between defenders of tradition and proponents of liberalized sexual practices.  In the process, the sex-behavior portions of folk psychologies were being modified at an accelerating pace.  The following sketch of changes during this four-decade period focuses on (a) examples of changes in sex-behavior custom and law and (b) likely causes for the changes.

## Changes in Sexual Behavior

Alterations in cultural beliefs relating to sexual behavior occurred in relation to (a) permissible sexual acts, (b) types of sex partners, and (c) marriage.

### Permissible sexual acts

In recent years, many states and nations have rescinded laws designed to prohibit people from engaging in sexual acts traditionally deemed "crimes against nature."    Some of the laws were broadscale, worded imprecisely so they could be applied to all sexual behavior except the one act that could produce pregnancy.  As a result, people would be punished for "any unnatural and lascivious" behavior.  By way of illustration, until 1992 it was illegal in the District of Columbia to copulate via any orifice except the vagina.  Despite the scrapping of such laws in most parts of the United States, by 1999 such broad restrictions were still in effect in 12 states and Puerto Rico. A Massachusetts law warns that an "abominable and detestable crime against nature, either with mankind or with a beast, shall be punished by imprisonment in the state prison for not more than 20 years" (Nathan, 1999, p. 16).

Other laws have focused on particular acts, with sodomy being the act most often targeted.  By the late 1990s, it was still a felony in the state of Virginia if a person "carnally knows any male or female person by the anus or by or with the mouth, or voluntarily submits to such carnal knowledge." In Michigan, oral-genital contact between consenting adults could result in a jail term of up to 15 years.

But increasingly, legislators and the general public in Europe and North America, as well as in certain nations in other regions of the world, have come to believe that what two consenting adults do in a bedroom is those individuals' private business.  As a first step toward the acceptance of this liberalized attitude, restrictive laws that remain on the books in many places have fallen into disuse—they are simply not enforced.   The next step beyond nonenforcement has been the elimination of the laws themselves, which has occurred with increased frequency.   From 1962 through 1999, sodomy laws were repealed by legislation in 25 U.S. states and invalidated by courts in 8 others.   However, sodomy laws remained intact in 18 states and Puerto Rico (American Civil Liberties Union, 1999).   But gradually, even those are being struck down.   In mid-2000 a Texas court of appeals declared that the state's sodomy law, in force since 1860, was unconstitutional ("Sodomy Law," 2000).

## Types of sex partners

The most vigorous groups behind the movement to liberalize sex laws have been homosexual organizations.   Not only have gay and lesbian activists sought to eliminate laws restricting sexual behavior, but they have also endeavored to convince the general populace that homosexuality is as respectable a lifestyle as heterosexuality.   These attempts have met with significant success.   In an international survey of legislative changes from the mid-1980s through the mid-1990s, Frank and McEneaney (1999, p. 912) reported that

> State policies on same-sex sexual relations changed rapidly between 1984 and 1995. Of the 86 countries for which we have data at both time points, 24 changed their policies regarding sex between men, sex between women, or both in just an 11-year period. Strikingly, nearly every change was one toward liberalization, with more than a quarter of the countries in our data set relaxing their policies during this period. In some cases, liberalization entailed merely the cessation of systematic police harassment, which accounts for Panama's policy shift on homosexual relations between women. In other cases, a legal prohibition was struck down and new legislation was passed, as when South Africa granted homosexual and heterosexual relations equal status under the new constitution. . . . In spite of the liberalizing trend, a good deal of variation remained in state policies by 1995. Liberalization had occurred in Hong Kong but not Singapore, in Ireland but not Italy, and in South Africa but not Nigeria.

In such countries as Denmark and Holland, which have liberal laws bearing on gays and lesbians, "the relative tolerance shown the homosexual is a by-product of [those societies'] emphasis on personal freedom rather than of any acceptance of the behavior. . . . [The] ideological pressure [behind such legislation] comes from above, from politicians and the higher strata of society" (Weinberg & Williams, 1974, p. 76).

## Marriage

Among the opportunities sought by gay and lesbian groups has been the right to become legally married—including the right to be wed in a church. Or, short of actual marriage, gays and lesbians wish to have same-sex partners receive the same financial benefits as heterosexual married couples, such as spousal support, inheritance, and family-member medical insurance.

The most successful of these demands has been the one concerning same-sex financial benefits. In Canada by 1994, a growing number of employers extended spousal benefits to their lesbian and gay workers. A Gallup poll showed that the Canadian public was almost evenly divided on the issue of whether same-sex couples should be given the same tax and employment benefits as heterosexuals; 49% favored the notion, 44% opposed it, and 7% expressed no opinion. Younger and better-educated respondents were more likely to back same-sex benefits. Among 18- to 29-year-olds, support rose to 64%. More than 40% of Canadians under the age of 40 accepted same-sex marriages, compared with only 29% of the general population (Steele & Nemeth, 1994, p. 42). In 1998, the Netherlands permitted same-sex partners to register as legal couples and claim pensions, social security, and inheritance (Deutsch, 2000, p. A12). In 1999, California Governor Gray Davis signed legislation that granted spousal benefits to same-sex couples and that fined business and property owners who considered sexual orientation in hiring or housing ("New Laws," 1999). In 2000, a Vermont law gave homosexual couples a "civil-union license" for financial benefits (Witham, 2000, p. 26).

Compared to the matter of same-sex benefits, the question of same-sex marriages has proven a far more divisive issue, one that has threatened to fracture several major religious denominations. In the United States in 1999, a group of 96 United Methodist clergy defied church rules and blessed the joining of Ellie Charlton, 63, and Jeanne Barnett, 68, at the Sacramento Convention Center in California. "O God, our maker, we gladly proclaim to the world that they are loving partners together for life." In response, the governing body of the United Methodist Church voted by a 2-to-1 margin to affirm its 1996 ban on ceremonies that "celebrate homosexual unions" by clergy or in sanctuaries; and they moved the ban to the *Book of Discipline* so it would be more legally binding. During the same period, after 15 homosexual marriages had been conducted in southern U.S. Presbyterian churches in violation of church orders, the Presbyterian Church (U.S.A.) ruled that the unions were not truly marriages and thus were not in violation of church law. But in 2000, the Presbyterian General Assembly voted to ask its regional bodies to approve an amendment prohibiting all kinds of same-sex ceremonies. That same year, the Episcopal Church General Assembly voted to let each diocese set its own policy regarding same-sex marriages, while the rabbis of Reform Judaism supported the proposal that "a same-gender couple is worthy of affirmation through appropriate Jewish ritual" and thus allowed the development of ceremonies. However, the two largest denominations in the United States—the Southern Baptist Convention and the Roman Catholic Church—continued to oppose any endorsement of homosexual unions (Witham, 2000, p. 26).

Outside of the jurisdiction of religious bodies, efforts to legitimate same-sex marriages have continued to gain ground. In late 2000, the Dutch parliament granted "registered same-sex partnerships" in the Netherlands the right to engage in full-fledged marriage, to obtain a divorce, and to adopt Dutch children. The legislation thus gave the nation's gay and lesbian couples more rights than in any other country. The new law represented a move toward a tolerance of homosexuals that had been building for many decades. Homosexuality between consenting adults had not been punishable in the Netherlands since 1809 when the Napoleonic Code was imposed. Studies in the 1960s of public attitudes showed that the populace in general was "apathetic toward homosexuals and not intolerant" while organized religion was "officially on record as being concerned with helping homosexuals and in general [not displaying] a moralizing stance toward them" (Weinberg & Williams, 1974, pp. 63-64).

The movement to extend a growing array of civil rights to homosexuals and bisexuals has been particularly strong in northwestern Europe. Both Norway and Sweden permitted gay couples to register their partnerships, and Denmark in 1989 became the first country to allow homosexual marriages (Deutsch, 2000, p. A12).

In summary, during the final decades of the 20th century, gays and lesbians were rapidly winning public acceptance and legal rights, but their status continued to be held in question within particular cultural groups. In effect, the sexual components of folk psychologies in many cultures were undergoing a significant change, with the shift more apparent among youths than among the elderly.

## Procreation Versus Erotic Pleasure

David Frank and Elizabeth McEneaney (1999) propose that the widespread condemnation of any form of sexual engagement other than the traditionally approved form derived from a cultural concept of sexual behavior that focused exclusively on the reproductive function—the creation of children—with no concern for erotic pleasure. Consequently, any sexual behavior outside of marriage or involving any parts of the body other than the sperm- and ova-producing equipment should be forbidden.

By contrast, in individually based sex-for-pleasure, a person need not be married to have legitimate sexual liaisons (indeed marriage often desexualizes a relationship). The purpose of sexual liaisons is rarely procreation, and thus the focal act may be of many sorts: manual, oral, anal, and even "virtual" sex are increasingly routine. . . . Accordingly, sexual encounters may involve more or fewer than two participants, who are male or female in any combination, and of any age beyond the age of consent. Birth control is de rigueur, and satisfaction is the preeminent goal. (Frank & McEneaney, 1999, p. 912)

Over the past two centuries, social attitudes associated with strict religious condemnation of pleasure in sexual behavior have relaxed, particularly in Europe and North America, thereby encouraging individuals to expect to enjoy sexual encounters. Furthermore, the practice of female circumcision in the Middle East and North Africa, which aims at reducing or eliminating the likelihood of women deriving pleasure from coitus, has been increasingly outlawed by governments and religious bodies, thus suggesting that it is normal and desirable for both men and women to engage in sexual acts for sensual satisfaction.

# 13

# Prohibitions

*What is forbidden and why?*

All societies ban certain acts and objects, and all propose consequences that people can expect if they violate those bans. The Polynesian word *taboo* and its variants (*tapu* or *tafu* in Tahitian and Maori, *tabu* in Tongan, *kapu* in Hawaiian) has long since been adopted into European languages to serve as a popular designator of proscribed behavior. Steiner's (1999, pp. 118-119) analysis of the meaning of *taboo* in Polynesia suggests that the term applies to things regarded as dangerous, particularly because they are either sacred or unclean. In other societies, the meaning has been extended to include additional things that appear to threaten people's welfare. Those things are objects and events mysteriously associated with damaged social relations, illness, death, or natural catastrophe (crop failure, earthquake, volcanic eruption, fire, flood). Sometimes, the threat is to the welfare of people in positions of power, so they outlaw behavior that would threaten their position of authority or privilege. Therefore, the function of prohibitions in folk psychologies is to warn people of events that can bring unwanted outcomes.

This chapter first focuses on forms and sources of prohibitions, then turns to functions that proscriptions are intended to serve in individuals' lives and in the society as a whole. The chapter's brief closing section concerns prohibitions and cultural change.

## FORMS AND SOURCES OF PROHIBITIONS

Prohibitions embedded in folk psychologies can appear in a variety of forms—as unwritten custom, oral or written history, aphorisms, moralistic anecdotes and stories as well as written rules, regulations, and laws.

Different prohibitions can be imposed by different sources of power or authority, such sources as parents, the school, the church, and the government (king, chieftain, legislature, town council, police, military). It is also the case that a given type of prohibition can be divided into levels of seriousness, with the levels usually differentiated by the severity of sanctions to be suffered by offenders. For example, parents' opinion about the comparative importance of the rules "Don't eat mashed potatoes with your fingers" and "Don't smoke marijuana" is reflected in more painful punishment for infractions of the latter than of the former. The school's view of the comparative significance of the rules "Don't chew gum in class" and "Don't bring a gun to school" is demonstrated in school authorities merely scolding a gum chewer but discharging a student from school for carrying a gun.

In religious bodies, the acts condemned by prohibitions are typically called *sins*. Sin, in its most general sense, is any violation of religious or moral principles. The fifth-century Christian cleric St. Augustine identified sin as "any thought, word, or deed, opposed to the law of God" (Kauffman, 1967, p. 394). Sin is thus properly viewed "as the violation of a personal bond with God, [and] not only as a wicked deed" (Pelikan, 1979, p. 3307). Among the best-known sins in Christian lore are the seven referred to as the *deadly* or *cardinal sins*, which Catholic theologians prefer to call *capital sins*. The modern-day list typically consists of pride, avarice, lust (inordinate or illicit sexual desire), anger, gluttony (including drunkenness), envy, and laziness (sloth) (Voll, 1979, p. 622). The adjectives *venial* and *mortal* identify two levels of gravity among sins. In Roman Catholic doctrine a venial sin is an improper act that can be forgiven because it was committed without the full exercise of the will or full awareness of its seriousness. Venial sin, although by no means trifle, is pardonable and thus does not deprive the soul of divine grace. A mortal sin, in contrast, is a very serious intentional transgression against God's law that "kills the soul by bringing about the loss of grace," thus eliminating any opportunity for the individual to enjoy an eternal heavenly life after death (Pelikan, 1979, p. 3307).

Governments (national, provincial, local) adopt regulations and laws that can cover a wide range of behaviors. Such directives are often divided into two major categories—civil and criminal. In the United States, civil law pertains primarily to disputes between individuals or organizations over such things as business contracts, property rights, divorce, real estate transactions, employment agreements, inheritance, personal injury, patents and copyrights, defamation of character, and the like. In contrast, criminal law concerns offenses against the public. A crime is any "action or instance of negligence that is deemed injurious to the public welfare or morals, or to the interests of the state and that is legally prohibited" (*Webster's*, 1989, p. 343).

Within any folk culture, crimes are typically classified according to their perceived seriousness, with levels of seriousness reflected in the harshness of sanctions imposed. Common categories of harshness in the United States are *felony, misdemeanor*, and *infraction*. Crimes that draw the greatest penalties are felonies. Although what specifically may be considered a felony can differ from one culture to another, typical felonious acts are murder, burglary, rape, and grand theft (large amounts of money or goods). Committing a felony can result in the malefactor's death, corporal punishment (whipping, cutting off the hands of a thief), an extended prison term, or the payment of a large monetary fine. Which of these sanctions will be applied depends on the particular society in which the crime was committed. Misdemeanors are less serious offenses. In the United States, misdemeanors can include such acts as petty theft (small amounts of money or goods), fighting at school, dumping waste matter in forbidden places, and failing to appear as a prosecution witness in a criminal trial (Calligan, 1992). The least serious crimes are often called *infractions*. They consist of minor breaches of the law for which the offender is usually not jailed. Such traffic violations as driving through a red light, speeding, or parking in a zone reserved for the handicapped are examples of infractions.

In summary, the prohibitions in a folk culture can appear in different forms, derive from diverse sources, and vary in how vital each is judged to be for people's welfare.

## FUNCTIONS OF PROHIBITIONS

As proposed in Chapter 2, the essence of every folk psychology is its cosmology—the cultural beliefs about which components make up the universe and how those components interact. What distinguishes one culture's prohibitions from another's are the two cultures' beliefs about (a) which dangerous things (concepts, objects, events) are thought to be real rather than just imaginary and (b) in what way those things are part of a causal chain. The question becomes: Which things are responsible for particular harmful outcomes? Thus, when the effect of one thing (a cause) on another is believed to be damaging (a harmful outcome), prohibitions are established to reduce the incidence of damage. So the purpose of cultural proscriptions is to protect people from such calamities as (a) personal misfortune, (b) harm to relatives and friends, (c) violations of etiquette, (d) social disorder, (e) alterations of the social structure, (f) mysterious bad fortune, and (g) retribution. The following pages offer examples of these functions in various folk psychologies.

## Personal Misfortune

Distressing happenings suffered by individuals can be of various sorts—illness, accident, financial setback, loss of friends and loved ones, damaged social relations, missing property, damaged reputation, and more. The cause-effect linkages and resulting prohibitions of one culture's folk psychology are often very different from another culture's, so that one society's array of prohibitions can be seen as quite odd and unreasonable by members of other societies. Consider, for example, the following potpourri of taboos.

Among the Inuit of northern Canada, if someone falls ill in a house, then fluids or particles that drop from the ceiling onto the sick person must not be wiped off lest the soul of the sick person is thrown out with the droppings. And when someone dies, the family of the deceased must not work for five days in order to allow time for the soul to have left the body (Riches, 1994, p. 391).

In the Yoruba culture of southwestern Nigeria, the king (*Oba*) is considered sacred, for he commands powers from the spirit realm. To ensure his longevity, he is obliged to observe prohibitions that protect him from sources of harm—sources from both the spirit world and the mundane world. For example, the king may not witness the birth of a child nor see the hairs of a newborn, which are "hairs of the spirit realm"— and ill fortune results if the king's spiritual self encounters other spirits. To eliminate the chance of the Oba seeing a newborn infant, an expectant royal wife is required to return to her maternal home to give birth, where she and her baby stay until the infant's head is shaved. The king is also prohibited from seeing or touching a dead body or from looking into an open grave, because doing so would threaten the "spiritual, life-giving power of the Oba. Hence, the sick are removed [from the palace] to be cared for in another dwelling until they recover" (Pemberton & Afolayan, 1996, pp. 93-94). To protect the king from worldly threats to his welfare, custom dictates that he be the sole male permitted to live in the palace. No one other than his children, his wives, women servants, and eunuch bodyguards may dwell there.

The personal misfortune that prohibitions are often intended to prevent is failure in occupational activities. Such proscriptions are particularly frequent in ventures over which people have limited control, so that success is heavily dependent on what people construe as fate, luck, or meddling spirits. Among the Indian tribes living on the northwest American plateau between the Rocky Mountains on the east and the Cascade Mountains on the west, both men and women were warned to abstain from sexual intercourse during the period preceding risky work and also to cleanse themselves with sweat baths. They apparently feared that the forces of nature would work against them if they attempted a hazardous undertaking in an impure state. For men, this meant avoiding sexual encounters before a fishing or hunting trip. For women, it meant avoiding sex prior to a root-digging excursion or a chancy food-preparation activity.

> Drying roots in an earth oven was a long and delicate task, sometimes ending in failure and the ruin of a large amount of food. The presence of men was judged a danger to the success of the undertaking. (Ackerman, 1995, p. 94)

## Harm to Relatives and Friends

In addition to avoiding personal disaster, people often are obliged to observe prohibitions designed to avert threats to persons and objects they respect and cherish.

In Native American cultures, peace within families and larger social groups depends on people observing a host of taboos specific to every activity and social relationship. Among the Delaware living in Oklahoma, Wisconsin, or Canada's Ontario province, a menstruating woman has traditionally been warned to stay away from men because, if she breathed on them, game animals could smell the taint at a distance and flee into the woods. Nor could a menstruating woman take part in tribal ceremonies. If she did participate, injury or other misfortune would visit members of her family. Likewise, no female herbalist could collect herbs during her catamenial period, since doing so would affront the spirit world and cause her medicines to spoil (Weslager, 1973, pp. 56, 60).

In California Yukot Indian tradition, fathers transmitted to all their children a totem symbol of a particular bird or animal that was the guardian spirit of the paternal line. Because that animal was considered to be part of the clan, family members were expected to dream about—and pray to—the totem, but were warned never to kill or eat members of the animal species to which their totem belonged (Wallace in Steadman, Palmer, & Tilley, 1996, p. 72).

The Skagit Indians in the state of Washington venerate species of animals considered to be people's guardian spirits. Consequently, children are trained to avoid harming such creatures as spiders, snakes, or ants that might stand for the spirit of the children's parents or relatives. Those species might, in time, even represent the child's own spirit (Collins, 1974, p. 214).

Failing to respect the sanctity of revered places or objects can be thought to invite disaster. According to Jorgensen (1980, p. 297), a Navajo recently explained that he had carelessly driven and twisted the opening of an empty beer can onto a fragile budding branch of a sacred evergreen tree at the time that his wife was pregnant. He blamed this rude act for causing his daughter to be born with one arm twisted and distorted in a manner similar to the damage to the tree.

As noted in Chapter 12, incest (sexual intercourse with a close relative) is proscribed in virtually all cultures. Only in very rare cases—such as the brother-sister matings in the royal families of ancient Egypt, Peru, and Hawaii—has marriage between primary members of a family been condoned. However, who is considered a close relative often differs among cultures. Navajo custom forbids marriage or sexual relations with any person from one's clan, thereby ruling out a large number of individuals as potential mates. According to Navajo tradition, anyone violating the ban risks going insane, dying, or producing deformed children. However, a man can marry or have intercourse with a kinsman's widow, two or more sisters, or a mother and her daughter, so long as they are not members of his own clan (Stone, 1997, p. 131). The Jewish Torah interdicts a man's copulating with his own mother, his daughter, his sister, his father's wife, his son's daughter, his father's sister, any other kinswoman, or a woman and her daughter (Maimonides in Thomas, 1997, p. 181).

According to Elkin (1964, p. 149), "The severest taboo [in Australian aborigine cultures] is that which is observed all over Australia between a man and his wife's mother. Typically, they must not look at one another, speak to one another, come close to one another, or mention one another's names." One explanation of this custom is that such a taboo helps prevent the possibility of a father producing his own wife. The reasoning behind this explanation is that in societies that practice gerontocratic polygyny, (a) a man is often as old as, or older than, his mother-in-law and (b) his mother-in-law may have promised him his wife at the time the wife was born or even before she was conceived. "It follows that if a man were to have sexual relations with a potential or actual mother-in-law, he might beget his own wife. The [mother-in-law] taboo seeks to render this impossible" (Hiatt, 1984, p. 183).

## Violations of Etiquette

Action that is not physically or economically harmful but that still deviates from what is thought proper for the occasion is condemned and exposes the actor to social sanctions. The sorts of behavior considered breaches of etiquette can vary from one culture to another. For example, personal cleanliness is a central value in Tahitian culture. Although

shabby clothing is forgivable; a public appearance in dirty clothing is not, unless one is returning from labor, in which case one is expected to return home and bathe before engaging in any extended social contact with others. . . . In the communities where my research was based, twice-daily baths are the norm" (Clark, 1994, p. 216).

In Japanese tradition, making slurping noises while eating can be regarded as a compliment to the skill of the cook, whereas in proper British society such noises are condemned as evidence of crude upbringing. Likewise, eating cooked rice with one's fingers is normal etiquette in Indonesia but a violation of good manners in Canada.

## Social Disorder

The intended function of many cultural prohibitions is to maintain trustworthy, amicable relations among members of the society. For example, six of the Ten Commandments of Judaic-Christian tradition are intended to protect the community from social disruption. Hence, Jews and Christians are advised to honor their parents and are warned not to kill, commit adultery, steal, lie about others, or yearn for others' possessions (*Holy Bible*, 1930, Exodus, 20: 12-17).

Laws and regulations often forbid particular behavior and language deemed harmful to individuals or the public good. During wartime, citizens who pass classified information to the enemy are subject to death or imprisonment for treason. Employees of business firms who sell trade secrets to competitors are subject to either legal or customary sanctions. Family members who consort with people considered by the family as dangerous or unworthy of the family's friendship may be ostracized by their relatives for threatening familial cohesiveness.

Efforts ostensibly designed to promote amicable social relations sometimes take the form of activists urging a society to adopt new prohibitions. An example is the social movement, particularly in North America during the 1980s and 1990s, that acquired the label *political correctness*. The movement sought to prohibit any language usage which might imply that one person's or one group's characteristics were more desirable than another's. Thus, words that might be interpreted as denigrating should be replaced by terms intended to suggest no evaluation—good or bad—of the people being described. Proponents of political correctness supported their proposals with the egalitarian rationale that everyone's characteristics are as desirable as everyone else's, and that such equality should be reflected in social discourse. This led to such neologisms as *survivor* (rather than *victim*, as in *incest survivor*), *differentially sized* (rather than *obese* or *overweight*), *undocumented workers* (rather than *illegal aliens*), *male sexual dysfunction* (rather than *impotence*), and *intellectually challenged* (rather than *mentally retarded*) (Leo, 1998, pp. 39-41). Strategies for getting such political correctness accepted as a cultural norm include (a) convincing authorities to pass regulations outlawing language considered offensive, (b) conducting public demonstrations that condemn individuals who continue to use objectionable social labels, and (c) urging the controllers of mass-communication media to publicize instances of harm done by socially unacceptable language.

In Chemehuevis Indian culture of the North American southwest, mentioning the names of the dead is forbidden, since doing so insults their living relatives. "To curse and revile an enemy, one mentions *father, your dead father's father, your dead mother's mother,* and so on. This constitutes the deadliest insult and the greatest provocation that can be offered" (Laird, 1976, p. 69).

## Social Structure

The term *social structure* refers to the pattern of relationships among individuals and groups as dictated by the society's customs and laws. Structural relations are not defined in terms of people as individuals but, rather, in terms of social categories and power/privilege relations among those categories. An individual's placement within those categories is based on such characteristics as the person's age, gender, ethnicity, social class, religious affiliation, wealth, political affiliation, occupation, citizenship, marital status, and level of education.

Two ways that prohibitions bear on the structure of a society are by (a) delineating the nature of the social structure and (b) protecting the existing structure from change.

### Defining a society's structure

Michael Lambek (1999) suggests that sociologists and anthropologists, who make it their business to understand social structure, typically base their judgments on positive signs and rules that dictate or imply people's rights and responsibilities in relation to each other. At the highest formal level, a nation's constitution is the document that describes these relationships. The Bill of Rights attached to the U.S. Constitution is a clear example. At the day-by-day, informal level of custom, structure is reflected in people's expectations about their own and others' rights and duties.

However, as Lambek illustrates with Malagasy culture on the island of Madagascar, the structure of some societies is more obviously reflected—not in positive signs and rules—but in prohibitions. Malagasy tradition, rather than telling people how they should act, tells them how they should not act. Prohibitions set boundaries that should not be breached, but they do not specify how to behave, so any actions that do not violate the taboos are acceptable. Consequently, social structure defined in terms of taboos conceivably offers people more options for action than does a structure defined as specific things that people are to do. "Rather than prescribing behavior, [a structure defined by prohibitions] merely sets the limits beyond which action is unacceptable" (Lambek, 1999, p. 246).

## Protecting the existing social structure

Two motives behind prohibitions against changing the structure of a society are (a) desires of people in positions of power and privilege to preserve their advantages for themselves, their associates, and their progeny and (b) desires of members of a group—ethnic, regional, kinship, religious, and the like—to protect the purity and unity of their group. Two popular strategies employed for resisting structural change are those of establishing the prohibitions as unwritten custom or as written law. Methods of convincing the public to abide by the prohibitions include (a) asserting that the proscriptions have been decreed by the supernatural forces that control the universe, (b) basing the proscriptions on the agreement of the majority of the citizens (democratic legislation), (c) citing tradition as the foundation for the interdictions, and (d) punishing people who engage in forbidden acts. The following examples illustrate prohibitions in various cultures intended to keep the existing social structure intact.

A prime example of the social-structure-maintenance feature of a folk psychology is the Hindu caste tradition. Although in recent times the limitations on people's rights and opportunities ingrained in the caste system have been officially outlawed by the government of India, the system continues very much in effect in daily social intercourse.

The caste system, which so dominated social life in India over the centuries, is founded on the conviction that one's status in the world is properly determined by a divinely ordered hierarchy of social classes or castes. The caste structure in its most basic form is composed of four well-defined upper strata plus one lowest stratum of outcasts referred to as *untouchables* or, in more recent and less degrading terminology, as *tribes* and *scheduled castes*.

Theoretically, the caste system consists only of the five major strata, kept pure by prohibitions on marriage across caste boundaries. But in reality, ever since Aryan tribes from the north invaded India 3,500 years ago, there has always been a substantial amount of intermarriage, resulting in groups recognized by names assigned to these mixed classes. Consequently, today there are around 3,000 recognized subcastes produced by complex permutations of marriage between castes, with most subcastes associated with particular occupations (Renou, 1961, p. 53).

The four top castes, ranging from the most privileged and honored at the top to the least privileged and least respected at the bottom, follow this order: (1) the Brahmans or priests who exercise spiritual power, (2) the Kshatriyas or warriors and administrators who wield secular power, (3) the Vaisyas or artisans and cultivators responsible for business and production functions, and (4) the Sudras who are expected to serve the three higher castes. It is estimated that in modern times about 20% of India's Hindus are in the upper three classes, whereas 60% are Sudras, and the remaining 20% in the scheduled castes and tribes (Shinn, Folan, Hopkins, Parker, & Younglof, 1970, p. 154).

Individuals are bound to their caste by birth. Strict rules are set out for the behavior of the members of each caste, with sanctions applied to anyone who engages in forbidden behavior. Since the time that caste restrictions were abolished by the government after World War II, sanctions have not been officially imposed, yet they continue to be applied in daily life through acts of prejudice and discrimination by a large portion of the Hindu population. Friendship patterns, marriage, educational and vocational opportunities, etiquette, control of wealth, and religious activities all reflect caste prohibitions regarding social relationships. Thus, in present-day India, the government—in keeping with the spirit of democratic equal rights that is reflected internationally in United Nations' pronouncements—has officially condemned traditional caste prohibitions, but those prohibitions continue to be a widely accepted feature of Hindu folk psychology. For members of the upper castes, preserving traditional proscriptions protects their positions of privilege as well as the purity and unity of their class.

## Mysterious Bad Fortune

Frequently, direct causes of the ill fate that people suffer are not apparent. In effect, people are unable to understand why a child died, why lightning struck a mosque, why a flock of sheep disappeared, why a monster appeared in a dream, and more. However, the observed appearance of two happenings within a limited time period (a certain kind of object, event, or behavior is followed by an unwelcome consequence) may convince some influential individual that, in an indirect and enigmatic way, the object, event, or behavior is actually to blame for the unwelcome outcome. The term *influential individual* here means a member of the society who is thought to command uncommon wisdom and whose opinions are so highly respected that they are regarded as authoritative and thus warrant widespread acceptance. As suggested in Chapter 4, such individuals often fill the role of priest, shaman, soothsayer, diviner, oracle, healer, spiritualist, seer, or political leader. Their opinions become elements of the culture's folk psychology.

The following examples are prohibitions in various cultures that are intended to safeguard people from adverse consequences of an assumed, but incomprehensible, origin.

In some Moorish tribes of Mauritania, donkeys are regarded as mystically ominous creatures. The call of a donkey is said to presage disaster that can be counteracted only by the hearer uttering a magic formula derived from Islamic tradition—"*Bisma el-lah er-rahman er-rahim*" (In the name of God the merciful, always merciful). Anyone who imitates a donkey's braying may be doomed to hell (Gerteiny, 1967, p. 76).

Furthermore, when a visitor among the Moors departs from a host's tent and inadvertently has left a belonging behind, the visitor is never to be called back. Instead, the host must pursue the visitor in order to return the forgotten item. This custom may derive from the fact that a camel will often become unruly if forced to change direction quickly, as would be required if the guest suddenly halted and turned back to the tent (Gerteiny, 1967, p. 77).

In recent years, a Hong Kong newspaper headline announced that "Bad *Fung Shui* Haunts Radio Station." The incident reported in the accompanying article concerned two deaths that had occurred at the studio of Radio/Television Hong Kong. The station's employees speculated that the deaths were the result of bad *fung shui* (ill fortune) caused by the studio's having been built over the mass grave of citizens who had been slaughtered during the World War II Japanese occupation of the city. Consequently, "the main gate to the studio was closed, as it remains today, in order to set the bad *fung shui* to rights" (Bloomfield, 1983, p. 23).

In gypsy societies, the fear that a dead person may return to the world of the living to cause trouble in the guise of a specter has led to a prohibition against ever mentioning the name of the deceased. It is imagined that saying the name may be interpreted by the dead as a summons to return to haunt the living. Consequently, when a gypsy dies, his or her name should never be uttered. Furthermore, people who happen to bear that same name are expected to adopt a new name or at least to refer to themselves henceforth by a nickname (Trigg, 1973, pp. 137-138).

## Avoid Retribution

*Retribution* means wreaking vengeance for wrongs that an individual or group is accused of committing. Folk psychologies typically include prohibitions whose purpose is to evade retribution from either mundane or supernatural sources.

The exact intent behind human-devised punishments for violating laws, rules, or customs is usually unclear. Is the purpose of punishment to deter the miscreants from further breaches of the same prohibition? Or is it to deter others from committing such an act? Or is the aim to educate wrongdoers—teach them a lesson? Or is it to get revenge—to pay the rascals back? Or is the intent some combination of these?

Although the true aims behind humans' aversive sanctions may not be apparent, there is a good reason to believe that those aims frequently include avenging an assumed wrong. Certainly that's true of the feuds, vendettas, wars of reprisal, and personal acts of retribution that fill the pages of literature and history. In ancient Greece, Homer wrote of Agamemnon's army retaliating against Troy for the kidnapping of Helen. During the Renaissance, Shakespeare dramatized Hamlet's efforts to vindicate his father's murder. In the 19th century novel *Moby Dick*, Melville described Captain Ahab's vengeful pursuit of the great whale that had taken his leg.

Whereas the true intent of sanctions that people impose on each other for misbehavior is often unclear, the intent of promised punishment from supernatural sources is usually evident—the intent is vengeance. For example, the Book of Psalms of the Jewish Bible reports that God punished the people of Israel for disobeying his dictates.

> [The Lord] was wroth, so a fire was kindled against Jacob, and anger also came up against Israel. . . . The wrath of God came upon them, and slew the fattest of them, and smote down the chosen men of Israel. (*Holy Bible*, 1930, Psalms 78: 21, 31)

In the New Testament of the Christian Bible, the apostle Paul is reported to have written to members of the church in Rome that "the wrath of God is revealed from heaven against all ungodliness and unrighteousness of men," with God's anger vented on those guilty of "fornication, wickedness, covetousness, maliciousness; full of envy, murder, debate, deceit, malignity; whisperers, backbiters, haters of God, despiteful, proud, boasters, inventers of evil things, disobedient to parents." Such sinners are deemed "worthy of death" (*Holy Bible*, 1930, Romans 1: 18, 29-30).

The principal totemic animal for North America's Ute Indians has been the bear, a creature particularly respected for robustness and prowess in both sexual and food-gathering pursuits. The Utes periodically performed bear dances to foster tribe members' good health, fertility for women, and hunting success for men. On these occasions, in order to avoid offending the bears and thus inviting ill fortune, girls who were experiencing their first menses were sequestered in a special hut built adjacent to the brush enclosure in which the dance was performed (Jorgensen, 1980, pp. 270-271).

Newcomb (1961, p. 216) reports that Kiowa braves on North America's Great Plains believed they could ward off sickness and become better warriors if they pledged to participate in the tribal Sun Dance that consisted of four days of debilitating stomping, leaping, and twisting. If warriors—when they had fallen ill or were in mortal danger during battle—had vowed to the mysterious powers of the universe that they would join in the Sun Dance, they dared not break their promise for fear calamity would beset them.

Not only may the ill fortune suffered by individuals be attributed to their having angered the gods, but also such widespread catastrophes as flood, drought, hurricane, and pestilence that befall an entire community can be blamed on the group's having disobeyed the proscriptions of powerful luminous forces.

In summary, then, the purpose of many of cultures' *thou-shalt-nots* is to prevent people from having to suffer vengeance.

## PROHIBITIONS AND CULTURAL CHANGE

The phenomenon of a folk belief changing as a result of a new law is illustrated in Chinese villagers' attitudes toward marriage between cousins. In traditional Chinese folk psychology, arranging marriages between individuals from families that were already linked by marriage was considered a very good thing, since the families were well acquainted and a new marriage would further strengthen the ties between two ancestral lines. Thus, weddings between first, second, or third cousins were encouraged, with first-cousin matches the most common. However, in 1981 a nationwide marriage law prohibited first-cousin marriages because of the chance that such matings might result in physically or psychologically impaired children. As evidence that traditional folk psychology was readily altered by the reasoning underlying the law, Cooper (1998, p. 381) reported that by the end of the 1980s "belief that such marriages run the danger of producing genetically flawed offspring is now nearly universal in [the rural village of] Dongyang" (Cooper, 1998, p. 381).

# 14

# Folk Psychologies' Significance and Trends

*Of what use is an understanding of folk psychologies, and what can be
expected of folk psychologies in the years ahead?*

The three purposes of this final chapter are to suggest why the study of
folk psychologies is important, to adopt hindsight for reviewing key
features of the book's preceding 13 chapters, and to adopt foresight for
speculating about the likely fate of folk psychologies in the future.

## THE STUDY OF FOLK PSYCHOLOGIES

Three vantage points from which to view the significance of studying
folk psychologies are those of (a) the functions that folk psychologies
perform in the lives of individuals and in the society as a whole, (b) how
knowing a variety of folk psychologies can enhance a person's understanding of, and interaction with, people of diverse cultural backgrounds, and (c) the relationship between folk psychologies and newly
created psychologies.

### Personal and Societal Functions of Folk Psychologies

For individuals, their culturally shared psychology usually serves several purposes. First, it simplifies the task of understanding the cause of
events, since it provides a ready-made explanation of why things occur
as they do. Because the culture's traditional explanation for happenings
furnishes an automatic guide to action, there is no need for people to
puzzle about how and why to behave in decision-making situations.

Subscribing to a culture's traditional worldview can also strengthen a
person's sense of belonging to a community. Members of a society, by
thinking alike, can take comfort in the feeling that they are part of a uni-

fied group in which people perceive life in a similar way. Furthermore, this shared worldview can support a person's confidence in the group's interpretation of events by supplying social confirmation of the interpretation's validity. If so many other members of the society—and particularly older, more experienced members—have held those beliefs, then those time-tested convictions must be true.

Folk psychologies also furnish benefits to the society as a whole. When people share the beliefs that comprise their culture's folk psychology, communication among them becomes quick and simple, because a few words or gestures can convey a mass of meaning. And folk beliefs held in common by members of a group can reduce the conflict experienced in group decisionmaking that would result if different members subscribed to different interpretations of life.

The widespread acceptance of a particular worldview also helps unify a society, promoting cohesion through the individuals' common shared values, conceptions of reality, and modes of communication. For example, one of the reasons that members of a cultural group feel bonded together is that all speak the same language.

## The Value of Knowing a Variety of Folk Psychologies

What value, then, does a person gain from learning about different folk psychologies? It seems apparent that knowing the content of various cultures' belief systems can enhance individuals' understanding of, and interaction with, people of cultural backgrounds different than their own. Specifically, becoming well-informed about folk psychologies can equip people to

- Recognize features of other people's worldviews that have resulted from those individuals' cultural backgrounds.
- Observe others' behaviors that reveal how their interpretations of life are similar to and different from one's own.
- Inquire of others to discover the nature of their customs and the sorts of rationales with which they support their beliefs and behaviors.
- Tolerate and respect others' beliefs and customs that pose no threat of harm to oneself or to others.
- Explain to others the nature of one's own cultural convictions and customs so that those others can understand and respect one's own view of life.

## The Relation of Folk Beliefs to Innovative Psychologies

The term *innovative psychologies* is used here to identify explanations of human thought and action that differ from a culture's traditional belief system. Novel theories can either be introduced from another culture or arise from within a culture in the form of proposals offered by one or more creative members of the society who have become dissatisfied with some aspect of the group's existing folk belief. Those inventive members usually fill such roles as those of religious leader, seer, philosopher, or scientist. The study of folk psychologies can contribute to people understanding the appearance of novel psychologies by suggesting which features of a given folk psychology are replaced by the innovator's proposal, why the change has been introduced, and what consequences are likely to result from adopting that unusual portrayal of human thought and action.

## HINDSIGHT

The following observations, drawn from a retrospective look at the preceding 13 chapters, concern (a) the overlap of chapter contents, (b) processes of change, (c) how increasing cultural diversity within a society affects folk psychologies, (d) the frequent personification of causal factors in folk psychologies, and (e) three additional propositions abstracted from the chapters' examples.

### Chapter Overlap

One obvious characteristic of the book's chapters is that examples of folk psychologies found in one chapter might serve equally well to illustrate matters discussed in other chapters. A folk belief that working on Sunday will offend God and result in punishment for the offender could serve equally well as an example in the chapters about reality, cause, and prohibitions. The description of a ceremony honoring ancestors could fit nicely into any of several chapters, such as those about cause, values, rituals, or time and life span. Thus, it is apparent that the chapters have not addressed entirely separate contents of folk beliefs. Instead, they have offered a diversity of perspectives from which human belief and behavior can be seen. The result is a multifaceted portrait of people's interpretations of life's events.

### Processes of Change

A second observation to be drawn from earlier chapters is that the process by which imported beliefs change traditional folk psychologies often results in a new syncretic perspective that differs from both the imported psychology and the culture's customary worldview. The new system incorporates only portions of the imported beliefs and melds them into the pattern of existing convictions. One way such melding can occur is illustrated in M. G. Smith's account of how a priest among the

Kadara of northern Nigeria translated a scientific explanation of illness into terms familiar in Kadara folk psychology as a means of convincing the populace to adopt hygienic drinking-water practices.

[The] village census in 1950 showed that over 60 percent of Kadara children of Kufana died within five years of birth, the overwhelming majority due to enteritis or dysentery. In the absence of hygienic wells, or hopes of their early installation, I consulted the Agwom (chief) and the Wuciciri (priest) of Kufana together about the problem. They agreed that we had to find some way of persuading the people to boil the water they gave their infants to drink, and that we should try to do so immediately. Adapting a basic Kadara belief, the Wuciciri undertook to promulgate a revelation received in a dream from an ancestor to the effect that, just as spirits of leprosy and smallpox lived in solid objects scattered in the bush, so the spirit of dysentery lived in water, and could only be driven out by boiling, when its exit is visible as steam. Thereafter, to prevent the spirit's re-entry, water once boiled should always be kept covered; and to avoid dysentery, only such water should be drunk. The Wuciciri also undertook to "test" the validity and reliability of this dream revelation by appropriate divinations and auguries shortly after its announcement. On this basis, within a few weeks, about one-third of the community was persuaded to adopt the new practice. (Smith, 1982, p. 19)

The fact that the Kadara were selective in accepting imported beliefs is attested by their adopting Christian moral precepts and the "this-wordly" teaching of the Christian churches as valid and binding" but by their explicitly rejecting the notion of heaven and hell, a notion that assumes individual immortality, which is a belief that conflicts with traditional Kadara folk psychology (Smith, 1982, p. 19).

A similar case of partial-adoption of new beliefs has been observed in the United States where certain Jewish and Christian sects accept some scientific observations about the nature of the universe but not others. Consider, for example, ideas relating to astronomy and to biological species. In the Judeo-Christian biblical version of the cosmos, the sky is not composed of gaseous matter and of empty space extending infinitely into the beyond. Instead, the sky is a canopy poised on the horizon, rather like an inverted teacup or blue hemispheric shell of solid matter (firmament) into which stars are implanted as specks of light.

And God made the firmament . . . and called the firmament Heaven. . . . And God said, Let there be lights in the firmament of the heaven. . . . (*Holy Bible*, 1930, Genesis 1: 6-7, 14)

Today this "firmament" proposal about the nature of the sky is rarely if ever accepted by American Jews and Christians. However, many fundamentalist Jews and Christians continue to believe in the biblical version of how species of animal life first appeared (each species created within a single day as a separate type) rather than believing in Darwin's proposal that the species gradually evolved over many millions of years from very simple biological cells.

> And God made the beast of the earth after his kind, and cattle after their kind, and every thing that creepeth upon the earth after his kind: and God saw that it was good. And God said, Let us make man in our image, after our likeness. . . . So God created man in his own image; male and female created he them. (*Holy Bible*, 1930, Genesis 1: 26-27)

The strength of this creationist belief among fundamentalist North Americans has been demonstrated periodically by such events as a widely publicized court case in 1925 aimed at prosecuting John T. Scopes, a high-school teacher, for teaching Darwin's theory in preference to the biblical description. In subsequent decades, the opposition to Darwinian theory did not abate among Christian fundamentalists. In the 1990s, Christian activists in various regions of the United States continued their attempts to prevent the teaching of Darwinism in the schools or, at least, to require that a biblical version of human origins be given equal classtime. In 1999, the issue of who determines science curricula in U.S. schools pitted creationists against evolutionists when the Kansas state board of education prohibited any mention of Darwin's theory on state achievement tests, thereby effectively eliminating the theory from the course of study. Critics of the decision charged that the board's move was an attempt on the part of religious fundamentalists to circumvent court rulings which, over the previous four years, had overturned legislation in New Hampshire, Ohio, Tennessee, Texas, and Washington designed to reduce or eliminate the teaching of Darwinism in public schools (Marcus, 1999, p. 32).

## Increased Cultural Diversity

At an accelerating pace, improvements in communication and transportation over the past two centuries have dramatically increased the interactions among peoples. In the 18th and 19th centuries, and during the first half of the 20th century, European, North American, and Japanese colonial powers gained control over many regions of the world, affecting the culture of the captured peoples by introducing—and frequently imposing—their own folk psychologies. Following World War II, most of the formerly colonized peoples gained political independence and, in many cases, sought to reassert their indigenous interpretations of life. However, in all such cases the influence of the introduced psychologies lingered on, and the resulting diverse worldviews continued side by side. In recent decades, interaction among peoples has been further hastened by growing migration and literacy, along with such technological innovations as radio and television, more convenient air transportation, and the computer Internet with its e-mail and chat groups. Consequently, as societies have become culturally more variegated, there has been greater need for people to understand and respect—or at least to tolerate—psychologies different from their own. The study of folk psychologies helps meet that need.

## Personifying Causes

A particularly salient feature of the psychologies described throughout this book is the high incidence of supernatural beings that are held responsible for instigating so many of life's events. A question may then be asked about why such paranormal beings—gods, spirits, jinns, angels, devils, and the like—are accorded so important a place in cultural beliefs about cause. In response, I would suggest that the habit of anthropomorphizing the causes of so many happenings is founded on individuals' commonsense interpretation of their own behavior and of the actions of people they encounter in daily life. That interpretation results from the commonsense notion that the cause of many life events involves a three-step process—someone has (a) an intent in mind (goal, aim, envisioned outcome) that leads to (b) behavior (action) that results in (c) an outcome. For instance, the logic of court trials is typically based on this line of reasoning. Trials are conducted not only to determine whether the law has been broken and who did the breaking, but also to reveal the motive (intent) that led to the behavior (action) that produced the unfortunate result. "He wanted revenge, so he spray-painted the defendant's car" or "She was desperately trying to feed her children, so she took the groceries without paying for them."

People can personify the cause of many additional phenomena by assuming a parallel between their own behavior and the way the physical world operates. They apply their three-step conception of cause to explain happenings that seem otherwise incomprehensible—a hurricane, crop failure, insanity, the elusiveness of game they hunt, accidents, the death of a child, the disappearance of valued possessions, and more. They account for such mysterious events by imagining that causal forces in the universe operate much the same way as persons. Like living humans, invisible forces harbor intentions that serve as motives for taking action to achieve desired outcomes. Hence, pestilence can be interpreted as punishment the spirits impose for a population's disobeying the spirits' commandments; and winning the lottery can be seen as the gods rewarding a self-sacrificing person for rescuing a child from drowning.

In summary, it seems natural for people to use their own experience as a proper analogy for explaining happenings whose causes are not directly apparent. The resulting explanations can become embedded in folk psychologies passed down through the generations. I would expect this tendency to continue into the future, but diminishing gradually as people become more aware of persuasive, empirically verifiable causes of events.

## Three More Propositions

The examples of folk psychologies portrayed in Chapters 2 through 13 appear to support the following propositions.

*Proposition 1.* People yearn for final, permanent answers about life. Consequently, they tend to hold fast to established traditions. Many folk beliefs, particularly those that have assumed the status of religious doctrine, seem highly resistant to the intrusion of opposing belief systems. People's desire to feel that they live in a comprehensible, predictable, and unchanging world encourages them to hold fast to tradition. That desire serves to perpetuate folk psychologies over extended periods of time.

*Proposition 2.* People wish to resolve discrepancies between their existing folk psychology and any of their observations of the world that could cast doubt on the validity of their folk beliefs. The term *cognitive dissonance* has been used to label this mental conflict over incompatible ideas, that is, the conflict between traditional modes of thought and other modes that are newly introduced. To resolve this conflict, people can either reject the innovations outright, replace their traditional beliefs with the new ones, or integrate selected portions of the new and old into a novel, blended conviction. Each of these solutions can be found existing side by side in most, if not all, cultures.

*Proposition 3.* Not everyone accepts the same sorts of evidence as trustworthy support for the beliefs they adopt. Therefore, when individuals choose between conflicting beliefs, their choice is often determined by their preferring one source of evidence over another. Some people accept the word of an authoritative figure—chieftain, shaman, priest, government official, professor, newspaper, television personality, scientist. Others trust their own direct experience—what they have seen with their own eyes. Consequently, within a particular culture, the different degrees of trust in folk tradition displayed by members of the group can often be explained by the kinds of evidence different people accept as convincing.

## FORESIGHT

Two trends from the past that seem bound to continue into the future, and to advance at a growing pace, are these:

- Across the world, the number of distinct folk psychologies will diminish.
- Within any given society—national, regional, local—the diversity of folk psychologies will increase.

Each of these trends can be seen as resulting primarily from (a) an assumed motivating force called *exploration drive* and (b) *technological innovations*.

The term *exploration drive* refers to people's desire and willingness to abandon their present familiar location and/or lifestyle in order to improve the quality of their life. In this effort, what people are seeking to escape and to replace with something better can differ from one person to another. An adventurous individual may seek to escape boredom by traveling to a foreign land. An unemployed peasant may head for the city in the hope of getting a job. A politically oppressed family may leave their homeland to seek safety in another country. Missionaries may feel duty bound to travel abroad to convert heathen to their own religious persuasion. Chiefs of state may send their armies to capture foreign territories and thereby increase the size and power of the empire they control.

Ever since prehistoric times, this postulated exploration drive has brought individuals into contact with cultures unlike their own, resulting in various consequences for folk psychologies. Four ways that such contact may affect people's psychologies can be labeled *parallel accommodation, domination, eradication,* and *integration.*

The term *parallel accommodation* is applied to societies in which two or more widely adopted cultural traditions continue side by side in an amiable—or oftentimes uneasy and contentious—relationship. An example of generally amiable arrangement would be the relationships among religious denominations in a typical North American town. An instance of a contentious relationship would be that between Jewish and Arab belief systems in Israel. Parallel accommodation can be either a long-lasting condition or merely a transition state on the way to one of the other three modes.

Domination is the pattern of cultural belief when two or more contending folk psychologies exist within a society, but one is far more widespread than others. An example would be Roman Catholicism in Spain and Portugal, where other religious denominations exist but are far less popular than Catholicism.

Eradication is the outcome of cultural contact when one belief or custom eliminates another. This has been the case with the languages and religions of nonliterate cultures, such as the cultures of Native American tribes whose belief systems and customs had traditionally been passed from one generation to the next in oral form. Without the historical permanence that written records provide, nonliterate cultures have a difficult time sustaining their belief systems against the onslaughts of cultures that command advanced methods of permanently recording, retrieving, and displaying the beliefs.

Integration occurs when elements of each of the contending cultures are combined to form an amalgam that differs in detail from any of the traditions that contributed to the mixture. For example, Bloomfield (1983, p. 36) proposes that present-day Chinese folk psychology is a "mélange of animism, Tao-Buddhism scraps and patches, folk myth and magic, and long centuries of supernatural practices."

It is also the case that a culture may display features of all four of these responses to cultural encounters. Thus, in some of their elements, the folk psychologies currently observed in a society may illustrate parallel accommodation, whereas in other elements they may exhibit dominance, eradication, and integration.

In thousands of non-Western societies, elements of once-dominant indigenous folk psychologies have been whittled away by intrusive foreigners imposing on those societies their own school curricula and highly influential mass-communication media—books, periodicals, movies, radio, television, and the Internet. As a consequence, the amount of original content of many folk psychologies has diminished, leaving the world with a progressively smaller number of distinct cultural worldviews.

Because advances in communication and transportation are appearing at a growing pace, the process of reducing the diversity of the world's folk psychologies can be expected to progress at an even more rapid rate in the future. In effect, people's ability to indulge their exploration drive will be increasingly facilitated by technological innovation.

These same factors—exploration drive and technological invention—that serve to decrease the variety of folk psychologies in the world tend to increase the variety of belief systems within particular societies, especially within large, urban communities. As Pakistanis immigrate to London and Liverpool, they bring into these settings Islamic and ethnic folk beliefs not available before. As Zen Buddhists from Nepal, China, and Japan settle in Los Angeles and Chicago, they not only form coteries of their own believers, but they also recruit into their ranks numbers of Americans originally reared in Baptist and Catholic families. As colleges in Sri Lanka, India, and Egypt adopt textbooks from Britain, Canada, and the United States, students are exposed to belief systems different from those of their home cultures. When computer users from around the world form chat groups on the Internet, they may expose themselves to cultural convictions of which they were formerly unaware.

This increased diversification of folk psychologies within a society is accompanied by advantages and disadvantages. One advantage is that individual differences in people's preferences for belief systems are better served by a multicultural environment than by a culturally monolithic society, since the multicultural setting offers more choices of what to believe. A second advantage is that such a society provides a subcommunity of people who subscribe to convictions similar to one's own, thereby providing individuals a source of support and satisfying interaction. However, a diversity of worldviews also increases the potential for conflict among members of the society who subscribe to different folk psychologies. In addition, diversity imposes on individuals the burden of having to select among alternatives, a burden not borne in societies that offer only one or two psychologies from which to choose.

Finally, as a closing note, I should mention once again that a central purpose of this book has been to enhance readers' ability to understand the varieties of folk belief that may be held by people whom they encounter in daily life, either directly or vicariously through such media as books, television, and the World Wide Web. The hope is that such an understanding will contribute to our interacting ever more amicably and constructively with others whose worldviews differ from our own.

# References

Acheson, J. M. (1981). Anthropology of fishing. In B. J. Siegel, A. R. Beals, & S. A. Tyler (Eds.), *Annual review of anthropology* (pp. 275-316). Palo Alto, CA: Annual Reviews.

Ackerman, L. A. (1995). Gender status in the Plateau. In L. F. Klein & L. A. Ackerman (Eds.), *Women and power in native North America* (pp. 75-100). Norman: University of Oklahoma Press.

Adams, K. M. (1997). Ethnic tourism and the renegotiation of tradition in Tana Toraja. *Ethnology, 36* (4), 309-320.

Agency for Cultural Affairs. (1972). *Japanese religion*. Tokyo: Kodansha International.

Alegría, J. A. (1974). *Psicología de las Mexicanas Coyacan*. Mexico City: Samo.

Ali, A. Y. (Ed.). (1979). *The glorious Qur'an* (Vols. 1, 2). Cairo, Egypt: Dar El Kilab Al Masri.

Allport, G. W. (1961). *Pattern and growth in personality*. New York: Holt, Rinehart, & Winston.

Almagor, U. (1978). *Pastoral partners*. Manchester, UK: Manchester University Press.

Almagor, U. (1985). The bee connection: The symbolism of a cyclical order in an East African age system. *Journal of Anthropological Research, 41* (1), 1-17.

Almunzri, A. (1977). *Saheeh Muslim*. Damascus, Syria: Al Makteb Elislami.

Alves, J. (1993). Transgressions and transformations: Initiation rites among urban Portuguese boys. *American Anthropologist, 95* (4), 894-928.

American Association of University Women. (1992). *How schools short-change girls: A study of major findings on girls and education.* Washington, DC: Author.

American Civil Liberties Union. (1999, October). *Status of U.S. sodomy laws.* [On-line]. Available: http://www.aclu.org/issues/gay/sodomy.html

Amish. (1994). In R. McHenry (Ed.), *Encyclopaedia Britannica* (Vol. 1, p. 343). Chicago: Encyclopaedia Britannica.

Angelino, H., & Shedd, C. (1955). A note on berdache. *American Anthropologist, 57,* 121-126.

Aoki, T. (1990). *Nihon bunkaron no henyou* (The transition of world conditions and the evaluation of Japanese culture). Tokyo: Chuokoronsha.

Bagdikian, B. (1990). *The media monopoly* (3$^{rd}$ ed.). Boston: Beacon.

Baker, L. R. (1999). Folk psychology. In R. A. Wilson & F. C. Keil (Eds.), *The MIT encyclopedia of the cognitive sciences.* Cambridge, MA: MIT Press.

Bank, B. J. (1985). Student sex and classroom behavior. In T. Husen & T. N. Postlethwaite (Eds.), *International encyclopedia of education* (Vol. 8, pp. 4878-4881). Oxford, UK: Pergamon.

Banks, C. G. (1992). "Culture" in culture-bound syndromes: The case of anorexia nervosa. *Social Science & Medicine. 34* (8), 867-884.

Barber, P. (1988). *Vampires, burial, and death.* New Haven, CT: Yale University Press.

Barlow, K. (1992). Dance when I die: Context and role in the clowning of Murik women. In W. E. Mitchell (Ed.), *Clowning as critical practice* (pp. 58-87). Pittsburgh, PA: University of Pittsburgh Press.

Barth, F. (1987). *Cosmologies in the making: A genrative approach to cultural variation in inner New Guinea.* New York: Cambridge University Press.

Barton, R. F. (1946). *The religion of the Hugaos* (Memoir 65). Washington, DC: American Anthropological Association.

Bautista, C. B. (1977). Women in marriage. In *Sterotype, status, and satisfactions: The Filipina among Filipinos.* Quezon City: Social Research Laboratory, Department of Sociology, University of the Philippines.

Becker, A. E. (1995). *Body, self, and society: The view from Fiji.* Philadelphia: University of Pennsylvania Press.

Beyer, L. E., & Liston, D. P. (1996). *Curriculum in conflict: Social visions, educational agendas, and progressive school reform.* New York: Teachers College Press.

Bianchi, S. M., & Spain, D. (1986). *American women in transition.* New York: Russell Sage Foundation.

Biebuyck, D. P. (1973). *Lega culture.* Berkeley: University of California Press.

Black, P. W. (1985). Ghosts, gossip, and suicide: Meaning and action in Tobian folk psychology. In G. M. White & J. Kirkpatrick (Eds.), *Person, self, and experience: Exploring Pacific ethnopsychologies* (pp. 245-300). Berkeley: University of California Press.

Blackwood, E. (1984). Sexuality and gender in certain North American tribes: The case of cross-gender females. *Signs: Journal of Women in Culture and Society, 10,* 27-42.

Blank, J. (1996, December 9). The body as temple, the body as prison: In India, a beauty crowned, a man in flames. *U.S. News & World Report, 121* (23), 84.

Blankenhorn, D. (1995). *Fatherless America.* New York: Basic Books.

Bloomfield, F. (1983). *The book of Chinese beliefs.* London: Arrow Books.

Bonvillain, N. (1998). *Women and men* (2nd ed.). Upper Saddle River, NJ: Prentice Hall.

*Book of Mormon, The* (1980). Salt Lake City, UT: The Church of Jesus Christ of Latter-Day Saints.

Boulding, E. (2000). *Cultures of peace.* Syracuse, NY: Syracuse University Press.

Bourque, L. N. (1995). Developing people and plants: Life-cycle and agricultural festivals in the Andes. *Ethnology, 34* (1), 75-87.

Brown, D. (1979). Umbanda and class relations in Brazil. In M. L. Margolis & W. E. Carter (Eds.), *Brazil: Anthropological perspectives* (pp. 270-304). New York: Columbia University Press.

Brown, M. E. (1987). Ropes of sand: Order and imagery in Aguaruna dreams. In B. Tedlock (Ed.). *Dreaming: Anthropological and psychological interpretations* (pp. 154-170). New York: Cambridge University Press.

Brown, M. E. (1989). *The spiritual legacy of the American Indian.* New York: Crossroad.

Brown, M. E., & Van Bolt, M. L. (1980). Aguaruna Jivaro gardening magic in the Alto Rio Mayo, Peru. *Ethnology, 19* (2), 169-190.

Bruner, J. S. (1990). *Acts of meaning/* Cambridge, MA : Harvard University Press.

Brunner, B. (Ed.). (2000). *Time almanac 2000.* Boston, MA: Information Please.

Bryce, R. (1996). Priest puts funeral prices on the Internet. *National Catholic Reporter, 32* (39), 5.

Bryson, J. B. (1991). Modes of response to jealousy-evoking situations. In P. Salovey (Ed.), *The psychology of jealousy and envy* (pp. 178-207). New York: Guilford.

Buck, W. (1976). *Ramayana*. Berkeley: University of California Press.

Buhler, G. (1886). *Manu Smriti—The Laws of Manu*, (Vol. 25, *The sacred books of the East*, F. M. Muller, Ed.). London: Oxford University Press.

Burridge, K. (1969). *Tangu traditions*. Oxford, UK: Oxford University Press.

Burridge, K. (1973). *Encountering aborigines: Anthropology and the Australian aboriginnal*. Oxford, UK: Pergamon.

Buss, D. M. (2000). *The dangerous passion*. New York: Free Press.

Cahn, Z. (1962). *The philosophy of Judaism*. New York: Macmillan.

Callender, C., & Kochems, L. (1983). The North American berdache. *Current Anthropology, 24,* 443-470.

Calligan, M. E. (Ed.). (1992). *1992 penal code: Abridged California edition*. San Clemente, CA: Quik-Code Publications.

Camilleri, C., & Malewska-Peyre, H. (1997). Socialization and identity strategies. In J. W. Berry, P. R. Dasen, & T. S. Saraswathi (Eds.), *Handbook of cross-cultural psychology* (pp. 41-67). Boston: Allyn & Bacon.

Cardes, C. (1983, November). Spanish research comes alive in Miami. *APA Monitor*.

Carucci, L. M. (1984). Significance of change or change of significance: A consideration of Marshallese personal names. *Ethnology, 22* (2), 143-155.

Chandler, T. A., Shama, D. D., Wolf, F. M., & Planchard, S. K. (1981). Multi-attributional causality for achievement across five cross-national samples. *Journal of Cross-Cultural Psychology, 12* (2), 207-221.

Chater, N., & Oaksford, M. (1996). The falsity of folk theor. es. In W. O'Donohue & R. F. Kitchener (Eds.), *The philosophy of psychology* (pp. 244-256). Thousand Oaks, CA: Sage.

Chavel, C. B. (1967). Foreword. In M. Maimonides, *Sefer Ha-Mitzvoth of Maimonides* (Vol. 1, pp. vii-xvi). London: Soncino Press.

Chelala, C. (1998). An alternative way to stop female genital mutilation. *Lancet, 352* (9122), 126.

Chen, W. T. (1963). *A source book in Chinese philosophy*. Princeton, NJ: Princeton University Press.

Chiasson, N., Dubé, L., & Blondin, J. -P. (1996). A look into the folk psychology of four cultural groups. *Journal of Cross-Cultural Psychology, 27* (6), 673-691.

Child marriages continue in India. (1994). *WIN News, 20* (3), 56.

Chilman, C. S. (1993). Hispanic families in the United States. In H. P. McAdoo (Ed.), *Family ethnicity* (pp. 141-163). Newbury Park, CA: Sage.

Chiñas, B. N. (1995). Isthmus Zapotec attitudes toware sex and gender anomalies. In S. O. Murray (Ed.), *Latin American male homosexualities* (pp. 292-302). Albuquerque: University of New Mexico Press.

Cho, O. L. (1986). The system of belief in Korean rural communities. In S. B. Han (Ed.), *Asian peoples and their cultures.* Seoul, Korea: Seoul National University Press.

Churchland, P. M. (1988). *Matter and consciousness* (Rev. ed.). Cambridge, MA: MIT Press.

Churchland, P. M. (1994). Folk psychology. In S. Guttenplan (Ed.), *A companion to the philosophy of mind* (pp. 308-316). Oxford: Blackwell.

Clark, S. S. (1994). Ethnicity embodied: Evidence from Tahiti. *Ethnology, 33* (3), 211-227.

Clay, B. J. (1986). *Mandak realities.* New Brunswick, NJ: Rutgers University Press.

Clayman, C. B. (1989). *The American Medical Association encyclopedia of medicine.* New York: Random House.

Clemmer, R. O. (1996). Ideology and identity: Western Shoshoni "cannibal" myth as ethnonational narrative. *Journal of Anthropological Research, 52,* 207-223.

Coberly, R. W. (1980). Maternal and marital dyads. *Ethnology, 19* (4), 447-457.

Cogan, J. C., Bhalla, S. K., Sefa-Dedeh, A., & Rothblum, E. D. (1996). A comparison study of United States and African students on perceptions of obesity and thinness. *Journal of Cross-Cultural Psychology, 27* (1), 98-113.

Collins, J. M. (1974). *Valley of the spirits.* Seattle: University of Washington Press.

Colson, E. (1960). Ancestral spirits among the Plateau Tonga. In S. Ottenberg & P. Ottenberg (Eds.), *Cultures and societies of Africa* (pp. 372-387). New York: Random House.

Comarow, A., Cohen, G., & Mulrine, A. (1999, May 17). Virtual funeral planning. *U.S. News and World Report, 127* (19), 135.

Combs, A. W., & Snygg, D. (1959). *Individual behavior.* New York: Harper & Row.

Contado, M. E. (1981). Power dynamics of rural families: The case of Samar barrio. *Philippine Sociological Review, 29* (1-4), 73-85.

Cooper, G. (1998). Life-cycle rituals in Dongyang County: Time, affinity, and exchange in rural China. *Ethnology, 37* (4), 373-394.

Counts, D. R., & Counts, D. A. (1992). Exaggeration and reversal: Clowning among the Lusi-Kaliai. In W. E. Mitchell (Ed.), *Clowning as critical practice* (pp. 88-103). Pittsburgh, PA: University of Pittsburgh Press.

Crocker, J. C. (1977). The mirrored self: Identity and ritual inversion among the eastern Bororo. *Ethnology, 16* (2), 129-145.

Dahl, O. (1999). *Meanings in Madagascar.* Westport, CT: Bergin & Garvey.

Dalai-Lama. (1998). Patience: A flash of lightning in the dark of night: A guide to the Bodhisattva's way of life. *Middle Way, 73* (1), 6-12.

Damon, W., & Hart, D. (1988). *Self-understanding in childhood and adolescence.* New York: Cambridge University Press.

Davies, C. (1990). *Ethnic humor around the world.* Bloomington: University of Indiana Press.

Delaisi de Parseval, G., & Hurtsel, F. (1987). Paternity "à la Française." In M. E. Lamb (Ed.), *The father's role* (pp. 59-87). Hillsdale, NJ: Erlbaum.

Delaware Diocese Seeing Decline in Use of Funeral Mass. (1999, Nov. 20). *America, 181* (16), 4.

Demerath, P. (1999). The cultural production of educational utility in Pere Village, Papua New Guinea. *Comparative Education Review, 43* (2), 162-192.

Denzin, N. K. (1997). *Interpretive ethnography.* Thousand Oaks, CA: Sage.

Derné, S. (1995). *Culture in action: Family life, emotion, and male dominance in Banaras, India.* Albany, NY: State University of New York Press.

Derrida, J. (1976). *Of grammatology* (Gayatri Chakravorty Spivak, Trans.). Baltimore, MD: Johns Hopkins University Press.

Deutsch, A. (2000, September 13). Netherlands gives gays right to marry, adopt. *San Francisco Chronicle,* A12.

Diaz-Guerrero, R. (1955). Neurosis and Mexican family structure. *American Journal of Psychology, 112,* 411-419.

Dodge, G. (1996). Laughter of the samurai: Humor in the autobiography of Etsu Sugimoto. *MELUS, 21* (4), 57-69.

Doloff, S. (1998). Racism and the risks of ethnic humor. *Free Inquiry, 19* (1), 11.

Downey, W. E. (1998). Secular rites: With the number of Christians declining, a new kind of funeral speaker has emerged. *Christian Century, 115* (11), 358-359.

Draitser, E. A. (1998). *Taking penguins to the movies: Ethnic humor in Russia.* Detroit, MI: Wayne State University Press.

Duggan, R. D. (1993). The age of confirmation: A flawed proposal. *America, 168* (20), 12-14.

Duncan, B., & McRae, J. A., Jr. (1978). *Sex typing and social roles.* New York: Academic Press.

Durst, W. (1997). Ibonics lesson. *Progressive, 61* (3), 14.

Egami, N. (1962). Light on Japanese cultural origins from historical archeology and legend. In R. J. Smith & R. K. Beardsley, *Japanese culture: Its development and characteristics* (pp. 11-16). Chicago: Aldine.

Eickelman, D. F. (1977). Time in a complex society: A Moroccan example. *Ethnology, 16* (1), 39-56.

Elkin, A. P. (1964). *The Australian Aborigines.* Sydney, Australia: Angus and Robertson.

Elmendorf, M. (1977). Mexico: The many worlds of women. In J. Giele & A. Smock (Eds.), *Women: Roles and status in eight countries* (pp. 129-172). New York: Wiley.

Erchak, G. M. (1992). *The anthropology of self and behavior.* New Brunswick, NJ: Rutgers University Press.

Erikson, E. H. (1987). *A way of looking at things: Selected papers from 1930 to 1980.* New York: Norton.

Esar, E. (1978). *The comic encyclopedia.* Garden City, NY: Garden City Books.

Estermann, C. (1976). *The ethnography of southwestern Angola* (Vol. 1). New York: Africana.

Female circumcision: Facts and myths. (1997, December 29). *Out! Magazine,* 1-2.

Feud. (1994). In R. McHenry (Ed.), *Encyclopaedia Britannica,* (Vol. 4, p. 755). Chicago: Encyclopaedia Britannica.

Firth, R. (1967). *Tikopia ritual and belief.* Boston: Beacon.

Fodor, J. A. (1987). *Psychosemantics: The problem of meaning in the philosophy of mind.* Cambridge, MA: MIT Press.

Ford, P. J. (1995). Female circumcision. [On-line]. Available: www.vanderbilt.edu/ AnS/philosophy/Students/FordPJ.HTM

Frank, A. W. (1979). Reality construction in interaction. In A. Inkeles, J. Coleman, & R. H. Turner (Eds.), *Annual review of sociology* (Vol. 5, pp. 167-191). Palo Alto, CA: Annual Reviews.

Frank, B. (1995). Permitted and prohibited wealth: Commodity-possessing spirits, economic morals, and the goddess Mami Wata in West Africa. *Ethnology, 34* (4), 331-346.

Frank, D. F., & McEneaney, E. H. (1999). The individualization of society and the liberalization of state policies on same-sex sexual relations, 1984-1995. *Social Forces, 77* (3), 911-913.

Free your mind: Japanese colleges are starting to rethink the cookie-cutter view of education and pay attention to creativity. (1999, May 3). *Time International, 153* (17) 48.

Freud, S. (1953). The interpretation of dreams. In J. Strachey (Ed.), *The standard edition of the complete psychological works of Sigmund Freud* (Vol. 4, pp. 1-228). London: Hogarth. (Original work published 1900)

Frugal funerals. (1996, December 16). *Maclean's, 109* (51), 16.

Fujita, S., Ito, K. L., Abe, J., & Takeuchi, D. T. (1991). Japanese Americans. In N. Mokuau (Ed.), *Handbook of services for Asians and Pacific Islanders.* Westport, CT: Greenwood.

Furnham, A., & Baguma, P. (1994). Cross-cultural differences in the evaluation of male and female body shapes. *International Journal of Eating Disorders, 15* (1), 81-89.

Galaty, J. G. (1998). The Maasai ornithorium: Tropic flights of avian imagination in Africa. *Ethonlogy, 37* (3), 227-238.

Gamson, W. A., Croteau, D., Hoynes, W., & Sasson, T. (1992). Media images and the social construction of reality. In J. Balake & J. Hagan, *Annual review of sociology* (Vol. 18, pp. 373-393). Palo Alto, CA: Annual Reviews.

Gaskell, G. A. (1981). *Dictionary of all scriptures and myths.* New York: Avenel.

Gates, B. (1995). *The road ahead.* New York: Viking.

Gazlay, K. (2000, November 19). Brits propose spanking limits. *San Luis Obispo Tribune,* pp. 1A, 6A.

Geertz, C. (1960). *The religion of Java.* New York: Free Press.

Geertz, C. (1983). *Local knowledge.* New York: Basic Books.

Geertz, C. (1995). "From the native's point of view": On the nature of anthropological understanding. In N. R. Goldberger & J. B. Veroff (Eds.), *The culture and psychology reader* (pp. 25-40). New York: New York University Press.

Gellner, D. N. (1994). Priests, healers, mediums, and witches: The context of possession in the Kathmandu Valley, Nepal. *Man, 29* (1), 27-48.

George, J. M. (1999). Indigenous knowledge as a component of the school curriculum. In L. M. Semali & J. L. Kincheloe (Eds.), *What is indigenous knowledge?* (79-94). New York: Falmer.

Gerber, E. R. (1985). Rage and obligation: Samoan emotion in conflict. In G. M. White & J. Kirkpatrick (Eds.), *Person, self, and experience: Exploring Pacific ethnopsychologies* (pp. 121-167). Berkeley: University of California Press.

Gerbert, E. (1993). Lessons from the *kokugo* (national language) readers. *Comparative Education Review, 37* (2), 152-180.

Gerteiny, A. G. (1967). *Mauritania.* New York: Praeger.

Ghosh, A. (1983). The relations of envy in an Egyptian village. *Ethnology, 22* (3), 211-223.

Gilligan, C. (1982). *In a different voice.* Cambridge, MA: Harvard University Press.

Gist, N. P. (1940). *Societies: A cultural study of fraternalism in the United States.* Columbia: University of Missouri Press.

Goodwin, G. (1942/1969). *The social organization of the Western Apache.* Tucson: University of Arizona Press.

Gold, S. J. (1993). Migration and family adjustment. In H. P. McAdoo (Ed.), *Family ethnicity* (pp. 300-314). Newbury Park, CA: Sage.

Goulet, J -G. A. (1996). The 'berdache'/'two-spirit': A comparision of anthropological and native constructions of gendered identities among the Northern Athapaskans. *Journal of the Royal Anthropological Society, 2* (4), 683-701.

Gregor, T. (1979). Secrets, exclusion, and the dramatization of men's roles. In M. L. Margolis & W. E. Carter (Eds.), *Brazil: Anthropological perspectives* (pp. 250-269). New York: Columbia University Press.

Guemple, L. (1995). Gender in Inuit society. In L. F. Klein & L. A. Ackerman (Eds.), *Women and power in native North America* (pp. 17-27). Norman: University of Oklahoma Press.

Hall, C. S., & Nordby, V. J. (1973). *A primer of Jungian psychology.* New York: Taplinger.

Hall, E. T. (1959). *The silent language.* New York: Doubleday.

Harkness, S., & Super, C. M. (1995). Child-environments' interactions in the socialization of affect. In M. Lewis & C. Saarni (Eds.), *The socialization of emotions* (pp. 21-36). New York: Plenum.

Harris, P. L. (1989). *Children and emotion.* Oxford, UK: Basil Blackwell.

Harwood, R. L., Miller, J. G., & Irizarry, N. L. (1995). *Culture and attachment.* New York: Guilford.

Hatch, E. (1987). The evaluation of wealth: An agrarian case study. *Ethnology, 26* (1), 37-50.

Henry, S. (1994). *The deep divide: Why American women resist equality.* New York: Macmillan.

Herbert, J. (1967). *Shinto: At the fountain-head of Japan.* New York: Stein & Day.

Hertz, R. (1960). A contribution to the study of the collective representation of death. In *Death and the right hand.* (R. Needham & C. Needham, Trans.). New York: Free Press.

Hess, R. D., Azuma, H., Kashiwagi, K., Dickson, W. P., Nagano, S., Holloway, S., Miyake, K., Price, G., Hatano, G., & McDevitt, T. (1986). Family influences on school readiness and achievement in Japan and the United States: An overview of a longitudinal study. In H. Stevenson, H. Azuma, & K. Hakuta (Eds.), *Child development and education in Japan.* New York: W. H. Freeman.

Hess, R. D., Chang, C. M., & McDevitt, T. M. (1987).   Cultural variables in family beliefs about children's performance in mathematics: Comparisons among People's Republic of China, Chinese-American, and Caucasian-American families. *Journal of Educational Psychology, 79,* 179-188.

Hiatt, L. R. (1984). Your mother-in-law is poison. *Man, 19* (2), 183-198.

Hill, S. (2000). The global view. *New Statesman, 129,* (4494), xxii-xxiii.

Ho, D. Y. F. (1987).  Fatherhood in Chinese culture. In M. E. Lamb (Ed.), *The father's role* (pp. 227-245). Hillsdale, NJ: Erlbaum.

Hofstede, G. (1980). *Culture's consequences: International differences in work-related values.*  Beverly Hills, CA: Sage.

Hollan, D. (1992a). Cross-cultural differences in the self. *Journal of Anthropological Research, 48* (4), 283-300.

Hollan, D. (1992b). Emotion work and the value of emotional equanimity among the Toraja. *Ethology, 31* (1), 45-56.

*Holy Bible.* (1930). (King James authorized version). Philadelphia: John C. Winston. (Original work published 1611)

Houghton, A. A., & Boersma, F. J. (1988). The loss-grief connection in susto. *Ethnology, 27* (2), 145-154.

Howard, A. (1990). Dispute management in Rotuma. *Journal of Anthropological Research, 46* (3), 263-292.

Hubbell, L. J. (1993). Values under siege in Mexico: Strategies for sheltering traditional values from change. *Journal of Anthropological Research, 49* (1), 1-17.

Hunt, H. (1989). *The multiplicity of dreams.* New Haven, CT: Yale University Press.

Hupka, R. B. (1991).  The motive for the arousal of romantic jealousy: Its cultural origin. In P. Salovey (Ed.), *The psychology of jealousy and envy* (pp. 252-270). New York: Guilford.

Hwang, C. P. (1987).  The changing role of Swedish fathers. In M. E. Lamb (Ed.), *The father's role* (pp. 115-138). Hillsdale, NJ: Erlbaum.

Hyönä, J., Destefano, C., Hujanen, H., Lindeman, J., Poskiparta, E., D'Heurle, A., & Niemi, P. (1995). Primers as socializing agents in American and Finnish schools. *Comparative Education Review, 39* (3), 280-298.

Inkeles, A. (1997). *National character.* New Brunswick, NJ: Transaction.

Inkeles, A., & Rossi, P. H. (1956). National comparisons of occupational prestige. *American Journal of Sociology, 61* (3), 326-339.

Irwin, K. (1972). *Laugh with the comedians.* London: Wolfe/Independent Television Books.

Ishii, B. (1987). *Taijinkankeito ibunkakomyunikeshon* [Intercultural communication]. Tokyo: Yuhikaku.

Iteanu, A. (1990). The concept of the person and the ritual system: An Orokaiva view. *Man, 25,* 35-53.

Iyer, K. B. (1969). *Hindu ideals.* Bombay, India: Bhratiya Vidya Bhavan.

Jackson, S. (1987). Great Britain. In M. E. Lamb (Ed.), *The father's role* (pp. 29-57). Hillsdale, NJ: Erlbaum.

James, W. (1961). *The principles of psychology.* New York: Holt, Rinehart, and Winston. (Original work published 1892)

Jamieson, K. H. (1994). *Beyond the double bind.* New York: Oxford University Press.

Jankowiak, W. R., & Fischer, E. F. (1992). A cross-cultural perspective on romantic love. *Ethnology, 31* (2), 149-155.

Jelen, E. (Ed.). (1990). *Women and social change in Latin America.* London: Zed Books.

Jenkins, C.A., & Bainer, D.L. (1990, March). *Common instructional problems in multicultural classrooms.* Paper presented at the Lily Conference on College Teaching, West Lake Arrowhead, CA.

Johnson, W. I. (1979). Work together, eat together: Conflict and conflict management in a Portuguese fishing village. In R. Andersen (Ed.), *North Atlantic maritime cultures* (pp. 241-252). The Hague, The Netherlands: Mouton.

Johnston, B. (1982). *Ojibway ceremonies.* Lincoln: University of Nebraska Press.

Jorgensen, J. G. (1980). *Western Indians.* San Francisco: W. H. Freeman.

Joshi, M. S., & MacLean, M. (1994). Maternal expectations of child development in India, Japan, and England. *Journal of Cross-Cultural Psychology, 28* (2), 219-234.

Judd, E. R. (1994). *Gender and power in rural North China.* Stanford, CA: Stanford University Press.

Junod, H. A. (1927). *The life of a South African tribe* (Vol. 1, 2nd ed.). London: Macmillan.

Just, P. (1991). Conflict resolution and moral community among the Dou Donggo. In K. Avruch, P. W. Black, & J. A. Scimecca (Eds.), *Conflict resolution: Cross-cultural perspectives* (pp. 107-143). Westport, CT: Greenwood.

Kakar, S. (1978). *The inner world: A psychoanalytic study of childhood and society in India.* New Delhi: Oxford University Press.

Kalland, A. (1996). Geomancy and town planning in a Japanese community. *Ethnology, 35* (1), 17-32.

Kato, G. (1973). *A historical study of the religious development of Shinto.* Westport, CT: Greenwood.

Kauffman, D. T. (1967). *The dictionary of religious terms.* Westwood, NJ: Fleming H. Revell.

Kehoe, A. B. (1995). Blackfoot persons. In L. F. Klein & L. A. Ackerman (Eds.), *Women and power in native North America* (pp. 113-125). Norman: University of Oklahoma Press.

Kelley, E. C. (1962). The fully functioning self. In A. W. Combs, E. C. Kelley, A. H. Maslow, & C. R. Rogers (Eds.), *Perceiving, behaving, becoming.* Washington, DC: Association for Supervision and Curriculum Development.

Kelly, R. (1976). Witchcraft and sexual relations. In P. Brown & G. Borchinder (Eds.), *Man and woman in the New Guinea highlands* (pp. 36-53). Washington, DC: American Anthropological Association.

Keppler, A. L. (1993). Poetics and politics in Tongan laments and eulogies. *American Ethnologist, 20* (30), 474-501.

Kim, Y. K. (1982). Several forms of Korean folk rituals, including shaman rituals. In S. Y. Chun (Ed.), *Customs and manners in Korea* (pp. 57-64). Seoul, Korea: Si-sa-yong-o-sa.

King, L. (1999). Learning through the soul: Concepts relating to learning and knowledge in the Mayan cultures of Mexico. *International Review of Education, 45* (3/4), 367-370.

Kirkpatrick, J. (1985). Some Marquesan understandings of action and identity. In G. M. White & J. Kirkpatrick (Eds.), *Person, self, and experience: Exploring Pacific ethnopsychologies* (pp. 80-120). Berkeley: University of California Press.

Klein, R. (1994). Big country: the roots of American obesity. *New Republic, 211* (12-13), 28-32.

Koestler, A. (1994). Humour and wit. In R. McHenry (Ed.), *Encyclopaedia Britannica,* (Vol. 20, pp. 682-688). Chicago: Encyclopaedia Britannica.

Kohlberg, L. (1976). Moral states and moralization: The cognitive-developmental approach. In T. Likona (Ed.), *Moral development and behavior.* New York: Holt, Rinehart & Winston.

*Kojiki* [Records of Ancient Matters]. (1958). Tokyo: Iwanami Publishing Company. *Koran, The.* (1844). (G. Sale, Trans.). London: Tegg.

Krögersonn, E. (1977). *Ostfriesenwitze.* Frankfurt am Main, Germany: Fischer.

La Fontaine, J. S. (1986). *Initiation.* Manchester, UK: Manchester University Press.

Laird, C. (1976). *The Chemehuevis.* Banning, CA., Malki Museum Press.

Lambek, M. (1999). Taboo as cultural practice among Malagasy speakers. *Man, 27,* 245-266.

Lao, T. (1963). *Tao te ching.* New York: Bantam.

Laszlo, V. S. (Ed.). (1993). *The basic writings of C. G. Jung.* New York: Modern Library.

Lau, D. C. (1963). Introduction. In T. Lao, *Tao te ching* (pp. 7-52). New York: Bantam.

Leach, E. R. (1961). Two essays concerning the symbolic representation of time. In E. R. Leach (Ed.), *Rethinking anthropology* (pp. 124-143). London: Athlone Press.

Lebot, V., Merlin, M., & Lindstrom, L. (1992). *Kava, the Pacific drug.* New Haven, CT: Yale University Press.

Lebra, W. F. (1966). *Okinawan religion.* Honolulu: University of Hawaii Press.

Lechuga, R. D., & Sayer, C. (1994). *Mask arts of Mexico.* San Francisco: Chronicle Books.

Lee, H. S. (1996). Change in funeral customs in contemporary Korea. *Korea Journal, 36* (2), 49-60.

Legman, G. (1969). *The limerick.* New York: Bell.

Leifer, R. (1999). Buddhist conceptualization and treatment of anger. *Journal of Clinical Psychology, 55* (3), 339.

Leis, N. B. (1982). The not-so-supernatural power of Ijaw children. In S. Ottenberg (Ed.), *African religious groups and beliefs* (pp. 151-169). Meerut, India: Archana Publications

Leo, J. (1998). *Two steps ahead of the thought police* (2nd ed.). New Brunswick, CT: Transaction.

Le Tendre, G. K. (1999). Community-building activities in Japanese schools: Alternative paradigms of the democratic school. *Comparative Education Review, 43* (3), 283-310.

LeVine, R. A. (1974). Gusii sex offenses: A study in social control. In N. N. (Ed.), *Perspectives on human sexuality* (pp. 308-351). New York: Behavioral Publications.

LeVine, R. A., & LeVine, B. B. (1963). Nyansongo: A Gusii community in Kenya. In B. B. Whiting (Ed.), *Six cultures: Studies of child rearing* (pp. 15-202). New York: Wiley.

LeVine, S., (1982). The dreams of young Gusii women: A content analysis. *Ethnology, 21* (1), 63-77.

LeVine, S. E., Correa, C. S., & Uribe, F. M. T. (1986). The marital morality of Mexican women: An urban study. *Journal of Anthropological Research, 42* (2), 183-202.

Levy, R. I. (1996). Essential contrasts: Differences in parental ideas about learners and teaching in Tahiti and Nepal. In S. Harkness & C. M. Super (Eds.), *Parents' cultural belief systems* (pp. 123-142). New York: Guilford.

Lévy-Bruhl, L. (1966). *How natives think* (R. L. Bunzel, trans.). New York: Washington Square Press.

Lewis, M. (1990). Self knowledge and social development in early life. In L. A. Previn (Ed.), *Handbook of personality* (pp. 277-300). New York: Guilford.

Lewis, M., & Saarni, C. (1985). Culture and emotions. In M. Lewis & C. Saarni (Eds.), *The socialization of emotions* (pp. 1-17). New York: Plenum.

Lin, H. Y. (1988). A Confucian theory of human development. In R. M. Thomas (Ed.), *Oriental theories of human development* (pp. 118-133). New York: Peter Lang.

Lin, H. Y., & Thomas, R. M. (1988). Confucianists' replies to questions about development. In R. M. Thomas (Ed.), *Oriental theories of human development* (pp. 244-268). New York: Peter Lang.

Lincoln, K. (1993). *Indi'n humor: Bicultural play in native America.* New York: Oxford University Press.

Lindholm, C. (1997). Does the sociocentric self exist? Reflections on Markus and Kitanyam's "Culture and the self." *Journal of Anthropological Research, 53,* 405-422.

LiPuma, E. (1994). Sorcery and evidence of change in Maring justice. *Ethnology, 33* (2), pp. 147-163.

Loizos, P. (1988). Intercommunal killing in Cyprus. *Man, 23* (4), pp. 639-653.

Lutz, C. (1985). Cultural patterns and individual differences in the child's emotional meaning system. In M. Lewis & C. Saarni (Eds.), *The socialization of emotions* (pp. 37-53). New York: Plenum.

Macintyre, M. (1992). Reflections of an anthropologist who mistook her husband for a yam: Female comedy on Tubetube. In W. E. Mitchell (Ed.), *Clowning as critical practice* (pp. 130-166). Pittsburgh, PA: University of Pittsburgh Press.

Malewska-Peyre, H., & Zaleska, M. (1980). Identités et conflits de valeurs chez les jeunes immigrés. *Pscyologie Française, 25*: 125-138.

Malinowski, B. (1922). *Argonauts of the western Pacific.* London: Routledge & Kegan Paul.

Malinowski, B. (1948). *Magic, science, and religion and other essays.* Garden City, NY: Doubleday.

Mandelbaum, D. G. (1988). *Women's seclusions and men's honor.* Tucson: University of Arizona Press.

Mangaoang, G. (1994). From the 1970s to the 1990s: Perspectives of a gay Filipino American activist. *Amerasia, 20,* 33-44.

Mao, Z. (1974). Remarks at the spring festival. In S. Schram (Ed.), *Chairman Mao talks to the people: Talks and letters, 1956-1971* (pp. 195-211). New York: Pantheon.

Marcus, D. L. (1999, August 30). Darwin gets thrown out of school. *U.S. News & World Report, 127* (8), 32.

Marcus, H. R., & Kitayama, S. (1991). Culture and the self: Implications for cognition, emotion, and motivation. *Psychological Review,* *98* (2), 224-253.

Marek, J. C. (1988). A Buddhist theory of human development. In R. M. Thomas (Ed.), *Oriental theories of human development* (pp. 76-115). New York: Peter Lang.

Marek, J. C., & Marek, S. (1988). Buddhists' replies to questions about development. In R. M. Thomas (Ed.), *Oriental theories of human development* (pp. 213-241). New York: Peter Lang.

Marek, J. C., & Thomas, R. M. (1988). Hindus' replies to questions about development. In R. M. Thomas (Ed.), *Oriental theories of human development* (pp. 189-212). New York: Peter Lang.

Maretski, T. W., & Maretski, H. (1963). Taira: An Okinawan village. In B. B. Whiting (Ed.), *Six cultures: Studies of child rearing* (pp. 363-539). New York: Wiley.

Marshall, M. (1996). Problematizing impairment: Cultural competencies in the Carolines. *Ethnology, 35* (4), 249-263.

Marshall, R. C. (1985). Giving a gift to the hamlet: Rank, solidarity, and productive exchange in rural Japan. *Ethnology, 24* (3), 167-182.

Martin, H. W., Richardson, C., & Acosta, V. R. (1985). Folk illnesses reported to physicians in the Lower Rio Grande Valley: A binational comparison. *Ethnology, 24* (3), 229-236.

Marx, K. (1977). Preface to "A critique of political economy." In D. McLellan (Ed.), *Karl Marx, selected readings.* Oxford: Oxford University Press. (Original work published 1859)

Maurial, M. (1999). Indigenous knowledge and schooling: A continuum between conflict and dialogue. In L. M. Semali & J. L. Kincheloe (Eds.), *What is indigenous knowledge?* (59-77). New York: Falmer.

McConnell, U. (1957). *Myths of the Mungkan.* Melbourne, Australia: University of Melbourne Press.

Medicalization of FGM. (1999). *WIN News, 25* (2), 1.

Merrill, W. (1987). The Raramuri stereotype of dreams. In B. Tedlock (Ed.). *Dreaming: Anthropological and psychological interpretations* (pp. 194-219). New York: Cambridge University Press.

Mesquita, B., Frijda, N. H., & Scherer, K. R. (1997). Culture and emotion. In J. W. Berry, P. R. Dasen, & T. S. Saraswathi (Eds.), *Handbook of cross-cultural psychology: Vol. 2. Basic processes and human development* (pp. 255-297). Boston: Allyn & Bacon.

Metcalf, P., & Huntington, R. (1991). *Celebrations of death* (2nd ed.). New York: Cambridge University Press.

Miller, P. (1963). *The New England mind: The seventeenth century.* Cambridge, MA: Harvard University Press.

Mitchell, H. (1991). Ethnic humor aound the world. *National Review,* *43* (11), 43-45).

Mitford, J. (1963). *The American way of death.* New York: Simon & Schuster.

Mitford, J. (1998). *The American way of death revisited* (Rev. ed.). New York: Knopf.

Modiano, N. (1974). *La educacion indigena en los altos de Chiapas.* Mexico City: INI.

Moms in the work force. (2000, October 14). *San Luis Obispo Tribune,* pp. A1, A4.

Monberg, T. (1991). *Bellona Island beliefs and rituals.* Honolulu: University of Hawaii Press.

Mosha, R. S. (1999). The inseparable link between intellectual and spiritual formation in individual knowledge in education: A case study in Tanzania. In L. M. Semali & J. L. Kincheloe (Eds.), *What is indigenous knowledge?* (pp. 209-225). New York: Falmer.

Mosko, M. S. (1992). Clowning with food: Mortuary humor and social reproduction among the North Mekeo. In W. E. Mitchell (Ed.), *Clowning as critical practice* (pp. 104-129). Pittsburgh, PA: University of Pittsburgh Press.

M'Timkulu, D. (1977). Some aspects of Zulu religion. In N. S. Booth, Jr. (Ed.), *African religions: A symposium* (pp. 13-30). New York: NOK Publishers.

Munn, N. D. (1986). *The fame of Gawa.* Cambridge, UK: Cambridge University Press.

Murdock, G. P., Wilson, S. F., & Frederick, V. (1978). World distribution of theories of illness. *Ethnology, 17* (1), 449-470.

*Mysteries of the ancient Americas.* (1986). Pleasantville, NY: Reader's Digest Association.

Nadel, S. F. (1960). Witchcraft in four African societies: An essay in comparison. In S. Ottenberg & P. Ottenberg (Eds.), *Cultures and societies of Africa* (pp. 407-420). New York: Random House.

Nagarajan, V. R. (1997). Inviting the goddess into the household: Women's kolams in Tamil Nadu. *Whole Earth, 49* (90), 49-53.

Nanda, S. (1997). The Hijras of India. In M. Duberman (Ed.), *A queer world.* New York: New York University Press.

Nash, J., & Safa, H. I. (1980). *Sex and class in Latin America: Women's perspectives on politics, economics, and the family in the third world.* Westport, CT: Bergin & Garvey.

Nathan, D. (1999). Sodomy for the masses. *Nation, 268* (14), 16.

Needham, R. (1967). Blood, thunder, and the mockery of animals. In J. M. Middleton (Ed.), *Myth and cosmos* (pp. 271-285). New York: Natural History Press.

Neff, D. L. (1987). Aesthetics and power in Pambin Tullah: A possession ritual in rural Kerala. *Ethnology, 26* (1), 63-71.

Neuer, R., Libertson, H., & Yoshida, S. (1979). *Ukiyo-e, 250 years of Japanese art.* New York: Mayflower.

Newcomb, W. W., Jr. (1961). *The Indians of Texas.* Austin: University of Texas Press.

Newell, P. (Ed.). (1972). *A last resort? Corporal punishment in the schools.* Middlesex, UK: Penguin.

Newland, A., & Uhlenbeck, C. (Eds.). (1990). *Ukiyo-e to shin hanza.* New York: Mallard Press.

New laws protect homosexuals. (1999). *Christianity Today, 43* (13), 17.

Nickel, H., & Köcher, E. M. T. (1987). West Germany and the German-speaking countries. In M. E. Lamb (Ed.), *The father's role* (pp. 89-114). Hillsdale, NJ: Erlbaum.

*Nihonshoki* [Chronicles of Japan]. (1958). Tokyo: Iwanami Publishing Company.

Niikura, R. (1999). Assertiveness among Japanese, Malaysian, Filipinio, and U.S. white-collar workers. *The Journal of Social Psychology, 139* (6), 690-699.

Nyamongo, I. K. (1999). Burying the dead, culture and economics: An assessment of two Kenyan cases. *International Social Science Journal, 51,* 255-261.

O'Connell, M. C. (1982). Spirit possession and role stress among the Xeside of eastern Transkei. *Ethnology, 21* (1), 21-37.

Oldenberg, H. (1886). *The Grihya-Sutras—Rules of Vedic domestic ceremonies.* (Vols. 29, 30, *The sacred books of the East*). Oxford, UK: Clarendon Press.

Oliver, D. L. (1989). *Oceania: The native cultures of Australia and the Pacific Islands* (Vol. 1). Honolulu: University of Hawaii Press.

O'Malley, W. J. (1995). Confirmed and confirming. *America, 172* (21), 16-19.

Ortner, S. B. (1978). *Sherpas through their rituals.* New York: Cambridge University Press.

Parker, R. G. (1995). Changing Brazilian constructions of homosexuality. In S. O. Murray (Ed.), *Latin American male homosexualities* (pp. 241-255). Albuquerque: University of New Mexico Press.

Parrott, W. G. (1991). The emotional experiences of envy and jealousy. In P. Salovey (Ed.), *The psychology of jealousy and envy* (pp. 3-30). New York: Guilford.

Pelikan, J. (1979). Sin. In P. K. Meagher, T. C. O'Brien, & C. S. Aherne (Eds.), *Encyclopedic dictionary of religion* (Vol. 3, pp. 3307-3308). Washington, DC: Corpus Publications.

Pemberton, J., III, & Afolayan, F. S. (1996). *Yoruba sacred kingship.* Washington, DC: Smithsonian Institution Press.

Piaget, J. (1948). *The moral judgment of the child.* Glencoe, IL: Free Press.

Pinto, N. R. S., & Baruzzi, R. G. (1991). Male pubertal seclusion and risk of death in Indians from Alto Xingu, central Brazil. *Human Biology, 63* (6), 821-834.

Place, U. T. (1996). Folk psychology from the standpoint of conceptual analysis. In W. O'Donohue & R. F. Kitchener (Eds.), *The philosophy of psychology* (pp. 264-270). Thousand Oaks, CA: Sage.

Pollock, D. (1995). Masks and the semiotics of identity. *Journal of the Royal Anthropological Institute, 1* (3), 581-597.

Poniewozik, J. (1998, December 21). "Today I am a man. Charge it!" *Fortune,* 44.

Popenoe, D. (1996). *Life without father.* New York: Free Press.

Powers, M. (1996). In the eye of the beholder. *Human Ecology Forum, 24* (4), 16-19.

Price, R. A., Charles, M. A., Pettitt, D. J., & Knowler, W. C. (1993). Obesity in Pima Indians: Large increases among post-World War II birth cohorts. *American Journal of Physical Anthropology, 92* (4), 473-479

Pusat Pengembangan Kurikulum dan Saran Pendidikan [Development Center for Curriculum and Educational Materials]. (1981). *Pola dasar pengembangan pendidikan luar biasa* [Basic pattern for developing special education}. Jakarta, Indonesia: Departemen Pendidikan dan Kebudayaan [Ministry of Education and Culture].

Queiroz, M. S. (1984). Hot and cold classification in traditional Iguape medicine. *Ethnology, 23* (1), 63-72.

Rahman, F. (1994). Islam. In R. McHenry (Ed.), *Encyclopaedia Britannica* (Vol. 22, pp. 5-6). Chicago: Encyclopaedia Britannica.

Rawson, P. S. (1994). Southeast Asian arts. In R. McHenry (Ed.), *Encyclopaedia Britannica* (Vol. 27, p. 835). Chicago: Encyclopaedia Britannica.

Reichard, G. A. (1950). *Navajo religion: A study of symbolism* (Vol. 1). New York: Pantheon.

Renou, L. (1961). *Hinduism.* New York: Braziller.

Revilla, L. A. (1997). Filipino American identity. In M. P. P. Root (Ed.), *Filipino Americans* (pp. 95-111). Thousand Oaks, CA: Sage.

Richards, G. (1996). On the necessary survival of folk psychology. In W. O'Donohue & R. F. Kitchener (Eds.), *The philosophy of psychology* (pp. 270-275). Thousand Oaks, CA: Sage.

Riches, D. (1994). Shamanism: The key to religion. *Man, 29* (2), 381-405.

Rix, S. E. (Ed.). (1988). *The American woman 1988-89: A status report.* New York: Norton.

Roberts, J. M., & Nutini, H. G. (1988). Witchcraft event staging in rural Tlaxcala. *Ethnology, 27* (4), 407-431.

Rodman, W. (1993). Sorcery and the silencing of chiefs: "Words the wind" in postindependence Ambae. *Journal of Anthropological Research, 49* (3), 217-235.

Romney, K., & Romney, R. (1963). The Mistecans of Juxtlahauca, Mexico. In B. B. Whiting (Ed.), *Six cultures: Studies of child rearing* (pp. 543-691). New York: Wiley.

Rorty, R. (1965). Mind-brain identity theory, privacy, and categories. *Review of Metaphysics, xix,* 24-54.

Rosenblatt, P. C., Walsh, R. P., & Jackson, D. A. (1976). *Grief and mourning in cross-cultural perspective.* Washington, DC: HRAF Press.

Rouse, I. (1963). The Carib. In J. Steward (Ed.), *Handbook of South American Indians* (pp. 547-566). New York: Cooper Square Publishers.

Rubin, R. (2000, October 2). The new economy goes global. *Newsweek, 136* (14), 74L.

Rushwan, H. (1995). Female circumcision. *World Health, 48,* 16-17.

Sanders, C. M. (1989). *The mourning after.* New York: Wiley.

Saposnik, I. (1998). These serious jests: American Jews and Jewish comedy. *Judaism: A Quarterly Journal of Jewish Life and Thought, 47* (3), 311.

Sargent, C. F. (1988). Born to die: Witchcraft and infanticide in Bariba culture. *Ethnology, 27* (1), 79-95.

Scheff, T. J. (1983). Toward integration in the social psychology of emotions. In R. H. Turner & J. F. Short, Jr. (Eds.), *Annual review of sociology* (Vol. 9, pp. 133-154). Palo Alto, CA: Annual Reviews.

Scherr, B. P. (1998) Taking penguins to the movies: Ethnic humor in Russia. *Russian Review, 58* (3), 495-496.

Schieffelin, E. L. (1985). Anger, grief, and shame: Toward a Kaluli ethnopsychology. In G. M. White & J. Kirkpatrick (Eds.), *Person, self, and experience: Exploring Pacific ethnopsychologies* (pp. 168-182) Berkeley: University of California Press.

Schultz, E. (1965). *Proverbial sayings of the Samoans.* Wellington, New Zealand: The Polynesian Society.

Segal, D. (1992). Excuuuse me: The case for offensive humor. *New Republic, 206* (19), 9-10.

Seyboldt, P. J. (1973). *Revolutionary education in China.* White Plains, NY: International Arts and Sciences Press.

Shakir, M. H. (Trans.). (1988). *The Qur'an.* Elmhurst, NY: Tahrike Tarsile Qur'an.

Sharp, H. S. (1995). Women and men among the Chipewyan. In L. F. Klein & L. A. Ackerman (Eds.), *Women and power in native North America* (pp. 46-74). Norman: University of Oklahoma Press.

Sharpsteen, D. J. (1991). The organization of jealousy knowledge: Romantic jealousy as a blended emotion. In P. Salovey (Ed.), *The psychology of jealousy and envy* (pp. 31-51). New York: Guilford.

Shaw, A. (Ed.). (1924). *The messages and papers of Woodrow Wilson.* New York: Review of Reviews Corporation.

Sherlock, C. (1997). The three refuges, the three signs of being, and the three fires. *Middle Way, 71* (4), 229-239.

Shinn, R. S., Folan, J. B., Hopkins, M. G., Parker, N. B., & Younglof, R. L. (1970). *Area handbook for India.* Washington, DC: U.S. Government Printing Office.

Shokeid, M. (1982). The regulation of aggression in daily life: Aggressive relationships among Moroccan immigrants in Israel. *Ethnology, 21* (3), 271-281.

Signorini, I. (1982). Patterns of fright: Multiple concepts of susto in a Nahua-Ladino community of the Sierra de Puebla (Mexico). *Ethnology, 21* (4), 313-323.

Silverman, E. K. (1997). Politics, gender, and time in Melanesia and aboriginal Australia. *Ethnology, 36* (2), 101-121.

Sinavaiana, C. (1992). Where the spirits laugh last: Comic theater in Samoa. In W. E. Mitchell, (Ed.). *Clowning as critical practice* (pp. 192-218). Pittsburgh, PA: University of Pittsburgh Press.

Skjonsberg, E. (1989). *Change in an African village: Kefa speaks.* West Hartford, CT: Kumarian Press.

Smith, J. E. (1959). *The works of Jonathan Edwards: Vol. 2. Religious affections.* New Haven, CT: Yale University Press.

Smith, M. G. (1982). Cosmology, practice, and social organization among the Kadara and Kagoro. *Ethnology, 21* (1), 1-20.

Smock, A. C. (1977). Ghana: From autonomy to subordination. In J. Z. Giele & A. C. Smock (Eds.), *Women: Roles and status in eight countries* (pp. 175-216). New York: Wiley.

Sodomy law's last stand. (200, July 28). *Advocate,* p. 13.

Spae, J. J. (1972). *Shinto man.* Tokyo: Oriens Institute for Religious Research.

Special education. (1981-1982). *Chinese Education, 14* (4), 49-52.

Spencer, B., & Gillen, F. J. (1968). *The native tribes of central Australia.* New York: Dover.

Spiro, M. E. (1997). *Gender ideology and psychological reality.* New Haven, CT: Yale University Press.

Stambach, A. (1998). "Too much studying makes me crazy": School-related illnesses on Mount Kilimanjaro. *Comparative Education Review*, 42 (4), 497-512.

Steadman, L. B., Palmer, C. T., & Tilley, C. F. (1996). The universality of ancestor worship. *Ethnology*, 35 (1), 63-76.

Steele, S., & Nemeth, M. (1994, May 16). Coming out: The state is out of the bedroom, but after 25 years, old attitudes still linger. *Maclean's*, 107 (20) 40-43.

Steiner, F. B. (1999). *Taboo, truth, and religion: Franz Baermann Steiner, selected writings* (Vol. 1) (J. Adler & R. Fardon, Eds.). New York: Berghahn.

Stephen, L. (1997). *Women and social movements in Latin America*. Austin: University of Texas Press.

Stevenson, M. S. (1970). *The heart of Jainism*. New Delhi, India: Munshiram Manoharlal. (Original work published 1915)

Stich, S. (1983). *From folk psychology to cognitive science*. Cambridge, MA: MIT Press.

St. John, D. P. (1989). Iroquois. In L. E. Sullivan (Ed.), *Native American religions: North America* (pp. 133-138). New York: Macmillan.

Stone, L. (1997). *Kinship and gender*. Boulder, CO: Westview.

Strathern, A. (1989). Melpa dream interpretation and the concept of hidden truth. *Ethnology*, 28 (4), 301-315.

Suhrawardy, A. A. al-M. (Ed.). (1941). *The sayings of Mohammad*. London: John Murray.

Takahata, A. (1999). Beyond efficiency and rationalization: A highly standardized educational system is slowly giving way to a more flexibly organized, creative, person-to-person style. *World and I, 14* (9), 318.

Tamadonfar, M. (1989). *The Islamic polity and political leadership*. Boulder, CO: Westview.

Thaman, K. H. (1993). Culture and the curriculum. *Comparative Education, 29* (3), 249-260.

Thomas, E. M. (1959). *The harmless people*. New York: Knopf.

Thomas, R. M. (1962). Reinspecting a structural position on occupational prestige. *American Journal of Sociology, 67* (3), 561-565.

Thomas, R. M. (1970). Who shall be educated? The Indonesian case. In J. Fischer (Ed.), *The social sciences and the comparative study of educational systems* (pp. 227-348). Scranton, PA: International Textbook Co.

Thomas, R. M. (1985). Christian theory of human development. In T. Husen & T. N. Postlethwaite (Eds.), *International encyclopedia of education* (Vol. 2, pp. 715-721). Oxford, UK: Pergamon.

omas, R. M. (1987). *From talking chiefs to videotapes: Education in American Samoa—1700s to 1980.* Washington, DC: ERIC (Document Reproduction Service, No. ED 273 544).

omas, R. M. (1988). A Hindu theory of human development. In R. M. Thomas (Ed.), *Oriental theories of human development* (pp. 29-73). New York: Peter Lang.

Thomas, R. M. (1997). *Moral development theories—Secular and religious.* Westport, CT: Greenwood.

Thomas, R. M. (2001). *Recent theories of human development.* Thousand Oaks, CA: Sage.

Todd, S. M., & Shinzato, S. (1999). Thinking for the future: Developing higher-level thinking and creativity for students in Japan and elsewhere. *Childhood Education, 75* (6), 342-345.

Tollefson, K. D. (1995). Potlatching and political organization among the Northwest coast Indians. *Ethnology, 34* (1), 53-73.

Tomlinson, S. (1982). *A sociology of special education.* London: Routledge & Kegan Paul.

Tong, R. P. (1998). *Feminist thought* (2nd ed.). Boulder, CO: Westview.

Tooker, D. E. (1992). Identity systems of highland Burma: "Belief," Akha zán, and a critique of interiorized notions of ethno-religious identity. *Man, 27,* 799-819.

Tooker, E. (1964). An ethnography of the Huron Indians, 1615-1649 (Bulletin 190). Washington, DC: U.S. Bureau of American Ethnology.

Toulmin, S. E. (1994). Philosophy of science. In R. McHenry (Ed.), *Encyclopaedia Britannica,* (Vol. 25, 652-669). Chicago: Encyclopaedia Britannica.

Trigg, E. B. (1973). *Gypsy demons and divinities.* Secaucus, NJ: Citadel.

Tynan, L. M. (1997). The status of FGM in the world today. *Off Our Backs, 27* (6), 8-11.

U.S. Census Bureau. (1999). *Statistical abstract of the United States.* Washington, DC: Author.

Valadez, A. A. (1986). *Confrontación: Historia de la investigación d e los sueños.* México City: Centro de Investigación y Estudio de los Sueños.

Valentine, E. R. (1996). Folk psychology and its implications for cognitive science: Discussion. In W. O'Donohue & R. F. Kitchener (Eds.), *The philosophy of psychology* (pp. 275-278). Thousand Oaks, CA: Sage.

van Buitenen, J. A. B. (Ed.). (1973). *The Mahabharata.* Chicago: University of Chicago Press.

Vivelo, F. R. (1977). *The Herero of Western Botswana.* St. Paul, MN: West.

Vogt, E. Z. (1965). Zinacanteco souls. *Man, 65* (29), 13-35.

Voll, U. (1979). Capital sins. In P. K. Meagher, T. C. O'Brien, & C. S. Aherne (Eds.), *Encyclopedic dictionary of religion* (Vol. 1, p. 622). Washington, DC: Corpus Publications.

Waldman, C. (1988). *Encyclopedia of Native American tribes.* New York: Facts on File.

Waley, A. (1938). *The analects of Confucius.* New York: Vintage Books.

Wallace, A. F. C. (1958). Dreams and the wishes of the soul: A type of psychoanalytic theory among 17th century Iroquois. *American Anthropologist, 60,* 234-248.

Ware, J. R. (1955). *The sayings of Confucius.* New York: New American Library.

Waters, F. (1950). *Masked gods.* New York: Ballentine.

Watkins, B., & Rothchild, N. (1996). *In the company of women: Voices from the women's movement.* St. Paul: Minnesota Historical Society Press.

Watson, G., & Goulet, J. G. A. (1992). Gold in; gold out: The objectification of Dene Tha accounts of dreams and visions. *Journal of Anthropological Research, 48* (3), 215-230.

Watt, W. M. (1994). Islam. In R. McHenry (Ed.), *Encyclopaedia Britannica* (Vol. 22, pp. 1-5). Chicago: Encyclopaedia Britannica.

*Webster's encyclopedic unabridged dictionary of the English language.* (1989). New York: Portland House.

Weinberg, M. S., & Williams, C. J. (1974). *Male homosexuals: Their problems and adaptations.* New York: Oxford University Press.

Weiner, J. F. (1991). *The empty place.* Bloomington: Indiana University Press.

Wellman, H. M. (1990). *The child's theory of mind.* Cambridge, MA: MIT Press.

Wertenbaker, L. (1974). *The world of Picasso 1881-1973.* New York: Time-Life Books.

Weslager, C. A. (1973). *Magic medicines of the Indians.* New York: New American Library.

Wilde, L. (1978). *The complete book of ethnic humor.* Los Angeles: Corwin.

Willems, P. (1996). War without end. *Middle East,* (262), 5-6.

Williams, J. E., Satterwhite, R. C., & Best, D. L. (1999). Pancultural gender stereotypes revisted: The Five Factor Model. *Sex Roles: A Journal of Research, 40* (7-8), 523.

Wilson, E. (1959). *Apologies to the Iroquois.* New York: Random House.

Wilson, G. (1960). An African morality. In S. Ottenberg & P. Ottenberg (Eds.), *Cultures and societies of Africa* (pp. 345-364). New York: Random House.

Wilson, J. W., & Neckerman, K. M. (1986). Poverty and family structure: The widening gap between violence and public policy issues. In S. H. Danziger & D. H. Weinberg (Eds.), *Fighting poverty* (pp. 232-259). Cambridge, MA: Harvard University Press.

Winiata, M. (1967). *The changing role of the leader in Maori society.* Auckland, New Zealand: Blackwood & Janet Paul.

Witham, L. (2000). Churches debate role of homosexual unions. *Insight on the News, 16* (29), 26.

Wollstonecraft, M. (1975). *A vindication of the rights of woman* (C. H. Poston, Ed.). New York: Norton.

World's way of death. (1998, November 14). *Economist,* 95.

Wundt, W. (1912/1916). *The elements of folk psychology* [Elemente der völkerpsychologie] (E. L. Schaub, Trans.). London: Allen & Unwin. (Original work published 1912)

Wundt, W. (1927). *Völkerpsychologie* (4th ed., 10 vols.). Leipzig, Germany: Kröner.

Yan, W. F., & Gaier, E. L. (1994). Causal attributions for college success and failure. *Journal of Cross-Cultural Psychology, 25* (1), 146-158.

Yee, T. T. (1984). Family stress: Appraising and coping processes. In G. Lim (Ed.), *The Chinese American experience.* San Francisco: Chinese Historical Society of America and Chinese Culture Foundation of San Francisco.

# Name Index

# Subject Index

Tamil, 130
Latin America, 161, 198
Laws, 21-22, 118, 148-149, 207, 263
Leader, 127-129
Learning materials, 64-68
Legaland, 67
Lengua, 104
Lenni Lenape, 114-115
Lepcha, 99
Lesbians, 13, 207, 259, 263-265
Liberia, 212
Libertarian, 12
Libya, 205
Life span, 9, 13, 27, 29, 235, 239-243, 283
Limerick, 178
Liminality, 221
Literature, 22-23
Love, 3, 159, 161-163, 169-170
Luo, 95-96, 242
Lusi-Kaliai, 181
Lutheranism, 28

Maasai, 218-219
Macedonia, 35
Machismo, 154-155
Madagascar, 162-163, 274-275
Madrasah, 62
Madurese, 153
Mae Enga, 261
Maghreb countries, 205
Magic, 17, 144, 289
Mahabharata, 22
Malagasy, 162-163, 274-275
Malaysia, 33, 80, 85, 104, 130-132, 229
Mandak, 144
Mandala, 9
Mandan, 35, 218
Manly hearted, 251
Manu Smriti, 21
Manus Islands, 64, 261
Maori, 9, 128-129, 267

Marquesas, 9, 170
Marianisma, 154-155
Maring, 150-151
Marriage, 264-265
  child, 230
Marshall Islands, 204
Marxism, 12, 66, 232
Masks, 82, 193, 199-201, 210
Masturbation, 256
Matrilineal, 125, 250
Matrilocal, 250-251
Mauritania, 138-139, 277
Mayan, 45-46, 68, 236
Mediterranean region, 104, 162
Mediums, 74-75, 93
Mehinaka, 216-217
Melanesia, 70, 73, 150, 225, 258
Melpa, 70-71
Melting pot, 207
Mennonites, 78
Menstruation, 103, 211, 271
Mental,
  functions, 4
  products, 1
Metempsychosis, 47
Methodist, 48, 264
Mexico, 68-70, 82, 136, 151-156, 220, 227-228, 236, 253, 257-258
Micronesia, 73, 131, 147, 195
Mind, 36
  products of, 2
  theory of, 3
Misdemeanor, 269
Mixed salad, 207
Mixtecan, 253
Mockery, 178, 181
Models, 19, 59-60, 64, 119, 152, 170
Modernism, 34
Mongo, 103
Mongolia, 12, 195
Mormon, 11, 12, 16, 243
Morocco, 166-167, 205, 237-238
Mosaic, 207

# About the Author

**R. Murray Thomas** (PhD, Stanford University) is an emeritus professor at the University of California, Santa Barbara, where for three decades he taught educational psychology and directed the program in international education. He began his 50-year career in education as a high school teacher at Kamehameha Schools and Mid-Pacific Institute in Honolulu, then continued at the college level at San Francisco State University, the State University of New York (Brockport), and Pajajaran University in Indonesia before moving to Santa Barbara.

His professional publications exceed 340, including 46 books for which he served as author, coauthor, or editor. His earlier books that relate to the contents of *Folk Psychologies Across Cultures* include:

*Social Strata in Indonesia—A Study of West Java Villagers* (1975)
*From Talking Chiefs to Videotapes—Education in American Samoa, 1700s-1980* (1987)
*Oriental Theories of Human Development* (editor, 1988)
*The Encyclopedia of Human Development and Education* (editor, 1990)
*Moral Development Theories—Secular and Religious* (1997)
*Human Development Theories: Windows on Culture* (1999)
*Comparing Theories of Child Development* (5th ed., 2000)
*Multicultural Counseling and Human Development Theories* (2000)
*Recent Theories of Human Development* (2001)